LIFE
APPLICATION®
BIBLE
COMMENTARY

ROMANS

Bruce B. Barton, D. Min.

David R. Veerman, M. Div.

Neil Wilson, M.A.R.

Series Editor: Grant Osborne, Ph.D.

 Tyndale House Publishers, Inc.
WHEATON, ILLINOIS

Editor: Philip Comfort, Ph.D.
Contributing Editors: James C. Galvin, Ed.D.; Linda K. Taylor; Ronald A. Beers

Life Application is a registered trademark of Tyndale House Publishers, Inc.

Library of Congress Cataloging-in-Publication Data
Barton, Bruce B., date
   Romans / Bruce B. Barton, David R. Veerman, Neil Wilson.
      p.   cm. — (Life application Bible commentary)
   Includes bibliographical references and index.
   ISBN 0-8423-2818-1 — ISBN 0-8423-2890-4
   1. Bible. N.T. Romans—Commentaries. I. Veerman, David.
II. Wilson, Neil S., date - III. Title. IV. Series.
BS2665.3.B345 1992
227' .107—dc20

Printed in the United States of America

07 06 05 04
14 13 12 11

CONTENTS

vii   Foreword
  ix   Introduction
  ix   Author
xiv   Setting
  xv   Audience
xviii   Occasion and Purpose for Writing
  xx   Message
xxvi   Summary
xxvii   Vital Statistics
xxvii   Outline
xxviii   Map
  1   Romans 1
  41   Romans 2
  61   Romans 3
  81   Romans 4
  97   Romans 5
113   Romans 6
131   Romans 7
147   Romans 8
175   Romans 9
193   Romans 10
207   Romans 11
229   Romans 12
245   Romans 13
259   Romans 14
271   Romans 15
287   Romans 16
297   Bibliography
299   Index

FOREWORD

The *Life Application Bible* Commentary series provides verse-by-verse explanation, background, and application for every verse in the New Testament. In addition, it gives personal help, teaching notes, and sermon ideas that will address needs, answer questions, and provide insight for applying God's Word to life today. The content is highlighted so that particular verses and phrases are easy to find.

Each volume contains three sections: introduction, commentary, and reference. The introduction includes an overview of the book, the book's historical context, a timeline, cultural background information, major themes, an overview map, and an explanation about the author and audience.

The commentary section includes running commentary on the Bible text with reference to several modern versions, especially the New International Version and the New Revised Standard Version, along with the New King James Version, accompanied by life applications interspersed throughout. Additional elements include charts, diagrams, maps, and illustrations. There are also insightful quotes from church leaders and theologians such as John Calvin, Martin Luther, John Wesley, A. W. Tozer, and C. S. Lewis. These features are designed to help you quickly grasp the biblical information and be prepared to communicate it to others.

The reference section includes a bibliography of other resources, short articles on specific topics, and an index.

INTRODUCTION

The courtroom is filled with intense drama as the lawyer for the plaintiff states the case for guilt and the lawyer for the defendant builds the case for innocence. Judge and jurors listen carefully in preparation for their verdict. Although Romans was not presented in court, this letter from Paul to the Roman believers reads like a lawyer's brief as Paul slowly and skillfully presents the case for the gospel. Paul was a scholar and a world traveler. He was a Pharisee and a Roman citizen. But most important, Paul was a follower of Jesus Christ. Because Paul had not visited Rome, he wrote this letter to introduce himself to the Roman believers and to prepare the way for his coming. And so, under the inspiration of the Holy Spirit, he clearly outlined the Christian message. His readers would know that this Roman citizen was *first* a citizen of the kingdom of heaven, a brother in Christ.

AUTHOR

Paul (Saul of Tarsus): Pharisee, apostle, pioneer missionary of the church.

Citizenship is a valuable possession—to claim a country, a nation, a people as your own. Consider the multitudes who poured through Ellis Island, and the thousands since, yearning to be Americans. Watch the Olympic celebrations—at every race, flags are waved enthusiastically for the winning athlete and country—and feel the pride when individuals proclaim their nationality. Our citizenship is integral to our identity, signifying who we are and where we belong.

Paul was a Jew, culturally and religiously, by birth and by choice. We know little of his early years except that he was from Tarsus, far north and west of Jerusalem, in Cilicia. When he comes onto the biblical scene at the confrontation with Stephen (Acts 7:58), we see Paul as a young Pharisee, zealous for the faith and giving his approval to Stephen's death. Later we learn that Paul had been trained by Gamaliel, the most respected rabbi of the day (Acts 22:3). Paul was so Jewish, in fact, that he became obsessed with eliminating the young Christian sect that he viewed as heretical (Acts 8:1-3; 9:1-2).

Paul outlined his Jewish connections in his address to the mob in Jerusalem:

- *I am a Jew, born in Tarsus of Cilicia, but brought up in this city. Under Gamaliel I was thoroughly trained in the law of our fathers and was just as zealous for God as any of you are today. I persecuted the followers of this Way to their death, arresting both men and women and throwing them into prison, as also the high priest and all the Council can testify. I even obtained letters from them to their brothers in Damascus, and went there to bring these people as prisoners to Jerusalem to be punished. (Acts 22:3-5 NIV)*

In addition, Paul had emphasized his Jewish credentials with the Corinthians to help refute his detractors: "Are they Hebrews? So am I. Are they Israelites? So am I. Are they Abraham's descendants? So am I" (2 Corinthians 11:22 NIV).

Paul was Jewish, but he was also a Roman citizen. The mighty Roman empire extended well beyond Italy, through Macedonia and Asia, all the way to the limits of Judea. Although all who lived in the conquered territory were under Roman domination, not everyone was a Roman citizen. That was a special privilege. A person could become a Roman citizen by birth (born to parents who were citizens) or by purchase. And with Roman citizenship came certain rights and guarantees (for example, the right to a fair trial and the right of passage).

We learn about Paul's Roman connection in the Jerusalem incident mentioned above. After hearing Paul say "Gentiles," the crowd became enraged and tried to seize him. This prompted the Roman commander to bring Paul inside, away from the mob, for questioning.

- *He [the commander] directed that he [Paul] be flogged and questioned in order to find out why the people were shouting at him like this. As they stretched him out to flog him, Paul said to the centurion standing there, "Is it legal for you to flog a Roman citizen who hasn't even been found guilty?"*

  When the centurion heard this, he went to the commander and reported it. "What are you going to do?" he asked. "This man is a Roman citizen."

  The commander went to Paul and asked, "Tell me, are you a Roman citizen?"

  "Yes, I am," he answered.

  Then the commander said, "I had to pay a big price for my citizenship."

"But I was born a citizen," Paul replied.

Those who were about to question him withdrew immediately. The commander himself was alarmed when he realized that he had put Paul, a Roman citizen, in chains. (Acts 22:24-29 NIV*)*

Later, Paul used his Roman citizenship again, this time to get to Rome:

- *Then Paul made his defense: "I have done nothing wrong against the law of the Jews or against the temple or against Caesar."*

  Festus, wishing to do the Jews a favor, said to Paul, "Are you willing to go up to Jerusalem and stand trial before me there on these charges?"

  Paul answered: "I am now standing before Caesar's court, where I ought to be tried. I have not done any wrong to the Jews, as you yourself know very well. If, however, I am guilty of doing anything deserving death, I do not refuse to die. But if the charges brought against me by these Jews are not true, no one has the right to hand me over to them. I appeal to Caesar!"

  After Festus had conferred with his council, he declared: "You have appealed to Caesar. To Caesar you will go!" (Acts 25:8-12 NIV*)*

So Paul had dual citizenship—in Israel and in Rome—and both were important to him. But Paul was a citizen of yet another nation, the kingdom of God. As this zealous Jew, armed with authority from the high priest, had journeyed to Damascus to root out and capture Christians, he was confronted by Christ (Acts 26:12-18). From that moment on, Paul had a new Emperor, a new Commander-in-chief. Shortly after that experience, Paul became totally dedicated to spreading the news of God's kingdom. He traveled extensively throughout the Mediterranean area, enduring incredible opposition and hardships to preach the good news about Christ and to establish churches (Paul lists many of these difficulties in 2 Corinthians 11:23-28). Paul's new King took precedence over any earthly authority, making his new citizenship more important than being a Jew or a Roman.

Paul used this truth about being a citizen of God's kingdom to challenge Philippian believers in their walk with Christ:

- *Our citizenship is in heaven. And we eagerly await a Savior from there, the Lord Jesus Christ, who, by the power that enables him to bring everything under his control, will transform*

> *our lowly bodies so that they will be like his glorious body.*
> *(Philippians 3:20-21* NIV*)*

Paul also spoke of heavenly citizenship to encourage the Ephesians: "Consequently, you are no longer foreigners and aliens, but fellow citizens with God's people and members of God's household, built on the foundation of the apostles and prophets, with Christ Jesus himself as the chief cornerstone" (Ephesians 2:19-20 NIV).

This was a remarkable man. As an educated and dedicated Jew, no doubt Paul could have risen to great power and influence in the Jewish community. As an articulate and talented Roman citizen, he probably could have achieved wealth and notoriety in the Roman world. Instead, he focused all of his talents, gifts, and energy on serving Christ (Philippians 3:12-14).

Often today, people who claim to be followers of Christ and citizens of heaven give their allegiance to earthly leaders instead of to God. They live by earthly standards and values instead of those of God's kingdom. Where is your allegiance? What evidence is there in your life that you are a citizen of heaven?

Paul's ministry. After his conversion to Christ (Acts 9:1-19), Paul spent three years in Damascus with Ananias and the other disciples in that city (Galatians 1:18). There his ministry began (Acts 9:20-23). Paul then returned to Jerusalem, sponsored by Barnabas who encouraged him and presented him to the apostles. But after attempts on Paul's life by his former associates, zealous Jews, he was sent by the apostles to Tarsus. (It would be fourteen years before he would return to Jerusalem—Galatians 2:1.)

Paul remained in the northern region for about eight years, becoming established in the faith and teaching in the churches, especially in Antioch (Acts 11:25-26). The church at Antioch then commissioned Paul and Barnabas, sending them on the first missionary journey (Acts 13:2-3), to Cyprus, Pamphylia, and Galatia (Acts 13:4–14:28). This trip occurred in A.D. 46–48. At each town, first Paul would attempt to reach the Jews with the gospel; then he would reach beyond the synagogue to the Gentiles, who responded in great numbers. The response of the Gentiles further enraged the Jews and even caused the apostles and other believers to question Paul's ministry. But the issue of taking the gospel to non-Jews was somewhat resolved at the Council of Jerusalem in A.D. 50 (Acts 15).

Paul took two other missionary trips, establishing churches in Ephesus, Philippi, Thessalonica, Corinth, and other cities along the Mediterranean coast and inland. These trips occurred in A.D. 50–52 and A.D. 53–57.

While on his third missionary journey, Paul became determined to return to Jerusalem, to deliver the money he had collected for believers there, even though he knew that enemies were waiting for him (Acts 20:22-24).

Paul's arrival in Jerusalem was peaceful at first (Acts 21:17-19), but when he was recognized at the temple, a violent mob seized him and tried to kill him (Acts 21:27-32). This led to his conversation with the commander and the beginning of his series of trials that eventually brought Paul to Rome in A.D. 59 (Acts 28:11-16).

Although under Roman guard in a house, Paul was able to continue his ministry while in Rome, teaching all who came to visit and listen. In addition, he was able to write the Prison Epistles: Ephesians, Philippians, Colossians, and Philemon. This arrangement lasted two years (Acts 28:17-31).

According to tradition, Paul was released after those two years. Some reasons for this tradition are as follows: (1) Luke does not give an account of Paul's trial before Caesar, and Luke was a detailed historian; (2) the prosecution had two years to bring the case to trial, and time may have run out; (3) in Paul's letter to the Philippians, written during his imprisonment in Rome, he implied that he would soon be released and would do further traveling; (4) Paul mentioned several places where he intended to take the gospel, but he never had visited those places in his first three journeys; and (5) early Christian literature talks plainly about other travels by Paul.

After his release, Paul probably left on another missionary journey, through Ephesus where he left Timothy (1 Timothy 1:3), then to Colosse (Philemon 22), and on to Macedonia. He may also have realized his goal of going to Spain (Romans 15:24, 28). Eventually he probably journeyed east and visited Crete (Titus 1:5), where he left Titus to organize and lead the church. During this time of freedom, Paul wrote 1 Timothy and Titus.

Eventually, Paul was arrested a second time and returned to Rome. This prison experience differed greatly from his first—this time Paul was isolated and lonely, awaiting execution (2 Timothy 4:9-18). However, he was able to write 2 Timothy. Paul was martyred in the spring of A.D. 68.

From beginning to end, Paul's ministry was focused on taking the good news of Christ to the world. Despite continual harassment and violent persecution, he courageously took every opportunity to tell others about the Savior, teaching, preaching, making his defense in court, and sharing one-to-one. Paul's identity and citizenship were found in Christ. He was committed to obeying God, his true Emperor, no matter what.

When Paul wrote to the church in Rome, therefore, he was writing first as a citizen of heaven. Yet Paul also was writing as a Roman citizen to people who lived at the apex of worldly power—the capital of the Roman empire. Paul had felt the tension between those allegiances; he knew the conflicts that his readers must be facing.

Although Paul had never visited Rome, he felt very close to the church there. Paul and those believers had much in common—many of the Roman Christians were Jewish, and they *all* were living in occupied territory.

Just a decade after writing this letter, tensions erupted into full-scale persecution under Emperor Nero, claiming the lives of thousands of believers, who were torn apart limb from limb, fed to lions, and crucified. In fact, during that horrible time, both Peter and Paul met their death. According to other historians (their deaths are not recorded in Scripture), Peter was crucified, and Paul was beheaded.

It cost dearly to identify with Christ in the first century. Paul and the early believers suffered greatly for being followers of Jesus, eventually dying for what they believed. Still they continued to hold fast to the faith and to proclaim God's Word. Our hardships are not nearly as severe, yet often we find excuses for *not* letting others know where we stand—just the hint of social embarrassment may cause us to remain silent. Instead, we should boldly and lovingly tell others God's good news of salvation in Christ, regardless of the cost. What in your words and life-style bears testimony to your faith? What is your plan for telling your friends and neighbors about Christ? Don't let anything hold you back. Let Paul's example inspire you to spread God's message of love and salvation.

SETTING

Written from Corinth in A.D. 57.

Paul had visited Corinth on his second missionary journey and established the church there (Acts 18:1-18). This was a difficult task because of opposition from local Jews and because of the city itself—Corinth was notorious for its great evil. As a seaport, Corinth was a cosmopolitan city and a major trade center. It was also filled with idolatry and immorality. The fledgling church struggled to resist the pressures of sin and thus survive. We see reflections of this struggle in Paul's first letter to the Corinthian church, 1 Corinthians.

During Paul's ministry in Corinth, he met Aquila and Priscilla, Jews who had left Rome following an order by Emperor Claudius (Acts 18:2). They were tentmakers, a trade that Paul also knew. While in Corinth, Paul stayed and worked with Aquila and Priscilla and had a tremendous effect on their spiritual growth (Acts 18:3). Later, this godly couple returned to Rome and became leaders in the church there (Romans 16:3-5).

Because of a number of problems in the Corinthian church, Paul felt compelled to write to them and to visit Corinth at least two more times (2 Corinthians 1:12-15). Paul's last visit came at the end of his third missionary journey (A.D. 57).

During this journey, Paul was collecting money for the church in Jerusalem, which was poor and struggling through a devastating famine. For three years of this trip, Paul ministered in Ephesus. But after a riot (Acts 19:23-41), he left for Greece, where he stayed for three months (Acts 20:2-3) before leaving for Jerusalem with the money he had collected (Romans 15:25-26). Much of the three months was spent in Corinth. That's when Paul wrote the letter to the Romans. Note the reference to Gaius, a Corinthian believer (1 Corinthians 1:14) who was known to the believers in Rome (Romans 16:23).

Although Paul had never been to Rome, he longed to go there (Romans 1:9-13). He was planning to visit the church on his way to Spain, after delivering the money to Jerusalem (Romans 15:25-29).

AUDIENCE

Christians in Rome. "To all who are in Rome, beloved of God, called to be saints" (1:7 NKJV).

The city of Rome. Rome was the capital city of the vast and mighty Roman empire, an empire that stretched from Britain to Arabia. Truly, all roads led to Rome. It would be natural, then, for Paul to want to visit this great city, not merely as a dutiful citizen or a curious tourist, but as a gifted evangelist who desired to reach the world for Christ.

Founded in 753 B.C., Rome was strategically located on the Tiber River at a ford that was indispensable for traveling between northern and southern Italy. In addition, the ridges surrounding the Tiber River valley provided hilltop fortifications against attack. In Paul's day, Rome was the largest city in the world, with a population of approximately one million. Wealthy and cosmopolitan, it was the diplomatic and trade center of the world. The Roman empire provided stability, order, and the rule of law for the conquered countries. The Roman peace made travel safe; Roman roads made it relatively swift and easy.

There is evidence for a Jewish colony in Rome dating to the second century B.C. The colony was small until Judea was incorporated into the Roman empire in 63 B.C., when Pompey called for the deportation of Jews to Rome. Then the Jewish population expanded. In 59 B.C., Cicero wrote that the Jews of Rome were a large, powerful, and influential group.

During the period of the Roman Republic (509–527 B.C.), the Romans adopted and "Romanized" Greek gods. Thus Zeus, the king of the gods, became Jupiter, Hera became Juno, Poseidon became Neptune, Hermes became Mercury, and Aphrodite became Venus. Emperor worship also was encouraged. This worship was enforced in varying degrees, depending on the emperor's disposition. Devout Jews had very different worship patterns and would never worship the emperor, so the Jewish community was often persecuted and was expelled from Rome several times. Aquila and Priscilla were driven from Rome by an edict from Claudius in A.D. 49. Each time, the expulsion edict would lapse and the Jews would return. This was the case with Claudius's edict.

What was it like to be a Christian in Rome? It was like being a distinct and oppressed minority. In many ways, Rome was a secular city, consumed with financial and political concerns. But Rome was also a very religious city. It's pagan religion centered around Jupiter and other gods and included many superstitions. The Romans regarded unusual occurrences as signs that the gods were displeased, and they looked to birds for signs to help them discover the will of the gods. Added to this religious potpourri were the superstitions and idols from conquered territories (colonies), brought to Rome by Greek settlers and traders. We get a glimpse of some of these pagan religious practices on Paul's missionary journeys (see Acts 13:6-12; 14:11-18; 16:16-18; 17:16-23; 19:23-41). Rome was filled with gods, and the prevailing thought was that all the gods were real. Thus, Jews and Christians who insisted on *one* God were viewed as atheists because they denied the existence of all the other deities.

Christians also came in conflict with Roman society because of their values. To Roman citizens, the highest allegiance was to the state. But for Christians, God took priority. To Roman citizens, non-Romans were distinctly inferior, and enslaving conquered peoples was the accepted way of life. The Romans were also very class conscious. Contrast these Roman social divisions with Paul's statement, "There is neither Jew nor Greek, slave nor free, male nor female, for you are all one in Christ Jesus" (Galatians 3:28 NIV). Clearly Christians stood out.

At first, Christianity was tolerated in Rome, as a sect of Judaism. But in the last few years of Emperor Nero's reign (he reigned from A.D. 54 to his death in A.D. 68), he authorized hunting down, torturing, and killing Christians. In A.D. 64, a large part of Rome was destroyed by a fire, thought by many to have been ordered by the emperor himself. Nero, however, accused the Christians in the city, giving him the excuse for any number of terrible atrocities. The secular historian Tacitus wrote:

- *Their death was made a matter of sport; they were covered in wild beast's skins and torn to pieces by dogs; or were fastened to crosses and set on fire in order to serve as torches by night . . . . Nero had offered his gardens for the spectacle and gave an exhibition in his circus, mingling with the crowd in the guise of a charioteer or mounted on his chariot. (Annals 15.44)*

During these terrible persecutions, Christians were forced to choose between the emperor and Christ; those who chose Christ often died for their faith. Both Peter and Paul are thought to be victims of Nero's terror. In 2 Timothy, Paul's last letter, written in about A.D. 67 from a Roman prison, we sense that Paul knows he is giving his final words to his young protégé. And the letters of Peter (1 and 2 Peter), thought to have been written at about the same time, also from Rome, contain many references to suffering.

With this backdrop of paganism and persecutions, it is no wonder that Rome was seen as the epitome of evil in the later Scriptures. Like Babylon, Rome became a symbol of paganism and opposition to Christianity. In the vision given to John by Christ and recorded as the book of Revelation, John gives a dramatic description of the fall of Rome—symbolized as Babylon (Revelation 17–18).

What was it like to be a Christian in Rome? The answer—very similar to what it is like today. Of course we don't have to deal with a Nero, a maniacal dictator breathing threats and carrying them out. But still, real Christians are a distinct minority in society. And we stand out if we stand for Christ. It is possible, of course, to be a *secret* believer, hiding our faith to avoid trouble. But that reaction is tantamount to denying our Savior. He died for us—we can live for him.

The church at Rome. The founders of the church at Rome are unknown. It was not started by Peter—his ministry was to Jews, and he seems to have settled in Rome just after Paul's arrival in about A.D. 60. And the church was not founded by Paul—he admits to not having been there (Romans 1:11-13; 15:23-24). Most likely, the church was begun by Jews who had been in Jerusalem for the Passover celebration and had been converted through Peter's powerful sermon and the outpouring of the Holy Spirit in A.D. 30 (Acts 2:5-40). These new believers were soon joined by travelers like Aquila and Priscilla who had heard the Good News in other places and had brought it back to Rome.

At first, of course, the Roman church was Jewish; that is, the members were Jews who had come to believe in Jesus as their Messiah. But over the subsequent twenty-seven years, many Christians from all parts of the Roman empire had migrated to Rome, some of them Paul's own converts and many of them Gentiles.

Paul's Roman letter is addressed, "To all who are in Rome, beloved of God, called to be saints" (1:7 NKJV). The recipients probably were a loosely knit fellowship of believers and not a highly organized church. That is, there were no ordained leaders by any title. And the Roman Christians worshiped in various homes and other meeting places, rather than in one church location (16:5, 14-16). But organized or not, this church had become large and influential—"your faith is proclaimed throughout the world" (1:8 NRSV).

The membership of the church reflected Roman society; that is, it was a cosmopolitan mix of believers from a wide variety of backgrounds and walks of life. From Paul's many references to Gentiles (1:5-8, 12-14; 11:13, 28-31; 15:15-17) and his personal greetings to many with Greek names (16:3-16), it seems clear that by the time of this letter, the church consisted of a majority of Gentiles, but with a strong Jewish minority (see 4:1; 7:1).

With such a diversity of cultures and nationalities in the Roman church, we might expect factions and divisions. Yet there seems to be unity in worship and outreach, even with no well-known, charismatic leaders. Surrounded by pagan influence, these believers made a significant difference in their city and were known all over the world for their faith (1:8). Contrast this with many churches in our world today that despite incredible resources are ineffective and fractured. What would it take for the faith of your church to be reported all over the world?

OCCASION AND PURPOSE FOR WRITING

The main purpose for Paul writing this letter at this time was to prepare the way for his visit to Rome, to let the believers in Rome know of his plans to come, and to enlist their support for his future ministry in Spain. Paul had longed to visit Rome, and, God willing, he would be there soon (1:10-13). He knew that Rome was the most important city in the empire, with influence spreading far and wide—ministering there would be strategic. But if that were Paul's only purpose, he could have merely sent a brief note to that effect with Phoebe, rather than giving her such a long letter to deliver (16:1-2).

One reason for Paul spending so much time on this letter is probably because he wanted to counteract any misunderstanding of his goals and his message—there was widespread slander directed at him by some fellow Christians and many Jews (for example, see 1 Corinthians 3 and 2 Corinthians 10–12). To most Roman Christians, Paul was just a name; they had never met him and had only heard about him. So Paul took time to build his credibility and authority by carefully setting forth his theology. It's as if Paul were saying, "Here's who I am, and here's what I believe."

Another purpose for Paul's writing was to solidify the Romans in their faith, since they had no apostolic leaders or teachers. He knew the inevitable conflicts that would arise for citizens of Christ's kingdom in the greatest city of the Roman empire. Also, from Priscilla, Aquila, and other friends in Rome, Paul had undoubtedly heard of the struggles and tensions the Roman believers were experiencing. And this was a church without a whole Bible—they had the Hebrew Scriptures (the Old Testament), but the Gospels hadn't been written, and the other Epistles had been sent to other churches. This letter, therefore, was the first piece of strictly Christian literature that these believers would see. So, under the inspiration of the Holy Spirit, Paul clearly and carefully crafted this theological masterpiece with the strong message of the sovereignty of God and justification by faith.

An important part of the faith-solidification process is to correct errors. So Paul's message included warnings of people "who cause divisions and put obstacles in your way that are contrary to the teaching you have learned" (16:17 NIV). Paul doesn't seem to have any specific situation or individuals in mind; rather, his warning is a general one that should be heard and heeded by all Christians. He warned of Judaizers (those who insisted on adherence to the Jewish laws, 2:17–4:25), antinomianists (those who would live with no laws or rules, 6:1–8:17), and legalists (those who would turn Christianity into a set of dos and don'ts, 14:1–15:13). Writing from Corinth, Paul was painfully aware of the influence of those false ideas, and he wanted to strengthen his readers against them.

Paul felt a unity with Roman believers even though he had met very few of them, and he wrote to strengthen their faith. They were members of the same family, citizens of the same nation, and subjects of the same King. The unity of the church is real, despite barriers of distance, language, and culture. All those who trust in Christ are members of God's family—brothers and sisters. How close are you to the rest of the family? What can you do to build their faith?

So Paul had many reasons for writing. Paul longed to visit his friends in Rome, to minister God's Word to his Christian brothers and sisters, and then to travel to Spain with their help and prayers (15:23-24).

MESSAGE

Sin, Salvation, Spiritual growth, Sovereignty, and Service.

Because Paul was introducing himself to the Romans, he carefully outlined his beliefs. And because Paul was writing to help strengthen the faith of these young Christians, he was careful to build his case slowly, starting with the basics. The result was a concise, logical, and well-ordered presentation of Christian theology. In short, Paul's message was, "I am not ashamed of the gospel, because it is the power of God for the salvation of everyone who believes: first for the Jew, then for the Gentile. For in the gospel a righteousness from God is revealed, a righteousness that is by faith from first to last, just as it is written: 'The righteous will live by faith'" (1:16-17 NIV).

Sin (1:18–3:20). Before announcing the good news, Paul gives the bad news: The whole human race stands condemned as sinners deserving God's wrath and punishment. In presenting this truth, Paul makes his case like a skillful lawyer, beginning with references to humankind in general and to the obvious sinners in the world.

Paul's readers were familiar with Greek and Roman paganism and idolatry and would certainly agree with his descriptions of their terrible sins. But then Paul moves to the other extreme, focusing on the Jews who were so careful to avoid sin by observing the law. He explains that even those who are religious stand condemned, just as they condemn others. By referring to both Gentiles and Jews, Paul speaks to both elements in the church and effectively heads off any judgmental finger pointing or holier-than-thou self-righteousness of one side over the other.

Paul's argument moves closer and closer to each reader until finally he says, "What shall we conclude then? Are we any better? Not at all!" (3:9 NIV). The final conclusion is that "there is no one

righteous, not even one. . . . There is no one who does good, not
even one" (3:10, 12 NIV).

Sin means refusing to do God's will and failing to do all that
God wants. Since Adam's rebellion against God, our nature is to
disobey him. Our sin cuts us off from God. Sin causes us to want
to live our own way rather than God's way. Because God is morally perfect, just, and fair, he is right when he condemns sin.

All human beings are sinners. All human beings are "guilty!"—
deserving the death penalty.

Importance for Today. It is easy to point judgmental fingers at
others, noting their sins and almost gleefully condoning their certain punishment. In doing so, we often compare ourselves to
them and thus excuse our own disobedience and shortcomings.
I'm not so bad, we think. *After all, I've never killed anybody.* But
the terrible truth is that every person has sinned, either by rebelling against God or by ignoring his will. Compared to God's
standard of perfection, we fall woefully short. Thus we stand condemned, no matter how religious we are.

Regardless of our background or how hard we try to live a
good and moral life, we cannot earn salvation or remove our sin.
Only Christ can save us.

Salvation (3:21–5:21). The Romans had a smorgasbord of gods
and religious beliefs from which to choose. It would be easy to be
confused about spiritual truth and eventually assume that one religion must be as good as another ("As long as you believe in
something") or to think that eventually everyone will be saved
("All religious roads lead to the same destination").

Paul's clear answer is NO! The only thing that we all have in
common is condemnation for our sins; we all stand guilty before
God.

But that bad news sets the stage for the Good News. Paul joyfully explains the rest of the story—that salvation is available
from God. This salvation (forgiveness and eternal life) comes
through faith (not by works) in Christ, and Christ alone. It is not a
reward for being good, observing the law, or being religious.
"This righteousness from God comes through faith in Jesus
Christ to all who believe" (3:22 NIV). And it is available to all
types of people—"There is no difference, for all have sinned and
fall short of the glory of God, and are justified freely by his grace
through the redemption that came by Christ Jesus" (3:22-24 NIV).
Our sin points out our need to be forgiven and cleansed. Although
we don't deserve it, God, in his kindness, reached out to love and
forgive us. He provides the way for us to be saved. Christ's death
paid the penalty for our sin.

In our pluralistic society that holds tolerance and openmindedness in high regard, a popular idea is that all religions are essentially the same and equally effective. Christians, therefore, are often seen as narrow and dogmatic when insisting that Christ is the *only* way to God. But that is what Jesus taught, and it is the truth that Paul affirms here in Romans.

Throughout the book of Romans, Paul stressed the relationship between law and grace. By *law* Paul usually meant the Mosiac law. He was painfully aware of the Jews' struggle to keep the law and the continuing conflict between Jewish and Gentile believers over the role of the law in God's plan. While affirming the importance of the law and of the Jews in God's plan (3:1-8), Paul proclaimed that salvation is open to all who believe (11:11-32) and that salvation is by grace through faith (3:22-24; 4:1–5:11).

Importance for Today. Although we may lose popularity for insisting that salvation comes only through faith in Christ, we must be steadfast in our commitment to the gospel because it is the *truth*. And we must explain that the exclusiveness of the message is far from being closed or narrow-minded—it is Good News. After recognizing our utter lostness in our sins, we can say, "Thank God there is *one* way!" By believing in Jesus Christ and accepting him as Savior, men and women can enter into a wonderful new relationship with God.

Spiritual Growth (6:1–8:17). After clearly setting forth the foundations of the faith (all are sinners; salvation is available through Christ), Paul turns his attention to the practical implications of being saved. This encompasses the rest of his letter to the Romans as he attempts to strengthen their faith. Paul moves from the theological to real life, into the day-to-day struggles of his readers.

First, of course, there is the matter of growth in the faith. Believing in Christ (being "saved") is only the beginning. New followers of Christ must mature in their relationship with God, continually turning away from sin and obeying God. This was important for the Roman Christians to understand, as they were surrounded by many pressures and temptations. It would be easy to give in to sinful desires in a society where pleasure was the principal good and where gratifying every lust of the flesh was the norm. And believers who had slipped back into sin might feel trapped, as though they couldn't escape sin's grasp.

So Paul explains that by God's power, believers are freed from the cycle of sin and death and are sanctified—made holy. This means they are set apart from sin and enabled to obey and to become more like Christ (6:1–7:6). In his explanation, Paul writes of slaves—an illustration that all Romans would understand because slavery was a vital part of Roman life. Paul's message was that Christians don't have to be slaves to sinful desires. Instead, they are free to obey God, to be *his* slaves instead, to do what he wants (6:15–7:6). Although breaking free of sin's grasp can be a struggle, Christians can be freed totally because of the work of Christ and through the power of the Holy Spirit (7:7-25). And when believers are growing in their relationship with Christ, the Holy Spirit frees them from the demands of the law and from fear of judgment (8:1-17).

Importance for Today. Human nature has not changed since the first century. Born sinners, men and women continue to live for self and to ignore God and his rules for living. Although the environment has changed radically through science and technology, the basic temptations have remained constant from then until now: "the desire of the flesh, the desire of the eyes, the pride in riches" (1 John 2:16 NRSV). People feel trapped in their sins, unable to break free of destructive habits, relationships, and obsessions.

Certainly our cities provide at least as many enticing temptations as did Rome. Flip on a television, peruse a magazine rack, check out the latest movie listings, and scan the headlines—we still crave sex, money, and power.

Paul's message to the Romans, therefore, is good news for us as well—faith in Christ gives us true freedom. We no longer have to give in to the desires of our sinful nature and to the evil influences around us. Not only can we have eternal life someday; we can have new life now. Through the power of the Holy Spirit, we can live the way God wants us to live. That's freedom!

Because we are free from sin's control, the law's demands, and fear of God's punishment, we can grow in our relationship with Christ. By trusting in the Holy Spirit and allowing him to help us, we can overcome sin and temptation. "Therefore, there is now no condemnation for those who are in Christ Jesus, because through Christ Jesus the law of the Spirit of life set me free from the law of sin and death" (8:1-2).

Sovereignty (8:18–11:36). One word that would epitomize the Roman government is *power*. The mighty Roman empire seemed to stretch forever, and its armies seemed invincible. Those who lived in Rome were continually reminded of Rome's power, with generals parading through the streets to celebrate their victories, thousands of men and women from conquered lands serving as slaves, and emperors demanding to be worshipped. Into this milieu, Paul sends the message of God's sovereignty.

This is a crucial truth for the Roman Christians to understand and believe, for it is at this point that the kingdom of God and the kingdom of Rome will come into the greatest conflict. Soon believers will have to choose between allegiance to Rome and allegiance to Christ. Knowing that God reigns triumphant will make that choice much easier.

God's sovereignty is also a message of hope. It would be easy for Roman believers to despair in the face of overwhelming opposition and persecution. We can almost hear them ask, "If God is in control, why doesn't he show himself and get rid of this evil and corruption?" "What about suffering? Why does God allow his people to suffer so much?" "And what is God's plan for the Jews, his chosen people?"

Paul answers by explaining that the world is not the way it should be and that this life is not all there is: "I consider that our present sufferings are not worth comparing with the glory that will be revealed in us. The creation waits in eager expectation for the sons of God to be revealed" (8:18-19 NIV).

In addition, God is working all things for good (8:28). His sovereign purpose in all that we are experiencing is to make us like Christ (8:29). And no matter what happens, "we are more than conquerors" (8:37) and can never be lost to his love (8:38-39).

Next, Paul explains how God's plan has worked in the past, through the Jews; (9:1-33) how his plan includes all who call on the name of the Lord, both Jews and Gentiles (10:12); and how God is in control of the present and the future (11:1-32).

Finally, overwhelmed by the awesome power and plan of God, Paul breaks into poetry: "Oh, the depth of the riches of the wisdom and knowledge of God! How unsearchable his judgments, and his paths beyond tracing out! 'Who has known the mind of the Lord? Or who has been his counselor? Who has ever given to God, that God should repay him?' For from him and through him and to him are all things. To him be the glory forever! Amen" (11:33-36 NIV).

Regardless of the present circumstances, believers can trust and take hope in the sovereignty of God. He is in control; his plan is at work; and he will work all things to his glory.

Importance for Today. Our world is also obsessed with power—in politics, business, and relationships. Power means control, influence, security, and ease. In the face of this lust for power, Christians can feel isolated and alone. And as a powerless minority, we can feel discriminated against and persecuted. Like the Roman believers, we need to hear Paul's message reaffirming the sovereignty of God, reminding us that our allegiance is not to the puny gods of this world and their hollow offers of power and prestige. No, we belong to the Sovereign of the universe.

We can take hope in knowing who God is and understanding his might. He has chosen us! We belong to him! He has great plans for us! He is working in all things for our good and his glory! He offers salvation to all who would come to him in humble faith! He is in control! Hallelujah!

Service (12:1–15:13). Paul has explained the gospel by describing the utter sinfulness and lostness of humankind and the wonderful good news that salvation is available to all (Jews and Gentiles alike) who trust Christ as Savior. Then Paul outlined the importance of growing in the faith—that begins with realizing our freedom from sin through the work of Christ and the power of the Holy Spirit. Next, Paul emphasized God's sovereignty, reminding believers of their allegiance and giving them hope when their world seemed to be caving in.

Paul's final theme is service: serving God and the other members of the body of Christ, the church. In many ways, the previous themes could be seen as personal and inward, focusing on what God is doing in and through the individual. Here, however, the focus is outward. Paul explains how believers should relate in society, to government (13:1-7) and to neighbors (12:9-21; 13:8-14). Paul also tells how they should relate to their brothers and sisters in Christ—encouraging Christians to use their spiritual gifts (12:3-8) and helping weaker members (14:1–15:13).

Although Christians made up a small minority of the population of Rome, still they could make a difference for Christ. How? By living as "transformed" men and women (12:2)—holding on to good (12:9), returning good for evil (12:17-19), helping those in need (12:20), being good citizens (13:1-7), and loving others as Christ would love them (13:8-14). And during these difficult days, with all the pressures and temptations of the surrounding society, it was important for Christians to be a unified (15:5) and loving body. Paul urges believers to humbly serve one another by avoiding arguments and judgments (14:13-18), working for peace and harmony (14:19), strengthening each other (15:1-2), and accepting each other (15:7).

If men and women truly honor Christ as Lord, it will show in their lives. They will be known for their love, in the community and in the church.

Importance for Today. Just before Jesus was arrested and crucified, he told his disciples that people would know that they were his followers by their love for each other (John 13:34-35). In essence, that is Paul's message to the Roman followers of Christ: "Let no debt remain outstanding, except the continuing debt to love one another" (13:8 NIV). That strong message is for us as well. If we are going to make any kind of impact in this world for Christ, we must love as Christ loved, helping those in need and serving with humility and grace.

This example of love must begin in our churches. Unity, encouragement, and support should be our goal, rather than the much-publicized arguments, splits, and even lawsuits. People will take seriously the claims of Christ when they see what he has done in the lives of those who bear his name—Christians ("one who belongs to Christ").

SUMMARY

Paul wrote to introduce himself to the Romans and to strengthen the faith of these young Christians. The result is a concise, logical, and well-ordered presentation of Christian theology.

Before announcing the good news, Paul gives the bad news: the whole human race stands condemned as sinners, deserving God's wrath and punishment. But that bad news sets the stage for the Good News. So Paul joyfully explains the rest of the story—that salvation is available from God through faith (not by works) in Christ, and Christ alone. Our sin highlights our need to be forgiven. God, in his kindness, provides the way for us to be saved.

Next Paul turns his attention to the practical implications of being saved. First, of course, there is the matter of growth in the faith. Believing in Christ (being "saved") is only the beginning. New followers of Christ must mature in their relationship with God, continually turning away from sin and obeying God. Through the power of the Spirit, believers are freed from the cycle of sin and death and are sanctified—made holy—set apart from sin and enabled to obey and to become more like Christ.

Paul then tells of God's sovereignty. Although the world is not the way it should be, God is working all things for good. God's plan has worked in the past, through the Jews; now it includes everyone who calls on the Lord's name—both Jews and Gentiles. God is in control of the present and the future too. Overwhelmed by the awesome power and plan of God, Paul breaks into song.

Finally, Paul turns to service, serving God and the other members of the body of Christ, the church. Paul explains how believers should relate to society, to government, and to neighbors. He also tells how they should relate to their brothers and sisters in Christ—encouraging Christians to use their spiritual gifts and to help weaker members. Then Paul concludes with personal greetings and final exhortations.

VITAL STATISTICS

Purpose: To introduce Paul to the Romans and to give a sample of his message before he arrives in Rome

Author: Paul

To Whom Written: The Christians in Rome and believers everywhere

Date Written: About A.D. 57, from Corinth, as Paul was preparing for his visit to Jerusalem

Setting: Apparently Paul had finished his work in the east, and he planned to visit Rome on his way to Spain after first bringing a collection to Jerusalem for the poor Christians there (15:23-28). The Roman church had a majority of Gentiles with a strong Jewish minority.

Key Verse: "Therefore, since we have been justified through faith, we have peace with God through our Lord Jesus Christ" (5:1 NIV).

Key People: Paul, Phoebe

Key Place: Rome

Special Features: Paul wrote Romans as an organized and carefully presented statement of his faith—it does not have the form of a typical letter. At the end of the letter, however, Paul does spend considerable time greeting people in Rome.

OUTLINE OF ROMANS

A. WHAT TO BELIEVE (1:1–11:36)
1. Sinfulness of mankind
2. Forgiveness of sin through Christ
3. Freedom from sin's grasp
4. Israel's past, present, and future
B. HOW TO BEHAVE (12:1–16:27)
1. Personal responsibility
2. Personal notes

THE GOSPEL GOES TO ROME

When Paul wrote his letter to the church in Rome, he had not yet
been there, but he had taken the gospel "from Jerusalem all the
way around to Illyricum" (15:19 NIV). He planned to visit and
preach in Rome one day, and hoped to continue to take the gospel
farther west—even to Spain.

Romans 1

As if proving that all roads did lead to Rome, the gospel born in Judea eventually made its way to the capital of the empire. It is not clear how soon the message about Christ actually arrived at Rome, but it produced results. By the end of the second decade following Christ's resurrection, there was an established group of Christians there. Several house-churches were probably meeting. Paul opens his letter to these Roman believers, most of whom he had never met, by explaining who he is and what his credentials are. Almost immediately, he directs their attention to the Lord Jesus Christ. Paul knew that the resurrected Christ was the most important common denominator for him and the believers in Rome. From that common ground he introduces his plan to visit them and then plunges into one of the most detailed explanations of the Christian faith found in the Bible.

1:1 Paul ... servant ... apostle ... set apart.NRSV In spite of the remarkable influence Paul had in the spread of the gospel and the writing of the New Testament, we know relatively little about him. He given the name Saul at birth, and he is called that until his conflict with Bar-Jesus at Paphos. At that time Luke wrote, "Then Saul, who also is called Paul" (Acts 13:9 NKJV). From then on, he was called Paul in Acts. As Saul, he was raised a strict Pharisee, from the tribe of Benjamin (Philippians 3:5), born in Tarsus and educated in Jerusalem under Gamaliel (Acts 22:3). Though born to Jewish parents, Saul was also a Roman citizen (Acts 22:27-28). In fact, we know him best by his last name, since *Paul* (Greek, *Paulos*) was probably his Roman surname. He would have been formally introduced as Saul Paul (*Saulos Paulos*). Out of this diverse background, God formed and called a valuable servant. And

God used every aspect of Paul's upbringing to further the spread of the gospel.

 LIABILITIES TURNED INTO ASSETS
In God's plans, no part of our background or upbringing is wasted. As with Paul, parts of our past that seem like a liability can be used by God. It is a humbling experience to look back over life and see how God has been able to turn even the difficult situations into good. Our own past makes us a wiser mentor or more merciful counselor to others we meet along the way.

Paul had friends in Rome, as Romans 16 shows, but he had not personally visited that church. So he begins his letter by formally presenting his credentials. While we no longer practice the custom of beginning a letter with a signature, we can see its benefits in Paul's writing. Knowing who is writing the letter focuses our attention, right from the beginning. And in the case of the New Testament letters, it establishes that the author's writing was under the command of Christ. The letters carry divine authority.

Long before Paul was able to call himself **a servant of Jesus Christ,**[NRSV] he gained a reputation as a great enemy of Christians. Paul was so zealous for the Jewish faith that he persecuted the followers of Jesus without mercy. He is first mentioned in Acts 8:1-3, where he approved of the stoning of Stephen. Later, on a journey to Damascus to capture believers there, Paul came face to face with Jesus Christ and became a believer himself—*a servant* and *an apostle.* Paul's own account of these events is recorded in Acts 26:9-18.

The word translated *servant* means "slave," one who is subject to the will and wholly at the disposal of his master. Paul, in using the term, expresses his absolute devotion and subjection to Christ Jesus. The New Testament teaches that the true leader is servant of all. Jesus exemplified this throughout his life (see Mark 10:35-45; Philippians 2:5-9). For a Roman citizen to identify himself as a servant was unthinkable. Paul could have introduced himself to these Romans as a Roman citizen, but instead he chose to speak of himself only as completely dependent on and obedient to his beloved Master. Because Paul was writing to a church made up of both Romans and Jews, he wisely emphasized, from his own life, the highest allegiance that ought to mark a believer.

WHAT IS A SERVANT?
What is your attitude toward Christ, your Master? Our willingness to serve and obey Jesus Christ enables us to be useful and usable servants to do work for him—work that really matters. Obedience begins as we renounce other masters, identify ourselves with Jesus, discover his will and live according to it, and consciously turn away from conflicting interests, even if these interests have been important to us in the past.

After establishing his identity as Christ's servant, Paul notes two important roles to characterize his life. Paul was **called to be an apostle** and **set apart for the gospel of God.**^{NRSV} His calling occurred when he saw the Lord Jesus on the road to Damascus (Acts 9:1-19). His call came directly from "Jesus Christ and God the Father" (Galatians 1:1) and was to him an assignment—he was responsible to teach the *gospel of God* (the good news of salvation in Jesus Christ) "among the Gentiles" (Galatians 1:16).

Paul was one of the few Christians who could speak of being literally called *(kletos)* by God. Jesus audibly spoke to Paul on the road to Damascus. The term is frequently used today to indicate when a believer senses God's direction in his or her life. In Romans, within several verses, Paul used the same term to identify his readers, "And you also are among those who are called *(kletoi)* to belong to Jesus Christ" (1:6). Further, they are "called *(kletois)* to be saints " (1:7). Responding to the gospel involves hearing God's most important call in our lives. Believers can speak confidently of being called in two distinct ways: we are called to belong to Jesus Christ, and called to be saints. We should use the term *called* with great caution, especially when we use it to refer to a role we have chosen or when we have been gradually led by God's Spirit. God's calls tend to be permanent; however, people often use the term to indicate responsibilities or jobs that they have no intention of doing permanently. The call to belong to Christ and the call to be saints ought to be our daily pursuit!

The title *apostle* designated authority to set up and supervise churches and discipline them if necessary. Even more than a title of authority, *apostle* means one sent on a mission, like an envoy or an ambassador. Paul represents himself with the credentials and responsibilities given to him by the King of kings as an ambassador to evangelize the Gentile world. Not only was he called, he was *set apart;* he regarded the communication of the gospel as a special sign on his life, a role given to him that he had not earned but was privileged to carry out. Elsewhere he wrote, "I have become its servant by the commission God gave me to present to you the word of God in its fullness" (Colossians 1:25 NIV).

THE PROPHETS WROTE OF GOD'S PLAN

Paul did not specify the passages from the prophets he had in mind when he wrote of "the gospel [God] promised . . . through his prophets in the Holy Scriptures," probably because of his readers' familiarity with those Scriptures (herein quoted from NIV). For these early Christians, the Old Testament continued to be their authority, and they knew of many references to God's plan and the Messiah. Here are several references that Paul might have pointed to:

Genesis 12:3	The Messiah would come from Abraham's line, and through the Messiah "all peoples on earth will be blessed."
Psalm 16:10	The promise of the resurrection given to David: the Messiah (the Holy One) would be resurrected.
Psalm 40:6-10	The Messiah would "desire to do your will, O my God, " and would accomplish that will so completely as to die on the cross.
Psalm 118:22	The Messiah would be rejected by his own people, but would become the "capstone, " the most important part of the church.
Isaiah 11:1ff.	The Messiah would be the "Branch " that will "bear fruit " in the form of believers. "The Spirit of the LORD will be on him.
Isaiah 49:5-6	The Messiah would gather Israel and be a light for the Gentiles.
Zechariah 9:9-11	The Messiah would come to his people "riding on a donkey, " which he did in his Triumphal Entry into Jerusalem.
Zechariah 12:10	The Messiah would "be pierced " on the cross, and many would mourn his death.
Malachi 4:1-5	The Messiah's arrival will be heralded by one like "the prophet Elijah, " who was to be John the Baptist.

1:2 The gospel he promised beforehand through his prophets in the Holy Scriptures.[NIV] Romans 16:22 informs us that Tertius was Paul's scribe for this letter. Remember that these words were written down as they were being spoken. For instance, the first six verses in this letter are one long sentence. Knowing Paul's style helps us follow some difficult sentences that were more easily grasped by Greek audiences. Here Paul abruptly changes the focus from himself to the gospel, then to the person it presents, then to the audience for whom the gospel is intended. As Paul warms to his subject, the letter quickly develops the tone of a sermon. Tertius's quill must have been flying across the papyrus.

> Here the door is thrown open wide for the understanding of the Holy Scriptures, that is, that everything must be understood in relation to Christ, especially in the case of prophecy.
> —Martin Luther

The Good News was promised by God and was not a new religion made up by Paul or anyone else. It was rooted in God's promises in the Old Testament to his people through his *prophets*. The gospel that Paul preached was in perfect continuity with God's earlier words in the Scriptures to his people, Israel. Both the Jews and Gentiles in the church of Rome needed to be reminded that the gospel is an ancient message of God's plan for his creation. This was on Paul's mind and is a recurring theme throughout the letter.

Even though the church in Rome consisted mostly of Gentiles and former converts to the Jewish faith, Paul reminded them all that in their acceptance of the gospel they were not casting off Moses and the law in order to embrace Christ. Rather, they were discovering and responding to the outworking of God's eternal plan. The prophets in the Old Testament announced the coming fulfillment of God's grace in Christ. The actual fulfillment of those prophetic statements confirmed God's involvement all along. This direct statement by Paul anticipates an important teaching that he would develop later in this letter.

1:3 **Concerning his Son.**NRSV After introducing the messenger (himself), the message (gospel), and the source (God), Paul turns to the subject of the message. In verses 3-5, Paul summarizes the good news about Jesus Christ, who came as a human by natural descent (1:3), was part of the Jewish royal line through David (1:3), died and was raised from the dead (1:4), and opened the door for God's grace and kindness to be poured even on the Gentiles (1:5). Paul is simply outlining what he will return to describe at length later in the letter.

As to his human nature, he **was a descendant of David.**NIV The central focus of the gospel is Jesus Christ, God's Son, who was both human and divine (see Luke 3:31; 2 Timothy 2:8). Jesus was born in David's line, in Bethlehem, and of David's tribe (Judah). King David, "a man after [God's] own heart," was promised a kingdom without end. In the birth of Jesus Christ, the eternal King of kings, that promise was fulfilled (2 Samuel 7:12-16). Jesus truly fulfilled the Old Testament Scriptures that predicted that the Messiah would come through David's line. With this statement of faith, Paul declares his agreement with the teaching of all Scripture and of the other apostles.

The unique dual nature of Jesus (the God-man) was a constant part of Paul's thinking. The historical human life of Christ was essential to the gospel. The Messiah was not a god like those of the Greeks and Romans, a product of legends. He was the flesh-and-blood founder of the Christian faith. Here Jesus is described as David's descendant *as to his human nature*, but the phrase is surrounded by the term *Son*, used both in verses 3 and 4 and connecting Christ's sonship with God. Maintaining a clear emphasis on both Christ's human nature and his divine nature is important for a complete understanding of the gospel. In Christ's humanity we see his identification with us and his excellence as our example. In Christ's divinity we see his worthiness to take our place in receiving the punishment for sin that is due us. We separate Christ's human and divine natures for understanding and discussion, but in fact, they cannot be separated. Jesus is and will always be the God-man, our Lord and Savior.

1:4 **According to the spirit of holiness.**^{NRSV} This expression completes a parallel reference to Jesus' dual nature. The two phrases use the Greek *kata*, which is literally translated by the words *according to*. Jesus was a descendant of David according to the flesh (*kata sarka*) and he was declared Son of God according to *the spirit of holiness* (*kata pneuma hagiousunes*). In short, Christ was fully human and fully divine. Jesus' entire life, from his human conception to his resurrection, was planned, promised, and fulfilled by God. There is some question over whether the expression *the spirit of holiness*, which is not capitalized in Greek, refers to the Holy Spirit acting through the Resurrection or to the spirit of Christ's holy character that, combined with the Resurrection, declares his Sonship. The NIV preserves the ambiguity in its text, while other translations (e.g., NRSV) sometimes make note of the difference. The emphasis of Paul's statement is that Jesus was clearly marked out as the Son of God when he rose from the dead.

Declared the Son of God.^{NASB} The term *declared* here does not mean that Christ somehow achieved or gained his Sonship. It

means that his nature as God's Son was made clear **by his resurrection from the dead.**^{NIV} He was, is, and will always be the Son
of God. Christ's resurrection unmistakably revealed that truth to
the world. At the time of his resurrection, Christ was glorified
and restored to his full rights and status as Son of God in power
(Philippians 2:4-9).

HE IS RISEN!
Our personal declaration or acceptance of Jesus as God's
Son does not affect the truth of who he is, but it certainly
makes a difference in our lives. In surrendering to that truth, we
place ourselves in a position where we can benefit from all
Christ offers. He is our Savior even before we accept him as
such; but until we accept him, we have not been saved. And
that is only the beginning. The faith that believers have in
God's guidance rests on the truth of Christ's resurrection.
The same power that raised Christ from the dead is the
power that operates in believers' lives not only to save, but
also to help them obey God and to give them victory over
death.

Jesus Christ our Lord.^{NIV} Jesus is eternal and exalted as Lord at
God's right hand (Psalm 110:1; Acts 2:33-35). The gospel message tells us about Christ, the Son of God, who humbled himself
and then was glorified by the Holy Spirit. When the gospel message is received, *Jesus* becomes *our Lord.* The message is true
(Jesus Christ is Lord), whether we believe it or not. But personally recognizing Jesus as *our Lord* is an important part of realizing that his authority extends to every area of our lives.

1:5 We have received grace and apostleship.^{NRSV} Having summarized the uniqueness of Christ, Paul briefly returns to his own experience. For him, the beginning was when he *received grace.*
Before Paul became an apostle, he was made a disciple, a follower of Christ. After personally receiving the gospel, he then
was sent out to tell others. Christians have both privilege and
great responsibility. Paul and the apostles received forgiveness
(*grace*) as an undeserved privilege. But they also were given the
responsibility of sharing the message of God's forgiveness with
others. God also graciously forgives our sins when we repent and
put our trust in Christ. In doing this, we are committing ourselves
to begin a new life. Paul's new life also involved a God-given responsibility—to witness about God's Good News to the world.
God's call may take many forms and many directions, but he

does call each believer to be an example of
the changed life that Jesus Christ has begun
and to spread the word.

In Paul's case, God's direction became
very clear. He was to **call people from
among all the Gentiles.**NIV While Paul
waited, blind and helpless, in Damascus,
the Lord told Ananias, "This man is my
chosen instrument to carry my name before the Gentiles and their kings and before the people of Israel" (Acts 9:15
NIV). Paul did carry the Good News
across the known world, speaking in
synagogues, convincing the Gentiles,
and even standing before kings. Paul
understood his calling, for in Romans
11:13 he states, "I am talking to you Gentiles. Inasmuch as I am the apostle to the
Gentiles . . ."

> This letter is not a tract to be put into the hands of the sinning man in order that, believing what it says, he may be saved. It is rather a treatise to be put into the hands of Christian men in order that they may understand the method of their salvation.
> —G.Campbell Morgan

Paul's introduction accounts for both the Jews and the Gentiles within the Roman church. He makes it clear that the gospel is the working out of God's plan first revealed to the
Jews. He also makes it clear that the gospel offered hope to
the Gentiles. "For God so loved the world that he gave his
one and only Son, that whoever believes in him shall not perish but have eternal life" (John 3:16 NIV). Paul was chosen to
be a key link in making sure that God's love for the world actually got announced to the world.

To the obedience that comes from faith.NIV This was the desired response to the gospel message and the goal of Paul's
ministry to the Roman Christians—that they would obey
God because of their faith in God. The only source for the
kind of obedience expected is faith in the one true God and
in Jesus Christ, his Son. Faith and obedience are inseparable.
Where one is lacking, the other will not be found either. Real
faith will always lead to obedience; real obedience *comes
from faith.*

Faith is a word with many meanings. It can mean faithfulness
(Matthew 24:45). It can mean absolute trust, as shown by some
of the people who came to Jesus for healing (Luke 7:2-10). It can
mean confident hope (Hebrews 11:1). Or, as James points out, it
can even mean a barren belief that does not result in good deeds

(James 2:14-26). What does Paul mean when he speaks of saving faith?

We must be very careful to understand faith as Paul uses the word because he ties faith so closely to salvation. It is *not* something we must do in order to earn salvation; if that were true, then faith would be just one more deed, and Paul clearly states that human deeds can never save us (Galatians 2:16). Instead, faith is a gift that God gives us *because* he is saving us (Ephesians 2:8). God's grace, not our faith, saves us. In his mercy, however, when he saves us, he gives us faith—a relationship with his Son that helps us become like him.

Even in Old Testament times, grace, not deeds, was the basis of salvation. As Hebrews points out, "it is impossible for the blood of bulls and goats to take away sins" (10:4). God intended for his people to look beyond the animal sacrifices to him, but all too often they required sacrifices. When Jesus triumphed over death, he canceled the charges against us and opened the way to the Father (Colossians 2:12-15). Because God is merciful, he offers us faith. How mistaken it is to turn faith into a deed and try to develop it on our own! We can never come to God through our own faith, any more than his Old Testament people could come through their own sacrifices. Instead, we must accept God's gracious offer with thanksgiving and allow him to plant the seed of faith within us.

1:6 You also . . . are called to belong to Jesus Christ.NIV Having stated the scope of his ministry, Paul goes on to include the Roman believers in God's plan. These believers may not have been called as apostles, as Paul was, but they certainly had been called to belong to Jesus Christ (see 8:28, 30 and the note on "called" in 1:1). Paul was reminding the Romans that the message of the gospel is larger than its messengers. Even though he had not been able to visit them personally, he was fully aware that they were among those God had intended to reach.

The word *belong* is implied, not stated in this verse. Paul uses the literal phrase "you are also called ones (*kletoi*) of (or by) Jesus Christ." Consequently, the meaning can be read two ways, both emphasizing a sense of belonging. First, being called points to Christ's desire to make them his own. Secondly, being called implies their response to Christ's call, so that they presently do, in fact, *belong* to Christ.

WHO HOLDS THE TITLE?
Applying the Scriptures involves discovering where we *fit* in God's plan. Here the message is direct—*you also!* The call echoes across the centuries and speaks to our own hearts and minds. We too have been *called to belong to Jesus Christ.* How have you responded to that call? Picture your life as a piece of valuable property—In whose name is the title?

1:7 **To all who are in Rome.**^{NKJV} In Paul's day, Rome had a population of approximately one million and was the largest city in the world. It was the capital of the Roman empire that had spread over most of Europe, North Africa, and the Near East. In New Testament times, Rome was experiencing a golden age. The city was wealthy, literary, and artistic. It was a cultural center, but it was also morally decadent. The Romans worshiped many pagan gods, and some of the emperors were also worshiped. Many Romans were naively pragmatic, believing that any means to accomplish a task or reach a goal was good. And for them, nothing worked better than physical might. The Romans trusted in their superior military power to protect them against all of their enemies.

In stark contrast to the Romans, the followers of Christ believed in only one God and lived by his high moral standards. In addition, Christianity was at odds with the Romans' dependence on military strength. Obedience to God will always challenge the prevailing attitudes and values of society. Christians in every age need to be reminded that God is the only permanent source of our security and salvation, and at the same time he is "our Father"!

The church in Rome was primarily made up of Gentiles (1:5-6, 13; 11:13; 15:15-16), although there were a number of Jewish Christians as well. Part of the church may have been Jews who became believers at Pentecost and returned to Rome with the Good News. Acts 2:10-11 states that among the great crowd in Jerusalem who heard Peter's speech were "visitors from Rome (both Jews and converts to Judaism)." In addition, travelers who had heard the Good News in other places brought it back to Rome (for example, Priscilla and Aquila—Acts 18:2; Romans 16:3-5).

Loved by God and called to be saints.^{NIV} The Christians in Rome were called to belong to Christ (1:6), and they were called to be saints (a common term designating believers). Paul describes those who have become Christians as people invited by Jesus Christ to become part of God's family and to be holy people (set apart, dedicated for his service). The reality of this invitation rests on the truth that people are *loved by God.* Before believers are called, they are loved. What a wonderful expression of what it means to be a Christian! In being reborn into God's family we have the greatest experience of love and the greatest inheritance. Because of all that God has done for us, we should strive to be his holy people.

GOD'S LOVE
Whenever we think that God's love for us depends on our behavior or spiritual success, we put ourselves in a hopeless situation because we can never be good enough to deserve God's love. As Paul later explains in this letter, God's love precedes everything. All of our attempts to earn his love will fail. That's because perfect love would require a perfect effort, clearly beyond us. It is also true that when we think of God's love as conditional, we unwittingly transform it into something much less than love.

Conditional love is an oxymoron. God's love is unconditional. The first delightful surprise in the gospel is that "God proves his love for us in that while we still were sinners Christ died for us" (Romans 5:8, NRSV). When you're feeling spiritually dull or anxious, ask yourself, "Have I begun to think of God's love as dependent on my effort?" Thank God for his unconditional, perfect love, and respond by living for him.

Grace and peace. *Grace* is God's unmerited favor; *peace* refers to the peace that Christ made between us and God through his death on the cross. Only God can grant such wonderful gifts. Paul wants his readers to experience God's grace and peace in their daily living. In these two words of greeting Paul is combining expressions from Jewish and Gentile customs. Jews wished each other *peace* (*eirene* or the Hebrew *shalom*); Gentiles wished each other *grace* (*charis*). Each of these common expressions gained considerable value in Christian use. Jesus said, "Peace I leave with you; my peace I give you. I do not give to you as the world gives. Do not let your hearts be troubled and do not be afraid" (John 14:27 NIV). The world offers a temporary and counterfeit version for each of God's wonderful gifts (for grace, luck; for Christ's peace, a fragile human calm). For believers, life's great blessings are not luck or chance, but God's grace; and even hardships have a gracious purpose behind them. For believers, Christ's peace is not escape from problems or turmoil, but an inner calm that permeates life itself. That is Paul's greeting and hope for all of us. Do grace and peace rule in your heart?

From God our Father and the Lord Jesus Christ.^{NKJV} By stating the divine source of grace and peace, Paul drew a forceful "bottom line" to his introduction. These last two qualities join the impressive list of wonders *from God our Father and the Lord Jesus Christ* that Paul has included in the last six breathless verses. Paul's calling and ours, the gospel itself, ancient promises, the plan of history, and the inclusion of both Jews and Gentiles in Christ's body have come from the divine source. The powerful message of these verses is a preview of all that follows.

PAUL DECLARES THE POWER OF THE GOSPEL / 1:8-17

After formally introducing himself, Paul expresses his feelings toward the Roman believers and his reasons for wanting to visit them. This would disarm objections that might be raised to his coming. Some believers in Rome might think that he was arrogant in trying to extend his influence all the way to the capital of the empire; others might think he was presumptuous in planning to teach the gospel to those who had already heard it; others might even be concerned that he lacked integrity for often expressing his desire to come to Rome but never getting there. Paul does not leave the Romans guessing—he tells them exactly why he wants to come.

Having placed himself and his motives before the Romans, Paul adds a final word to his introduction that vividly summarizes the content of his letter. He declares the power of the gospel. Romans 1:16-17 is considered one of the most profound and concise statements of Christianity ever written.

After quickly sketching the truth that God has made himself known to everyone, Paul explains that human beings consistently have turned their backs on God's self-revelation. Paul's word pictures present God as the powerful and gracious Creator who does

> The chief purpose of this letter is to magnify sin and to destroy all human wisdom and righteousness, to bring down all those who are proud and arrogant on account of their works. We need to break down our "inner self-satisfaction." God does not want to redeem us through our own, but through external righteousness and wisdom; not through one that comes from us and grows in us, but through one that comes to us from the outside; not through one that originates here on earth, but through one that comes from heaven.
> —Martin Luther

not force himself on his creation. As the letter continues, Paul provides vivid and detailed descriptions of our sinful world. But alongside his picture of human hopelessness, Paul emphasizes God's message of hope in Christ.

1:8 I thank my God through Jesus Christ for all of you.^{NRSV} Consistent with the style of ancient letter writing, Paul moves on from his greeting to state the motives for his letter. He mentions two: First, a word of thanks and later, a word of hope. Just as it was *through* Jesus Christ that Paul *received grace and apostleship* (1:5), it is also *through Jesus Christ* that Paul thanks God for the faith of the Roman believers. Paul's phrase emphasizes the truth that Jesus Christ is the one and only mediator between God and people—through Christ, God sends his love and forgiveness to us; through Christ, we offer praise and thanksgiving back to God (see 1 Timothy 2:5). Paul gave God the glory for these Roman believers and their faith. Their faith *had* encouraged him and *would continue* to encourage him (see Acts 28:15).

Your faith is being reported all over the world.^{NIV} Living in the Western world's political power center, Roman Christians were highly visible. Fortunately, their reputation was excellent; their strong faith was making itself known around the world. To have a thriving church in Rome and to have Christians living pure lives in an evil city bore strong testimony to their faith!

WHAT'S THE REPORT ON YOUR FAITH?
A visitor to your town stops by the local restaurant for lunch and casually asks the waitress to tell him about the church in town. How would the waitress describe the church you presently attend? When people talk about your congregation or your denomination, what do they say? Are their comments accurate? What features would you want them to notice? What is the best way to get the public to recognize your faith? How often does your church seriously evaluate its impact on the community?

1:9-10 God, whom I serve with my whole heart in preaching the gospel of his Son, is my witness.^{NIV} Paul is here telling his readers that his service to God in preaching the gospel has always been a heartfelt act of devotion. He calls upon God, who called him to this devoted service, to be his witness.

How constantly I remember you in my prayers.^{NIV} Paul was a man of prayer. Paul prayed for the Romans the same way that he prayed for the Ephesians (Ephesians 1:15-16), the Philippians (Philippians 1:3-4), the Colossians (Colossians 1:3-4), and the Thessalonians (1 Thessalonians 1:2-3). We would expect Paul to pray for his own converts and the churches he helped establish, but these words show that he also prayed for those outside his immediate acquaintance and responsibility. Paul had not personally visited these believers, so he had not yet been able to prove his love for them, but he appeals to God as his *witness*, confirming his constant prayers for the believers in Rome.

HABITUAL PRAYER
In addition to teaching the importance of prayer, Paul's practice also emphasizes the need for habitual prayer. How faithful are you in praying for other believers? What groups of Christians do you care enough about to regularly pray for them?

I pray that now at last by God's will the way may be opened for me to come to you.^{NIV} This is Paul's second motive for writing. He hoped to travel soon to Rome. For a long time, Paul had wanted to visit the empire's capital city, but he had been prevented from doing so (see also 1:13; 15:22; Acts 19:21; 23:11; 28:14-16). Here Paul expresses his continued desire to go, but only if God wills it.

When Paul finally did arrive in Rome, it was as a prisoner (see Acts 28:16). When writing this letter, he had no idea how, *by God's will, the way* to Rome would *be opened.* Paul prayed for a safe trip, and he did arrive safely—after getting arrested, slapped in the face, shipwrecked, and bitten by a poisonous snake. But along the way God also accomplished many things in and through Paul's life. (See Acts 21–28 for Luke's account of the journey.)

PRAYERS ANSWERED
When we sincerely pray, God will answer, although sometimes with timing and in ways we don't expect:
■ He uses different strengths than the ones we might rely on.
■ He has a different timetable than the one we might imagine.
■ He may use different training than the ways we have prepared ourselves.
■ He may use different opportunities, jobs, and careers than the ones we might have anticipated.
■ He may well use someone else whom we influence to accomplish what we thought was our job.

**1:11 May share with you some spiritual gift to strengthen
you.**NRSV Paul's continual prayers for the believers in Rome
had built up a strong desire to see them. Having prayed so
often for them, he wanted to visit them in order to minister to
them. Paul proposed a trip to Rome to serve, not to be served.
He fully intended that his visit would benefit the believers
there.

What *spiritual gift* did Paul want to impart? This was not a
particular empowering to do something; rather, it was an insight or teaching based on the needs that Paul would find
when he got to Rome. It would deepen their faith. Paul
wanted his readers to further understand what their faith
meant in their families, in their businesses, and in other relationships. If they were clear on those basics, their church
would be made strong, and their strengthened faith could
hold up under any circumstance. This letter to them certainly
worked toward that end, but Paul also hoped that the spiritual effects of his intended visit would be powerful and mutual.

THE STRENGTH OF PRAYER
Concerned prayer often gives birth to responsible plans for effective action. Acting before praying or without praying can lead
to disaster. But praying can develop in us a deeper awareness
of those priorities and people that God cares about. Praying
makes us open to what God wants us to do. Spending time
with those for whom we are praying can increase our understanding of their needs, deepen our love for them, and make
our prayers for them more specific.

1:12 Mutually encouraged by each other's faith.NRSV Paul prayed
for the chance to visit these Christians so that he could encourage them with his gift of faith and be encouraged by theirs. As
God's missionary, he could help them understand the meaning
of the good news about Jesus. As God's devoted people, they
could offer him fellowship and comfort. Paul makes it clear
that he will not come as simply the teacher and giver—he will
be open to be given to and encouraged as well. When Christians gather, everyone should give *and* receive. Our mutual
faith gives us a common language and a common purpose for
encouraging one another. To help evaluate the effects of our
ministry, we can ask, "What would encourage Paul about our
church?"

THE MUTUAL ENCOURAGEMENT OF FAITH
Paul fully anticipated that as he worked to strengthen the faith of his brothers and sisters in Rome, his faith would also be encouraged. Our desire to serve must never render us unwilling to be served. In order for the body of Christ to function smoothly, each member should serve in his or her own special way, and each should receive the service of others. Encouragement comes (1) when we hear from others about God's faithfulness in times of trouble; (2) when we experience the sacrificial service of other believers; and (3) when we are lifted by others' praise, knowing that tomorrow they may be lifted by our praise.

1:13 **I planned many times to come to you (but have been prevented from doing so until now).**NIV As explained in verse 10 above, Paul had tried to come to Rome, but had been hindered.

That I may reap some harvest among you.NRSV Paul's original plan was to include Rome in his missionary efforts. Although the church had been established there without his efforts, that fact did not discourage Paul from wanting to visit. Even with several house churches in Rome, Paul is most likely thinking here of the community rather than the church specifically. Paul's hope is for a harvest of the unsaved masses in Rome.

In the Old Testament, *harvest* referred to God's judgment, a time of doom for rebels and unbelievers (Jeremiah 8:20; Hosea 8:7). Jesus used it to represent a harvest of souls. In that sense evangelism is a harbinger of the end times and signals the defeat of Satan (Matthew 3:12; 13:24ff.).

Just as among the other Gentiles.NKJV By the end of his third missionary journey, Paul had traveled through Syria, Galatia, Asia, Macedonia, and Achaia. The churches that he had begun in these areas consisted mostly of Gentile believers. Paul could make statements like these without a hint of pride. He is making it clear that God directed him into ministry to the Gentiles and that the *harvest* came from God. He is simply saying, "I've always known that sooner or later I would end up in Rome. In fact, I've looked forward to seeing what God would accomplish through me there!"

LOOKING AHEAD
Paul was always looking ahead. He made plans to touch people's lives. It is much too easy for us to settle into a spiritual routine of church attendance and religious habits. Without conscious intention, our discipleship can degenerate into comfortable patterns that may make us feel good but do little to accomplish the tasks God wants. Preparation for church ought to involve more than wondering what we will get out of the preacher's sermon. Instead, we should consider what we will offer the rest of the believers. Do we prepare to give them encouragement? Do we anticipate a harvest among others? Ministering to others may result in having our own needs met in the process.

1:14 **I am obligated both to Greeks and non-Greeks, both to the wise and the foolish.**NIV One of the primary cultural divisions in Paul's world was linguistic—those who spoke Greek and those who didn't. Although Paul, as a Jew, might be expected to divide the world into "Jews and Gentiles," at this point he purposely looks through Gentile eyes to see the world as they see it. The expression *Greeks and non-Greeks* summarizes the *Gentiles*, among whom Paul hoped to have a *harvest* (1:13). But Paul's analysis of people went far beyond language. The labels he uses merely convey the breadth of his concern for all people. He desires a *harvest* among those known to be *wise* but who are lost because of their worldly wisdom. He desires the same for the *foolish* who might be considered by others unworthy or even unable to receive the gospel.

What was Paul's obligation? *Obligated* translates from the Greek "debtor" (*opheiletes*). After his experience with Christ on the road to Damascus (Acts 9), Paul's goal in life was to spread the Good News of salvation. He was partly obligated to Christ for being his Savior, and he was partly obligated to the entire world because it reminded him of his former lostness. Paul met his obligation by proclaiming Christ's salvation to all types of people—both Jews and Gentiles—crossing cultural, social, racial, and economic lines. Furthermore, Paul is also basing his obligation on the unique role that God had called him to play. Paul's upbringing allowed him to straddle the barriers that existed between the major cultural groups of his time. When he realized Christ had

> There was, accordingly, among the nations of antiquity, one system for the learned and another for the illiterate. An opposite mode of procedure belongs to true Christianity. Without distinction, it professes an equal regard for all human beings and its message is characterized as "glad tidings to the poor."
> —W. Wilberforce

"broken down the dividing wall" (Ephesians 2:14, NRSV) between these cultures, Paul also realized that he had been raised and called to carry the message of reconciliation through Christ to both sides. He literally owed it to them!

We also are *obligated* to Christ because he took on the punishment we deserve for our sin. We are *obligated* because God provided for our salvation and then somehow got the message to us. We are acting on that obligation whenever we become willing vehicles of God's message in the lives of others. Later in Romans, Paul uses the same Greek word, *opheiletes,* when he states, "Let no debt remain outstanding, except the continuing debt to love one another, for he who loves his fellowman has fulfilled the law" (13:8). Although we cannot repay Christ for all he has done, we can demonstrate our gratitude by showing his love to others.

> In a civilization like ours, I feel that everyone has to come to terms with the claims of Jesus Christ upon his life, or else be guilty of inattention or of evading the question.
> —C. S. Lewis

1:15 **Eager to preach the gospel . . . at Rome.**[NIV] Paul has an *obligation* (1:14), but he is *eager* to fulfill it! Paul had already visited some of the most beautiful cities of the world—Athens, Corinth, Ephesus—yet he carried an unfulfilled desire to minister in one of the most populated, corrupt places on earth. Neither the power nor the hostility of Rome intimidated Paul. He was convinced the gospel must be taken everywhere, specifically to the large and needy metropolitan areas of the world. Paul knew that the gospel had already gained a foothold in Rome—the believers to whom he was writing had heard and had responded. But Paul wanted to explain and teach that gospel more fully. This letter to the Romans is the introductory statement of all that Paul wanted these believers to understand more fully. Referring, for the second time in this letter so far, to the *gospel*, Paul turns his full attention to the message that he feels driven to declare.

EAGERNESS

Paul was eager to preach the gospel. Is our Christian service done in a spirit of eagerness? Or do we serve out of habit, a feeling of obligation, or perhaps even with a feeling of reluctant duty (much like a child who has to take a bath)? When we fully understand what Christ has done for us and what he offers to others, we will be motivated to share the Good News. Ask God to rekindle that fresh, eager attitude that wants to obey him and to tell others about Christ.

1:16 **I am not ashamed of the gospel.** Verses 16 and 17 summarize the thrust of the rest of Paul's letter and give the reason behind Paul's missionary zeal. Paul was ready, even eager (1:15) to preach at Rome. And he was *not ashamed of the gospel*, even though the gospel was held in contempt by those who did not believe; even though those who preached it could face humiliation and suffering. Paul was not intimidated by the intellect of Greece nor the power of Rome. When describing to the Corinthians the typical attitudes toward the gospel, Paul wrote, "we proclaim Christ crucified, a stumbling block to Jews and foolishness to Gentiles," (1 Corinthians 1:23 NRSV). Paul was not ashamed, because he knew from experience that the gospel had the power to transform lives, so he was eager to take it to as many as would listen. This verse marks the beginning of Paul's extended explanation of the gospel. Reading, understanding, and applying the gospel faithfully can also bring us to that point of being unashamed of what God has said and done.

HELPING YOUNG BELIEVERS
One reason that the exuberance of those first days of knowing Christ tends to fade is because of the reception from other believers as well as from the unbelieving world. Becoming *ashamed* of the gospel is an attitude young Christians often learn from those who have been believers the longest. Faint praise, condescending responses, and averted eyes all combine to give the young believer the subtle but crushing hint that enthusiastic comments about what Christ has done for him or her need to be toned down. Paul was *eager* to speak and unashamed of his message. It was life to him, and he knew it would be life to others. In what ways do you sometimes seem to be ashamed of the gospel? What young or recent believers need you to rejoice with them in their new faith?

Many believers in Christ want to keep their faith a secret, carefully avoiding situations where they might be identified as a Christian. They are afraid of being embarrassed. These feelings are based on real though often exaggerated possibilities. They cause us to be silent when we ought to speak. They cause us to be anonymous Christians in most parts of our life. Shame grows when we think:

- People will openly ridicule our faith.

- Friends might desert us if they know we are Christians.

- Christians have a reputation as poor examples or hypocrites.

- Our faith is something private rather than public.

- Our success or achievement is worth more to us than having others know we are Christians.

Whatever the superficial reasons for being ashamed of the gospel, they all arise from misunderstanding or forgetting the radical, eternal, and awesome nature of God's message and what it tells us about him.

It is the power of God for the salvation of everyone who believes.NIV The Greek word for power (*dynamis*) is the source for our words *dynamite* and *dynamic*. Dynamite was not invented by Nobel until 1867, so it is obvious that Paul did not have that specific picture in mind. Instead, the inventor of the explosive took its name from the Greek. But the parallel is instructive. The **gospel** can be like spiritual dynamite. Under certain circumstances it has a devastating, even destructive effect, demolishing world views and traditions—paving the way for new construction. Placed inside a stone-hard heart that is resistant to God, it can shatter the barrier. God's power in the gospel is not only explosive; it also overcomes evil. Dynamite must be carefully handled, but it is very effective when put to its proper use. Keeping dynamite under lock and key, hidden by those who know about it, may keep it from being misused, but it also prevents the dynamite from doing what it was designed to do. The dynamite of the gospel deserves to be respectfully treated, but effectively used! Furthermore, it must never be used as a weapon, but as a constructive power.

The word *dynamic* also reminds us of another aspect of the gospel. While bringing spiritual life to a person, we cannot always predict the course it will take. Paul knew that Christians have the responsibility to proclaim the gospel whenever and wherever they can. Believers are not to be ashamed about its simplicity or universality—the gospel's effectiveness can be entrusted to God. Until we are convinced that the gospel is dynamic and effective, we will tend to be ashamed to pass it on. What has the gospel done in you? If the gospel is a message you know, but not a power that has changed you, it will matter little what you do with it.

The only way to receive salvation is to believe in Christ. This offer is open to all people. The gospel is powerful because the power of God resides in it by nature. This *power* is not descriptive of *how* the gospel is effective, but a guarantee that it *is* effective. The gospel is the inherent power of God that gives salvation to all who accept it. Its power is demonstrated not only by accomplishing the *salvation* of a person, but also in its undiminished capacity to do this for *everyone who believes*. What then is *salvation*? It is the forgiveness of sins, but it goes even deeper—to a restoration to wholeness of all that sin has defaced or destroyed. And salvation can only happen when a person *believes*. Having made this point, Paul continues to expand on the effectiveness of the gospel in verse 17.

First for the Jew, then for the Gentile.^{NIV} The Jews were given *first* invitation because they had been God's special people for more than 2,000 years, ever since God chose Abraham and promised great blessings to his descendants (Genesis 12:1-3). God did not choose them because they deserved to be chosen (Deuteronomy 7:7-8; 9:4-6), but because he wanted to show his love and mercy to them, teach them, and prepare them to welcome his Messiah into the world. He chose them not to play favorites, but so that they would tell the world about his plan of salvation. Being *first*, then, is simply a statement about the order of God's plan, rather than an indication of relative value. Paul later makes the case in Romans 4 that when God chose Abraham, the father of the Jewish nation, he was still a Gentile. God chose Abraham to bring into being a nation through which he would work to bring salvation to the world. That nation came to be the Jews. The entire plan has been an expression of God's love.

For centuries Abraham's descendants had been learning about God by obeying his laws, keeping his sacrifices and feasts, and living according to his moral principles. Often they forgot God's promises and requirements and had to be disciplined; but still they had a precious heritage of belief in the one true God. Of all the people on earth, the Jews should have been the most ready to welcome the Messiah and to understand his mission and message—and some of them were. The disciples and Paul were faithful Jews who recognized in Jesus God's most precious gift to the human race (see Luke 2:25, 36-38). The Jews were given the first opportunity to receive the Messiah during his ministry on earth (John 1:11) and during the days of the early church (Acts 1:8; 3:26). Although Paul was commissioned as the apostle to the Gentiles (Acts 9:15), even he followed this pattern. Whenever Paul went to a new city, he recognized his obligation to carry the gospel to the Jews first (Acts 13:45-46; 28:25, 28).

1:17 In it the righteousness of God is revealed.^{NRSV} The gospel tells us how we, sinners as we are, can be declared righteous before God; and it tells how God, who is righteous, can vindicate sinful people. What then is *righteousness?* This is precisely what Paul explains in detail in this letter, especially for the benefit of the Gentiles in the church who would have been unfamiliar with the concept.

The phrase *righteousness of God* can mean "God's righteousness" or "the righteousness God gives those who believe." Paul had both definitions in mind. Righteousness is an aspect of God's character, his standard of behavior, and a description of all that he wishes to give to us. The gospel shows how righteous God is in his plan for us to be saved, and also how we may be called righteous. This *righteousness from God* is the righteousness he bestows on people; in other words, it is God's provision for justifying sinners. The way for sinners to become righteous before God is *revealed* in the gospel. We could not know about this righteousness were it not for the gospel. Luther defined this as a "righteousness valid before God, which a man may possess through faith." When God declares us righteous, we have been made right with him. (See also Isaiah 46:12-13; 61:10.)

> Faith is different from truth. The one is a gift of God and the other is human. "The righteous will live by faith" (Romans 1:17). This is the faith God himself puts into our hearts, although he often uses proof as the instrument. "Faith comes from hearing the message" (Romans 10:17). But this faith dwells in our hearts, and helps us to say not "I know," but "I believe."
>
> —Blaise Pascal

A righteousness that is by faith.NIV Our righteousness begins because of God's faithfulness to his promises; it moves on in our response of faith and is a continuing process through life. Thus it is by faith **from first to last.**NIV Faith—unconditional trust—is the appointed way of receiving God's righteousness. Faith in what? Faith in the fact that Jesus Christ took our sins upon himself, taking the punishment we deserved, and in exchange making us righteous before God. By trusting in Christ, our relationship with God is made right both for now and for eternity.

The expression *by faith from first to last* translates what in Greek is literally "from faith to faith." It is also possible to translate this as "through faith for faith" (NRSV). In this expression some have seen Paul's description of the development of faith from beginning to maturity. Others think that Paul might be outlining the transmission of faith from the faithful proclaimer to the faithful responder. The thrust of the phrase, however, indicates that our relationship with God begins and exists by faith. When it comes to our relationship with God, we never initiate; we always respond. We love because he first loved us. Every obedience in the Christian life is based upon a simple trust that God has set us free in Christ to love, instead of leaving us hopelessly trapped in our feeble efforts to be righteous by our own strength. Today, Paul might have written, "When it comes to righteousness, the bottom line is always faith."

LETTING GOD WORK IN YOU
The righteousness that the gospel offers to us is like a spiritual suit of armor. It covers us (see Ephesians 6:10-18). In fact, when we are surrounded by God's righteousness, our first discovery is that the armor is far too big for us. We do not come anywhere near measuring up to the grace that God has given to us. The Christian life begins when we receive the gift and goes on as we grow into the armor that God designed for us. God calls us righteous when we clearly don't deserve the title. He also calls us saints, holy and clean, long before we exhibit those characteristics. In grateful response, let us allow God to develop those qualities in us. Each day we should ask, "How am I fitting into what God has designed for me?"

As it is written: "The one who is righteous will live by faith."^{NRSV} Paul is quoting from Habakkuk 2:4—this quotation is used again in Galatians 3:11 and Hebrews 10:38. Righteousness by faith was not a new idea—it is found in the writings of the prophets, with which the Jewish believers would be familiar. Even though Paul was taking pains to carry out his mission of carrying the gospel to the Gentiles, he was determined to hold up its connection with the plan and promise God had begun with the Jews. Paul quotes this verse and amplifies what he means by saying that faith is *from first to last.*

The one who is righteous will live by faith. There are two ways to understand this statement: (1) "the righteous by faith will live"—i.e., one's faith in God makes him righteous before God, and as a result, he has eternal life or (2) "the righteous will live by faith"—i.e., those made right with God live their Christian lives by remaining faithful to God. In summary, this expression means Christians will live because of God's faithfulness and because of their response of faith in God; as a result, they will have eternal life and experience fullness in life.

- Faith is personal trust in God.

- Faith is the source of the believer's new life in Christ.

- Faith justifies us, saves us, and gives us new life and a new life-style.

GOD'S ANGER AT SIN / 1:18-32

The remainder of the first chapter paints a picture of the human predicament before a holy God. These verses, when they are read aloud, sound like a list of charges being read in court. All people everywhere deserve God's condemnation for their sin. They know they are not acknowledging their creator and are deliberately disobeying his standards. The consequences have been disastrous. Sin continues to increase. Before detailing God's way of salvation, Paul first sets out to convince people of their lost condition and their need for a Savior.

Paul's description of the case against humanity can be outlined in three steps: (1) Man demonstrated an *aversion* to faith in God alone. (2) This was followed almost immediately by a *diversion* from God's way of thinking. (3) This led to *perversions* in relations with God (idolatry) and in relations among people (immorality). The evidence against humanity requires the verdict of guilty as charged.

1:18 **The wrath of God is revealed . . . against all ungodliness and unrighteousness of men, who suppress the truth.**NKJV As God's righteousness was revealed (1:17), so was his wrath. The flip side of God's righteousness is his wrath against evil. Certain aspects of human character elicit God's wrath. It is the response of his holiness to all wickedness and rebellion.

Why is God angry with sin? Because people have substituted the truth about him with a fantasy of their own imagination (1:25). They have suppressed the truth God naturally reveals to everyone in order to believe anything that supports their own self-centered life-styles. *Ungodliness* means lack of reverence for God, even rebellion against him; *unrighteousness* refers to unjust actions between people. As always, the human predicament has both a vertical and horizontal aspect. Once humans have abandoned God, it will not take long for the effects to be felt in their relationships with each other. The *truth* is the reality that there exists a God who deserves worship and obedience.

Attempts to *suppress the truth* recall our earliest ancestors' efforts to avoid discovery of their disobedience. When Adam and Eve were confronted with sin, they confirmed their rebellion by denying and excusing their wrongdoing. That tendency to cover up is still prevalent today. It takes the gospel, backed up by the effective working of God's Spirit to bring men and women to the place of confession and forgiveness.

God cannot tolerate sin because his nature is morally perfect. He cannot ignore or condone such willful rebellion. He wants to remove the sin and restore the sinner, but the sinner must not distort or reject the truth. But God's anger erupts against those who persist in sinning.

While we do not have many idol-worshiping religions in our neighborhoods, we do find those who supress the truth about God. These people

- replace God with the worship of success, property, and wealth,
- demote God by elevating their own homespun philosophies, and
- ignore God by devoting themselves to family, leisure, and career—rejecting his claim on their lives.

1:19 **What can be known about God is plain to them.**NRSV Verses 19 and 20 give four characteristics of the *truth* as revealed in nature: (1) It is **plain** and **clearly seen**—it is visible. (2) It is **understood**—any wise person who sees the truth will also reflect on it and come to a conclusion about it. (3) It has been **since the creation of the world**—it is constant, ongoing, changeless. (4) It reveals God's **eternal power and divine nature** (NIV)—for an understanding of God's love and grace one must look into the Scriptures and at God's Son.

What we can know from creation about God has been revealed by God. The clues to God's existence and character have traditionally been called general revelation. Humans have never discovered God on their own. God could have kept humans in ignorance about himself. But he chose to reveal himself, generally in nature and specifically through the Scriptures and Jesus Christ. Because God has made certain facts about himself plain to them, people will someday have to give an account before God of why they chose to ignore his existence and his character.

But how could a loving God send anyone to hell, especially someone who has never heard the Good News of Jesus? In fact, says Paul, in the creation God has revealed himself plainly to *all* people. Also, everyone has an inner sense of what God requires, but they choose not to live up to it. Put another way, people's moral standards are always better than their behavior. If people suppress God's truth in order to live their own way, they have no excuse. They know the truth, and they will have to endure the consequences of ignoring it.

1:20 God's invisible qualities—his eternal power and divine nature—have been clearly seen, being understood from what has been made.^{NIV} The paradox can't be missed—God's *invisible qualities* are *clearly seen.* How? God created the world with natural processes, with cause and effect. In the same way that observing a painting leads a person to conclude that there is an artist, so to observe the tremendous creation is to conclude that there is a supreme Creator, one with eternal power and divinity. This is part of the truth that unsaved people are suppressing.

Psalm 19:1-4 says, "The heavens declare the glory of God; the skies proclaim the work of his hands. Day after day they pour forth speech; night after night they display knowledge. There is no speech or language where their voice is not heard. Their voice goes out into all the earth, their words to the ends of the world" (NIV). One look at creation in all its splendor tells people that a mighty power made this world—but not just an abstract, impersonal force; rather, a personal God. Thus, creation shows both God's eternal power and his divine nature. Indeed, nature reveals a God of might, intelligence, intricate detail, order, beauty, and power; a God who controls powerful forces. God's qualities are revealed through creation (Acts 14:17), although creation's testimony has been distorted by the Fall. Adam's sin resulted in a divine curse upon the whole natural order (Genesis 3:17-19), thorns and thistles were an immediate result, and natural disasters have been common from Adam's day to ours. Nature itself is eagerly awaiting its own redemption from the effects of sin (8:19-21; Revelation 22:3).

Then why do we need missionaries if people can know about God through nature (the creation)?

- Although people know that God exists, they suppress that truth by their wickedness and thus deny him. Missionaries can point out their error.

- Although people may believe there is a God, they refuse to commit themselves to him. Missionaries can help persuade them.

- Missionaries can convince people who reject God of the dangerous consequences of their actions.

- Though nature reveals God, people need to be told about Jesus and how through him they can have a personal relationship with God.

- Missionaries are needed to help the church obey the great commission of our Lord (Matthew 28:19-20).

Knowing that God exists is not enough. People must learn that God is loving. They must understand what he did to show that love to us. They must be shown how to accept his forgiveness of their sins. (See also 10:14-15.)

They are without excuse.NKJV Does anyone have an excuse for not believing in God? The Bible answers an emphatic *no*. God has revealed his existence (or divine nature) in his creation. The fact that general revelation is not effective in convincing humans does not mean it is not true. The argument that design implies a designer is not an argument people *can't* accept; it is an argument people *refuse* to accept. Every person, therefore, either recognizes or rejects God. Does anyone have an excuse for his or her actions? Again the Bible answers *no*. Each person

> As a person would be foolish to look for money only to look at it, without trying to get it into his possession, so the heathen, though they knew God, were satisfied with and gloried in the mere knowledge of him. They left out of mind his worship, in particular, the inward dedication to God, whom they knew.
> —Martin Luther

knows enough about God to be careful of his or her conduct. Those who take the wrong path have chosen to do so. Don't be fooled. When the day comes for God to judge our response to him, there will be no excuses. We must give our devotion and worship to him—today.

1:21 **Although they knew God.**NKJV Their denial of their own awareness of God is what left people without excuse. When Paul says that men *knew God* he is not describing a knowledge that could save them but a knowledge that simply recognized God's existence. He was describing an awareness of God, that, if not suppressed would be nurtured by God. The writer of Hebrews spoke of this basic knowledge in stating, "And without faith it is impossible to please God, because anyone who comes to him must believe that he exists and that he rewards those who earnestly seek him" (Hebrews 11:6 NIV). But since human beings have, in fact, suppressed the truth about God, the following calamities ensued: (1) people could not glorify (worship) a God they didn't believe existed; (2) people could not be or feel thankful to a nonexistent deity; (3) people's thinking became pointless, for it lacked a starting point; and (4) the light of truth in people's hearts went out.

They neither glorified him . . . nor gave thanks.^{NIV}

They neither glorified him . . . nor gave thanks.[NIV] When people refuse to recognize God as Creator, they will also fail to glorify or thank him for his gifts—food, clothing, shelter, even life itself. When they neglect God, they open the door to evil. To omit what is good inevitably leads to committing what is evil. Ingratitude may seem like a small thing, but it begins the downward spiral into depravity. To forget to thank God for all he is and all he has done reveals a dangerous self-centeredness. This causes futile thinking and planning, darkness, pride, blindness, and finally total departure from God that bursts into a flood of sin.

Thinking became futile.[NIV] When God is declared "absent" in human thought, humans lose much more than they bargained for. Truth and absolutes are quickly abandoned. Something or someone must be at the center of life, so humans make themselves central. Then everything they try is futile in giving satisfaction. Like Solomon they discover that everything is "meaningless! Meaningless! . . . Utterly meaningless!" (Ecclesiastes 1:1-2 NIV). Living for self or for some other idol is utterly futile (see Daniel 5:23ff.). When we abandon God, we lose our standard or reference point from which to work. When anything goes, everything is futile.

Foolish hearts were darkened.[NKJV] The *heart* is the seat of feeling, intelligence, and moral choice. Their hearts are *foolish* because they refuse to recognize God (see 1:22). Futile thinking is followed by futile living. Then both mind and heart become devoid of light. When confused thinking becomes a permanent mind-set, people are unable to turn to God.

DOWNWARD SPIRAL
Paul portrays the inevitable downward spiral into sin. First people reject God; next they make up their own ideas of what a god should be and do; then they fall into sin—sexual sin, greed, hatred, envy, murder, fighting, lying, bitterness, gossip. Finally they grow to hate God and encourage others to do so. God does not cause this steady progression toward evil. Rather, when people reject him, he allows them to live as they choose. God gives them up or commits them to experience the natural consequences of their sin. Once caught in the downward spiral, no one can pull himself or herself out. Sinners must trust Christ alone to put them on the path of escape.

1:22 Claiming to be wise, they became fools.[NRSV] Paul continues his description of the inevitable results of the denial of God by stating that even though thinking will become futile and hearts will be darkened, some people will still claim to be wise. Without answers based on the reality of God, people seek heroes among those who will boldly say there are no answers. Under such circumstances, it is seen as a sign of sophistication and intelligence to refuse to acknowledge God's existence. But by biblical definition, anyone saying he or she cannot believe there is a God, or refusing to believe in God, is admitting to being a fool. The psalmist expressed it: "The fool says in his heart, 'There is no God'" (Psalm 14:1 NIV). The evidence of God's existence is so plain and clear that to ignore it is totally foolish.

To some people, statements like these by Paul appear to be out of line because they appear to be intolerant of other religions and views. The objection is often voiced in a question: "Well, after all, the point is that people are naturally somewhat religious; so isn't the most important thing not what religion you follow, but that you follow some religion?" The fallacy behind the question is that it still assumes that man is at the center, not God. The emphasis is not on believing what is true but on believing. Paul was speaking in a world that was inundated with gods. He would have been horrified to think that anyone would understand him to be saying that a little religion is a good thing! To Paul, even a lot of religion was bad if it was not true.

Christianity does not try (though some have tried in its name) to legislate people into being Christians. But while Christians know they cannot force anyone to believe, they are, with Paul, unashamed to claim that Jesus Christ is the answer. We may not coerce, but we must try to convince!

1:23 Exchanged the glory of the immortal God for images.NRSV Whether they claim it or not, people are religious beings. By their very nature, they are bound to worship and serve something beyond themselves. It may be another idea of God, a person, a thing, or even some false notion that no God exists. Anyone who rejects the Creator will end up worshiping the creature. And how foolish that they turn their backs on the Creator in order to worship something created, something that can die, decay, and disappoint.

Images resembling a mortal human being.NRSV In other words, a human being may be worshiped instead of God. But God is immortal—incorruptible, imperishable; the images are *mortal*—liable to decay. Some of these images not only looked like humans; they were humans. Such was the case in ancient Rome, where some of the Caesars were worshiped as gods. In our day, modern paganism subtly worships its human images—certain people and their power. Paul shows how the scale of images descends from **man** to **birds and animals and reptiles.** NIV Whether the images were created by man out of wood, stone, or metal or are humans raised to the status of gods, they lacked the glory that belongs only to God. These manufactured gods might inspire fear or reverence, but they clearly do not deserve worship. And because they were created by humans, they owe their existence to humans. This places people in control of their own gods. Faced with God's glory, humans know who is in control. This God is not an invention of human thought or hands. He is the one who reveals himself to human beings in such a way that people realize they are, themselves, merely pale images of the majestic being that is God. He alone is to be worshiped.

How can intelligent people turn to idolatry? Idolatry begins when people reject what they know about God. Instead of looking to him as the Creator and sustainer of life, they see themselves as the center of the universe. They soon invent gods that are convenient projections of their own selfish plans and decrees. These gods may be wooden figures, or they may be things we desire—such as money, power, or comfort. They may even be misrepresentations of God himself—a result of making God in their image, instead of the reverse. The common denominator is this: Idolaters worship the things God made rather than God himself. It is a tendency that we must constantly watch for in ourselves.

 IDOLATRY CHECK
Here are some questions to help you see if your attitudes are like idolatry.
- Who created you?
- Whom do you ultimately trust?
- To whom do you look for ultimate truth?
- To whom do you look for security and happiness?
- Who is in charge of your future?
- What do you think you can't live without?
- Who do you think you can't live without?
- What priority in your life is greater than God?
- What dream would you sacrifice everything to realize?
- Is God first place in your life?

1:24 God gave them over in the sinful desires.NIV The point that God *gave them over* is repeated twice (1:26, 28). God left those who spurned him to their own desires. Without his guidance, they degenerated into ruinous moral practices. As Paul's thoughts unfold, he pictures God releasing people to *sinful desires*, "shameful lusts" (1:26) and "a depraved mind" (1:28). This rush into sinful patterns can be seen in societies as well as in individuals. When people and nations refuse to repent, sin takes over and draws people into a life where there is no sense of right and wrong. Without God's remedy, his righteousness, the end is destruction. Because Paul's purpose is to expound on the "righteousness from God" (1:17), he focuses on present, ongoing consequences of sin, rather than the ultimate results. Here and in the list to follow, Paul is essentially saying, "Look around! The evidences are everywhere that God, in his wrath, is allowing sinful nature to run its course. Humanity is in trouble!"

Sinful desires (*epithumia*) is not simply a term implying sexual desire. It is sometimes translated "lusts" (1:24 NRSV) and sometimes translated "coveting" (7:7). In the Greek Old Testament, *epithumia* is used in the tenth commandment, "You shall not covet your neighbor's house. You shall not covet your neighbor's wife, or his manservant or maidservant, his ox or donkey, or anything that belongs to your neighbor" (Exodus 20:17 NIV). *Sinful desires*, then, cover a wide range of lusts. In verses 29-31 Paul continues to list the shocking consequences of human desire operating without godly control.

> I willingly believe that the damned are, in one sense, successful, rebels to the end; that the doors of Hell are locked on the *inside*. They enjoy forever the horrible freedom they have demanded, and are therefore self-enslaved just as the blessed, forever submitting to obedience, become through all eternity more and more free.
> —C.S.Lewis

For the degrading of their bodies with one another.[NIV] Any kind of sexual behavior that deviates from that originally designed by God devalues the God-given use of our bodies.

God does not vindictively cast rebels into sin or stop giving love and instead dole out suffering and punishment. But if people persist in fleeing from God, he loves them enough to grant them their wish, though it is not his ultimate purpose. With the restraints removed, sometimes the consequences of rebellion will cause people to reconsider God.

WHEN GOD LETS GO
In an unexpected way, God proves his love by letting go. If nothing else, consequences prove to us that our choices matter. Like the wise parent, God persistently expresses his love, but not in such a way that obedience becomes a requirement he expects rather than response we freely make. We, like the Prodigal Son (Luke 15:11-32), demand our freedom, take for granted all God has given us, and squander our inheritance of life, only to wonder why we feel such loneliness and despair. It may well be, as Jonathan Edwards preached, that it is a terrible thing to be sinners in the hands of an angry God. But it is even more terrifying to find ourselves sinners whom God has reluctantly given over to our own pursuits. Our awareness of sin is a golden opportunity for repentance.

Here Paul introduces the subject of *sexual impurity.* He returns to it in verses 26 and 27. The context indicates that he is referring in part to cultic prostitution and the fertility cults that made use of temple prostitutes in their rites. Throughout history, paganism has shown a remarkable capacity for substituting the pursuit of sexual pleasure for the pursuit of holiness. Rejection of God is often accompanied by deification of sex or reproduction. Paul, writing from Corinth, the home of the temple of Aphrodite, was surrounded by evidences of the horrible evil of such belief (see also 1 Corinthians 6:9-10; 2 Corinthians 12:21). Because people ignored their innate awareness of godly restraints, personal desire became the standard of behavior. Paul did not hesitate to point out the devastating effects of sin on the most personal aspects of human life. Without God's righteousness, wrong rules.

WHY IS SEXUAL SIN SO POWERFUL?
The Bible frequently urges believers to avoid sexual sin. Did God, the creator of sex, decide he had made a mistake? Definitely not! God invented sex as a pleasurable part of the unique relationship between women and men, who are made in his image. Like most gifts, sex has proper and improper uses. What was created to be an expression of fidelity, intimacy, comfort, and sheer pleasure can also be the expression of selfishness, betrayal, deception, and manipulation. In its rightful place sex builds self-worth and deepens intimacy. Used wrongfully, it destroys people and relationships, undermining trust and acceptance. Sex is a wonderful gift to be shared by those for whom God designed it.

Because sex is such a powerful and essential part of what it means to be human, it must be treated with great respect. Sexual desires are of such importance that the Bible gives them special attention and counsels more careful restraint and self-control than with any other desire. One of the clearest indicators of a society or person in rebellion against God is the rejection of God's guidelines for the use of sex.

1:25 Exchanged the truth about God for a lie.^{NRSV} Just as people exchanged the glory of God for lackluster images (1:23), they also traded what can be known about God for a deliberate distortion. This lie is the belief that something or someone is to be worshiped in place of the one true God. This is what will ultimately lead to the end of the world—people will follow and worship the man of lawlessness who will lead them to destruction (2 Thessalonians 2:3-12).

People tend to believe lies that reinforce their own selfish personal beliefs. Today more than ever we need to be careful about the input we allow to form our beliefs. With TV, music, movies, and the rest of the media often presenting sinful life-styles and unwholesome values, we find ourself constantly bombarded by attitudes and beliefs totally opposed to the Bible. Be careful about what you allow to form your opinions. The Bible is the only standard of truth. Evaluate all other opinions in light of its teachings.

Worshiped and served created things rather than the Creator.^{NIV} These people have completely turned their back on God and replaced him with other objects. And what they have decided about God will decide their character and life-style. Some people are extremely devoted to their self-made gods. It was to very religious people that Jesus said, "You belong to your father, the devil, and you want to carry out your father's desire" (John 8:44 NIV).

Who is forever praised. Amen.^{NIV} Although many may refuse to acknowledge God's existence, that doesn't change the truth of his existence and the fact that he will indeed be *forever praised.* God's worthiness to be *praised* is not affected by human beings' rebellion or their poor choices. God will be *praised* forever, though there are many who, by their deliberate exchange of truth for lies, will not be present to participate.

:26-27 For this reason.^{NKJV} Paul has just finished describing in general terms what happens to people who do not acknowledge God's law as the standard for moral behavior. They turn from their

Maker and worship what has been made, sometimes including themselves.

There have always been those willing to believe that human desires are self-regulating. They do not believe that any action they enjoy could possibly be wrong. They believe that people would not really desire something unless it was good for them. Somehow the fact that every person has violated that principle escapes them. The more blatant examples of evil are considered exceptions rather than the rule. In so doing, they make every person an exception, for as Paul writes later, "All have sinned" (3:23). When our wants become our ruler and our desires our authority, we quickly become slaves to the next appealing offer.

God gave them over to shameful lusts.^{NIV} Unlike verse 24, where God is described as releasing people to pursue their sinful desires, Paul is now speaking specifically about immoral relations. When the desire for the true God is rejected, other gods are raised up. When the desire for God is rejected, other desires take control. Why are *shameful lusts* the result? When people refuse God and his standards, when they are left to themselves as their own gods, nothing can stop them from seeking to fulfill their passions. Paul indicates that sexual passion, out of control, leads to *shameful lusts* and other destructive results (see 1:29-31).

> And yet, temptations can be useful to us even though they seem to cause us nothing but pain. They are useful because they can make us humble, they can cleanse us, and they can teach us. All of the saints passed through times of temptation and tribulation, and they used them to make progress in the spiritual life. Those who did not deal with temptations successfully fell to the wayside.
> —Thomas á Kempis

Their women exchanged natural relations for unnatural ones . . . . The men also abandoned natural relations.^{NIV} Not only was shameful lust the result, but perversions of sex became rampant. God's plan for natural sexual relationships is his ideal for his creation. It is the height of foolishness to think that any sex act is acceptable as long as "no one gets hurt."

Paul's treatment of homosexual behavior falls in the middle of two other major areas that he presents as evidence of the "godlessness and wickedness of men," (1:18). The first is sinful worship; the third is a whole list of personal and relational sins. It is important to note that Paul is using homosexual practices to indicate the *extent* to which sin has brought chaos into every area of life. He writes that as a result of *shameful lusts*, no person, relationship, or part of creation has been left untouched. (See 7:7ff. for more on *lusts*, and 8:18ff. for more on sin's effect on creation.) There is no hint here of a hierarchy of sin, with pagan worship being at the bottom, followed by homosexual practice, followed by "lesser sins." All sins grow out of human rebellion against God. The fact of sinfulness is a much more important discovery for a person to make than recognizing the particular acting out of that sinfulness. Repentance and restoration comes more quickly from the question, "What must I do to be saved?" than from the question, "Exactly how deeply have I sinned in comparison with any one else?"

Homosexuality (to exchange or abandon natural relations of sex) was as widespread in Paul's day as it is in ours. Many pagan practices encouraged it. God is willing to receive anyone who comes to him in faith, and Christians should love and accept others no matter what their background. But homosexual behavior is strictly forbidden in Scripture (see Leviticus 18:22). Paul is writing this letter from Corinth, a city infamous for deviant sexual behaviors. According to 1 Corinthians 6:9-11, some of the Corinthian believers may have been converted out of a homosexual life-style. Paul was able to say of them and many other sinners (i.e., adulterers, thieves, drunkards, the greedy), "And that is what some of you were. But you were washed, you were sanctified, you were justified in the name of the Lord Jesus Christ and by the Spirit of our God" (1 Corinthians 6:11 NIV).

Homosexuality is considered an acceptable practice by many in our world today—even by some churches. But society does not set the standard for God's law. Many homosexuals believe that their desires are normal and that they have a right to express them. But God does not obligate nor encourage us to fulfill all of our desires (even normal ones). Desires that violate God's laws must be controlled. God offers freedom from those sins through Jesus Christ and power to control our desires through the Holy Spirit.

HELP FOR SINNERS
A person with homosexual desires can and must resist acting upon them. We may not all be tempted the same way, but we all must recognize and defeat temptation. We must depend on God's help. Jesus knows about temptation! "Because he himself suffered when he was tempted, he is able to help those who are being tempted" (Hebrews 2:18 NIV). We can consciously avoid places or activities that we know will kindle temptations of this kind. We must not underestimate the power of

Satan to tempt us, nor the potential for serious harm if we yield to these temptations. Once we are believers, Satan's objective is to make us doubt our true identity in Christ (see 2 Corinthians 5:17). God can and will forgive sexual sins just as he forgives other sins. We must surrender ourselves to the grace and mercy of God, asking him to show us the way out of sin and into the light of his freedom and his love. Prayer, Bible study, and strong support in a Christian church can help us to gain strength to resist these powerful temptations. If we are already deeply involved in homosexual behavior, we ought to consider seeking help from a trustworthy, professional, pastoral counselor.

Received in themselves the due penalty for their perversion.NIV Sin has a penalty, and the punishment is in keeping with the offense. The natural result of a person's sin pays that person back for what he or she has done. The exact consequences of sin are not predictable, but they are inevitable. These people cannot call themselves helpless victims; a sinful choice was made, and it carries its *penalty.* Unfortunately, the *due penalty* also has a way of spilling over into other lives. The connectedness of everything in creation makes it almost impossible to confine sinful penalties. Often a truly painful consequence is seeing how a sin we unleashed effects others.

> A law broods over human existence, a law which is at the same time a divine act: Such as thou makest thy God, such wilt thou make thyself.
> —Godet

1:28 **They did not like to retain God in their knowledge.**NKJV Humans sat in judgment on God to decide whether he fit the qualifications of a God that would be to their liking; they decided he did not meet those qualifications and so dismissed him from their lives. They had the knowledge (they were not ignorant), but they did not want to use it.

In our own times we have seen a belittling of God as no more than a pale extension of our wishful thinking, someone made in our image. Yet those most vocal in condemning the authoritative Christian view of God have been busy at work creating people who think of themselves as gods. Paul's discussion is not out of date. The same rebellion against God is alive in the human heart.

He gave them over to a depraved mind, to do what ought not to be done.NIV For the third time, Paul describes God's action as "giving them over." Each time, the action is introduced by recalling humanity's rebellion against God.

Each expression serves as an outline point under Paul's main theme, which is to explain the ways that the "wrath of God is being revealed" (1:18) in the lives of people. This last time, Paul introduces a host of behaviors which demonstrate that human behavior is a result of man's way of thinking becoming *depraved.*

People do not turn away from God all at once; there is a progression. They may have started with some knowledge of God, but then they chose not to glorify him nor thank him. This led to questions and doubts that led them to no longer recognize God as God—they refused "to retain the knowledge of God" (NIV). And when they chose to reject God, God allowed them to do it. Their minds became *depraved,* and they lost the ability to distinguish between right and wrong. When the conscience is perverted, there is little hope. *To do what ought not to be done* indicates that the people were doing things not just offensive to God, but also offensive by human standards.

God does not usually stop us from making choices against his will. He lets us declare our supposed independence from him, even though he knows that in time we will become slaves to our own rebellious choices—we will lose our freedom not to sin. Does life without God look like freedom to you? Look more closely. There is no worse slavery than slavery to sin.

:29-31 **Filled with . . .** The term suggests a state of being filled to the point of overflowing. Once the mind of man had become depraved (1:28), it followed that the creative power of thought was turned to the pursuit of evil. Paul listed over twenty different ways in which the mind can be focused once it has turned away from God. (For similar lists, see 1 Corinthians 6:9-10; Galatians 5:19-21; and Colossians 3:5.) The following catalog may not be in any particular order, but it emphasizes the extent of the evidence against humanity. Who cannot find in himself more than one among these qualities (quoted from NIV)?
Every kind of wickedness—The opposite of righteousness, the absence of justice.
Evil—What is sinister and vile.
Greed—Relentless urge to get more for oneself.
Depravity—A condition of moral evil.
Envy—Desire for something possessed by another.
Murder—Greed, envy, and strife, left unchecked, could lead even to killing another in order to obtain what is desired.

Strife—Competition, rivalry, bitter conflict.

Deceit—To trick or mislead by lying.

Malice—Doing evil despite the good that has been received.

Gossips—They create problems by rehashing idle talk or rumors concerning others' private affairs.

Slanderers—Destroy another's good reputation.

God-haters—Not only do they ignore God; some actively hate him and attempt to work against any of his influences.

Insolent—Arrogant behavior toward those who are not powerful enough to fight back. This particularly refers to a person's attempt to shame another without mercy.

Arrogant and boastful—Making claims of superior intelligence or importance.

Invent ways of doing evil—Trying new kinds of perversions.

Disobey their parents—When God's authority is tossed aside as worthless, parental authority cannot be far behind. How unfortunate that the parents, in many cases, had set the example. By ignoring God's authority, they set the example for the children to ignore parental authority.

Senseless—Unable to discern spiritual and moral things.

Faithless—Not keeping one's promises or doing one's duties; unreliable, untrustworthy.

Heartless—Unfeeling, unkind, harsh, cruel.

Ruthless—Without pity or compassion; merciless.

> The principle of holiness leads to the exhortation, "Be not conformed to this world; but be ye transformed by the renewing of your mind, that ye may prove what is the will of God" (Romans 12:2). It is a very important consideration that we are consecrated and dedicated to God. It means that we will think, speak, meditate, and do all things with a view to God's glory.
> —John Calvin

1:32 They know God's decree that those who practice such things deserve to die.[NRSV] In the previous verses Paul pointed out several different ways that God "gives people up" to pursue their desires. He was convinced that each person in rebellion against God perceives the final outcome of that rebellion. But even the finality of death is ignored by many.

How did they know of God's death penalty? Human beings, created in God's image, have a basic moral nature and a conscience. This truth is understood beyond religious circles. Psychologists, for example, say that the rare person who has no conscience has a serious personality disorder, one that is extremely difficult to treat. Most people instinctively know when they do wrong—but they may not care. Some people will even risk an early death for the freedom to indulge their desires now. "I know it's wrong, but I really want it," or "I know it's dangerous, but it's worth the risk." For such people, part of the "fun" is going against God's law, the community's moral standards, common sense, or their own sense of right and wrong. But deep down inside they know that sin deserves the death penalty (6:23).

MORAL ALTERNATIVES

Having rejected God and his standard, people turn to a variety of sources for authority to back up what they want to do. Here are some of the most common "moralities" vying for our attention:

- Statistical morality. This approach depends on accepting the premise that the right thing to do is what most people are doing. Its motto is Everybody Is Doing It! Statistical morality makes extensive use of opinion polls, talk shows, and telephone surveys. The approach practically guarantees that a person can do just about anything he or she wants to do and claim personal morality.
- Emotional morality. This approach relies heavily on feelings. What feels good is right, and what feels bad is wrong. The term that most accurately describes the spirit behind this "morality" is selfishness. Emotional morality rejects almost any action that involves personal sacrifice.
- Situational morality. Also called make-it-up-as-you-go-along morality, situational morality relies on the belief that a person can figure out on the spot how they should behave, rather than having a decided standard of behavior in force in every situation. The worst experience for a situationalist is to be at the mercy of another situationalist.
- Sensitive morality. This approach to morality accepts the idea that there are no absolute standards of right and wrong, only personal standards. Holders of this position believe in minding their own morality and not questioning or contradicting the behavior of others. Sensitive moralists never offend anyone. They believe that each person has a right to his or her personal morality and not even God should dare to interfere.

Not only must we be watchful of the effects of these thought patterns in those around us; we must be alert for their influence in our own thinking. The best guard for our minds is saturation with God's Word. "Don't let the world around you squeeze you into its own mould, but let God re-mould your minds from within, so that you may prove in practice that the plan of God for you is good, meets all his demands and moves towards the goal of true maturity" (Romans 12:2 Phillips).

Continue to do these very things ... approve of those who practice them.[NIV] Not only have they turned their backs on God and realized that their deeds deserve the ultimate penalty of death; they also are continuing in their sin and encouraging it in others. The fierce defense of certain life-styles should not surprise us. People in rebellion against God have a lot at stake. Agreeing in any way with God's analysis of their lives would require them to repent, to change. It is not unusual for us to reinforce our own choices, good or bad, by urging others to make the same choices. Even when we are not sure we have made the right choices, convincing others to do what we have done increases our sense of security. In response, God's Word reminds us that gaining the whole world, or convincing many others that we are right, means nothing if our Creator says we are wrong. Claiming our way is right in the face of God's disagreement places us in danger of losing our soul. Jesus said, "What good is it for a man to gain the whole world, and yet lose or forfeit his very self?" (Luke 9:25 NIV).

The cause for the appalling condition of our world—the horrible perversions and the rampant evil—lies in people's rebellion against God. Although knowledge of God is accessible, people turn their backs on it, close their minds to it, and go their own way, worshiping whatever they choose. With this stroke, Paul places the final touches on the dismal picture of man's condition apart from God. From here, he will move on to deal with those who might use their knowledge of God as an excuse for missing his righteousness.

Romans 2

Having painted in large strokes the fate of humankind apart from God, Paul abruptly switches his attention to a new audience. He shapes his next thoughts in a style used widely at that time, called the *diatribe*. In a diatribe, the writer verbally attacks and attempts to destroy the ideas of the opposition. The anticipated questions or objections of the opposition are expressed or noted and then answered or refuted. Paul probably did not have an individual, but a character type in mind as he began his diatribe.

There may have been a single destination for Paul's letter, but he knew that his readers would be quite varied: Roman citizens, transplanted Jews, slaves of various types, other races of Gentiles, former Jewish converts, and unbelievers. When Paul's letter was read in the Roman church, no doubt many heads nodded as he condemned idol worship, homosexual practices, and violence. But what surprise his listeners must have felt when he turned on them and said, in effect, "You have no excuse. You are just as bad!" Paul's emphasis was that *nobody* is good enough to save himself or herself. If we want to avoid punishment and live eternally with Christ, we must depend totally on God's grace, whether we have been murderers and molesters or have been honest and hardworking citizens. Paul is not discussing whether some sins are worse than others. Any sin should cause us to depend on Jesus Christ for salvation and eternal life. We have all sinned repeatedly; salvation comes only through faith in Christ.

2:1 You, therefore, have no excuse, you who pass judgment.[NIV] Paul's style, as mentioned above, is *diatribal*—words are placed in the mouth of an imagined person who asks questions or raises objections, only to be refuted.

The critic here is Jewish, for Paul is focusing primarily on Jews in his words *you . . . have no excuse* (see 2:17). Paul had criticized the horrible evil of the Gentiles, their sins of idolatry and homosexuality and their general life-style. This Jewish critic nodded in agreement as Paul exclaimed that "those who do such things deserve death" (1:32), because the critic assumes that he is free from such vices, and thus free from their well-deserved judgment. But then Paul says that he has no right to pass judgment, because he is just as guilty.

In whatever you judge another you condemn yourself.^{NKJV} A person may feel self-righteous because he is not guilty of the sins for which he judges others. But no one is guiltless—all have sinned. By our very capacity to judge others we demonstrate that we are responsible to judge ourselves. To judge another is to presume that you have nothing to be judged in yourself—that attitude reveals a sinful and hardened heart (see 2:5).

You, the judge, are doing the very same things.^{NRSV} The critic, and Jews in general, were not guiltless. They were doing the *same things* but needed to be reminded or made aware of it (as is often the case with the examples given of greed, gossip, and arrogance). Their attitude condemns others' sins but somehow overlooks those sins in themselves (see Matthew 7:2-3).

JUDGING OTHERS
The verb for "do" is the same one used in 1:32—Paul's accusation cannot be missed. Whenever we find ourselves feeling justifiably angry about someone's sin, we should be careful. We need to speak out against sin, but we must do so with a spirit of humility. Often the sins we notice most clearly in others are the ones that have taken root in us. If we look closely at ourselves, we may find that we are committing the same sin. The unrighteous excuse themselves while condemning others. The truly righteous overlook faults in others but try to see their own faults.

Why is Paul going against the Jews here? He is anticipating the Jewish argument. Even though the Jews were probably a minority in the Roman church, they were growing. In addition, the Gentiles had heard of Paul and no doubt were wondering where he stood on this issue.

2:2 God's judgment against those who do such things is based on the truth.^{NKJV} Paul assumes that all his readers will agree with him regarding God's *judgment*. Human judgment is based on prejudice and partial perception; *God's judgment* is based on the truth—he judges on the basis of the facts about what we do. We only know in part, but God knows fully. Whereas our judgment of others is imperfect and partial, his is perfect and impartial.

RIGHTEOUSNESS AND WICKEDNESS

It is God who passes judgment on righteousness and wickedness, not people. The book of Proverbs often compares the life-styles of the wicked and the righteous and makes a strong case for living by God's pattern.

	Righteous	*Wicked*	*Proverbs references*
Outlook on life	Hopeful	Fearful	10:24
Response to life	Covered with blessings	Covered with violence	10:6
How they are seen by others	Conduct is upright	Conduct is devious	21:8
Quality of life	Stand firm	Swept away	10:25
Short-term results	Walk securely	Will be found out	10:9
Long-term results	God protects them	God destroys them	10:29
Eternal expecta-tions	Attain life	Go to death	11:19
God's opinion of them	Delights in the good	Detests the perverse	11:20

The truth of God's judgment was clearly demonstrated in the Old Testament (see Deuteronomy 31:15-22; Psalms 75:2-8; Isaiah 1:2-20; Zephaniah 1:14-18) and often reflected in the New Testament (see Matthew 12:36; John 12:44-50; 2 Corinthians 5:10; James 2:13; 2 Peter 3:3-9; Revelation 14:6-7). Not only is God capable of judging rightly; eventually he will judge the entire human race at the Day of Judgment (Matthew 11:24).

2:3 Do you think you will escape God's judgment?[NIV] Seven times in the first three verses, Paul used various forms of the Greek word for *judgment* (*krima*). Though human beings pass judgments, their judgments are judged by God. When we stand condemned before God, we have no higher court of appeal.

This is the first of two rhetorical questions. Paul ridicules the idea that a person might *escape God's judgment* by correctly analyzing the wrong in others. The very fact that we can see the sins in others leaves us with no excuse before God. Those Jews, who were guilty of the same sins for which God was condemning the Gentiles, would not escape God's judgment. Their national heritage could do nothing to save them, even though many Jews thought their privilege of birth ensured entrance into God's kingdom (Matthew 3:8-9). All people, Jews and Gentiles, have sinned, and all stand condemned before God. Paul repeats this theme over and over.

HOW CAN WE ESCAPE?

We cannot escape God's righteous judgment by avoiding or resisting it. We find our only hope in submitting to his verdict. If God says we have sinned, we must agree. When we agree with his judgment, we obtain his mercy. When we agree that we are lost, we find a savior. We escape God's judgment by accepting it and claiming God's mercy and grace that wait for us. As a result, those who have experienced God's forgiveness overlook the faults in others while they recognize their own faults. On the other hand, those who have not yet received forgiveness are prone to excuse themselves while condemning and blaming others. This last group of people have not escaped God's judgment.

2:4 **Do you show contempt for the riches of his kindness, tolerance and patience?**[NIV] Paul immediately follows his first rhetorical question with a second. While the first one emphasizes the unavoidability of God's judgment, the next one emphasizes the vast spiritual benefits a person gives up by judging others. Paul wants his readers to understand that judging others shows *contempt* for God's *kindness, tolerance and patience.* God demonstrates *his kindness* in giving us life and its fullness to enjoy; he is tolerant and patient as he bears our ingratitude and sin. He postpones punishment in order that his kindness will lead people to *repentance* (see 2 Peter 3:15). But Paul was concerned that these Jews, overconfident in their special status with God and unwilling to repent of sin, were showing contempt for God's blessings. So Paul reminds them that God's kindness is also meant to lead *them* to repentance, because all people need to repent!

AMAZING PATIENCE
It is easy to mistake God's patience for approval of wrong living. Self-evaluation is difficult, and it is even more difficult for us to expose our conduct to God and let him point out where we need to change. But as Christians we must pray constantly that God will show us our sins, so that he can remove them and heal us. Unfortunately we are more likely to be amazed at God's patience with others than humbled at his patience with us.

2:5 Hard and impenitent heart.^{NRSV} This kind of person has sat in self-righteous judgment of others for too long and has lived as described in verse 4—by showing contempt for all God has given (see also Deuteronomy 10:16 and Jeremiah 4:4). People receive blessings but stubbornly continue in sin, refusing to repent. It is difficult for self-righteous people to repent. Proverbs 26:12 says, "Do you see a man wise in his own eyes? There is more hope for a fool than for him" (NIV).

Storing up wrath for yourself.^{NRSV} Paul's readers who boasted of their faith yet continued to sin were inviting retribution and ironically were contributing not to their benefit but to their own judgment when *God's wrath* would be poured out upon them.

CRIME AND PUNISHMENT
We tend to expect punishment and consequences to follow immediately or closely behind sin. So we usually suspect that suffering is the result of some sin recently committed. Suffering is not always a consequence—see John 9 for a vivid example from Christ's ministry. Passages like this make it clear that immediate punishment for sin would mean that humans would rarely live long enough to repent. Consequences occur frequently enough and intensely enough to work alongside God's patience to bring us to repentance. It may be a popular lifestyle to "play now and pay later," but when it comes to God's judgment, the price is too high: eternal punishment. When we repent, we are given life, now and forever.

The day of God's wrath, when his righteous judgment will be revealed.^{NIV} Though we do not know the date of the *day of God's wrath*, we do know that no one will escape that final encounter with our Creator, and that we are called to live with this day in mind. A summary of the biblical counsel on what our attitude ought to be is "the day of the Lord is near" (see Isaiah 13:6;

Ezekiel 30:3; Acts 2:20; I Corinthians 1:8; 2 Corinthians 1:14;
1 Thessalonians 5:2). Though some are quick to point out that
thousands of years have passed since these warnings were given,
believers maintain that the warnings are valid. In the end, what
matters most is not exactly when in history the *day of God's
wrath* arrives, but that the clock is ticking. "Man is destined to
die once, and after that to face judgment" (Hebrews 9:27 NIV).
We do not know the *day* of the Lord, nor the day of our own
death. We will treat both days with more respect if we call them
"near." On this day, the wicked will be punished and the righteous will be rewarded.

**2:6 God "will give to each person according to what he has
done."**NIV God's judgment will be impartial, and it will be according to what people have done. Final judgment will be
based upon character. All people will be held accountable for
the truth that was available to them and what they did with it.
(See also Job 34:11; Psalm 62:12; Proverbs 24:12; Jeremiah
17:10; 32:19; Matthew 16:27; 2 Corinthians 5:10; Revelation
20:12; 22:12.)

The moment when all doubt is removed will coincide with the
moment when faith is no longer possible. What we have actually
done in life will be the basis of God's judgment. There will be no
last-minute negotiations. See Ezekiel 33:30-33 for a prophecy
against people who hedge at religion. When we know what God
desires, we are responsible for how well we obey.

**2:7 To those who by persistence in doing good seek glory, honor
and immortality.**NIV This *doing good* is a result of new life in
Christ. Real faith generates good works in a believer's life. *Persistence* is a characteristic of the growing and progressing Christian (see Luke 8:15; Hebrews 12:1; James 1:3). We must persist
in doing good and in believing in Christ (see John 6:28-29).
Again Paul is emphasizing God's impartial treatment of all his
creatures. He is not contradicting his previous statement that
salvation comes by faith alone (1:16-17). The gospel simply informs us about the proper sequence for *doing good* as a response
to God's grace rather than as a way of gaining God's grace. Paul
told the Ephesians, "For it is by grace you have been saved,
through faith—and this not from yourselves, it is the gift of
God—not by works, so that no one can boast. For we are God's
workmanship, created in Christ Jesus to do good works, which
God prepared in advance for us to do," (Ephesians 2:8-10 NIV).

LIVING OUR FAITH
We are not saved by good works, but when we commit our lives fully to God, we want to please him and do his will. As such, our good works are a grateful response to what God has done, not a prerequisite to earning his grace (see also 3:20). Think of what God has done for you. Then respond to God's loving acts by trusting and obeying him fully, living out your faith.

He will give eternal life.NRSV Persistence and hope in God are rewarded by meeting the goal—glory, honor, and immortality in eternal life. In the end, people will receive what they really want. If we desire to be with God, he will gladly fulfill our wish; but if our inmost desire is to keep God at arm's length, the distance will be preserved forever. Many people want it both ways: They think that eternal life might be nice as long as God doesn't interfere with their present life. But we must choose. Will we persist in wanting our own way, or in wanting God's way? Jesus himself defined the nature of *eternal life* in his prayer for believers: "Now this is eternal life: that they may know you, the only true God, and Jesus Christ, whom you have sent" (John 17:3 NIV).

2:8 **For those who are self-seeking and who reject the truth and follow evil.**NIV Paul still has in mind the self-confident, self-righteous person, who through his own self-seeking has actually turned away from the truth and who resisted the gospel, and is following his own evil path. This attitude of *self-seeking* can be illustrated in the actions of the worker who is adamantly insistent and protective of his own rights and benefits as an employee, while at the same time he has no concern for the welfare of the company for which he works or the quality of the product he makes. He sees no farther than his own well-being. Selfish interests frequently do lead to a rejection of the truth and a pattern of doing evil.

Wrath and fury.NRSV In the previous verse, eternal life is promised to those doing good. Here, God's wrath and anger are promised to those who have turned from him, yet are claiming to have a special place with him. They will receive the wrath and anger that they thought would fall on others.

2:9 **Anguish and distress for everyone who does evil.**NRSV God's impartiality and our behavior ensure the final results. There will be suffering and affliction for those who reject God. In simple terms,

Jews or Gentiles who do evil, even if they don't perceive it that way, will receive the consequences of final judgment. We must recognize the absolutes of the human condition apart from God before we will take seriously God's offer of salvation.

First for the Jew, then for the Gentile.^{NIV} Just as the gospel and salvation came first for the Jew and then for the Gentile (1:16), so will judgment by God. Those self-righteous Jews who thought they were somehow protected from judgment because of their heritage will not only find that they will be judged; they will be first in line!

2:10 **Glory, honor and peace to everyone who works what is good.**^{NKJV} In contrast to verse 9, Jews or Gentiles who do good (those who fulfill the law in Christ), no matter how incomplete they may feel that goodness to be, will receive a reward. As with the consequences of evil, there may be immediate benefits of a right relationship with God, but the full measure of *glory, honor and peace* is for the future.

We might misread a phrase like *who works what is good* so that it becomes "who does the best he or she can." But Paul was not comparing various human behaviors and creating a scale of good and evil. This passage describes God's righteous judgment on those who have done what is good or evil. God's perception penetrates what we perceive as gray areas. His view of us is crystal clear.

Some have suggested that Paul might have had a broader group in mind here than those whose faith in Christ generates good works. Added possibilities have been: (1) those faithful Jews and moral Gentiles who did good before Christ came; (2) those non-Christians who responded to the limited light given them; and (3) those who actually did good by their own will and effort (a group Paul will shortly prove has no members). Within the context, however, these possibilities seem secondary. Paul's main point is that God's judgment is based on truth and results, not on who we are, where we came from, our upbringing, or our intentions. The final question will be, What did you do with what you knew?

2:11 **God does not show favoritism.**^{NIV} God shows no favoritism for Jew over Gentile when it comes to judgment for sin, no matter what the Jews had come to assume or expect. This personally addresses those who adopt Israel's mind-set that religious heritage guarantees salvation. This verse answers the most common perception on how God will judge. God is usually pictured as the deity who grades on the curve. In this scenario, everyone gets a goodness grade in comparison with everyone else. Somewhere in the middle of the system is the passing line. Everyone below the line fails, while everyone above passes. Those holding this idea almost always express the hope that they are somehow just above the passing line, but they have no way of really knowing. They blatantly hope that God will show favoritism. Romans 2:11 obliterates that hope. There is no passing line. Instead, sin has created a moral chasm over which no one can leap. The gospel gives us a way to reach the other side. God offers us something far better than favoritism. He offers grace. Having Christian parents or attending the church of our ancestors does not guarantee one's salvation. Salvation is given to individuals on the basis of personal faith in Jesus Christ.

2:12 All who have sinned apart from the law will also perish apart from the law.NRSV Gentiles will be judged on the basis of the knowledge available to them. They won't be condemned for failing to conform to a code of laws they knew nothing about. They will not perish because they didn't have the Jewish law; they will perish because they have sinned.

All who have sinned under the law will be judged by the law.NRSV Jews will be judged by God's written law because they had been trained in it. They will be judged for sinning against the law that they knew so well. The Jews are not better or more secure because they possess God's law; in fact, some Gentiles may be better off at the last judgment than some Jews.

People are condemned not for what they don't know, but for what they do with what they know. Those who know God's written Word and his law will be judged by them. Those who have never seen a Bible still know right from wrong; they will be judged guilty because they did not keep even the standards of their own conscience.

2:13 It is not those who hear the law who are righteous.NIV Those faithful Jews who attend the synagogues every Sabbath and hear God's law read over and over may consider themselves to be righteous, but just hearing is not enough, because . . .

It is those who obey the law who will be declared righteous.NIV Those who do good (2:10) and those who obey the law will be declared righteous—this includes both Jews and Gentiles (see also

Leviticus 18:5 and James 1:22-25). Paul seems to offer a way of righteousness by works or law, but he is simply indicating humanity's hopelessness. By the time any person would be able to obey the law perfectly, he or she would have already sinned and thus would have canceled his or her opportunity. We must resist the tendency to make this statement achievable by subtly changing it to "those who try to obey the law." The obedience that Paul describes is perfect and well beyond our reach. Our righteousness must be sought and found elsewhere. Paul effectively closes many appealing doors while he describes the only one that leads to eternal life.

FAMILIARITY AND CONTEMPT
For some people, familiarity with the Scriptures has led to contempt. The Word of God has been heard, but not obeyed. In some places, the gospel has been present for generations, but the life-changing message has been buried under the weight of traditions and structures. These people will be judged, just as will the Jewish people of Paul's day. People today often substitute church size, a pastor's popularity, the number of Bibles owned, and other religious facts and assets for their personal accountability before God. Paul wanted his readers to be able to answer this question: "How can I be declared righteous?" It is a question we also must answer.

2:14 When Gentiles, who do not possess the law, do instinctively what the law requires, these, though not having the law, are a law to themselves.NRSV Some Gentiles who did not know anything about God's law had moral sensitivity and lived as though following it. They had the law of conscience. The knowledge of God's character was available to them, for they knew within their hearts the difference between right and wrong. Their moral awareness will serve in place of the law to judge them.

Paul does not attempt to prove that people are incapable of any good. His point is that not one of us is capable of perfect goodness. At the human level, we all behave more or less in line with the standards of our society. But righteousness is not determined by what most people do, or even by what most people think might be possible for someone who tries very hard. Righteousness is God's standard, God's character. Comparisons with others are of no help when we measure ourselves before God's standard. Ultimately, whatever our background, we will be held accountable by God for our life.

BROKEN LAWS
If you travel around the world, you will find evidence in every society and culture of God's moral law. For example, all cultures prohibit murder, and yet in all societies that law has been broken. We belong to a stubborn race. We know what is right, but we insist on doing what is wrong. It is not enough to know what's right; we must also do it. We must admit to ourselves and to God that we fit the human pattern and frequently fail to live up to our own standards (much less to God's standards). That admission is what the Bible calls repentance. It is the first step to forgiveness and healing.

2:15 **The requirements of the law are written on their hearts.**[NIV] All cultures and nations, no matter how different, have a common recognition that some things are right and others are wrong. Gentiles who do not know God's law have a moral sensitivity in their hearts that matches what God's law requires. Solomon realized this when he recorded that God "has made everything beautiful in its time. He has also set eternity in the hearts of men; yet they cannot fathom what God has done from beginning to end" (Ecclesiastes 3:11 NIV).

Their conscience also bearing witness.[NKJV] A conscience is an inward monitor that lets us know when we have done wrong. What the law does for the Jew, the conscience does for the Gentile.

Their thoughts now accusing, now even defending them.[NIV] There is an inward struggle as their conscience may accuse them, and at times they may try to defend their actions against their conscience. Their thoughts act as moral functions that recognize a law.

> First, . . . human beings, all over the earth, have this curious idea that they ought to behave in a certain way, and cannot really get rid of it. Secondly, . . . they do not in fact behave in that way. They know the Law of Nature; they break it. These two facts are the foundation of all clear thinking about ourselves and the universe we live in.
> —C.S.Lewis

2:16 **The day . . . when God . . . will judge the secret thoughts of all.**[NRSV] On that day, those who are deserving will be declared righteous (2:13). The only way to truly judge a person is to judge the *secrets* of the heart, conscience, and thoughts. Some actions that appear good may be wrongly motivated; other, less visible actions may be done with good intentions. In this manner, both Jews and Gentiles will be judged—and some Gentiles will be clearly seen as "doers of God's law," whether they knew that law or not. In the end, *God will judge.* Nothing will have to be explained to God. His judgment will be perfect, based on his perfect knowledge of every action and every motive.

Through Jesus Christ, as my gospel declares.NIV God will judge *through Jesus Christ* (see John 5:27). The *gospel* Paul preached included the wonderful message that though judgment is inevitable, it will be conducted through Christ's mediation. For those who are trusting in Christ for their righteousness, God's judgment does not include the fear of exposure and punishment. As Paul later says joyfully, "Therefore, there is now no condemnation for those who are in Christ Jesus" (8:1).

GOD'S LAW IS BROKEN / 2:17-29

Paul knew that among those in Rome who would vigorously agree with his first chapter, there would be legalistic Jews, proud of their heritage as God's chosen people. But their agreement with his case would surely turn to anger as they realized that they were being included in the judgment, as equal members in the fallen human race. Possessing God's law increased both privilege and responsibility. Because these Jews knew more, they were expected to do more. At first they thought they were Paul's allies, but suddenly they were confronted by him.

For Paul, this was familiar territory. Throughout his ministry the antagonism from Jewish leaders had steadily grown (see Acts 13:42-52; 14:1-4; 17:1-5). In their eyes, he was a heretic for continuing to hold up Jesus as the Messiah, and they were in-

The frightened men of Christ's day, groaning under the intolerable social security of the Roman peace, turned to their law and found only a tangle of gobbledygook. Like us, they could obey it blindly or reject it blindly; but they could not possibly make sense of it. Something new had to be added for that. And, again like us, they did not want negative commandments at all. They wanted a positive law, to put some heart back into them. They could not get it from the scribes and Pharisees; nor for that matter, from their neighbors, the skeptical Greek philosophers and scientists; nor from the Roman theorists of law and government. Nor can we.

—Joy Davidman

sulted by his open offer of salvation to the Gentiles. Even among early Christians, there were struggles to understand that a person did not have to become Jewish in order to be accepted by God. The first churchwide council (Acts 15:1-35) addressed this question. Their answer focused on the relationship of Gentile converts to the Jewish laws. The council made no statement regarding the expected behavior of Jewish believers. But Paul held the view that being Jewish did not automatically mean God's acceptance. By the time he wrote Romans, his approach was to confront the attitude even before it surfaced. His diatribe gains in intensity as he focuses on what he sees as a major barrier between Gentiles and Jews.

In these verses, Paul continues to argue that all stand guilty before God. After describing the fate of the unbelieving, pagan Gentiles, he moves to the religiously privileged. Despite their knowledge of God's will, they are guilty because they, too, have refused to live by their beliefs. Both here and later, Paul makes it clear that the law was much more effective in confronting sinfulness than it was in motivating righteousness.

Those of us who have grown up in a Christian family are the religiously privileged of today. Paul's condemnation applies to us if we do not live up to what we know.

2:17 **If you call yourself a Jew.**^{NRSV} The imagined ally turned adversary is directly addressed as Paul points out that Jews had the divine law, worshiped the one true God, knew right from wrong, and yet regarded themselves better than all those who didn't have the law (i.e., were not Jews). Paul set up the conclusion of his argument by subtly calling into question the identity of his adversary. He listed a series of descriptive phrases following his initial *if.* Paul is creating an argument that asks bluntly, "If you claim to be Jewish, why don't you live up to the name?" We who claim to be Christians, do we live up to this name?

The phrase **boast of your relation to God** ^{NRSV} is literally, "boast in God." The same expression appears in the book of Jeremiah; "This is what the Lord says: 'Let not the wise man boast of his wisdom or the strong man boast of his strength or the rich man boast of his riches, but let him who boasts boast about this: that he understands and knows me, that I am the Lord, who exercises kindness, justice and righteousness on earth, for in these I delight,' declares the Lord" (Jeremiah 9:23-24 NIV). The kind of knowing and boasting described here is a sham without a life that demonstrates the knowledge.

BEING GENUINE
Paul lists the qualities of legalistic Jews in almost complementary terms. Many of the characteristics are good. Being a Jew wasn't bad—Paul and Jesus shared that identity. Having the law, claiming to know God, understanding his will—all these were good qualities, but only if they were genuine. The effect is the same as if an appraiser were to come to your house to examine what you thought were priceless family heirlooms. After describing each of the exquisite jewels, he announces, "These are beautiful pieces. Too bad they are only costume jewelry." God knows what we are, not just what we claim to be.

2:18 **Know his will and determine what is best.**^{NRSV} Knowing God's will is the result of having been **instructed by the law.**^{NIV} The phrase *determine what is best* is literally, "approve what is excellent." Paul is saying that God's Word is not only a record of God's will; it is also a guideline to determine what course of action is best for us. Through God's Word we can be trained or *instructed* in how to appreciate what is good. Yet how often do we, surrounded by a wealth of spiritual resources, live no differently than our pagan neighbors! We need to put our knowledge into action.

2:19 **Are confident.**^{NKJV} Paul sees these people as dangerously self-confident. It was apparent from their lives that they could not back up their claims. Paul's sarcasm here parallels Jesus' words to the Pharisees, "Woe to you, teachers of the law and Pharisees, you hypocrites! You travel over land and sea to win a single convert, and when he becomes one, you make him twice as much a son of hell as you are" (Matthew 23:15 NIV). These people saw themselves as **a guide to the blind,**^{NKJV} but Jesus repeatedly called them "blind guides" (Matthew 15:14; 23:16, 24). They claimed to be **a light**^{NKJV} but were unwilling to recognize the light of the world (John 9:5, 39-41).

DELUSIONS OF THE SELF-RIGHTEOUS
Those who are privileged with religious knowledge, exposure to good teaching, and familiarity with the truth are also those most capable of self-deception. These errors often seem reasonable or unimportant, but they turn out to be poison for the soul. We must be on guard lest we convince ourselves that:
- our years of service will outweigh our spiritual downfalls.

- God will overlook some sins because we have built up such "spiritual equity" in other areas.
- we have given so much, so God is obliged to help us.
- our relationship with spiritual giants will rub off on us and make us more acceptable to God.

The self-righteous prove that their judge is easy to convince.

2:20 An instructor . . . a teacher.[NKJV] The Jews that Paul had in mind considered themselves not only separate from the Gentiles, but also capable of teaching those whom they considered mere children in spiritual matters. These people knew they had the truth and were proud of it! But assuming the teaching role carries with it heavy responsibility, especially in spiritual training. James wrote, "Not many of you should presume to be teachers, my brothers, because you know that we who teach will be judged more strictly" (James 3:1 NIV). Knowing what ought to be taught is only one part of being an effective teacher. Practicing what is taught is the clearest test of a teacher. If you are a teacher, can you pass this test?

2:21 You . . . who teach others, do you not teach yourself?[NIV] Paul suggests that anyone proud of his spiritual background should take a careful look at himself. The Jews *were* called to be guides of the Gentiles, and salvation is of the Jews (John 4:22), but their response to God's plan for them had made them arrogant. The Jew of whom Paul was thinking possessed the law and was confident that this position allowed him to teach all those who were ignorant without the law. However, Paul's questions were designed to force the listener to realize that not all Jews could claim such superiority. Many did not understand God's law, had false confidence in it, and could not apply it readily to their daily life. Without God's Spirit and the gospel, they had neither superiority nor all the answers. Having, knowing, and reading the law are not enough. The law says not to steal, yet some Jews were stealing. The law says not to commit adultery, yet some Jews were doing just that (see 2:22). The law says to abhor idols, yet some Jews acted in sacrilege, robbing their own temple by withholding tribute money (see Acts 19:37).

The Jews needed to teach *themselves,* not others, by their law. They knew the law so well that they had learned how to excuse their own actions while criticizing others. But the law is more than legalistic minimum requirements—it is a guideline for living according to God's will. It is also a reminder that we cannot please God without a proper relationship to him. As Jesus pointed out, even withholding what rightfully belongs to someone else is stealing (Mark 7:9-13); and looking on another person with lustful, adulterous intent is adultery (Matthew 5:27-28). Before we accuse others, we must look at ourselves and see if that same sin, in any form, exists within us.

2:22 **You who say that people should not . . . do you?**ᴺᴵⱽ Paul's scathing criticism of hypocrisy continues. He is not content to point out the general principle that it is much easier to tell others how to behave than to behave properly ourselves. He applies the principle with specific illustrations: teaching, theft, adultery, idolatry, lawlessness. What is preached ought to be practiced, or it will return as judgment on the one who preaches.

> We make an idol of truth itself, for truth apart from charity is not God by his image. It is an idol we must not love or worship for its own sake. Still less must we worship its opposite, which is falsehood.
> —Blaise Pascal

The question, **do you rob temples** seems an unexpected break in the logic. But perhaps the point Paul is making involves the contrast between claiming to **abhor idols**, while in private valuing them so highly that they become worth stealing.

It is easier to say the right words than to live them. When we advise others, we must be willing to live by our own advice. Otherwise we are hypocrites. Do our actions match our words?

DOUBLE LIFE
While Christians continue to stand against adultery, more reports come in of Christian leaders who are guilty of sexual sin. Every pastor and minister needs to be accountable to his church. If you suspect a fellow Christian of sexual sin or are tempted yourself, consider these four steps:
1. Admit that sexual temptation is a compulsion that you are unable to overcome by yourself.
2. Consider the dangers to yourself, your spouse, your family, and your church—not to mention the one you desire to be with.
3. Realize the temptation will not go away.
4. Seek help from someone outside the church whom you trust.

2:23 **You who brag about the law, do you dishonor God by breaking the law?**ᴺᴵⱽ Jews were doing more than boasting about the law one moment and breaking it the next. They were dishonoring God. The unmerited honor that God had given Jews by choosing them was being treated with unhealthy pride and outright disrespect. Arrogance regarding a person's standing before God is dangerous. Paul could plainly see this danger in many of his fellow Jews.

Each of the preceding verses touches on matters in the Ten Commandments. Theft, adultery, idolatry, and dishonoring God were all prohibited. By using questions, Paul is able to confront individuals. His assumption is not that every reader would answer yes to each question, but that each reader would find his life spotlighted at least once. This last of Paul's rhetorical questions marks a turning point in his comments concerning the law. Following verse 24, Paul brings into the discussion the role of the ceremonial law, represented by circumcision. This shift highlights Paul's awareness of the tension between the law as a written code of God's standard of righteousness and the law in its ceremonial and symbolic purpose. As Paul would develop at length, the gospel provides for people a way of salvation that cannot be achieved by keeping ethical or ceremonial laws.

2:24 **"God's name is blasphemed among the Gentiles because of you."**[NIV] Those who glory in God's law and brag about their relationship to him and then live in disobedience bring God into disrepute among unbelievers. Paul quotes from Isaiah 52:5, written about Israel's exile to foreign lands. It was the Jews' rampant evil and flouting of God's law that led to the exile. They had boasted about being God's chosen people, but because of their sin, their nation was destroyed. The Gentiles despised a God who, it appeared, could not save his own people. Paul's parallel was that Jews were again resting with false confidence on their being "chosen" and their possession of God's law. Their sins were still causing Gentiles to sneer at a God who would choose such a nation.

STAKE YOUR CLAIM
If we claim to be one of God's people, our life must reflect what God is like. When we do not live up to our spiritual claims, we dishonor God's name, discourage other believers, and give people reason to speak evil of God. Genuine confidence in God yields humility, not arrogance. Knowing God means that we know ourselves as humans more clearly. The world is sickened by false spirituality but will often respond gladly to the example of simple, genuine faith in Christ.

2:25 **Circumcision indeed is of value if you obey the law.**[NRSV] Circumcision was fundamental to the Jews—it symbolized the covenant between God and Abraham's descendants (Genesis 17:9-14). It was the expression of Israel's national identity and was a requirement for all Jewish men. Circumcision was a physical reminder to Jews of their national heritage and privilege. Many were confident that it sealed their position with God. But just as having the law did not make a person right before God, neither was circumcision in itself a cause for confidence. To be circumcised was only worthwhile if God's law was followed (see Galatians 5:3). To be circumcised and yet break God's law was no better than not being circumcised at all. What God desires is a pure and obedient heart.

The futility of substituting the symbol for the reality it represents was clear even in the Old Testament. Moses knew that obedience was much more than submitting to the ceremonial law. He wrote, "Circumcise your hearts, therefore, and do not be stiff-necked any longer" (Deuteronomy 10:16 NIV). Jeremiah echoed the same concern: "Circumcise yourselves to the LORD, circumcise your hearts, you men of Judah and people of Jerusalem" (Jeremiah 4:4 NIV).

If you break the law, you have become as though you had not been circumcised.NIV Symbols require some sense of reality in order to be significant; otherwise they are empty. Signing a contract does not take the place of doing the work. In fact, signing a contract and then refusing to carry out its terms is considered a serious breach. It is worse than a failure. It is a deception.

UNDERSTANDING THE MEANING
Substituting the symbol for the reality it represents is like deliberately writing checks on a bank account with no money in it. The problem really isn't the ease with which checks can be written, nor the existence of bank accounts. The problem is the deceitfulness of the human heart, willing to be false rather than admit poverty of any kind.

Christians are as guilty in treating the sacraments in this way as the Jews were in substituting the keeping of ceremonial laws for real obedience. Baptismal vows, marriage vows, and membership vows are only as real as the intentions behind them and the actions that are carried out as a result. Professing one life-style but living another; making a promise but not fulfilling it; claiming a symbol but violating its meaning—when we treat God with this kind of dishonor, we deserve his judgment.

2:26 **If those who are not circumcised keep the law's requirements, will they not be regarded as though they were circumcised?**NIV Paul had already pointed out that circumcision was a valuable part of a system governed by obedience. Where there was no obedience, circumcision was of no value. By the

same logic, when obedience was present, the real objective
was accomplished, even though circumcision had not occurred. In other words, a Gentile who kept *the law's requirements* was as good in God's sight as a law-abiding,
circumcised Jew.

2:27 **The one who is not circumcised physically and yet obeys
the law will condemn you who, even though you have the
written code and circumcision, are a lawbreaker.**NIV A Gentile who kept the law would be in a position to condemn a Jew
who broke it, no matter how well that Jew knew the law. The
Jew who required strict observance to every letter of the law,
but was not a doer of the law, was actually a transgressor of
that law because he had missed the point.

We must keep in mind that Paul is dealing here with absolutes. Obedience is not a matter of degrees. James saw this
clearly: "For whoever keeps the whole law and yet stumbles
at just one point is guilty of breaking all of it" (James 2:10
NIV). The sharp division that the law creates reveals the startling nature of the gospel. The righteousness we might try to
create by living up to the law, circumcised or not, leads to
hopelessness. Perfect obedience is beyond us. But the "righteousness revealed from God" (1:17) is by faith and gives us
hope. One of the best reminders of our undeniable need for
God's grace is to simply read the Ten Commandments out
loud to ourselves.

2:28 **A person is not a Jew who is one outwardly, nor is true circumcision something external and physical.**NRSV Paul is adamant: The circumcision that God wanted was not cutting the flesh, and cutting the
flesh did not fulfill the law. Paul is not inventing new theology, but
urging his readers to re-examine the testimony of the Old Testament
Scriptures. God has always wanted inward circumcision, the circumcision of the heart—something only the Holy Spirit can accomplish
(see Deuteronomy 10:16; 30:6; Jeremiah 4:4; Ezekiel 36:26-27;
Galatians 6:15).

2:29 **A person is a Jew who is one inwardly, and real circumcision is a
matter of the heart—it is spiritual and not literal.**NRSV To be one
of God's children was not merely to be a circumcised Jew, but to be
one who loved God and followed his laws. The kind of Jews God
wanted were not those people tied to a heritage, rather people whose
lives were pleasing to God.

Such a person receives praise not from others but from God.NRSV The Jews got their name from their ancestor Judah; and his name was associated with the verb *praise* (see Genesis 29:35; 49:8). The person whose heart is right with God because of God's Holy Spirit will be of great value to God. A Jew transformed by God's Spirit would be living up to his name, for he would be praiseworthy in God's eyes. He would fulfill what the law required but was powerless to produce.

Romans 3

Having firmly described the shared sinful condition of humankind, Paul turns to several thoughts about the unique benefits of being Jewish. He wants to remind his Jewish brothers that their lack of faith has not hindered God's plan. Paul does not want his people to miss the significance of God's faithfulness. In spite of their failures, God still allows them to be the people of the Messiah. In fact, the Jews' lack of faith is a clear witness to the absolute need for a Savior. Neither they nor we can save ourselves. God's faithfulness is our only hope.

3:1 What advantage then has the Jew, or what is the profit of circumcision?[NKJV] Paul's conversation with his Jewish critic continues into this chapter. At the end of chapter 2, Paul had clearly stated that true "Jewishness" is not a matter of heritage, but a matter of one's relationship with God, and that true circumcision is not on the body, but on the heart. The Jewish response might have well been, "If that's true, then is there any advantage to being a part of the Jewish nation or, for that matter, in being physically circumcised?" Paul gives his response.

YOUR ADVANTAGE
What a depressing picture Paul is painting! All of us—pagan Gentiles, humanitarians, and religious people—are condemned by our own actions. The law, which God gave to show the way to live, exposes our evil deeds. Is there any hope for us? Yes, says Paul. The law condemns us, it is true, but the law is not the basis of our hope. God himself is. He, in his righteousness and wonderful love, offers us eternal life. We receive our salvation not through law but through faith in Jesus Christ. We do not—cannot—earn it; we accept it as a gift from our gracious Father.

3:2 Much, in every way . . . . The Jews were entrusted with the oracles of God.[NRSV] Paul answers yes, there are advantages for those members of God's chosen nation. (1) They were entrusted with God's laws (Exodus 19–20; Deuteronomy 4:8). (2) They were the race through whom the Messiah came to earth (Isaiah 11:1-10; Matthew 1:1-17). (3) They were the beneficiaries of covenants with God himself (Genesis 17:1-16; Exodus 19:3-6). Later in Romans, Paul returns to this theme and lists several other benefits of being Jewish: "Theirs is the adoption as sons; theirs the divine glory, the covenants, the receiving of the law, the temple worship and the promises. Theirs are the patriarchs, and from them is traced the human ancestry of Christ, who is God over all, forever praised! Amen" (9:4-5 NIV). But these privileges did not make them better than anyone else (see 3:9). In fact, the privileges made the Jews even more responsible to live up to God's requirements.

Paul himself was a Jew, and even though he became a dynamic Christian, he did not turn his back on his heritage. In fact, he realized that the prophets, the law, and God's plan all pointed to fulfillment in Jesus Christ. Therefore, he could confidently state that being a Jew and being circumcised did have meaning, but only as part of God's total plan. The Jews were *entrusted with* God's words, preserving them until the coming of Christ, who was the fulfillment of the prophetic Scriptures.

3:3   **Some did not have faith . . . Will their lack of faith nullify God's faithfulness?**NIV While it was true that many Jews were not faithful to God or to what they had been entrusted, that didn't change the fact of God's faithfulness. Many Jews rejected the gospel and thus failed to understand their own Scriptures. But Israel's unfaithfulness did not determine God's faithfulness. God had always been faithful to Israel, despite the nation's failings, and God would continue to be faithful to his covenant with them.

Paul later encouraged Timothy by writing, "Here is a trustworthy saying: If we died with him, we will also live with him; if we endure, we will also reign with him. If we disown him, he will also disown us; if we are faithless, he will remain faithful, for he cannot disown himself," (2 Timothy 2:11-13 NIV). God's faithfulness is still far ahead of our obedience. In fact, it is futile to try to make God's faithfulness in any way dependent on the quality of our faith or obedience. Our experience of following Christ in this life will always include a mixture of faith and faithlessness.

GREAT IS HIS FAITHFULNESS
When the gospel and the faithfulness of God are the central themes of Christian churches, spiritual growth takes place. Even though some will lack faith, God will remain faithful. We must not forget that the beginning of our own faith was God's loving faithfulness: "But God demonstrates his own love for us in this: While we were still sinners, Christ died for us" (Romans 5:8). As long as God is faithful, there is hope for those moving out of faithlessness and into faith.

3:4 Certainly not! Indeed, let God be true but every man a liar.NKJV In the strongest terms he could use, Paul wanted to drive home the point that the combined self-justification of the whole world could not stand up to God's truth. If God and every person were to disagree, there still would not be any doubt about who was right. The fact that many people are unfaithful (see Psalm 116:11) by suppressing the truth (1:18), exchanging the truth for a lie (1:25), and rejecting the truth (2:8), doesn't change the deeper fact of God's faithfulness. God's purpose for Israel and his plan for all people remained unshaken.

GUILTY AS CHARGED
Our world, which worships at the shrine of public opinion, where truth is determined by percentages rather than absolutes and where might claims to be right, needs to be reminded again and often that we will not appear before God to state our case. We will come before God with our guilt proven. Any hope other than God's mercy in Christ will prove to be false.

Psalm 51, from which Paul chose to quote (verse 4), is one of the profoundly confessional passages in the Old Testament. It records the repentance of David following his confrontation with the prophet Nathan over his sin with Bathsheba. In the revelation of his sin David realized, as all of us must, that there is no denial before God. He sees even those things that we hide so well in ourselves and perhaps even come to believe never happened. Kings were used to getting their way. We tend toward the same arrogance. Before God it carries no weight at all.

3:5 Our unrighteousness brings out God's righteousness.NIV The apologist in Paul can foresee further objections arising. He poses them in the question of this verse. He understands that people are usually more willing to rationalize than repent, and that their minds will be pondering ways to elude God's righteous judgment. Paul knows they are thinking, *If God's faithfulness is not dependent on my faithfulness, then why should I be faithful? And if my sinfulness makes God look so good, then why should he punish me?* I'm actually helping him out! This was an attempt to make it seem unjust for God to punish sinners. (Paul seemed so embarrassed to even use this kind of reasoning that he explained that he was merely **using a human argument.**NIV)

Is God unjust to punish the unrighteous? Many believe that God's wrath contradicts his loving nature. But God judges based on his own character, not on society's norm for fairness. God is not accountable to some external, vague notion of fair play. His personal moral uprightness is the standard by which he judges.

BRINGING OUT THE BEST
In what ways does our unrighteousness bring out God's righteousness?

- Our awareness of sin causes us to repent, resulting in salvation.
- Our repeated failures result in a new consciousness of sin and an awareness of our need for God's help.
- Our deepened understanding of sin confirms the truth that victory and spiritual growth come from God's strength rather than ours.
- God's forgiveness becomes part of our testimony to others (God has done this for me, and he will do it for you).
- In the light of God's righteousness, our tendency to sin teaches us humility.

3:6 **How could God judge the world?**NRSV This answers the questions in verse 5. God is just, and he is the Judge of all creation. Eventually the final day of reckoning will come when God will "give to each person according to what he has done" (2:6). God must and will judge sin—he has the right to judge the world because he is God, and he is holy and just. Paul answers by reaffirming God's character. He reminds his readers that no person can be an exception to God's laws; that would violate God's character and disqualify him as the Judge.

People who make themselves final arbiters of God's laws usually make a mockery out of righteousness. The kind of thinking that Paul challenges is the same religious reasoning that Jesus confronted during his ministry. These questions attempt to project our difficulties in understanding God into real philosophical problems for God. But what are problems for us are not so for God. Our simplistic case studies are laughable. Note, for example, the Sadducees who approached Jesus with the hypothetical case of the

GOD'S JUSTICE

Wrong view	*Correct view*

LAW OF FAIRNESS	GOD
GOD	JUSTICE

There is a law of fairness or justice that is higher and more absolute than God. It is binding even for God. God must act in response to that law in order to be fair. Our response is to appeal to that law.	God himself is the standard of justice. He uses his power according to his own moral perfection. Thus, whatever he does is fair, even if we don't understand it. Our response is to appeal directly to him.

married woman who had been progressively widowed by seven brothers (Matthew 22:23-33). In the minds of Jesus' questioners, the resolution of such a complicated relationship actually called into question the possibility of the resurrection. Jesus not only eliminated the problem, but he also addressed the real issue, "You are in error because you do not know the Scriptures or the power of God" (Matthew 22:29 NIV).

3:7 If my falsehood enhances God's truthfulness . . . why am I still condemned?NIV This is the same question from verse 5, posed with different words. The root problem is in people's misunderstanding of God's righteousness when he is patient to both unfaithful Jews and sinful Gentiles. Jews cannot condemn Gentiles; both are in the same predicament. Both need to rely on God's righteousness in his dealings with them and then choose to trust him or face his inevitable wrath for their sins.

WHY WORRY ABOUT SIN?
Some people may think that they don't have to worry about sin because: (1) it's God's job to forgive; (2) God is so loving, that he won't judge us; (3) sin isn't so bad—it teaches us valuable lessons; or (4) we need to stay in touch with the culture around us. It is easy to take God's grace for granted. But God cannot overlook sin. Sinners, no matter how many excuses they make, will have to answer to God for their sin.

3:8 Why not say—as we are being slanderously reported as saying . . . "Let us do evil that good may result"?NIV The gospel

Paul preached was being misconstrued because he argued that obeying the law would not bring salvation. Paul, and possibly the Roman Christians, had heard this objection from Jews who were accusing him of teaching lawlessness. If Jews or Gentile Christians interpreted Paul's words that God is faithful despite people's faithlessness to mean that God's laws need not be followed, then they could reach this incorrect conclusion. Paul touches on the issue here and will return to it in detail in chapter 6. He wants his readers to appropriate the true freedom that Christ offers without slipping into lawlessness. He dismisses this perverse reasoning with the terse words, **Their condemnation is deserved.**NIV

ALL PEOPLE ARE SINNERS / 3:9-20

Paul applies the concept of depravity he taught in 1:18-32 to the Jews in these verses. Paul now brings to a close the lengthy introduction of the charges against humanity that he began back in 1:18. He continually maintains that everyone stands guilty before God. Paul exposes the common excuses of people who refuse to admit they are sinners: (1) "There is no God," or "I follow my conscience"—1:18-32; (2) "I'm not as bad as other people"— 2:1-16; (3) "I'm a church member," or "I'm a religious person"— 2:17-29. By the end of this section he again declares that no one will be exempted from God's judgment on sin. Every person must accept that he or she is sinful and liable for God's condemnation. Only then can they understand and receive God's wonderful gift of salvation.

I'M NOT SO BAD
Paul uses the Old Testament references in this passage to show that humanity in general, in its present sinful condition, is unacceptable before God. The personal danger is revealed when we catch ourselves thinking, *Well, I'm not too bad. I'm a pretty good person.* These verses provide a checklist for character evaluation. They apply to us. Have we ever lied? Have we ever hurt someone's feelings by our words or tone of voice? Are we bitter toward anyone? Do we become angry with those who strongly disagree with us?

In thought, word, and deed, we, like everyone else in the world, stand guilty before God. We must remember who we are in his sight—alienated sinners. We must not deny that we are sinners. Instead, we ought to allow our desperate need to point us toward Christ.

3:9 Are we better than they? Not at all.^{NKJV} To the question of
whether there was any value in being a Jew, Paul had said yes (3:2).
But to the question as to whether Jews are better than Gentiles, Paul
answers no. The reason? **Jews and Gentiles alike are all under
sin.**^{NIV} Both need God's grace. Gentiles have no excuse (1:20), and
neither do Jews (2:1).

3:10 As it is written. There can be no more argument about special privileges for the Jews, for from their own Scriptures Paul strings together a series of verses outlining universal indictment. The
advantage of being a Jew does not apply to salvation. All have
sinned; no one is righteous. No one can earn right standing with God.

As is the pattern throughout the New Testament, writers do not always quote word for word from the Old Testament. Their notions
about making exact citations were less stringent than ours. And because writers were probably working from memory as often as they
were working with a text before them, their quotations tend to be al-
lusions more than they are direct references. At other times their
quotes may have been exact to the translation they did have before
them, such as the Greek version of the Old Testament.

WE ALL FALL SHORT
This list of sins, quoted from the Old Testament, tends to strike
us as harsh and unfair. We can usually spot one or two for
Which we can claim exemption. *After all*, we think, *we don't kill
or openly practice deceit.* But, as Scripture often requires us to
do, a second look is helpful. The implications of the list are diffi-
cult to avoid. They force us to ask ourselves:
- How well do we understand God? (3:11)
- How diligently are we seeking God? (3:11)
- How much goodness would God find in our daily life? (3:12)
- In the wake of our actions and words, do we leave people
  helped or hurting? (3:13-15)
- What is our record of peacemaking? (3:17)
- In what sense do we fear God? (3:18)
Paul's point, of course, is that an honest look at the facts of sin-
fulness will inevitably include us under God's judgment.

3:11 No one who seeks God^{NRSV}—from Psalm 14:2. How fortunate
that our reluctance to *seek* God did not prevent him from seeking
us! Once we have been found by God, our motivation to seek him
comes into force. Having been found by his grace, we look for
evidences of his presence everywhere. Seeking is a way of expressing what is most important to us. Jesus said, "But seek first
his kingdom and his righteousness, and all these things will be

given to you as well" (Matthew 6:33 NIV). This kind of seeking means training ourselves to turn to God first for help, to fill our thoughts with his desires, to take his character for our pattern, and to serve and obey him in everything. The writer of Hebrews notes, "And without faith it is impossible to please God, for whoever would approach him must believe that he exists and that he rewards those who earnestly seek him" (Hebrews 11:6 NRSV). The rewards of seeking come after the spiritual birth through faith.

3:12 All have turned away, they have together become worthless[NIV]—from Psalm 14:3. The failure to seek God does not leave a person immobilized; rather, it sets him or her on a course of destruction. Whatever does not include the seeking of God ends up being *worthless*.

3:13 They use their tongues to deceive[NRSV]—from Psalm 5:9. Jesus made it clear that the indications of sinfulness come from inside of us. "What goes into a man's mouth does not make him 'unclean,' but what comes out of his mouth, that is what makes him 'unclean'" (Matthew 15:11 NIV). Up until this verse, the evidence of rebellion has been mainly evident between a person and God. Here Paul begins to point out that sinfulness corrupts human relationships too. The gift of communication becomes twisted into a weapon to *deceive* others.

3:14 Mouths are full of cursing and bitterness[NRSV]—from Psalm 10:7. Eventually, rebellion against God shows itself by tainting the way a person speaks. How often do we consider how clearly speech patterns reveal people who are desperately lost? *Cursing and bitterness* may strike us first as offensive expressions, but they are also clues about a person's inward condition.

> Here the apostle plainly declares that: (1) The good effect of a lie is no excuse for it. (2) It is a mere slander upon Christians to say, "They teach men to do evil that good may come, or do the evil themselves—their damnation is just. This is peculiarly applicable to those who tell lies in order to do good thereby. It follows that officious lies, as well as all others, are an abomination to the God of truth. Therefore, there is no absurdity, however strange it may sound, in that saying of the ancient Father, "I would not tell a willful lie to save the souls of the whole world."
> —John Wesley

3:15-17 Swift to shed blood . . . the way of peace they have not known[NKJV]—from Isaiah 59:7-8. Rebellion against God leads to violence against others. The shameful milestones of history are marked with bloodstains from the atrocities committed by those who freed themselves from God. There is always talk of peace, but apart from God, there can be no real *peace*.

3:18 **There is no fear of God**NKJV—from Psalm 36:1. To fear the Lord is to recognize God for who he is: holy, almighty, righteous, pure, all-knowing, all-powerful, and all-wise. When we regard God correctly, we gain a clearer picture of ourselves: sinful, weak, frail, and needy. When we recognize who God is and who we are, we will fall at his feet in humble respect. Only then will he show us how to choose his way.

> Because of the universal fact of sin, the way of acceptance with God by reason of our works of righteousness is closed—the notice is clearly worded: No Road This Way.
> —F. F. Bruce

Paul's brief tour of truth ends almost full circle. He began with the fact that no one is like God (who is righteous), and he ends with the parallel truth that we lack *fear of God*. Some people lack this fear out of ignorance, while others, through familiarity with God, lose the sense of humble awe that ought to characterize a person's attitude before God.

3:19 **Whatever the law says, it says to those who are under the law.**NKJV The verses quoted from the Scriptures (*the Law*) in verses 10 to 18 condemn all people, but especially those under the law, the Jews.

Every mouth may be silenced.NRSV Those who read the verses quoted in 10-18 are silenced. There are no more excuses to be made, no more self-defenses uttered. No one can answer to God; everyone is liable for judgment. And if the Jews— God's special chosen people—can say nothing in their own behalf, then no one can.

The whole world may be held accountable to God.NRSV In the silence filling the court, one thought is clear: guilty as charged. That accountability of guilt must be answered, even though every explanation and excuse had failed. But one question might remain, "Why are we accountable to *God* rather than, say, our better selves or some standard of righteousness?" We are *held accountable to God* because he is our Creator, the personal source behind the standard (*law*), and the faithful Judge. We owe our existence and obedience to this One.

SILENT BEFORE GOD
The last time someone accused you of wrongdoing, how did you react? With denial, argument, and defensiveness? The Bible says the world stands silent and accountable before Almighty God. No excuses or arguments are left. Have you reached the point with God where you are ready to put away your defenses and await his decision? If not, you need to ask what is keeping you from admitting your sin to him. For the person who has submitted to God, the following verses are truly good news!

3:20 **No one will be declared righteous.**^{NIV} With this flat, all-inclusive statement, Paul closes his opening arguments that describe the state of human lostness. The purpose of the law is not to bring salvation, but to make us aware of sin.

In his sight. Paul knows that it isn't very difficult to gain the acclaim of others. His point is that the only declaration of righteousness is the one that comes from God, and it will not come as long as we insist on trying to live up to the standards of the law in our own strength.

By observing the law.^{NIV} In the phrase *by observing the law,* Paul means keeping certain traditions, such as circumcision, in order to be identified as a Jew and so remain under God's covenant promises. These traditions have to do with identifying with God's people and maintaining relationship within that people. Again Paul drives the point home: being a knowledgeable, faithful, and law-keeping Jew doesn't make a person righteous.

Through the law we become conscious of sin.^{NIV} The law was not meant to become something the Jews boasted about; rather, it was given to eliminate anyone's boasting and to make all people aware of sin and their constant need for God's grace. The law shows us where we do wrong, but it doesn't enable us to do right.

TWO FUNCTIONS OF GOD'S LAW
First, the law shows us where we go wrong. Because of the law, we know we are helpless sinners, and we must come to Jesus Christ for mercy. For example, without a speed limit, we wouldn't be breaking the law by going fast. No one receives a

reward for consistently driving below the posted limit. But anyone driving over the limit is a lawbreaker.

Second, the moral code revealed in the law can serve to
guide our actions by holding up God's moral standards. We do
not earn salvation by keeping the law (no one except Christ
ever kept or could keep God's law perfectly), but we do
please God when our lives conform to his revealed will for us.

Later in the letter (see 7:1-25) Paul returns to this matter
of the usefulness of the law. Concern about the law is actually
the backdrop for the entire letter. Paul needs to explain in detail that his objective is not to undermine the law, but to un-
derline its real purpose. Paul's ministry exemplified the
wonderful truth Jesus claimed when he said, "Do not think
that I have come to abolish the Law or the Prophets; I have
not come to abolish them but to fulfill them" (Matthew 5:17
NIV). Until Jesus came, the law provided a strict measurement of God's just and righteous character. With the coming
of Christ, God's mercy was also demonstrated. The law expressed the righteous requirements of God; Christ provided a
way that we might be declared righteous. God's mercy had always been present; in Christ it became evident.

CHRIST TOOK OUR PUNISHMENT / 3:21-31

Like the swelling waves of the tide, Paul's argument rolls over the predicament of the human race. After each wave of the gospel, the waters
recede to reveal a new aspect or depth of the problem of sin. This wave-
like approach to Paul's letter provides a number of views of the same
issues, with slightly different emphases. Having stated such a strong
case for our universal indictment under the law, Paul now turns to
God's gracious alternative plan.

GOOD NEWS
After all the preceding bad news about our sinfulness and
God's condemnation, Paul gives the wonderful news. There is
a way to be declared not guilty—by trusting Jesus Christ to
take away our sins. Trusting means putting our confidence in
Christ to forgive our sins, to make us right with God, and to empower us to live the way he taught us. God's solution is available
to all of us, regardless of our background or past behavior.

3:21 **But now.** With this sharp expression Paul alerts his readers to an important shift in subject. They would still be trying to absorb the im-

HOW CAN GOD ACCEPT US?

The Problem:
We resist God.
We ignore God.
We attempt to deceive God.
We work against God's interests.
We acknowledge God only when we are in trouble.
We consider our plans and desires before God's.
We do not love God with all our heart, soul, and mind.

How can we even hope to have an intimate relationship with God, or to go to heaven after this life?

False Solutions:	*True Solution:*
Deny there is a God, but create our own god out of something or someone else.	Recognize the answer to our problem is faith and trust in Christ.
Live in guilt, punishing ourselves or masking the guilt behind alcohol and drugs.	Accept God's gracious gift of forgiveness, believing in his love.
Use religion (works, church attendance, service) as a substitute for faith, loving God, and obeying him.	Realize that God is willing to declare us not guilty, and that he alone can do that.
Assume or vaguely hope God will save us anyway.	Live in the freedom provided by God, enjoying the opportunity to express our thanks by obedience rather than trying to earn his acceptance.
Conclude God is too demanding and live in despair or apathy.	Humbly accept the fact that Christ's substitution for us accomplished what we could not have done for ourselves.

pact of the Old Testament testimony against them. It was a teachable moment—an instant when the mind has been opened to a new view of familiar ideas and is vulnerable to significant application. Paul's apologetic handling of the law is similar to Jesus' approach with his parables, taking what was merely familiar to his readers and then shocking them into understanding. At this point, they are perhaps ready to hear the gospel. For them, Paul's *but now* is a signal of hope.

Righteousness from God . . . has been made known.^{NIV} Paul reintroduces the phrase he used in 1:17, *a righteousness from God.* Whereas the law was God's righteous standard, the righteousness required to live up to it was not within man's capacity. God, the measure of righteousness, had to provide a means of righteousness. Paul is convinced beyond doubt that this means of *righteousness from God* has, in fact, *now* been given. The phrase *been made known* (*pephanerotai*) can also be translated "manifested," "disclosed," or "revealed." These meanings are consistent with Paul's claim that this *righteousness from God* had been acknowledged by those who served God in the past. The gospel is not a recent creation by God to respond to human failure. It was part of the plan all along, *but now . . . made known.*

Apart from law . . . to which the Law and the Prophets testify.[NIV] In Greek grammar, *apart from law* follows immediately after *but now.* Paul emphasizes a different way of seeing the same issue. Whereas the law provided a measurement of the distance between God and his creatures, this *righteousness from God, apart from law,* provides a means to cross the distance. *Apart from law* indicates the same source but an independent working. There is a way to be righteous before God. It is not by obeying the law, by being "Jewish" (see 3:20), yet it has always been in *the Law and the Prophets*, for they pointed to it. The gospel is the fulfillment of the Law and the Prophets.

3:22 Righteousness from God comes.[NIV] Because of its content, many translators make this verse an independent sentence, but it is actually a continued phrase begun in verse 21. The word *comes* is not in Greek, but some term of arrival or appropriation is made necessary **to all who believe.** The process that Paul is describing involves God's revelation of his *righteousness*, its confirmation by the Law and Prophets, and its reception by individual believers.

Through faith in Jesus Christ for all who believe.[NRSV] The way to acceptance by God is the way of faith in Jesus Christ. *Faith in*, (believing in) Jesus Christ means putting our confidence in him to forgive our sins, to make us right with God, and to empower us to live the way he taught us. God's solution is available to all of us regardless of our background or past behavior. And this way is open to *all who believe*—both Jews and Gentiles.

No difference.[NIV] A more accurate word is probably "distinction" (NRSV). This word emphasizes the fact that *faith in Jesus Christ* is the only requirement for receiving God's righteousness. It also anticipates Paul's description of our common state as sinners. We all begin in the same place spiritually, and there is only one way out, *faith in Jesus Christ.*

Faith in Jesus Christ doesn't mean we understand everything that Christ has done for us, but it does mean that we believe he has done everything for us!

3:23 **All have sinned and fall short of the glory of God.** Paul has made it clear thus far in his letter that there is no difference between Jews and Gentiles when it comes to final judgment—everyone has sinned. Therefore, no one can share in the **glory of God** by virtue of their sinlessness. If the law measures the distance between God and his creatures, then human righteousness is our attempt to bridge that distance by our own efforts. Paul is correct—we all *fall short.* But what is this *glory of God* that we do not reach on our own? The word *glory* (*doxes*), from which we derive the word *doxology,* refers to the wonderful and awe-inspiring but indescribable presence of God himself. We tend to think of *glory* in terms of brightness, but it is certainly more than that. It is utter wholeness, completeness. Sin keeps us from the presence of God. What ought to catch our attention is the fact that our common sinfulness keeps us from reaching the place that we were created to experience. And one of the anticipations of faith in Jesus Christ is that we will share fully in the *glory of God* (see Romans 8:18, 29-30; Philippians 3:21; 2 Thessalonians 2:14).

Sinning confirms our status as sinners, and sin cuts us off from our holy God. Furthermore, sin leads to death (because it disqualifies us from living with God), regardless of how great or small each sin may seem. Sins are deadly, but sinners can be forgiven. There are no distinctions: we have all sinned; we all need a savior; Jesus Christ is the Savior; through faith we can receive his salvation.

3:24 **Justified freely by His grace.**^NKJV Just as there is no distinction in our fallenness, Paul writes, so there is no distinction in the source of our justification. God justifies us;

> In order that he alone might be righteous, it was necessary for God to deliver the whole human race to death on the cross in the judgment of his wrath. The death of Jesus is the manifestation of God's righteousness, it is the place where God has given gracious proof of his own righteousness, the place where alone the righteousness of God will dwell. By sharing in this death we too become partakers of that righteousness.
>
> — Dietrich Bonhoeffer

he declares us "not guilty" for our sins. When a judge in a court of law declares the defendant "not guilty," all the charges are removed from the person's record. Legally, it is as if the person had never been accused. When God forgives our sins, our record is wiped clean. From his perspective, it is as though we had never sinned. We do not have to anxiously work while hoping that in the end we will have been good enough to meet God's approval. Instead, God takes those who believe in his Son, Jesus Christ, justifies them, and then calls them righteous before they've even begun to live for him. Our righteousness before God depends entirely on him and can only be accepted as a gift from him. God *by His grace* assures us of our acceptance and then calls us to serve him as best we can out of sheer love for him.

Through the redemption that came by Christ Jesus.NIV The word *redemption* refers to the cost paid by Christ to set sinners free from slavery to sin. Christ paid the debt we owed for violating the righteous demands of the law. In Old Testament times, a person's debts could result in his being sold as a slave. The next of kin could redeem him (buy his freedom). Christ purchased our freedom, and the price was his own life. Christ has provided all that we need to stand in God's presence as though we have never done wrong. What he did for us becomes our own when we put our faith in him.

3:25 God presented him as a sacrifice of atonement.NIV In describing how God provided us with undeserved righteousness, Paul alludes to the sacrificial system in the Old Testament (see Leviticus 17:11). Only now, the life offered as sacrifice is not a spotless animal, but Christ. God removed our punishment through the perfect sacrifice of Jesus Christ, a sacrifice that involved his death, the shedding of his blood. The classic theological term for this process, (*sacrifice of atonement*) is *propitiation* (*hilasterion*). The word signifies a substitutionary sacrifice whereby sinful people can be reconciled to a righteous God. It is used to describe how Christ took our place in receiving the wrath of God poured out for sin. On the cross, Jesus stepped into the line of fire in front of us and absorbed the wrath aimed at us. Because of what Jesus did on the cross, God can accept those who put their trust in Jesus.

Through faith in his blood.NIV Why blood? God had said from the beginning, "For the life of a creature is in the blood, and I have given it to you to make atonement for yourselves on the altar; it is the blood that makes atonement for one's life" (Leviticus 17:11 NIV). But the blood Paul mentions here is a particular *blood*—it is *his*, that is, Christ's *blood*. Only the sacrificial death of Christ on the cross was the effective atonement for our sins. Christ stands in our place, having paid the penalty of death for our sin, and he completely satisfied God's demands. Our faith is in that atonement. It is faith that humbly accepts what has been done on our behalf. As Paul states in 5:9, "Since we have now been justified by his blood, how much more shall we be saved from God's wrath through him!" (For more on Christ's sacrificial death, see 1 Corinthians 5:7; 10:16; Ephesians 1:7; 2:13; 5:2; Colossians 1:20).

> Although our view of the sublimest things is limited and weak, it is most pleasant to be able to catch but a glimpse of them.
> —Thomas Aquinas

Demonstrate his justice . . . left the sins committed beforehand unpunished.NIV What happened to people who lived before Christ came and died for sin? If God condemned them, was he being unfair? If he saved them, was Christ's sacrifice unnecessary? Paul shows that God forgave the sin of all who believe at the cross of Jesus. Old Testament believers looked forward in faith to Christ's coming and were saved, even though they did not know Jesus' name or the details of his earthly life. Unlike the Old Testament believers, we know about the God who loved the world so much that he gave his own Son (John 3:16). The question to answer is, Have you put your trust in him?

God is just, both in his inherent character, and in his dealings with sinners. Christ's death relates to both the past and the present. God did not completely reject his people, the Jews, even though they constantly rejected him. He was not being unfairly generous; rather, he was looking forward to the time when Jesus' death would be effective for all those who believed in God *before* Jesus came, as well as those who come after. The timeliness of Christ's death as part of God's plan and of his death as applying even to the sins of the past was a matter that Paul considers at length in the next chapter.

3:26 **To demonstrate at the present time his righteousness.**NKJV God maintains his righteous character by providing Christ as the perfect and complete sacrifice for sin. While his full justice demanded full payment for sin, he also provided the full payment for those who put their trust in Jesus Christ.

To be just and the one who justifies those who have faith in Jesus.NIV God is just—his answer for dealing with sin always has been death (in the Old Testament, the sacrifice of animals), and he has dealt with sin once and for all in the same manner, except this time, through the death of his own Son. Jesus' death atones for the believer's sins and destroys the power of sin in the believer's life. The only answer to humanity's plight—that is, death because of sin—was given by God in the death and resurrection of Jesus Christ. This action fulfilled God's own law and his promises to Israel. The way to receive this answer for ourselves through faith in Jesus Christ.

Paul does not hesitate to emphasize God's divine consistency. God was able *to be* perfectly *just*, and at the same time be active as the one who *justifies* those who trust what he accomplished through Jesus. A god of mechanical and impersonal justice would have left us without hope. But God has revealed himself as personal and loving, while remaining *just*.

3:27 **Boasting . . . is excluded.** In conclusion, Paul writes that since there are no exceptions in God's plan (3:22), since person must begin with the same realization (3:23) and pass by the same way (3:24-26), there is no room for personal pride. There can be no boasting by Jews or Christians about their heritage, their law, or their works. Instead, God's law is to be understood in terms of faith. The law is "done" or "observed" by faith.

At this point, Paul begins to focus on the word *law* in a way that anticipates his further discussion of the fact that the requirement of faith was already in place when the law was given. He writes, literally, "So, where is the boasting? Excluded. On the basis of what law? Of works? No, but on the basis of the law of faith." Paul is confronting the reduction of God's standard to a list of actions by emphasizing a deeper "law," the requirement of faith.

Why is faith the law of God's kingdom?

- Faith eliminates the pride of human effort, because faith is not a deed that we do.

> Should he grow so foolish, however, as to presume to become righteous, free, saved, and a Christian by means of some good work, he would instantly lose faith and all its benefits, a foolishness aptly illustrated in the fable of the dog who runs along a stream with a piece of meat in his mouth and, deceived by the reflection of the meat in the water, opens his mouth to snap at it and so loses both the meat and the reflection.
>
> —Martin Luther

- Faith exalts what God has done, not what people do.

- Faith admits that we can't keep the law or measure up to God's standards—we need help.

- Faith is based on our relationship with God, not our performance for God.

3:28 A person is justified by faith apart from works prescribed by the law.^{NRSV} Most religions prescribe specific duties that must be performed to make a person acceptable to God. Christianity is unique in teaching that the good works we do will not make us right with God. No amount of human achievement or progress in personal development will close the gap between God's moral perfection and our imperfect daily performance. So there can be no basis for pride. Good deeds are important, but they will not earn us eternal life. We are saved only by trusting in what God has done for us through Jesus Christ (see Ephesians 2:8-10).

3:29 Is God the God of Jews only?^{NRSV} Again, the Jews cannot claim sole propriety of God or deny that Gentiles can also receive God's saving grace. The Old Testament consistently recorded God's inclusion of the Gentiles in his plans. God had promised Abraham, "All peoples on earth will be blessed through you" (Genesis 12:3 NIV). The fact that the Jews had been chosen for special service to the rest of the world had become horribly twisted into prideful separation from the world. Paul reminds his readers of this fact and develops the thought in the next part of his letter.

We must not think that God belongs to our group only. Our church or denomination cannot contain all of Christ's fullness. Only the complete body can complement the head, Jesus Christ.

3:30 There is only one God.^{NIV} A key Hebrew scripture reads: "Hear, O Israel: The Lord our God, the Lord is one" (Deuteronomy 6:4 NIV)—a prayer uttered by pious Jews every day. Paul simply states the logical necessity. If God really is the one and only God, then he is God of all his creation and calls both Jews and Gentiles to faith in him. The question of justification will not be settled by God according to those who have and have not been circumcised, but rather by their faith, whatever their physical lineage.

3:31 Do we, then, nullify the law by this faith? ... We uphold the law.^{NIV} Paul envisions the Jewish critic raising these last concerned and valid questions: "Does faith wipe out Judaism, cancel our Scriptures, end our customs? If we are saved by faith, does that mean we no longer need to obey God's laws?" Paul answers, "Absolutely not!" In fact, only when we trust Jesus can we fulfill the righteous requirements of the law. The law is not something that only the Jews can "do" for God; the law is for both Jews and Gentiles and can only be "done" through faith in Christ. Faith returns the law to its proper place and role in God's plan for people. Faith does not wipe out the Old Testament; rather, it makes God's dealings with the Jewish people understandable. (See also 5:20-21; 8:3-4; 13:9-10; Galatians 3:24-29; 1 Timothy 1:8.)

In order to show the priority of faith, Paul feels compelled to turn his readers' attention to the origins of the Jewish race. He invites Abraham to make a contribution to the discussion by providing proof that faith was already the sole requirement between God and his creatures long before the Mosaic law was given.

Romans 4

Paul had already stated that "a righteousness from God, apart from law, has been made known, to which the Law and the Prophets testify" (3:21 NIV). Now he continues to show the Jews from their own Scriptures that a person is justified by faith and not by works. Abraham is Paul's first example. Paul knows that if he can make a convincing case for Abraham's justification by faith, Jews might be more open to considering the claims of the gospel. After all, if the ancestral father of the Jewish nation did not attempt to earn his way into God's favor, neither should his offspring. Paul was anxious that his fellow Jews discover what he and their father Abraham had discovered—that justification comes by faith.

4:1 Abraham, our forefather.^{NIV} Paul continues his conversation with his Jewish questioner by mentioning Abraham, the great patriarch of the Jewish nation, and calling him "our" forefather. But Paul's intended audience is much broader. He wants to make it clear that Abraham is forefather to all *believers*, whether Jews or Gentiles. So his question, "What did Abraham discover?" while appealing to Jewish readers, introduces the possibility of Abraham's fatherhood in other ways. Paul does this by literally calling Abraham "our forefather after the flesh."

According to Jewish tradition, Abraham had been chosen by God for his unique role in history because he was the only righteous man alive at the time. Abraham was the epitome of what it meant to be a Jew, and he was the first Jew, the father of all Jews. John the Baptist had warned that being descendants of Abraham did not settle matters with God (see Luke 3:7-9). Jesus had anticipated the broader application of Abraham's faith when he told certain Jews, "If you were Abraham's children . . . then you would do the things Abraham did" (John 8:39 NIV). Clearly there was more to being a child of Abraham than simply being able to trace one's genealogy back to him.

The Jews remembered that God had said, "Abraham obeyed

me and kept my requirements, my commands, my decrees and my laws" (Genesis 26:5 NIV). But this estimate of Abraham's life came long after his initial venture by faith, acting solely on the basis of God's promise. Along his way Abraham became God's friend and received promises and covenants, especially the covenant of circumcision. Yet Paul wants to impress upon his readers the point that what Abraham had **discovered**[NIV] about faith and righteousness is worth being discovered by everyone.

4:2 If Abraham was justified by works, he has something to boast about.[NRSV] It may seem harsh to describe someone who is sincerely and fearfully trying to earn God's approval as "a person who wants to have **something to boast about.**" But Paul did not hesitate to point out faulty ideas and ways of thinking. Whether a person is sincerely or arrogantly wrong doesn't change the fact that he or she is wrong. If God could be put in debt to any person, he would not be God. The idea of earning one's salvation is based on the erroneous assumption that people can somehow cause God to owe them something because of something they have done. The picture of a person standing before God and asking to be given "only what I deserve" is wrong in two ways: (1) It fails or refuses to recognize the depth of human sinfulness, and (2) it displays a disregard for the holiness and majesty of God. Being given only what we deserve would result in our worst nightmare. Trying to earn God's favor may come from pride or misunderstanding, but it is neither effective nor right.

If Abraham was accepted by God because of what he did, then he would have something to boast about. This was the traditional rationale for religious pride that Paul expects from his Jewish questioner. Many Jews saw Abraham as justified by his works, especially in his obedience to God's command to sacrifice Isaac. They believed that he had every reason to boast in his relationship with God. As Abraham's descendants, they believed that they also had reasons for pride. But Paul knocks down that argument by saying . . .

> It is like the proffered hand of a drowning man that makes it possible for the lifeguard to save him. There is nothing meritorious in the act of a drowning man stretching out his hand in order to be saved. It is the efficient medium through which he is saved. Thus, the act of faith on the sinner's part is not meritorious but only the efficient medium through which God is able to save him.
> —Kenneth Wuest

But not before God. There can be no boasting about anything when it comes to God. The pride of the Jews in their special status before God and in all their laws had made them unable to see that the only way to be justified before God is by humble faith.

4:3 **"Abraham believed God, and it was credited to him as righteousness."**NIV To underscore his point, Paul quotes directly from Genesis 15:6. Having given the human answer in verse 2, Paul now introduces God's answer. Jewish teachers interpreted this Old Testament verse to refer to Abraham's faithfulness to God's covenants. Paul, however, puts this verse in a new light with his understanding of the gospel. Abraham's works or obedience were not credited as righteousness, but his *faith* was. From this verse, Paul goes on to emphasize that belief, or faith, on Abraham's part did not earn right standing with God; instead, Abraham's faith was simply an affirmative response to God's promise that Abraham's seed would be multiplied as the stars in heaven and the sand on the seashore (Genesis 15:5).

Paul uses the term *it was credited* (*elogisthe*) to describe how God treats human faith. Other translations have *counted* or *reckoned.* God credited righteousness to Abraham's account. God gives us everything based on our allowing him to do so. The moment that we stop trying to be good or pretending to be good and simply submit ourself before God's mercy, he responds by saying, "Now, that's good!"

 WHAT DOES THE SCRIPTURE SAY?
If our defense of the faith relies too heavily on our own thinking, we will fail. Too often we have our unanswered questions or doubts simply because we have failed to find out what God's Word has to say. For the believer, the Bible is the most immediate source of authority. We must realize that we have not honestly or carefully responded to a question or problem until we have asked, "What does the Scripture say?"

4:4 **Now to one who works, wages are not reckoned as a gift but as something due.**NRSV Paul illustrates the difference between faith and effort by describing the process of employment. An employer cannot call an employee's pay a present if it has been earned. The employer is obligated to pay for work that has been completed. The wages are the agreed-upon amount, not a gift. If a person could earn right standing with God by his or her works (doing good, obeying the law), salvation wouldn't be free; it would be God's obligation, like payment for our efforts.

Faith is crucial in Christianity because it bases righteousness (right standing and right relationship with God leading to right behavior) on trust in God's unconditional love rather than on performance (works). If righteousness were based on works, our actions would require God to bless us. God would then be subject to a breach of contract suit on our part if he failed to reward our good works. Such a system would actually reverse our roles, making us divine and God merely our servant.

4:5 **But to one who without works trusts him who justifies the ungodly, such faith is reckoned as righteousness.** In contrast to the wage earner is the sinner (the *ungodly*) who trusts in God. This person *does not work*—in other words, he or she has come to God because of faith and has not performed any rituals or followed any laws. God will justify that person; his or her *faith is reckoned as righteousness.* How could God do this? Paul explains further in 5:6, "Christ died for the ungodly." Of course, the justified person is expected to no longer be wicked, but his justification is not based on good or evil actions.

In the following verses, Paul shows how even Abraham was called righteous *before* he was given the covenant of circumcision—thus proving that it was not the act of circumcision that saved him, but the fact that he *believed God* (4:3). Abraham was not "wicked"; in fact, he was very pious. The point is that Abraham was justified without regard to works performed;

> God does not accept the person on account of his works, but he accepts the works on account of the *(believing)* person.
> —Martin Luther

thus, the opportunity to be justified is equally available to all people.

In Luke 18:9-14, Jesus told the parable of two men who prayed— a Pharisee and a tax collector. The Pharisee prayed, telling about his own merit (fasting and tithing). The tax collector could only pray for mercy. Jesus said, "I tell you that this man [the tax collector], rather than the other, went home justified before God" (NIV). The humble tax collector was justified by his faith.

SAVING FAITH
When some people learn that they are saved by God through faith, they start to worry. *Do I have enough faith?* they wonder, *Is my faith strong enough to save me?* These people miss the point. It is Jesus Christ who saves us, not our feelings or actions, and he is strong enough to save us no matter how weak our faith is. Jesus offers salvation as a gift because he loves us, not because we have earned it through our powerful faith. What, then, is the role of faith? Faith is believing and trusting in Jesus Christ and reaching out to accept his wonderful gift of salvation.

4:6 David says the same thing.^{NIV} Next Paul quotes from Psalm 32 (written by David) to develop his explanation of how God **credits righteousness apart from works.**^{NIV} David had written of the blessedness of those whose sins were forgiven and covered, whose sin God would not count against (or *credit* to) them. Paul is saying that God's forgiveness of sins by his sheer grace is the same as crediting righteousness given to people apart from their works. He will explain this in coming verses.

THE JOY OF FORGIVENESS
King David was guilty of terrible sins—adultery, murder, and lies—yet he experienced the joy of forgiveness. We too can have this joy when we:
- stop denying our guilt and recognize we have sinned,
- admit our guilt to God and ask his forgiveness, and
- let go of our guilt and believe God has forgiven us.

This can be difficult when a sin has taken root and grown over many years, when it is very serious, or when it involves others. Remember, Jesus is willing and able to forgive every sin. In view of the tremendous price he paid on the cross, it is arrogant to think that any sins are too great for him to cover. Even if your faith is weak, your conscience is sensitive, and your memory haunts you, God's Word declares that sins confessed are sins forgiven (1 John 1:9).

4:7-8 Blessed are those . . . whose sins are covered.^{NKJV} Paul uses David's thoughts to describe the fate of sin in the light of God's grace. In these two verses, sins are *forgiven, covered,* and *never counted against* the sinner (NIV). Apart from any effort on our part, and not based on anything good we have done, our sins are forgiven, buried, and never exhumed.

Blessed (makarios) is one of those theological words that is easier to use than understand. It is often translated "happy" or "fortunate." We tend to think of a "blessing" as a positive experience, position, or personal state. This understanding makes it difficult to understand the biblical contexts of *blessed* that include experiences and personal states that we can only describe as painful and even life-threatening. When Jesus said, "Blessed are you when people insult you, persecute you and falsely say all kinds of evil against you because of me," (Matthew 5:11 NIV) he was certainly not referring to good feelings. Perhaps our emphasis needs to be more on blessing as a particular awareness of God's grace, rather than an emotional condition. Whether or not our immediate experiences in life are positive and exciting, we ought to be constantly conscious of God's grace.

PAINFUL PASSAGES
The idea of being rewarded by God for our good acts has a certain appeal, especially during those times when things are going well. But sooner or later, every person experiences loss, confusion, and failure. Some of these painful passages are:

- Watching adult children turn away from their upbringing
- Enduring the death of a spouse or other loved one
- Having financial reversals
- Experiencing illness and pain
- Losing a job
- Growing old

At these times we lose control over the circumstances and outcomes in our lives. And that's when we need God's grace. In our times of weakness we are acutely reminded of how desperate our position would be if we actually were required to earn God's acceptance. For believers, difficult experiences can be opportunities to renew an awareness of God's grace.

4:9 Is this blessedness only for the circumcised?^{NIV} The word *blessedness* refers to verses 7 and 8. Does being forgiven of sins and not having them held against us depend on whether we are circumcised? Is an awareness of God's grace only possible to those who have been circumcised?

Abraham's faith was credited to him as righteousness.^{NIV} It was Abraham's *faith*, not his faithfulness to certain rituals, that made him righteous. The critical question is: If Abraham was justified by faith, then why did God initiate the rite of circumcision? Paul uses the term *circumcised* to refer to the whole of the law, because circumcision implies a desire to live under the demands of the law.

REMINDERS
Rituals did not earn any reward for Abraham; he had been blessed long before the circumcision ceremony was introduced. Abraham found favor with God by faith alone, before he was circumcised. Genesis 12:1-4 tells of God's call to Abraham when he was seventy-five years old; the circumcision ceremony was introduced when he was ninety-nine (Genesis 17:1-14).

Ceremonies and rituals serve as reminders of our faith, and they instruct new and younger believers. But we should not think that they give us any special merit before God. They are outward signs and seals that demonstrate inward belief and trust. The focus of our faith should be on Christ and his saving actions, not on our own actions.

10   Credited . . . after he was circumcised, or before?NIV When did this
happen? When did Abraham believe God and have righteousness credited to him? Before or after circumcision? Paul immediately answers his
own question—**It was not after, but before!**NIV God called Abraham in
Genesis 12 (when Abraham was seventy-five years old), declared him
righteous in Genesis 15, then introduced the circumcision ceremony in
Genesis 17 (when Abraham was ninety-nine).

Paul shows here that there is more to answering the question
"What does the Scripture say?" (4:3) than just quoting a verse. The
context helps determine the meaning. The traditional interpretation
of Genesis 15:6 was in error by neglecting the context of Abraham's
life. Paul is basing his applications on not only what God said about
Abraham, but when he said it. In one case, the application is that justification is by faith, not works. In the other case, because the timing
meant Abraham was still a Gentile when the promise was given, the
application is that the opportunity to believe extends to everyone.

11   A seal of the righteousness that he had by faith.NRSV Abraham's
circumcision sealed the righteous standing he already had with
God because of his faith. God said, "You are to undergo circumcision, and it will be the sign of the covenant between me and you"
(Genesis 17:11 NIV). His circumcision was a seal and a sign.

**Father of all those who believe, though they are uncircum-
cised.**NKJV So, Abraham was also the "father" of the Gentiles who,
although not circumcised and not part of the Jewish nation, could
still have *righteousness credited to them* when they believed in
God. Faith then, precedes and supercedes circumcision.

12   Also the father of the circumcised.NIV Abraham is truly "our
forefather" (4:1), for he is father of all who believe in God. Abraham is father of uncircumcised believers because he was uncircumcised when he was considered righteous; he is the father of
circumcised believers not simply because of common Jewish heritage, but because they both had faith in God.

In the final analysis, Abraham's righteousness was not dependent on his being circumcised. Being circumcised was a sign to
Abraham that he had been accepted by God. The Jews were to remember that circumcision was a sign, not a substitute for faith.

Walk in the steps of the faith.NKJV Everything that God had
given the Jews (the Law, circumcision, sacrifices, feasts, etc.) better informed their faith, but never removed their need to respond
personally in faith, as Abraham had done. By responding to God

STEPS OF ABRAHAM'S FAITH

Abraham's faith was tested a number of times. Each response was a step of faith. Some of these steps were not what we would call big tests, but together they establish a picture of Abraham as a man of genuine faith. After the last test, God said, "Now I know that you fear God, because you have not withheld from me your son, your only son" (Genesis 22:12 NIV). Note that these "steps" are not "works" in that they earn God's approval; rather, they are the natural outworking of the inward faith that God counts as righteousness.

Abraham's faith-steps can have applications for us:

Reference/Step	*Application*
Genesis 12:1-7–At God's direction, Abraham left Ur and Haran for a destination unknown.	Do I trust God with my future? Is his will part of my decision making?
Genesis 14:17-24–Abraham gave a tithe of loot to the godly king of Salem, Melchizedek, but he refused the gift from the king of Sodom.	In my dealings with people, am I careful to give proper honor to God and refuse to receive honor that belongs to him?
Genesis 15:1-6–Abraham trusted God's promise that he would have a son.	How often do I consciously reaffirm my trust in God's promises?
Genesis 15:7-11–Abraham received the Promised Land by faith, though God warned him the fulfillment would not come for many generations.	How have I demonstrated my continued trust in God during those times when I have been required to wait?
Genesis 17:9-27–At God's command, Abraham circumcised every male in his family.	In what occasions in my life have I acted simply in obedience to God?
Genesis 18:22-33–Abraham prayed for Sodom.	Am I a person who cares for people in spite of their sinfulness?
Genesis 20:1-17–Abraham admitted to wrongdoing and took the actions necessary to set things right.	When I sin, do I tend to cover up or admit my fault? When needed, do I accompany my apology with restitution?
Genesis 22:1-12–Abraham prepared to sacrifice his son Isaac.	How have I demonstrated that I will not allow anything in my life to come before God?

in faith, both circumcised and uncircumcised people are literally "keeping in step with Abraham's footsteps of faith." The faith that Jews and Gentiles should imitate is the faith that Abraham had before he was circumcised.

4:13 Not through law that Abraham . . . received the promise. ^{NIV} What promise? "Abram believed the LORD" (Genesis 15:6 NIV), and what he believed was God's promise **that he would be heir of the world.**^{NIV} God had said, "I will make you into a great nation and I will bless you; I will make your name great, and you will be a blessing. I will bless those who bless you, and whoever curses you I will curse; and all peoples on earth will be blessed through you" (Genesis 12:2-3 NIV) And "[God] took [Abraham] outside and said, 'Look up at the heavens and count the stars—if indeed you can count them . . . . So shall your offspring be'" (Genesis 15:5 NIV). This promise was made to Abraham many years before the requirement of circumcision, and hundreds of years before the giving of the Ten Commandments (Exodus 20). Abraham believed God's promise, even though it was also made when he was almost one hundred years old and did not yet have any children.

That Abraham would be *heir of the world* is not explictly stated in the Old Testament, but it is implicit in the three promises God made to him: (1) he would have many descendants (Genesis 12:2; 13:16; 15:5; 17:4-6), (2) he would possess the land of Canaan (Genesis 13:15-17; 15:17-21; 17:8), and (3) he would be a medium of blessing to all the people of the earth (Genesis 12:3; 18:18; 22:18).

4:14 If those who live by law are heirs, faith has no value and the promise is worthless.^{NIV} The expression *those who live by law* refers to the Jews. If living by the law makes the Jews the only heirs of God's promises, then Abraham's faith and God's promises are worthless. Why would God make a promise conditional on obedience to laws that would be given over four hundred years later? The law cannot bring blessing or righteousness, instead . . .

4:15 Law brings wrath.^{NRSV} If the law does not bring righteousness, then why does it exist? The law brings wrath. In other words, in a world where people can make real choices, the law's presence automatically includes the possibility of failure and the consequences that would follow. The law's function is to help people realize their great sinfulness and to impose penalties on those who transgress it. But if **there is no law, neither is there viola-tion.**NRSV If no one defines right and wrong, then no one knows the difference, and no one can sin. Or, in terms of the gospel, if the punishment required by the law is diverted to Christ, then we are judged "not guilty."

WHAT WE HAVE AS CHILDREN

As Adam's children we have	As God's children we have
Ruin (5:9)	Rescue (5:8)
Sin (5:12, 15, 21)	Righteousness (5:18)
Death (5:12, 16, 21)	Eternal life (5:17, 21)
Separation from God (5:18)	Relationship with God (5:11, 19)
Disobedience (5:12, 19)	Obedience (5:19)
Judgment (5:18)	Deliverance (5:10-11)
Law (5:20)	Grace (5:20)

4:16 **The promise comes by faith ... by grace ... guaranteed to all Abraham's offspring.**NIV What God gives by grace can only be accepted by faith. The promise given to Abraham that he and his countless offspring would inherit the world (4:13) refers to his spiritual offspring, those who follow his example of faith.

Father of us all.NKJV Abraham is the father of all who come to God in faith, whether they are Jews or Gentiles.

Paul explains that Abraham had pleased God through faith alone, before Abraham had ever heard about the rituals that would become so important to the Jewish people. We too are saved by faith plus nothing. It is not by loving God and do-ing good that we are saved; neither is it by faith plus love or by faith plus good deeds. We are saved only through faith in Christ, trusting him to forgive all our sins.

4:17 **"I have made you a father of many nations."**NKJV The promise (or covenant) that God gave Abraham said that Abraham would be the father of many nations (Genesis 17:2-4) and that the entire world would be blessed through him (Genesis 12:3). This promise was ful-filled in Jesus Christ, who was from Abraham's line. Not only was Abraham the physical father of God's chosen nation, the Jews, he was also the father of God's people today, the church. Paul points out that the promise to Abraham to be the father of many nations ex-tends beyond Israel to all the nations of the world.

**The God who gives life to the dead and calls things that
are not as though they were.**^{NIV} Paul switches quickly into a
description of God. Abraham and Paul believe in the same
God, so what is the character of the God in whom they believe? Paul answers this question because believers need to
have a clear understanding of the God being trusted. Paul's
words here may seem awkward to us, but they were very familiar to the Jews. He is not introducing a new concept of
God; this was the very same God whom the Jews had always
worshiped. Paul's explanation of the God in whom Abraham
trusted is consistent with how the Jews had always understood God, a fact that Paul makes clear here. God is Creator—the giver and sustainer of life. He can bring the dead
back to life, and can bring into existence what previously did
not exist (see also Deuteronomy 32:39; 1 Samuel 2:6).

Here are four examples of God's life-giving power:
1. Abraham's body and Sarah's womb conceived in old age
   (Romans 4:18-21).
2. God reversed Abraham's intention of sacrificing Isaac (Hebrews 11:17-19).
3. God made Abraham the father of many nations (Romans 4:17).
4. God raised Jesus from the dead (Romans 4:23-25).

God has demonstrated his power. We know he can do the
impossible!

4:18-19 **Against all hope, Abraham in hope believed.**^{NIV} Abraham
believed God's promise that he would become **the father of
many nations.**^{NIV} He believed it *against all hope*; that is, beyond any possible natural hope, because he was past the age
of being able to father a child (**he was about a hundred
years old**), and his wife was well past childbearing age
(**Sarah's womb was also dead** ^{NIV}). Yet Abraham realized
that God's ability to fulfill his promises outweighed the circumstances. So, Abraham's faith was not a leap into the
dark or an irrational decision, but rather a deliberate choice
not to place confidence in his senses or experience and instead to place his confidence in God and his word. Abraham
had nothing to hang on to but God's promise, but that was
enough, so . . .

4:20 **He did not waver through unbelief.**^{NIV} Abraham was able to
take God at his word, so he did not waste time wavering, wondering, and worrying. He was not like the "double-minded man"
(James 1:6-8 NIV), who constantly vacillates between belief and

unbelief. Instead, Abraham persisted in believing; thus, his faith was strengthened. He was able to trust in God to do what seemed humanly impossible, and even to glorify God before the results were apparent.

In spite of all this, Abraham was clearly human and imperfect. He had his weaknesses (fears) and bad habits (lying under pressure). The Bible describes Abraham with all his flaws, but as a man a faith. Thus, Abraham's faith could not have been anything but simple trust in God. Yet God honored that. Abraham is a model not just for the Jews, but for all people as a person of faith who realized he was totally dependent on his Creator for all things, even life itself.

Wavering is vacillating between choices, fluctuating in our resolve, and faltering in our commitment. Here are some warnings for the wavering:

- Do you waver in your opinion?
  Seek counsel from God's Word.

- Do you falter in your allegiance?
  Place your will under God's control.

- Do you hesitate in your decision making?
  Trust God and follow him.

Strengthened in his faith.[NIV] When we act upon trust, it becomes stronger. Exercised faith develops persistence. As Abraham encountered obstacles, his faith saw him through, and his confidence in God grew. When we meet and overcome opposition, we strengthen our spiritual muscles. Victories over temptations urge us on to new resolutions. Faced with the facts that would lead Abraham to doubt, he still maintained his trust. He may have hesitated or questioned his own ability, but he maintained his trust in God. When God's promises conflict with the hard facts, our stronger faith will enable us to obey him.

4:21 **Being fully convinced that God was able to do what he had promised.**[NRSV] Surrounded by a society fully immersed in paganism, where gods came by the dozens and were subject to human manipulation, Abraham dared to trust a God he could not control. Abraham did not say, "Well, we'll see what happens," or "Sounds nice, but we're too old, remember?" Instead, he chose to follow God, whom he believed could and would do what he had promised. Abraham's faith was in God alone. And Abraham never doubted that God would fulfill his promise. Abraham's life was marked by mistakes, sins, and failures, as well as by wisdom and goodness, but he consistently trusted God. His faith was strengthened by the obstacles he faced, and his life was an example of faith in action. If Abraham had looked only at his own resources for subduing Canaan and founding a nation, he would have given up in despair. But Abraham looked to God, obeyed him, and waited for God to keep his word.

ARE YOU FULLY OR PARTLY CONVINCED?
With the world seemingly packed with new idols and pagan ide-ologies, believers find themselves more and more in Abraham's place. So we must remember the character of this God whom we trust. And we should ask ourselves, "At what points in my life are my convictions about God's power and faithful-ness being put to the test?" Our trust in God will be demon-strated in these and other areas:

- Knowing that God's forgiveness is complete
- Believing that life extends beyond this one, in heaven or hell
- Being convinced that our life has significance
- Believing that our individual acts of service are meaningful
- Being confident that our needs will never exhaust God's love
- Knowing that our future is safe in God's protection
- Trusting that God will watch over our loved ones

4:22 This is why "it was credited to him as righteousness."[NIV] Abra-ham's faith, detailed above, was exactly the kind of faith God wanted and accepted when he declared Abraham "righteous" (4:3). It was this "fully convinced" faith that Paul called for when he preached the gospel—faith that relies on nothing but God; faith in God, who gives life, sustains life, and has power to keep his prom-ises.

4:23 Not for him alone.[NIV] That Abraham's faith was credited to him as righteousness (Genesis 15:6) describes not only how Abraham became righteous, but also how all his descendants (spiritual de-scendants, see 4:16) can become righteous before God. What makes us acceptable to God is not our works, but simply exercis-ing the kind of faith Abraham had.

4:24 But also for us.[NKJV] The underlying message of Romans 4 is the trustworthiness of God's Word. Paul has taken his readers back into their own history and challenged them to base their hope on the written record. Not only was God's transaction with Abraham universally valid; it was preserved in the Scrip-ture for later generations to read. Paul began this chapter with a crucial question, *What does the Scripture say?* (4:3); he made a transitional statement in verse 23, *The words . . . were* *written not for him alone;* now he applies the principle to *us* and to those **who believe in him.** For Paul, the past and the Scriptures were not just the inherited religious trappings of a particular group of people. They were examples and a record of who God is and how he relates to his people. That same God wants to deal with Paul's readers on the same basis—faith. Paul expressed this same principle in another letter when he wrote, "These things happened to them as examples and were written down as warnings for us, on whom the fulfillment of the ages has come" (1 Corinthians 10:11 NIV).

Who raised up Jesus our Lord from the dead.NKJV Abraham had to simply trust in God. That trust was confirmed in the immediate promises Abraham witnessed God fulfill in his lifetime. But he faced death without seeing all the promises fulfilled, nor understanding how God would fulfill them. The writer of Hebrews described the quality of this faith in glowing terms: "All these people were still living by faith when they died. They did not receive the things promised; they only saw them and welcomed them from a distance. And they admitted that they were aliens and strangers on earth" (Hebrews 11:13 NIV). Now Paul directs his readers to the same Abrahamic faith, but clearly focussed on God's fulfillment of the great promise, the blessing of the entire world through the gift of Jesus.

> Christ's death is the death of sin, and his resurrection is the raising up of righteousness. For by his death Christ has atoned for our sins, and through his resurrection he has procured for us righteousness. Christ's death does not merely signify, but has effected the remission of our sins. Christ's resurrection is not merely the pledge of our righteousness, but also its cause.
> —Martin Luther

GOD LOVES US, BUT CAN HE SAVE US?
Here Paul explains the importance of our faith including an understanding of God's omnipotence. We are to believe in a God who makes and keeps promises and whose power is awesome. That power was nowhere more clearly demonstrated than when God *raised up Jesus . . . from the dead.* That same power is applied to our forgiveness, our salvation. We turn to him *against all hope* (4:18), knowing that our only hope is in his power to do what we cannot possibly do—make ourselves acceptable to God. Do you believe in the infinite power of God to save you?

4:25 **Who was handed over to death for our trespasses and was raised for our justification.**NRSV Jesus died for our sins, taking the penalty we deserved, according to God's plan (see 3:23-26). Just as God brought life from Abraham and Sarah (even though they thought they were "dead" and unable to have children), so God raised Jesus back to life. His resurrection brought us justification before God, for the Resurrection proved the efficacy of Christ's death and demonstrates that Jesus, the living One, can make us right with God. As Abraham had faith that God would do as he promised, so all believers have faith that Jesus' death cleansed us of our sins and made us right with God. Now, by our union with Christ, we can live a righteous life.

THE GREAT EXCHANGE
When we put our faith in Christ, an exchange takes place. We give Christ our sins, and he gives us his righteousness and forgiveness (see 2 Corinthians 5:21). There is nothing we can do to earn this. Only through Christ can we receive God's righteousness. What an incredible bargain! But sadly, many still choose to pass up this gift to continue enjoying their sin.

Romans 5

Having demonstrated that what was real for Abraham can be real for everyone, Paul launches into one of his stirring summary statements. Abraham's life illustrates the truth that faith may require human action, such as waiting for a promised child, but that the effective part of faith is its connection with God. Faith like Abraham's never requires blind trust, but trust with eyes wide open. Paul goes on to say that if we have faith, we can experience a different life. It will not be easy, but it will be a life full of peace with God, joyful hope, personal development, growing awareness of God's love, and continued reconciliation with him.

One of the remarkable consistencies in Paul is how he links faith, hope, and love together. Rarely does he mention one without the other two. First Corinthians 13:13 is the best reference (see also Galatians 5:5-6; Colossians 1:3-8; 1 Thessalonians 1:2-3; 2 Thessalonians 2:13-17; 1 Timothy 6:11-17; Titus 3:4-8). Romans 5:1-11 begins by stating that personal faith is necessary for justification (5:1). This is followed by the response of rejoicing "in the hope of the glory of God" (5:2 NIV). But faith and hope do not exist alone, since "God has poured out his love into our hearts" (5:5 NIV). For Paul, wherever faith is present, there also are hope and love. The greatest, however, is love (see 5:8).

Paul introduces some difficult concepts in this chapter. He demonstrates the truth of the gospel in ways that stretch our thinking. To begin to understand the next four chapters, it helps to keep in mind the two-sided reality of the Christian life. On the one hand, we are complete in Christ (our acceptance with him is secure); on the other hand, we are growing in Christ (we are becoming more and more like him). At the same time, we have the status of kings and the duties of slaves. We feel both the presence of Christ and the pressure of sin. We enjoy the peace that comes from being made right with God, but we still face daily problems that help us grow. If we remember these two sides of the Christian life, we will not grow discouraged as we face temptations and problems. Instead, we will learn to depend on the power available to us from Christ, who lives in us by the Holy Spirit.

5:1 **Therefore, since we are justified by faith.**^{NRSV} With the word *therefore*, Paul indicates a conclusion based on his previous argument. In chapter 4, Paul showed how sinners, both Jews and Gentiles, are justified by faith. The Chamula culture of southern Mexico has no single word in their language for "faith." In fact, when translators discovered a phrase to accurately convey the meaning, they crossed a major hurdle in translating the New Testament for that people group. For the Chamulas, "faith" is taking-seriously-what-God-has-obligated-himself-to-do. Bringing their insight back into English can deepen our understanding of faith. In this way, Romans 5:1 could be paraphrased, "Therefore, since we have been justified through taking seriously what God has obligated himself to do, we have peace with God through our Lord Jesus Christ."

> Since God *now* has justified us by faith, and not by works, we have peace with him both in heart and conscience, though not with man and with the flesh, nor with the world and the devil. Believers have all the more trials.
>
> —Martin Luther

Here he begins to describe how justification affects our relationship with God. First, there is peace with God through our Lord Jesus Christ.^{NRSV} Peace anticipates Paul's claim that we have been reconciled with God (5:10). Peace (eirene) means there is no more hostility between us and God, no sin blocking our relationship with him. More than that, a new relationship has been established, so we no longer dread the outcome of judgment but live under the protection established by God. Paul's readers were intimately acquainted with the *Pax Romana* (Roman Peace), enforced by the power of Rome. It represented about as much security as the world could offer. While living under this uneasy peace, Jesus had told his disciples, "Peace I leave with you; my peace I give you. I do not give to you as the world gives. Do not let your hearts be troubled and do not be afraid" (John 14:27 NIV). Peace with God is only possible through Christ, because on the cross he met the conditions required for peace. Not only was "the punishment that brought us peace" (Isaiah 53:5 NIV) borne by him, but he also fully lived up to his given title, Prince of Peace (Isaiah 9:6). (See also Ephesians 2:14; Colossians 1:20.)

There are a few ancient manuscripts that read "let us have peace" rather than *we have peace*. While that reading makes sense, it weakens the point Paul is making by shifting the thought from accomplished fact to potential experience. The basic teaching is that *through our Lord Jesus Christ* peace is established between us and God, whether or not we feel it from moment to moment. In Christ we claim *peace with God*, even when we are experiencing turmoil.

5:2 Access . . . into this grace.NKJV One of the strongest characteristics of Hebrew writing was the habit of poetic repetition, expressing the same idea twice in order to emphasize its importance or illuminate the truth from a different angle. Paul's writing often reflects this style. In 5:1-2, Paul expresses three parallel, though not identical, thoughts: *justified by faith; peace . . . through . . . Christ; through whom . . . access . . . into this grace.* The relationship that is created in Christ Jesus between us and God is wonderful and complex. Yet the offer of salvation through trust in Christ remains simple enough for a child to grasp. Like a jeweler displaying his most precious gem, Paul never tires of showing a new angle of the gospel so that the light can strike it in a new way. Not only has Christ justified and reconciled us to God, but he also has given us personal access to God. The grace of God initiating our salvation is the same **grace in which we stand.**NKJV We require that gracious acceptance every day of our lives as believers, just as truly as we needed it the moment we believed. We have been brought into a place of favor with God. Instead of being his enemies, we are his friends—in fact, his own children (John 15:15; Galatians 4:5).

The word *access* (*prosagogein*), has also been translated "introduction" (NASB), "brought us into" (TLB), "been allowed to enter" (NEB). The use can include permission to enter or the act of entering itself. Paul does not have in mind the believer standing outside of God's grace with permission to enter, but rather that through Christ we are ushered into God's very presence. The thought is

> Into the depth of our predicament the word is spoken from on high: *By grace you have been saved!* To be saved does not just mean to be a little encouraged, a little comforted, a little relieved. It means to be pulled out like a log from a burning fire. You have been saved! We are not told: you may be saved sometimes, or a little bit. No, you *have been* saved, totally and for all times. You? Yes, we! Not just any other people, more pious and better than we are, no, we, each one of us.
> —Karl Barth

not about possible *access* to God, but accomplished *access* to
God. Having been introduced to grace, we now . . .

Rejoice in the hope of the glory of God.NIV Mankind was created for glory (more about this will be said in chapter 8) but, because of sin, had fallen "short of the glory of God" (3:23). It is
God's purpose to recreate his image, his glory, fully in us. One
version has this phrase, "The hope we have of sharing God's
glory" (TEV). Because of Christ, we now *hope* for (anticipate, look forward to) the time when we will share Christ's glory. This *hope*
helps us overcome our present frustrations when we fail to be all
that we want to be or all that God wants us to be.

Paul mentions three occasions for rejoicing:

1. *In the hope of the glory of God* (5:2). Anticipating our future
   with God ought to bring moments of joy. We stand in God's
   grace, and the outcome of our lives is secure in his hands.
2. *In our suffering* (5:3). Paul's contemporary, James, also understood this: "Consider it pure joy, my brothers, whenever you
   face trials of many kinds" (James 1:2 NIV). Both writers make
   it clear that we are not to be glad *for* our suffering, but to be
   glad that suffering can perfect a person's faith.
3. *In God* (5:11). Our faith in Jesus Christ frees us to deeply enjoy our relationship with God. We no longer need to be haunted
   by thoughts of judgment; now we can reflect upon and respond
   to his grace. As Paul wrote to the Philippians, "Rejoice in the
   Lord always. I will say it again: Rejoice!" (Philippians 4:4 NIV).

5:3 Rejoice in our sufferings . . . suffering produces perseverance.NIV
Suffering was a normal experience for first-century Christians. On
their first missionary journey, Paul and Barnabas preached in several
cities, and many people became believers. But, as was always the
case, there was an immediate backlash of persecution against believers. That is why Paul and Barnabas "returned to Lystra, Iconium and
Antioch, strengthening the disciples and encouraging them to remain
true to the faith. 'We must go through many hardships to enter the
kingdom of God,' they said" (Acts 14:21-22 NIV). Paul well understood the meaning of suffering for the faith (see, for example, 2
Corinthians 11:21-33). The key was that he learned to rejoice because he knew that *suffering produces perseverance*—the ability to
face difficulties without giving in. For Christians, suffering does not
negate the reality of God's love, but provides the occasion to affirm
and apply it. This character quality of *perseverance*, or endurance, is
not an end in itself (see 1 Peter 1:6-7). It is one step in a process that
eventually strengthens our hope (5:4).

DON'T JUDGE TRIBULATION BY ITS OUTWARD APPEARANCE
We *rejoice in suffering* not because we like pain or deny its tragedy, but because we know God is using life's difficulties and Satan's attacks to build our character. That is one of God's loving purposes. Our problems will develop perseverance which, in turn, will strengthen our character, deepen our trust in God, and give us greater confidence about the future. It is likely that our patience will be tested in some way every day. Rejoicing begins by thanking God for these opportunities to grow and then facing them, relying on his strength.

SUFFERING WITH CHRIST

If we serve the Lord, suffering is unavoidable. As we bring Christ's message to the world, we will face oppression. Christ participates with us when we suffer.

Colossians 1:24
"Now I rejoice in what was suffered for you, and I fill up in my flesh what is still lacking in regard to Christ's afflictions" NIV.

Until all the world knows him, there is always more work to do. As we work for him, we can face suffering joyfully because we know people are being saved as a result of our work.

Philippians 1:29
"For it has been granted to you on behalf of Christ not only to believe on him, but also to suffer for him" NIV.

Our suffering and how we handle it are signs to others that we belong to Christ.

Philippians 3:10
"I want to know Christ . . . and the fellowship of sharing in his sufferings, becoming like him in his death" NIV.

Sharing in Christ's mission for the world implies that we must share in his sacrifice. We must be ready to give up plans, pleasure, and even our life in order to serve him.

1 Peter 2:21
Christ suffered for you, leaving you an example, that you should follow in his steps" NIV.

Christ never sinned, yet he suffered so we could be set free. We should face suffering as he did—with patience, calmness, and confidence that God is in control of the future.

1 Peter 4:13
Rejoice that you participate in the sufferings of Christ, so that you may be overjoyed when his glory is revealed" NIV.

God strengthens us by his Holy Spirit when we face persecution for him. We know that one day he will overcome all suffering when we are with him in glory.

5:4 Perseverance, character.NIV Endurance, in turn, deepens character. The word *character* (*dokime*) includes the idea of "approved as a result of testing." A person with this kind of *character* is known for his or her inward qualities rather than any outward appearances. There is a progression that begins with suffering and ends with character. Suffering is like the pressure put on carbon to produce a diamond. As we persevere, we are being formed and molded on the inside—God is producing his character within us.

The end result of this chain reaction is *hope*—confidence that God is in control and will see us through. God's work in us now, conforming us "to the likeness of his Son" (8:29), gives us a glimpse of the wonderful things he has in store for us in the future.

> We rejoice in suffering not because pain in itself is good, but because it is the engraver's tool with which God creates lines of beauty on the life.
> —Kenneth J. Foreman

If we can maintain our love for Christ and see his work through all our difficulties, the result is increased faith, hope, and love. The difficulties of life are not random, meaningless, or wasted when we are trusting God. Our *hope* needs to grow and develop with the rest of our spiritual being. Rejoicing during suffering will increase our endurance and strengthen our overall character, leading to a more mature *hope*. (See also Ephesians 4:2-5; Colossians 1:4-5.)

BASICS OF CHRISTIAN CHARACTER
As Paul states clearly in 1 Corinthians 13:13, faith, hope, and love are at the heart of the Christian life. Our relationship with God begins with faith, helping us realize that we are delivered from our past by Christ's death. Hope grows as we learn all that God has in mind for us; it gives us the promise of the future. And God's love fills our lives and gives us the ability to reach out to others.

Since faith, hope, and love are essential characteristics of the Christian life, their opposites (doubt, despair, and hatred) can devastate any relationship with God. We must guard against them and help those who struggle with those devastating feelings. We must not avoid or fear those experiences that will cultivate in us a godly character.

5:5 Hope does not disappoint us.NRSV Our hope in God's promises will never disappoint us by being unfulfilled. When our hope is in God, we are absolutely assured that he will fulfill all that he has promised—we will be resurrected to eternal life and will be with him in glory. The first *hope* Paul mentioned (5:2) is one that primarily looks to the future, when we will share in God's glory; this *hope*, the maturing product of a life trusting God, focuses on the more immediate experience of God's love. So *hope*, for the believer in Jesus, includes a future worth rejoicing over and a present that will not *disappoint* either!

God has poured out his love into our hearts by the Holy Spirit, whom he has given us.^{NIV} It is the Holy Spirit who has filled our hearts with God's love and who continues to encourage us as we hope in God. (See also John 7:38; Romans 8:35; 2 Corinthians 5:14; Titus 3:5-6.) Paul wrote to the Corinthians, "[God] anointed us, set his seal of ownership on us, and put his Spirit in our hearts as a deposit, guaranteeing what is to come" (2 Corinthians 1:21-22).

5:6 Christ died for the ungodly. Paul wants to make sure that there is no misunderstanding about who Christ actually died for—*the ungodly.* Nor can there be any doubt about who *the ungodly* are, for Paul uses the same terminology at the end of 5:8, exchanging *us* in place of *the ungodly.*

We can have hope in God because of the nature of his love. God's plan, from the beginning, was to send his Son to die for us, **at just the right time, when we were still powerless.**^{NIV} The *right time* refers to both the timing in history and the timing in God's plan (see Galatians 4:4). In the face of our powerlessness, God was fully in control. The events in human history did not determine the plan of salvation; the plan of salvation was designed by God to happen *at just the right time.*

We are saved only because God took the initiative and demonstrated his incredible grace and love by sending his own Son to take the punishment we deserved. And he did this while we were *powerless* (unable to do God's will because of the power of sin in our lives) and *ungodly* (constantly living independently of God, as described in 1:18ff.).

5:7 For a good person someone might actually dare to die.^{RSV} The highest expression of human love is when someone gives his or her life so that another person can continue to live. People are able to understand sacrificial love, even though it is rarely practiced. This kind of sacrificial gesture is almost always dependent on a relationship that already exists between the one sacrificing (parent, friend, lover, fellow soldier) and the one benefited. People do not readily die for their enemies. But God's love stands in stark contrast to even the deepest expression of human love because . . .

5:8 God demonstrates His own love.^{NKJV} People do not have to hope
blindly that God loves them; he has openly demonstrated it.

While we were still sinners, Christ died for us. Christ's death is
the highest manifestation of God's love for us. While we were rebellious and despicable, Christ died for us so that we could come
to God, find peace with him, and become heirs of his promises.
Christ did not die so that we could be made lovable; Christ died
because God already loved us and wanted to bring us close to
himself. No matter how lonely or alienated we feel, we have the
unalterable objective fact that Christ died for us. Everytime we
celebrate communion, we hear the words from Jesus, "this is my
body broken for you; this is my blood shed for you."

GOD LOVES THE REBELS
God sent Jesus to die for us, not because we were good
enough, but because he loved us so much. Whenever we feel
uncertain about God's love for us, we should remember that he
loved us even before we turned to him. If God loved us when
we were rebels, he can surely strengthen us now that we love
him in return. Because our knowledge of God's love is based
on his demonstration, all doubts ("How do you know God loves
you?") can be directly answered: "I know God loves me because Jesus died for me."

5:9 Justified by his blood. God bases our justification on the sacrificial
death of Christ on the cross (see 3:25). Because God is holy, he
could not accept us by simply disregarding or ignoring our sins. Instead, those sins had to be dealt with. And God did this through the
sacrificial death of his Son. Again, this justification is God's approval,
given to us only on the basis of what Christ did. It is an acquittal that
sets free all of us who were otherwise hopeless prisoners of sin.

Saved from God's wrath.^{NIV} Those who have been justified and
pronounced righteous are also delivered from God's wrath at the final judgment. The comparison implies that justification is a present
event, while the full display of God's wrath will come only in the future. As much as we are amazed at the justification we have in
Christ, how **much more** will we stand in awe when we realize the
magnitude of God's wrath from which we have been saved.

5:10 Enemies ... reconciled to him through the death of his Son.
Alongside the theme of justification, Paul introduces the theme of
reconciliation. Our peace with God has legal as well as relational as-

pects. We were enemies because we were rebels against God. "Once you were alienated from God and were enemies in your minds because of your evil behavior. But now he has reconciled you by Christ's physical body through death to present you holy in his sight, without blemish and free from accusation" (Colossians 1:21-22 NIV). Because of Christ's death, we are reconciled—our proper relationship with God has been restored.

Much more. As in verse 9, Paul is using a comparison of wonder. He holds up one wonderful idea for consideration (our reconciliation with God through Christ's death) and immediately follows with an even *more* wonderful thought of what Christ's life accomplishes for us and in us.

Reconciled. Those who are reconciled (*katallasso*) are those who were once enemies of God but have now been brought into a relationship of peace with God. There are two steps in the reconciliation process: (1) God made the first move toward reconciliation by sending his Son to die on the cross (see 2 Corinthians 5:19), and (2) believers then accept the work Christ has done for them and thereby become reconciled to God (see 2 Corinthians 5:20). Reconciliation removes the hostility and establishes unity between believers and God.

Saved by his life.NKJV Because Christ's death accomplished our reconciliation with God, so *his life*—his present resurrection life in which he intercedes for us (see Hebrews 7:25)—insures our complete and final salvation. The reality of Christ's *life* was the source of some of Paul's most memorable words, as in Galatians 2:20, "I have been crucified with Christ and I no longer live, but Christ lives in me. The life I live in the body, I live by faith in the Son of God, who loved me and gave himself for me" (NIV).

POWER RESERVES
The love that caused Christ to die is the same love that sends the Holy Spirit to live in us and guide us every day. The power that raised Christ from the dead is the same power that saved us and is available to us in our daily lives. We can be assured that having begun a life with Christ, we have a reserve of power and love to call on each day for help to meet every challenge or trial. We can pray for God's power and love as we need it.

5:11 Rejoice in God.NIV It is not enough to list the marvelous facts of our relationship with God. Knowing all that God has accomplished should cause us to be filled with joy. Paul has already told his readers that they should rejoice in the hope of glory (5:2) and in their sufferings (5:3). Now he exclaims that they should rejoice *in God*. We rejoice in God because Christ took our sins upon himself and paid the price for them with his own death, instead of punishing us with the death we deserve (see introduction to this chapter).

We have now received reconciliation.NRSV Through faith in *his* work, we become his friends (*received reconciliation*) and are no longer enemies and outcasts.

> The true Christian life, which begins with a supernatural transition, consists and continues in a supernatural *transfusion*. The very life and nature of Christ are transfused into the inmost being of the Christian believer by the Holy Spirit. Thus our Savior's word is fulfilled: "Because I live, ye shall live also" (John 14:19).
> —J. Sidlow Baxter

ADAM AND CHRIST CONTRASTED / 5:12-21

Having linked Jews and Gentiles through Abraham to the promises of God, Paul now shows how the gospel applies to all humankind. Paul made important points by going back to Abraham; but by going back to Adam, he will draw conclusions that affect the fate of every person.

Twice in the last paragraph Paul expressed one idea and then followed it with an equally marvelous parallel idea (from the NIV): "Since we have now been justified by his blood, how much more shall we be saved from God's wrath," (5:9); and "If . . . we were reconciled to him through the death of his Son, how much more. . . shall we be saved through his life!" (5:10). Here, in verses 12-21, Paul also uses a series of parallels, only this time they express ideas moving in opposite directions: "Just as sin entered the world . . . and . . . death came to all men" (5:12) . . . "how much more did God's grace and the gift . . . overflow to the many" (5:15); "For if. . . death reigned through that one man, how much more will. . . righteousness reign in life through the one man, Jesus Christ" (5:17 NIV); and "For just as . . . many were made sinners, so also. . . many will be made righteous" (5:19). Paul shows that all of us are affected by Adam's disobedience and Christ's obedience.

5:12 **Sin came into the world through one man.**NRSV This *one man* is Adam, who sinned against God and brought alienation from God and death to all humanity (Genesis 2–3). God had warned Adam, "You must not eat from the tree of the knowledge of good and evil, for when you eat of it you will surely die"

(Genesis 2:17). Because Adam disobeyed God's command, the judgment of both spiritual and physical death fell on him and all his descendants—**death spread to all men, because all sinned.**[NKJV] Death is the consequence of being under the power of sin. "In Adam all die" (1 Corinthians 15:22 [NIV]). It was not in God's original plan for human beings to die, but it was the result when sin entered the world. Inevitably, the gift of life we bequeath to our children includes with it the sting of death. All human beings have two characteristics in common: They are sinners, and they will die.

5:13 **Before the law was given, sin was in the world.**[NIV] Verses 13-15 are a lengthy parenthesis to Paul's statement beginning in verse 12. God's law was not given until the time of Moses, so the people who lived between Adam and Moses did not have any specific laws to obey or break. Paul explains that **sin is not taken into account when there is no law.**[NIV] What Paul is saying is that the *sin* that was in the world was the *power* or *force* that causes people to act independently of God. All people are under the power of sin, and all people act in rebellion against God. Those sins did not count the same as Adam's sin because they were not deliberate actions against God's commands (as was Adam's, see 5:12) because there were no commands. Thus, they were *not taken into account.* Paul continues this thought in 5:20 and in chapter 7, when he describes the law's role in defining sin. *Sin was in the world* from the beginning, but it came into sharp focus when the law was given.

With this statement, Paul follows through his argument from chapter 2 regarding the pride of the Jews in their role as keepers of God's law. The very fact that they had the law, and that it is the law that makes people accountable for sin, means that the Jews' sin was deadly—they were certainly in as much need of redemption as the rest of the world.

5:14 **Death reigned . . . even over those who did not sin by breaking a command.**[NIV] Adam had knowingly broken a specific command (5:12). His descendants who lived prior to the time of Moses could not break any specific laws because there were none. But they still sinned, witnessed by the fact that *death reigned.* Adam's descendants had sinned with Adam (5:12). Death is the result of Adam's sin and ours, even if our sins don't resemble Adam's. For thousands of years, the law had not been explicitly given, and yet people died. The law was added (5:20) to help people see their sinfulness, to show them

the seriousness of their offenses, and to
drive them to God for mercy and pardon.
This was true in Moses' day and in Paul's
day, and it is still true today. Sin is a deep
rupture between who we are and who we
were created to be. The law points out our
sin and places the responsibility for it squarely on our shoul-
ders, but it offers no remedy.

> Christ is much
> more powerful to
> save, than Adam
> was to destroy.
> —John Calvin

Adam . . . a pattern of the one to come.^{NIV} Paul uses the
word *pattern* (*typos*), or "type" to describe Adam's role in history
compared with Christ's. Adam, the first man, was a counterpart
of Christ, whom Paul calls "the last Adam" in 1 Corinthians
15:45. Adam's one act determined the character of the world;
Christ's one act determined the character of eternity. In modern
terminology, we could say that Adam was a flawed prototype, but
Christ was the perfect original. Just as Adam was a representative
of created humanity, so is Christ the representative of the new,
spiritual humanity.

5:15 **The free gift is not like the trespass.**^{NRSV} The gift from God
through Christ (justification) has a greater but opposite effect
than the trespass of Adam and its consequences. Yet in each case,
the act of one affected the lives of **many**.

Many died by the trespass of the one man.^{NIV} Because of
Adam's sin, death entered the human race, and since then all peo-
ple have died (with the Bible's exceptions of Enoch and Elijah).
All people will die until the end of this age.

**The gift that came by the grace of . . . Jesus Christ, over-
flow to the many.**^{NIV} God's gift because of his grace—salvation and eternal life—overflows to the entire human race. It
is available to all, but not everyone will choose to receive it.
    Every human being is born into Adam's physical family—
the family line that leads to certain death. All of us reap the
results of Adam's sin. We have inherited his guilt, the tendency to sin, and God's punishment. Because of Jesus, however, we can trade judgment for forgiveness. We can trade
our sin for Jesus' goodness. Jesus offers us the opportunity
to be born into his spiritual family—the family line that begins with forgiveness and leads to eternal life. If we do nothing, we have death through Adam; but if we come to God by
faith, we have life through Christ.

5:16 **Judgment followed one sin and brought condemnation.**^{NIV}
God passed judgment on Adam's one sin of disobedience. As a result, Adam and the entire human race received condemnation.

The gift followed many trespasses and brought justification.^{NIV} Everyone since Adam has sinned, and yet Christ overcame those *many trespasses* and brought justification to those who accept him. The result of sin is death; the gift of God—his justifying sinners—results in reigning forever with Christ.

5:17 **By the trespass of the one man, death reigned through that one man.**^{NIV} By capitulating to sin Adam allowed the whole human race to succumb to death. Death is inescapable; it comes to every living thing. We all live close to the valley of the shadow of death. And the reign of death over creation began because of Adam's sin.

Will those who receive.^{NRSV} The only condition upon these wonderful provisions of grace is that we receive them by faith. God's love and Christ's work are for all men and women, but they are appropriated by faith.

Reign in life through the One, Jesus Christ.^{NKJV} Those who believe in Christ will become rulers, reigning in his kingdom of life, where there is no death (Revelation 1:6). What a promise this is to those who love Christ! We can reign over sin's power, over death's threats, and over Satan's attacks. Eternal life is ours now and forever. Though this promise has its greatest fulfillment in the future, it also has a significant immediate impact. In Christ, death loses its sting (see 1 Corinthians 15:50-57). We are still subject to the physical suffering and death brought by sin in the world, but we are free from the eternal spiritual separation that we would experience outside of Christ. Also, in the power and protection of Jesus Christ, we can overcome temptation (see 8:17 for more on our privileged position in Christ).

5:18 **Just as the result of one trespass was condemnation.**^{NIV} Paul emphasizes the contrasting roles of two single agents, Adam and Christ. Adam's sin brought *condemnation* on the human race. Christ's sinless sacrifice, or as Paul writes, his **one act of righteousness** opened the way for **justification that brings life.**^{NIV}

5:19 **By the one man's disobedience the many were made sinners.**^{NRSV} The same statement is made in different words: Here

Adam's trespass is called "disobedience," and it resulted in all people becoming sinners and thus unacceptable to God. The word *trespass* describes the specific act of Adam's sin, while *disobedience* describes its intent. The original temptation downplayed the importance of the act (see Genesis 3:1-7) and focused attention on the desired ends: "You will be like God" (Genesis 3:5 NIV). Temptation still takes that same form, rationalizing deliberate disobedience to God in pursuit of some supposedly higher ideal. Ends and means do not justify one another. In Adam's case, neither the ends (*disobedience*) nor the means (*trespass*) turned out to be right.

By the one man's obedience the many will be made righteous.NRSV Again, in contrast, here the act of righteousness is called Christ's "obedience." Adam's response to temptation was "My will be done"; but Christ's prayer to God was "Thy will be done" (Luke 22:42). Because of Christ's *obedience*, those who believe *will be made righteous*. Becoming righteous is both an immediate standing before God and an ongoing process to be completed when he returns.

5:20 **Law was added so that the trespass might increase.**NIV This statement is certainly not what Paul's Jewish readers expected to hear. Paul had already explained that the law was ineffective for salvation, but now he says that rather than being an antidote for sin, it actually *increases* sin! Paul is winding up the argument he has been carrying on through the first five chapters of his letter. The purpose of the law for his own people, the Jews, had been to make them aware of their need for salvation; thus, their trespass was increased. Sin was present from Adam, but the giving of the law was like having a huge spotlight turned on—the sinfulness of people became all the more defined (see also Romans 7:7-13). The solution to sin was not law, but grace.

Where sin increased, grace increased all the more.NIV No matter how much people sin, God's grace is greater. There are occasions of insight in life when people realize in a new way the reality of their sinfulness. Sometimes, reflecting on the commandments reminds us of our tendency to fall. Our consciences also flare with guilt from time to time. At other times, a loving friend may confront us with a sinful act or habit. When our awareness of sin increases, we need to ask God to help us see that his grace is always greater in its capacity to forgive than our capacity to sin.

OPEN ARMS

As sinners, separated from God, we see his law from below. Sometimes it seems like a ladder to be climbed to get to God. Perhaps we have repeatedly tried to climb it, only to fall to the ground every time we have advanced one or two rungs. Or perhaps the sheer height of the ladder is so overwhelming that we have never even started up. In either case, what relief we should feel to see Jesus with open arms, offering to lift us above the ladder of the law, to take us directly to God. Once Jesus lifts us into God's presence, we are free to obey—out of love, not necessity, and through God's power, not our own. Then we know that if we stumble, we will not fall back to the ground. Instead, we will be caught and held in Jesus' loving arms.

5:21 **As sin reigned in death, so also grace might reign through righteousness to bring eternal life.**[NIV] Our age is characterized by sin and inevitable death; but the age to come will be characterized by grace, righteousness, and eternal life. It is common to call the ultimate struggle that is going on in the universe "the conflict between good and evil." Paul was picturing here the outcome of the war between the kingdom of grace and the kingdom of sin. Until Christ, the war appeared to be decided, because *sin reigned in death.* But Christ's death and resurrection provided the decisive victory by which *grace* will *reign.* Under the reign of grace, a *righteousness* is declared that will *bring eternal life.*

This ends the first section of Paul's letter and his explanation of the law and its relation to salvation. But the law is not set aside as old and worthless. Paul will explain, in coming chapters, the role of the law for believers.

Romans 6

Up to this point in his letter, Paul has shown people's need for salvation, God's gift of that salvation through the death of his Son, and God's grace in forgiving the sins of all who accept him. Paul's focus was on *justification*. This next section of the letter (chapters 6–8) deals with *sanctification*—God progressively separating believers from sin and making them more like himself. Justification is the first moment of sanctification; it is when we pass, through Christ, from death to life. Sanctification is the step-by-step process when the Holy Spirit works in our lives and conforms us into the image of Christ (8:29). Paul's discussion of sanctification follows this outline: chapter 6 explains that believers are free from sin's control; chapter 7 discusses the continuing struggle believers have with sin; and chapter 8 describes how believers can have victory over sin. The key point to realize is that all believers have a new nature and the Holy Spirit within, yet they also have the old, human nature with its capability to sin. These opposites are in constant tension, yet God promises help and victory.

Paul begins this chapter by describing the miraculous power of the gospel; it sets people free from sin's control. It's not that Christians don't or can't sin anymore, but that they are free to choose between doing wrong and doing right. This Christ-bought freedom brings great responsibility. Believers must use their God-given opportunity to make right choices, replacing sinful thoughts and actions with righteous ones. Failure to do so means remaining enslaved to sin. But the rewards of serving God include abundant joy and eternal life.

6:1 Shall we go on sinning so that grace may increase?[NIV] Paul realized that his statement in 5:20, "Where sin increased, grace increased all the more" (NIV), would be interpreted by some to suggest that they ought to sin more in order to experience more grace. "If God loves to forgive, why not give him more to forgive?" would be their erroneous reasoning.

Paul may well have been thinking of actual problems in Corinth, where he was staying. He may have known individuals who thought that because forgiveness is guaranteed, they could sin as much as they wanted. Such an attitude—deciding ahead of time to take advantage of God—shows that a person does not understand the seriousness of sin. God's forgiveness does not make sin less serious; Christ's death shows the dreadful seriousness of sin. Jesus paid with his life so we could be forgiven. The availability of God's mercy must not become an excuse for careless living and moral laxness.

As in Corinth, we live in a world marked by increased tolerance. Being surrounded by temptations and examples of sinful behavior will increase the tendency to justify sin. Our freedom in Christ should not be used as an excuse to sin, nor should our life of obedience to Christ degenerate into legalism. We should resist sin and increase our appreciation of God's grace.

6:2 **By no means!**NRSV Paul denies the possibility outright. The idea that someone would claim to believe the gospel while planning to continue in sin is preposterous to Paul. He knew people would think that way and would be wrong. The point of the gospel was not to find an excuse for sin, but to give freedom from sin.

Died to sin. To make his answer clear, Paul introduces a new concept—we *died* in relation *to sin*. Up until this point he has written about the accomplishments of Christ's death. Here he teaches that because Christ died for our sins, those who believe in him actually *died to sin.* How have we died to sin?

- In the legal sense, we died in the sight of God's judgment.

- In the conversion sense, believing in Christ is dying to sin.

- In the baptismal sense, that burial implies we have died with Christ.

- In the moral sense, sinful desires may be present, but they are mortally wounded.

Such grace is *costly* because it calls us to follow, and it is *grace* because it calls us to follow *Jesus Christ.* It is costly because it costs a man his life, and it is grace because it gives a man the only true life. It is costly because it condemns sin, and grace because it justifies the sinner. Above all, it is *costly* because it cost God the life of his Son; "ye were bought at a price," and what has cost God much cannot be cheap for us. Above all, it is *grace* because God did not reckon his Son too dear a price to pay for our life, but delivered him up for us.
—Dietrich Bonhoeffer

- In the resurrection sense, we exchange our sinful life for Christ's resurrection life.

  Paul speaks of this death as fact and concludes, therefore, that believers cannot **live any longer in it**.^{NKJV}

LIVING IN SIN OR DYING TO SIN

Living in sin describes a life-style of habitual sinful practices. It is a life where sin reigns. Death is the currency of that kingdom. The subjects are slaves, and their future is hopeless. Why would anyone, given their freedom, want to remain in such a place, living such a life?

Dying to sin describes the most frequent way a slave gained freedom (by dying) to illustrate one aspect of the salvation that God has given us through Christ. The problem of sin is so deeply rooted in us that radical action is required to eliminate it. In another place, Paul described this process: "For he has rescued us from the dominion of darkness and brought us into the kingdom of the Son he loves" (Colossians 1:13 NIV). Unless we consider ourselves dead to sin (6:11), sin will continue to influence us.

6:3-4 **Baptized into Christ Jesus ... baptized into his death.**^{NIV} Baptism is a picture of a spiritual truth. In the very early church, baptism followed a person's decision to trust in Christ (see, for example, Acts 2:41; 8:37; 9:18; 10:48), marking these first generation believers as followers of Christ, members of the Christian community. Paul assumes that these Roman believers were baptized at conversion and would vividly recall the experience. Those who believe in Christ are *baptized into* him and *baptized into* his death; in other words, they are united with him. As he died, we die to our old, sinful life-style, and a *new life* begins. Immersion may have been the form of baptism—that is, new Christians were completely buried momentarily in water. They understood this form of baptism to symbolize being buried with Christ, thus the death and burial of the old way of life. Coming up out of the water symbolized resurrection to new life with Christ, as well as the promise of a future bodily resurrection—**as Christ was raised from the dead ... we too may live a new life.**^{NIV} If we think of our old, sinful life as dead and buried, we have a powerful motive to resist sin. We can consciously choose to treat the desires and temptations of the old nature as if they were dead. Then we can continue to enjoy our wonderful new life with Jesus (see also Galatians 3:27; Colossians 3:1-4).

> If, then, you died in your baptism, stay dead!
> —Chrysostom

For Paul, the practical insight demonstrated by baptism is a dual identification with Christ, not only in his dying for us, but also in his life-giving resurrection. Paul wants to convince believers that sin is no longer a desirable or necessary life-style. It is time to stop living in sin and start living in Christ (see also 2 Corinthians 5:17; Galatians 2:20; Ephesians 4:22; Colossians 3:9).

Subsequent traditions on the mode of baptism have obscured Paul's point and created unnecessary division among believers. The animosity and outright ferocity between people who claimed Jesus as Lord but baptized differently have been a shameful stain on the history of the church. Various modes of baptism (sprinkling, pouring, or immersing) and the timing of baptism (child or believer) all have eloquent if not entirely persuasive defenders. As believers, we have "One Lord, one faith, one baptism" (Ephesians 4:5), but the Scriptures consider these single facts in different ways. So, for instance, the Bible describes both a physical aspect of baptism (what is done with water—Matthew 28:19; Galatians 3:27) and a spiritual aspect of baptism (what the Holy Spirit does—Matthew 3:6; Acts 1:5; 1 Corinthians 12:13).

In the light of the development of baptismal practices throughout Christendom, Paul's comment on baptism in Romans allows for a question to be asked, while still honoring honest differences of tradition. Paul's question could be phrased, "However and whenever you were baptized, did it in fact unite you with Christ and result in a new life for you?"

6:5 **United with him like this in his death.**NIV *United (sumphutoi gegonamen)* literally means, "we have become grown together." Our baptism painlessly acts out the union that Christ painfully made real. *Like this (homoiomati)*, or "likeness," implies a willing submission, or conformity to God's plan. His plan was that in Christ's death, believers would also die (to sin and to rebellion against God). Paul told the Philippians, "I want to know Christ and the power of his resurrection and the fellowship of sharing in his sufferings, becoming like him in his death" (Philippians 3:10 NIV). Dying to sin is a lifelong process. When we accept Christ and die to our old nature, we begin a life of continually dying to the enticements of the world and living to please the One to whom we belong.

United with him in his resurrection.NIV As Christ was resurrected, believers also will be resurrected from death to eternal life with God. What people do with Christ now will greatly influence what happens to them later. The sobering corollary to this equation is that those who have not died with Christ will not live with him either.

UNITED WITH CHRIST
The concept of being *united with* Christ has been called our "mystical union" with him. As we contemplate what Christ has done for us on the cross, we are like an audience that has just watched an amazing feat of strength. The response is automatic; "How did he do that?" Faith can ask how, but it is not deterred by an inability to understand fully. Ultimately it is a more crucial step to believe in Christ and what he has done for us than to be able to explain aspects of how he accomplished the work of grace. Not understanding everything is no excuse for withholding belief.

UNITED IN CHRIST

CRUCIFIED TOGETHER	*Old Identity* Sin dies; the old slave master died; the power and lordship of sin have been destroyed; we are free from the obligation, addiction, and necessity to sin. If sin is dead, it can no longer rule.
RESURRECTED TOGETHER	*New Identity* We have new life, a new master, new fellowship with God, and new union with Christ. We have been set free to serve.
WORKERS TOGETHER	*New Service* We have new direction, new purpose, new gifts, and new power to accomplish Christ's work (see 1 Corinthians 3:9).

6:6 **Old self was crucified.**^{NRSV} The *old self,* literally "old man" (*palaios anthropos*), is the believer before he or she trusted Christ, the person who was ruled by sin and was God's enemy (5:10). Some think that Paul distinguishes between two parts or two natures in man; so it is debated whether the new nature replaces the old nature or whether the new nature is added to the old. But the "old man" and the "new man" are not parts of our personality; rather, they describe our orientation to the old life in Adam or the new life in Christ.

Though we personalize the *old self* individually in this verse, Paul probably has in mind our corporate sinful humanity in Adam. This takes us back to chapter 5, where Christ died for the sins of Adam and his descendants, including each of us. To put the choice another way, either we die with Christ or we die with Adam. That *old self was crucified*—he considers us to have died the same death as Christ when Christ was crucified. Why? This was the only way that the **body of sin might be destroyed** (NRSV), the only way our sinful nature could be set aside so that God's nature could live through us.

As a result, believers need **no longer be slaves of sin.**NKJV History records instances where slaves who were set free continued to live as if they were slaves. Either they could not believe they were free, or they were so conditioned to slavery that they could not imagine freedom. Likewise, until we accept our emancipation through Christ, we will remain slaves. But once we have accepted God's gracious gift of emancipation, we will be able to participate fully in a new life of obedience. As slaves to sin, we are set free by Christ before we can begin to live free. Paul wrote to the Galatians, "I have been crucified with Christ and I no longer live, but Christ lives in me. The life I live in the body, I live by faith in the Son of God, who loved me and gave himself for me" (Galatians 2:20 NIV). The power and penalty of sin died with Christ on the cross. We are no longer slaves to our sinful nature; we can choose to live for Christ.

CHOOSING TO LIVE FOR CHRIST
The power and penalty of sin died with Christ on the cross. Our "old self," our sinful nature, died once and for all, so we are freed from its power. The "body of sin" is not the human body, but our rebellious, sin-loving nature inherited from Adam.
    Though our body willingly cooperates with our sinful nature, we must not regard the body as evil. It is the sin in us that is evil. And it is this power of sin at work in our body that is defeated. Paul has already stated that through faith in Christ we stand acquitted, "not guilty" before God. Here Paul emphasizes that we need no longer live under sin's power. God does not take us out of the world or make us robots—we will still feel like sinning, and sometimes we will sin. The difference is that before we were saved we were slaves to our sinful nature, but now we can choose to live for Christ.

6:7 **Anyone who has died has been freed from sin.**NIV During slavery, freedom was rare except through death. Death brings about a release that cannot be reversed. The tense of the expression has been freed indicates a past action that has a continuing effect—we have been freed from sin and will continue to enjoy that freedom. We died to sin, but we are constantly being freed from sin. We are not yet sinless, but sin no longer has control over us. With our death to sin, we are free to begin our new life in Christ. Our former master (sin) has been bankrupted; we do not need to live in fear of its power. We are free from what we were in Adam, but we are prone to act like we used to in Adam.

6:8 Died with Christ . . . will also live with him.NRSV We are identified with Christ in his death, yet we continue to live in the world. Believers are in a transition period, suspended between their death to sin's power (yet still being tempted by sin) and their sharing of Christ's resurrection, beginning at the moment of conversion and continuing into eternity. Because we died with him, the present and the future are sure—we *will also live with him.*

For Paul, the Resurrection had immediate by-products. It was not just a guarantee of eternal life in the future. His teaching of conversion included the strong idea that new life in Christ (this side of physical death) is already the beginning of resurrected living. This truth is evident when Paul says, "Since, then, you have been raised with Christ, set your hearts on things above, where Christ is seated at the right hand of God" (Colossians 3:1 NIV). Getting used to this new life requires that believers "put to death . . . whatever belongs to [their] earthly nature" (Colossians 3:5 NIV). The old life has been exchanged for the new life; old habits and patterns must also be exchanged for new habits and patterns.

NEW LIFE
Because of Christ's death and resurrection, his followers need never fear death. Allowing this truth to permeate our being will change the way we live. We know that we will *live with* Christ in eternity, but we also live with him today. That assurance frees us to enjoy fellowship with him and to do his will. This will affect all our activities—work and worship, play, Bible study, quiet times, and times of caring for others. When we know that we don't have to fear death, we experience a new vigor in life.

6:9 Will never die again.NRSV Jesus experienced physical death and was resurrected to eternal life; therefore, he cannot die again. Jesus' resurrection was a victory over death, so *death no longer has mastery over him* (NIV). Paul concluded that dying with Christ, then, ends the mastery of death over us as well.

6:10 **The death he died, he died to sin, once for all.**NRSV Because believers are living in a time of transition, this verse offers advice in how that time should be spent. Just as Christ died to deal with sin once for all, so we have died to sin. This *once for all* (*ephapax*) emphasizes the finality and completeness of Christ's work. When Christ groaned from the cross, "It is finished!" (John 19:30), he knew that the sacrifice was complete, *once for all* (see Hebrews 7:27). Unlike Christ, we will still fall into sin's traps now and then; but like Christ, we constantly focus on living for God.

It is uncertain exactly what Paul meant by **the life he lives, he lives to God.**NRSV The immediate context seems to indicate that Christ suffered a temporary limitation by experiencing death for us, but he is now totally unlimited in direct communion *to God.* Christ humbled himself to the point of death even though he was God; but having completed his task, he reclaimed his divine state (see Philippians 2:6-11).

God's great plan was to liberate us from sin's ruling power. Thus our perspectives, attitudes, relationships, and desires will change, in light of the incredible events that have taken place on our behalf—death to sin and the ability to come to God and live for him.

6:11 **Count yourselves dead to sin but alive to God.**NIV If we have identified with Christ, what is true for him can be true for us. This identification starts in our minds by an act of mental reckoning or accounting. Indeed, the Greek word for *count* (*logizesthe*) means "to consider, reckon, declare." We can consider ourselves dead to sin. In other words, just as a dead body cannot respond to temptations or enticements, neither can we respond to them. But we are *alive to God* because we have been given new life and a new lifestyle, and we have been given the sure promise of eternal life (see also Ephesians 2:5; Colossians 2:13).

A NEW START
Count yourselves dead to sin means that we should regard our old sinful nature as dead and unresponsive to sin. Because of our union and identification with Christ, we are no longer obligated to follow through with those old motives, desires, and goals. So let us consider ourselves to be what God has, in fact, made us. We have a new start, and the Holy Spirit will help us become what Christ has declared us to be.

6:12 **Do not let sin reign in your mortal body.**NKJV If we are dead to sin, how can sin still reign? As explained in verse 7, we have died

WHAT HAS GOD DONE ABOUT SIN?

He has given us	Principle	Importance
New life	6:2-3 Sin's power is broken. 6:4 Sin-loving nature is buried. 6:6 We are no longer under sin's control.	We can be certain that sin's power is broken.
New nature	6:5 Now we share his new life. 6:11 We look upon our old self as dead; instead, we are alive to God.	We can see ourselves as unresponsive to the old power and alive to the new.
New freedom	6:12 We do not let sin control us. 6:13 We give ourselves completely to God. 6:14 We are free. 6:16 We can choose our own master.	We can commit ourselves to obey Christ in perfect freedom.

to sin, but we are constantly being freed from sin. When sin reigns, people have no choice but to **obey its evil desires** (NIV) because they are "slaves to sin" (6:6). Believers have died to sin, but as long as we live in our mortal bodies, we will have the compulsion to sin. But only because we have died to sin do we have the power to no longer let it reign over us. We are, in fact, free from our slavery. But each day we must reject our old slave ways.

HOW TO REVOLT AGAINST THE REIGN OF SIN IN OUR BODIES
- Identify personal weaknesses.
- Recognize temptations.
- Confront sinful desires.
- Stay away from known sources of temptation.
- Practice self-restraint.
- Consciously invest time in good habits and service.
- Depend on grace.
- Let the peace of Christ rule in your heart!

6:13 **Do not offer the parts of your body to sin.**NIV While we are in our bodies, there will always be the chance that some actions will be sinful or used as a tool to distort our relationship with God or with others. Because our bodies are mortal (6:12) (decaying and dying), we should not yield to sinful desires and temptations. Why yield to a decaying master? Why offer the parts of our bodies to sin, something to which we have died? Instead, Paul tells believers, **Offer yourselves to God** and **Offer the parts of your body to him as instruments of righteousness.**^{NIV} We have a choice. We have been given new life by God; thus, our bodies are to be given to him to use for promoting righteousness. We are to refuse sin and instead be wholly committed to living for God. We make these choices moment by moment. Later, Paul will return to this thought by saying, "Therefore, I urge you, brothers, in view of God's mercy, to offer your bodies as living sacrifices, holy and pleasing to God—this is your spiritual act of worship" (12:1 NIV).

WHO'S IN CONTROL?
Both times that Paul writes *instruments* (*hopla*), he uses a word that can refer to a tool or a weapon. Our skills, capabilities, and bodies can serve many purposes, good or bad. In sin, every part of our bodies are vulnerable. In Christ, every part can be an instrument for service. It is the one to whom we offer our service that makes the difference. We are like lasers that can burn destructive holes in steel plates or do delicate cataract surgery. Under whose control will we continue to place our lives?

6:14 **Sin shall not be your master.**^{NIV} Sin cannot and will not ever again reign over us and enslave us because we **are not under law, but under grace.** What does it mean that we are not under the law?

- We are not under the law's demands, as were the people of the Old Testament.

- We are not under curse implied by the impossible standard of the law (see Galatians 3:10-14).

- We are not under its system of requirements, the ceremonial laws that had to be meticulously kept.

- We are not under the fear of failing the just standard of the law.
  If believers were still under the law, then the sin would have to be master. By itself, the law produces both the proof and the acute awareness of sin but cannot direct or motivate a person to do what is right. Believers are under grace because only grace can overcome sin. Only by living in that grace can we defeat the power of sin in our lives. Paul doesn't make *grace* our master, in

opposition to sin; our new master is God. When our lives are under the law alone, sin is our master. But when we live under grace, our master is God. As an effective motivator we find grace (that gives us God's love, mercy, and acceptance) to be much more powerful than the law (that brings fear, guilt, and judgment). The first allows room for failure and growth, while the second accepts nothing short of perfection.

MAKE HEAVENLY TRUTH AN EARTHLY REALITY

Truth	Reality
We must . . .	
count ourselves dead to sin but alive to God (6:11).	When sin presents itself to tempt us, we must show our new I.D. stamped "In Christ." Sin's power is no longer valid.
not let sin reign, but allow Christ to reign as Lord (6:12).	We must forget our past master and fight against Satan's designs for our lives.
not offer our bodies to sin, but offer ourselves to God (6:13).	We must place our whole self at Christ's disposal for service, and then serve him in love.
remember we are not under law, but under grace (6:14).	We should not obey God out of obligation or fear, but out of love, remembering all that he has done for us.

SLAVES TO RIGHTEOUSNESS / 6:15-23

Paul begins this section in almost the same way as the last one. He wants to make sure there is no misunderstanding of the nature of grace. It is not the chance to do anything we want. Rather, it is the opportunity to live the way God wants us to live. Pure freedom is not humanly possible, for our interrelationships and complex make-up require that we live with limits. We will serve something or someone. In the past section, Paul has described our natural state apart from Christ as being in slavery to sin. Freedom under grace is not another term for ourselves in control. As soon as we attempt personal independence, we are back under the control of sin. The fact that we are creatures implies our need for mastery. Ultimately, there are only two masters: sin and the Lord Jesus Christ. The choice is clear and required. The only rightful master is our Creator!

6:15 Shall we sin because we are not under law but under grace?^{NKJV}
Paul's wording in verse 14—that seems to set the law against

grace—probably surprised his readers. It would look as though Paul was replacing the law with grace, thus giving people no law and, therefore, freedom to sin. This almost repeats the question in verse 1, and Paul's response is the same: **By no means!**NRSV As the argument develops, however, there is clearly a different matter at stake. In verse 1, Paul was challenging the crude assumption that sinning will give God the opportunity to exercise more grace. Here, Paul is guarding against the assumption that because sin is no longer our master, we can indulge in sin without fear of being controlled by it. Being under grace and under the mastery of Christ allows us the freedom not to sin. Any attitude that welcomes, rationalizes, or excuses sin is not grace, but slavery to sin itself.

THE MASTER
If we're no longer under the law but under grace, are we now free to sin and disregard the Ten Commandments? Paul says, "By no means!" When we were under the law, sin was our master, for the law could not help us overcome sin. But now that we are bound to Christ, he is our Master, and he gives us power to do good rather than evil.

6:16 **You are slaves of the one whom you obey.**NRSV All human be- ings are enslaved. While this idea clashes with our goal of in- dependence, the fact is that we were created for interdepen- dence. Paul is using a "human term" (6:19) to make an impor- tant spiritual point. Life is filled with choices about who and what we will obey. Another way of expressing Paul's phrase is, "You are a slave to whomever or whatever you commit yourself to obey." This means that friendships, goals, employ- ment, citizenship, membership, education, career, debt, and marriage all include aspects of slavery. We should choose our slavery wisely. When sin is our master, we have no power ex- cept to do what it bids us. We are **slaves to sin, which leads to death.**NIV But when we choose to obey the one who created us, and thus become slaves to obedience, we will discover that it is a slavery that **leads to righteousness.**NIV There are only two ultimate choices and no middle ground. This is as Jesus said, "No one can serve two masters" (Matthew 6:24 NIV). To refuse to allow God to be master over your life is to choose slavery to sin. But believers have been transferred, so to speak, to a new master, and must do his bidding. While service to sin leaves us powerless and leads to death, service to God leads to righteous- ness and eternal life.

WHAT ARE THE CHARACTERISTICS OF OBEDIENCE?
- Willing loyalty
- Quick responsiveness
- Intuitive understanding
- Readiness to change
- Eagerness to learn

How many of these qualities are part of our relationship with God?

6:17 **Used to be slaves to sin.**^{NIV} Before accepting the salvation offered through Christ, all believers were enslaved to sin (Paul graphically portrayed that fact in chapters 1 and 2). But now they have a new master.

Wholeheartedly obeyed the form of teaching to which you were entrusted.^{NIV} The *form of teaching* (*tupon didache*) entrusted to the Roman believers was the good news that Jesus died for their sins and was raised to give them new life (see 1 Corinthians 11:2; 2 Thessalonians 2:15; 3:6). Paul may even be referring to some widely used declaration of the faith similar to what is recorded in 1 Corinthians 15:1-11. In any case, this message abolished the slavery to sin that they had lived under, and it outlined a new way of living—under grace.

To best describe his reader's way of obeying, Paul uses the word *wholeheartedly*. He had already stated this fact in his greeting (1:8), but the encouragement bears repetition. To obey wholeheartedly means to give oneself fully to God, to love him "with all your heart and with all your soul and with all your mind" (Matthew 22:37 NIV). This obedience from the heart changed their lives—forever.

CHANGE OF HEART
We were wholehearted sinners, even if only in our desires. Now we are to be wholehearted servers, but doing so requires grace, repentance, forgiveness, the Lordship of Christ, the power of the Holy Spirit, restraint of our desires, and disciplined effort.

6:18 **Having been set free from sin, have become slaves of righteousness.**^{NRSV} It is impossible to be neutral. Every person has a master—either God or sin. A Christian is still able to sin, but he or she is no longer a slave to sin. This person belongs to God. Believers are set free from the control of their evil desires and their selfish habits, free to become enslaved to righteous living. We serve the righteous God who is in the process of transforming us to become more like him so that we can one day share in glorious resurrection to eternal life. That's not a bad master to have!

6:19 **Human terms.** Paul emphasizes that he is using an analogy in case any of his readers fail to understand his meaning. Anyone living in Rome knew about slavery. There were more slaves than citizens in the empire. Paul's letter to Philemon illustrates some of the complexities faced by Christians living in a society where slavery was a way of life. For all of the horrors of slavery, there were instances where the relationship between slaves and masters was quite positive. In the church, the presence of Christ in people's lives had an amazing leveling effect between people of different social strata.

When people are enslaved to sin, however, they are held in bondage to a master who seeks their destruction. But to be "enslaved" to God is very different. He does not keep us in his service against our will—rather, we desire to please him in everything we do. Paul repeats the analogy of verses 16-18 as he explains that those who "used to be slaves to sin" (6:17) would act in **impurity** and **ever-increasing wickedness.**[NIV] But believers, those who "have been set free from sin" (6:18), can act in **righteousness leading to holiness.**[NIV] Athletes place themselves under the control of a master-coach who has a purpose and a training plan. Paul has shown that we all belong (we're born that way) to the team that practices the training plan of sin. The longer sin is practiced, the "better" we become at it, until we have become fully trained in wickedness. The gospel, however, brings us news of a gracious coach and a new training plan. This coach freely accepts those who realize they don't want to be part of the old team and aren't fit to be on the new team, but are willing to accept the opportunity as a gift. After they

> What else do worldlings think we are doing but playing about when we flee what they most desire on earth, and what they flee, we desire? We are like jesters and tumblers who, with heads down and feet in the air draw all eyes to themselves. . . . Ours is a joyous game, decent, grave, and admirable, delighting the gaze of those who watch from heaven. This chaste and religious game he plays who says, "We are made a spectacle to angels and to men."
> —Bernard of Clairvaux

become members of the new team, they find a lifelong and challenging training plan, gradually taking them from wickedness-fitness to holiness-fitness. The training plan requires obedience to the gracious coach, Jesus Christ.

Holiness (*hagiasmos*), frequently translated "sanctification," refers to the progressive goal of salvation, our growth into persons who exhibit more and more of the character of Christ in the way we live.

> We must love God, before we can be holy at all; this being the root of all holiness. Now we cannot love God, till we know he loves us.
> —John Wesley

6:20 **Slaves to sin . . . free from the control of righteousness.**NIV The freedom that people experience when they are slaves to sin is the antithesis of genuine freedom. It is such a distortion of the meaning of liberty that it causes people to be glad that they are not constrained by the very things that would be very healthy and positive limits. What significance could there possibly be in the happiness of the person who spray-painted the warning signs, scaled the retaining wall, and spit on the offered helping hand in order to leap from the top of the building. The cost of freedom from *righteousness* is more than we can afford to pay.

6:21 **What benefit did you reap at that time from the things you are now ashamed of?** NIV It is possible to read this verse in Greek more than one way. It depends on how the phrases are punctuated. The question is, When Paul referred to his readers' present shame, did he have in mind (1) shame over their past slavery to sin, (2) shame over the consequences (*benefit* or "fruit") of their past slavery to sin, or (3) both?

The choices appear in different translations. For example:
1. NIV reads, "What benefit did you reap at that time from the things you are now ashamed of?"
2. NEB reads, "And what was the gain? Nothing but what now makes you ashamed."
3. TJB reads, "And what did you get from this? Nothing but experiences that now make you blush."
4. NRSV reads, "So what advantage did you then get from the things of which you now are ashamed?"

Attempts to translate choice (3) (i.e., "What fruit did you reap in the past? Aren't you ashamed of all that?") require a grammatical indiscretion. Theologically, the experience of shame ought to embrace both our past condition as sinners and the sins that were committed. Practically, it is often difficult to separate them (i.e., are we ashamed of being covetous in the past, or of the specific time we coveted our neighbor's boat?).

Practical considerations may motivate choice (1), but the overall structure and logic of Paul's writing in this section strongly suggest choice (2). The logical progression in verses 21-22, then, moves from *conditions* to *evidences* to *results*. Paul was teaching the Roman Christians that it was appropriate for them to feel ashamed of their pre-Christian actions, and Paul was encouraging them to seek the benefits of high moral living now that they served Christ.

> The beginning of our recovery and salvation is the restoration which we obtain through Christ. . . . This is the end of regeneration, that Christ may form us anew in the image of God.
> —John Calvin

Conditions	Evidences	Results
Slaves to sin/ Free from righteousness	Fruit toward shame	Death
Free from sin/ Slaves to God	Fruit toward holiness	Life

6:22 The benefit you reap leads to holiness.^{NIV} The benefits are immeasurable for those who are enslaved to God and set free from sin. The word *benefit* (*karpon*) is better translated "fruit" because it refers to more than one thing. What *leads to holiness* begins with a righteousness that is declared by God and based on faith in Jesus Christ. This echoes the theme of Paul's example of Abraham; "Abraham believed God, and it was credited to him as righteousness" (4:3). Faith makes us righteous in God's eyes and challenges us to realize that righteousness in practical living. Believers go on to *holiness* and **eternal life**—holiness is gained as a process over our entire life wherein we become more Christlike and set apart for his service; eternal life begins at conversion and, despite the physical death we will inevitably face, continues beyond the grave.

6:23 The wages of sin is death. This result of sin is not just physical death—everyone dies physically, believers and unbelievers alike. This refers to eternal separation from God in hell. This is the wage that a person receives for his or her rebellion against God.

Those in hell will find no comfort in the truth that they have been paid exactly what they earned.

The free gift of God is eternal life.^{NRSV} But instead of wages, those who believe receive a gracious gift from God—eternal life. *Eternal life* does not mean endless life on earth, but resurrection from death to eternal glory with God. Because eternal life is a gift, we cannot earn or purchase it. It would be foolish for someone to offer to pay for a gift given out of love. To be a gift, it must be given and received *freely*. A more appropriate response to a loved one who offers a gift is grateful acceptance. Our salvation is a gift of God, not something of our own doing (Ephesians 2:8-9). He saved us because of his mercy, not because of any righteous acts on our part (Titus 3:5). How much more we should accept with thanksgiving the gift that God has freely given to us.

THE CHOICE
You are free to choose between two masters, but you are not free to adjust the consequences of your choice. Each of the two masters pays with his own kind of currency. The currency of sin is death. That is all you can expect or hope for in life without God. Christ's currency is eternal life—new life with God that begins on earth and continues forever with God. What choice have you made?

Romans 7

Chapter divisions can be helpful, but at times they artificially break the text in ways that foster disjointedness. For instance, Romans 7 and 8 should be read as a unit, rather than as independent sections. Looking at either chapter alone creates an imbalance. Together they present two sides of the human experience—our struggle and our means of victory.

In chapter 6, Paul explained how Christ delivered us from sin: When he died, we also "died" to sin. But while we are alive in our bodies, we must continue to deal with our sin nature and its attempts to control our thoughts and actions. To describe this tension between our old and new natures, Paul used the analogy of slavery to sin versus slavery to God. He begins chapter 7 by arguing the same point, using the analogy of marriage: Just as death breaks the marital vow, so death with Christ breaks our "marriage" to sin. We were bound to sin because we failed to keep the law. The problem is not with the law; it is within us.

In chapters seven and eight Paul uses the word *law* in four different ways: (1) the Mosaic law (7:7ff.), (2) civil law (7:1-6), (3) the Old Testament Scriptures (7:22), and (4) a governing principle as in "the law of gravity" (7:21, 23, 25; 8:1-4). The last expression is the one used in phrases like "the law of my mind" (7:23), "the law of sin and death" (7:25; 8:2), and "the law of the Spirit of life in Christ Jesus" (8:2). The "law" in these expressions refers to something that always works.

7:1 **The law has authority over a man only as long as he lives.**[NIV] Paul continues his thought from 6:14, "For sin shall not be your master, because you are not under law, but under grace." Obviously, the law has authority only while someone is alive—a dead body cannot be expected to follow any laws, nor can it make restitution for sins committed. Paul's word for *has authority* (*kurieuei*) includes the idea of "master"—literally, "The law lords it over a person."

Paul's rhetorical question creates a chilling afterthought. Death brings an end to the *authority* of the law, but what remains is judgment. Death removes a person from the frying pan of the law, but then drops him or her into the fire of judgment. But if a person can get out from under the *authority* of the law without coming under the judgment of law, that would be good news!

7:2 **A married woman is bound by the law to her husband.**^{NRSV} The marriage vows bind a woman to her husband while he lives. If he dies, she is free from her vows to him.

CHECK YOUR SERVE
Paul uses marriage to illustrate our relationship to the law. When a spouse dies, the law of marriage no longer applies. Because we have died with Christ, the law can no longer condemn us. We rose again when Christ was resurrected, and now we belong to Christ. His Spirit enables us to produce good fruit for God. The result is that we serve God, not by trying hard to obey a set of rules, but out of renewed hearts and minds that overflow with love for him. Why do you serve God?

7:3 **Called an adulteress.** If the wife leaves her husband for another man, she is called an adulteress (except for the provisions described in Matthew 19:9 and 1 Corinthians 7). The Greek word for *called* means "to be publicly known as" or "to receive the stigma of." If this woman is widowed, she is free to marry another man and not be an adulteress.

Again, Paul was having to put this in "human terms" (6:19), by developing an analogy from common living to emphasize his lesson. Having begun the theme of marriage, Paul wants his readers to remember that under normal circumstances any breaking of the marriage vows would be adultery. Having stated that fact, Paul explains its significance.

7:4 **Died to the law . . . that you may belong to another.**^{NRSV} Just as death breaks the bond between a husband and wife, so a believer's "death" (death to his old self) breaks his bond with the law. The old contractual arrangement had to be completely severed before the new one could begin. This had to be as final as death. Jewish believers could not live with a dual allegiance. They could not be under the lordship of Christ and the lordship of the law. Total commitment to Christ cannot coexist with a total commitment to the law. That would be spiritual adultery. A believer belongs fully to Christ. This happens **through the body of Christ**, that is, because of Christ's death on the cross. The believer is then freed to *belong to another*, to Christ.

Bear fruit to God.^{NKJV} Just as there is fruit (i.e., children) from a marriage, so there is fruit from our relationship with Christ. In 6:20-21, Paul reminded the Romans that their old life had borne fruit that was reason for shame. But now there are prospects for a harvest of good. Only by belonging to Christ can we do good works and live a life pleasing to God. This is how we serve in the new way of the Spirit (7:6). (See also Galatians 5:22-23; Philippians 1:11.)

A NEW WAY OF LOOKING
When a person dies to the old life and belongs to Christ, a new life begins. The unbeliever's mind is centered on his or her own personal gratification. Those who don't follow Christ have only their own self-determination as their source of power. By contrast, God is at the center of a Christian's life. God supplies the power for the Christian's daily living. Believers find that their whole way of looking at the world changes when they belong to Christ.

7:5 **When we were controlled by the sinful nature**^{NIV} or, "When we were in the flesh."^{NKJV} Paul reminds his readers that the law did little more for them than fuel their passion for sin. They were under the authority of the law, but they disobeyed it. In the New Testament, when Paul used the term *flesh* (*sarx*), translated here as *sinful nature*, he had two concepts in mind: (1) basic humanity, or the mortal body (see 2 Corinthians 4:11; 10:3; Galatians 2:20; Philippians 1:22, 24), and (2) the human tendency to be dominated by desire and sin (see 8:7; Galatians 3:3, 5:24). Here, Paul is using the second meaning.

Bear fruit for death.^{NRSV} The only fruit produced by a life that is under the law is sin and death. Why? Because **sinful passions aroused by the law were at work in our bodies.**^{NIV}

- The law had authority, but it did not effectively control human passions.

- Sinful passions rebel against the law, seeing it as a "to do" list rather than God's standard to be obeyed.

- Sinful people, unwilling to obey God, are just as unwilling to obey his law.

The law restrains us and teaches us God's will, but it also reveals and stimulates our sinful nature. At the same time it identifies sin, it also generates sin.

Paul expands on these thoughts at length in verses 7-13.

WHY DO WE ENJOY DOING WRONG
JUST FOR THE SAKE OF IT?
- It temporarily satisfies our itching desires.
- It provides an instant and intense sense of power.
- Passionate wrongdoing can be intoxicating and addictive.
- It feels good to rebel.
- We easily jump to a host of wrong conclusions:
  - If one cookie tastes good, the whole bag will taste better.
  - If some of anything is satisfactory, then a lot of the same thing will be intensely satisfactory.
  - More is always better than less.
  - Wanting really isn't different than needing.
  - Nothing is wrong unless you get caught.
- Once an improper desire is seriously considered, it quickly intensifies in appeal and power

7:6 **Serve in the new way of the Spirit.**[NIV] This statement anticipates the spiritual solution to the problems Paul will address in this chapter. Because we have been **released from the law**, we no longer have to obey **in the old way of the written code**.[NIV] In other words, the law is not erased, but it is no longer to be obeyed on the superficial level of "works" (the way of obedience familiar to the Jews). Nor are we freed from all responsibility to serve.

SLAVERY VS. SPIRITUAL FREEDOM

Slavery under the law	New Way of the Spirit
Guilt	Love
Restraint	Joy
Sacrifices	Peace
Ceremonies	Patience
Emphasis on sin	Kindness
Rule keeping	Goodness
External pressures	Faithfulness
Failure	Gentleness
Hopelessness	Self-control

- We have been released from the penalty of the law.

- We are cleansed from sin and counted as righteous.

- We are free from the external regulations that must be fulfilled in order to be right with God.

- We are free from the ceremonial regulations that pointed to Christ (sacrifices and symbols—Hebrews 10:1-18) because Christ has fulfilled them.

God still desires our moral obedience, but we are to serve Christ out of love as our chosen master. Our focus should be on his desires, not on a list of commands. We have been released *so that* we can *serve in the new way of the Spirit* living within us, guiding us, and showing us how to please God. We are still called to serve, but our master is gracious, and we are no longer trapped by the cycle of effort, failure, and guilt.

FREED TO SERVE
Some people try to earn God's approval by keeping a set of rules (e.g., obeying the Ten Commandments, attending church faithfully, or doing good works), but all they earn for their efforts is frustration and discouragement. However, because of Christ's sacrifice, the way to God is already open—we can become his children simply by putting our faith in Christ. No longer trying to reach God by keeping rules, we can become more and more like Jesus as we live with him day by day.

Let the Holy Spirit turn your eyes away from your own performance and toward Christ. He will free you to serve him out of love and gratitude. This is living "in the new way of the Spirit."

THE STRUGGLE WITHIN / 7:7-25

But where does the law fit into all this? In this section, Paul shows that the law is powerless to save sinners (7:7-14) and lawkeepers (7:15-22). Even a person with a new nature (7:23-25) experiences ongoing evidence of the law's inability to motivate him or her toward good. The sinner is condemned by the law; the lawkeeper can't live up to it; and the person with the new nature finds that his or her obedience to the law is sabotaged by the effects of the old nature. Once again, Paul declares that salvation cannot be found by obeying the law. No matter who we are, only Jesus Christ can set us free. Yet the law, because it is God's law, is not then cast aside as useless. In the next chapters, Paul grapples with the complexity of life under grace and the believer's relationship to God's law.

WHY DO GOD'S LAWS AROUSE OUR SINFUL DESIRES?
Because sin in us seizes the opportunity and becomes:

- a sharpshooter, picking the best time and place for a kill
- a magnet, creating an attraction as the object comes near
- a temptress, working seduction at the point of need
- a lawyer, trapping a victim in his own arguments
- an engineer, building elaborate traps
- an army, occupying undefended areas in our morality
- a guerrilla, instigating rebellion behind the scenes

7:7 **Is the law sin?**[NKJV] Because the law arouses sin (7:5) and because we have been released from the law (7:6), does that mean the law is the same as sin? Paul again answers his own question, **Certainly not!**[NKJV] Instead, the law is both holy (7:12) and spiritual (7:14). The law itself is not sin, but it does tell us what sin is. Paul uses coveting (Exodus 20:17; Deuteronomy 5:21) as an example—**I would not have known what coveting really was if the law had not said, "Do not covet."**[NIV]

Paul deliberately chose the last commandment as an example. That particular commandment was unique among the laws in the decalogue, and it obviously had a significant effect on Paul himself. The tenth commandment focuses entirely on our inward nature. At a superficial level, we may claim to have lived up to the first nine, but the last commandment exposes our intentions with shameful clarity. Paul claims that no sooner had he discovered that commandment than "every kind of covetous desire" (7:8) assaulted him. His "sinful passions" (7:5) suddenly became clear. In telling him not to covet, the law had introduced Paul to the darkest desires. But still Paul could maintain his firm belief that God's law itself was sinless. The bright light that revealed a world of filth was not itself evil for having done so.

There are four major interpretations of the meaning of this section. All are ways of attempting to understand how Paul might have been using "I" in these verses. They also rise from difficulties in reconciling the picture that has emerged through history of Paul as a Christian superhero with the person revealed by these verses, who is experiencing deep and agonizing struggles with sin. The four main explanations are as follows:

> The end of the whole thing is that we arrive at an inward situation and not merely an outward one. Actually we break this last commandment, not to covet, before we break any of the others. Any time that we break one of the other commandments of God, it means that we have already broken this commandment, in coveting.
> —Francis Schaeffer

1. "I" is autobiographical, but most likely positioned in the past—Paul is recalling his childhood or preconversion experiences. At the bar mitzvah ceremony, the Jewish child becomes responsible for keeping the law.

2. "I" is Paul speaking for Adam at the fall in the Garden of Eden and identifying the universal human struggle with sin.

3. "I" is Paul speaking for the Jewish nation and identifying the unique struggle with sin created for Jews by the presence of the law of God that was given on Mount Sinai.

4. "I" is Paul speaking for every person's experience under the law.
Each interpretation finds some validity in the text, and none
can be discounted outright. When they are compared to each
other, we find that 2 and 4 are almost identical and that 1 and 3
could easily fit as subpoints under 2. Each, however, may give us
some insight into the depth of human predicament under the law
and under grace. But after each approach has been tried, the application question must still be asked: "In what ways is the 'I' me?"

The Jewish law, a superficial adherence to the law, or nominal
Christian life cannot deal with the force of our sinful desires.
Only the lordship of Christ and the power of the Holy Spirit can
give us the victory.

7:8 **Sin, seizing the opportunity.**[NIV] "Opportunity" is the translation
of a Greek word (*aphormen*) that was used as a military term—it
denotes establishing a bridgehead as preparation for making an attack. Sin uses the law to get a point of attack against us. The commandment "Do not covet" doesn't cause people to covet, but it
arouses within them **every kind of covetous desire.**[NIV] Then sin
(or our capacity to sin) seizes the opportunity that arises when the
law gives a prohibition, but offers no method of resistance. Instead of reading the law as a warning, sin reads the law as a welcome. Prohibiting something often makes people want to do that
very act. When those desires are acted upon, they are sinful.

Apart from the law sin lies dead.[NRSV] Without the law, sin goes
unnoticed, unknown. Some sins may not even present a problem
until they are prohibited.

READING THE SIGNS
Where there is no law, there is no sin, because people cannot
know that their actions are sinful unless a law forbids those actions. God's law makes people realize that they are sinners
doomed to die, yet it offers no help. Sin is real, and it is dangerous.
Imagine a sunny day at the beach. You plunge into the surf,
then you notice a sign on the pier: No Swimming. Sharks in
Water. Your day is ruined. Is it the sign's fault? Are you angry
with the people who put it up? The law is like the sign. It is essential, and we are grateful for it—but it doesn't get rid of the
sharks.

7:9 **I was alive apart from law; but when the commandment
came, sin sprang to life and I died.**[NIV] Paul's intimate, personal
expressions in the remainder of this chapter have given rise to nu-

merous interpretations. Commentators sound like the Ethiopian eunuch questioning Philip on the road to Gaza, "Tell me please, who is the prophet talking about, himself or someone else?" (Acts 8:34 NIV). The descriptions of someone alive apart from the law and later "deceived" (7:11) parallel the fall of humanity into sin recorded in Genesis. But whether Paul is simply telling his own story or retelling Adam's story in the first person, the application is the same. Before we realize the seriousness of the law and of sin, we believe ourselves to be "alive." But when the significance of the command not to covet, for example, becomes clear to us, we suddenly realize our sin and "die"—we sense the outcome of death, the inevitable result of sin (6:23).

The other issue in this extended passage (7:9-25) is its timing in Paul's life. In this verse, written in past tense, the events clearly precede conversion. Within a few verses, however, Paul shifts to the present tense. In this case, the term *tense* is particularly appropriate, since Paul reveals himself to be a person intimate with soul agony. We should listen carefully to what Paul says, within the context that he says it, before we allow theological priorities to shift our understanding.

7:10 The very commandment that promised life proved to be death to me.NRSV Paul is probably referring to a well-known Old Testament passage, "Keep my decrees and laws, for the man who obeys them will live by them. I am the LORD" (Leviticus 18:5 NIV). The commands were given to help people know how to live, but because of sin, those same commands brought only a heightened awareness of the inevitability of death.

7:11 Sin . . . deceived me. Sin deceives people by misusing the law. It is filled with false promises and deceptions:

- Sin promises to satisfy our desires even more than the last time.

- Sin promises that our actions can be kept hidden, so no one will know.

- Sin promises that we won't have to worry about consequences.

- Sin promises special benefits: wisdom, knowledge, and sophistication.

- Sin promises power and prestige in exchange for cooperation.

Don't buy the lie.

In the Garden of Eden (see Genesis 3), the serpent deceived Eve by taking her focus off the freedom she had and putting it on the one restriction God had given. Since that time we have all been rebels. Sin is tempting precisely because God has said it is wrong. When we are tempted to rebel, we need to look at the law from a wider perspective—in the light of God's grace and mercy. If we focus on his great love for us, we will understand that he only restricts us from actions and attitudes that ultimately will harm us.

How did sin use the commandment as an opportunity both to deceive and to kill? Perhaps Paul had thought of the commandments in general to justify himself as righteous, in which case he was deceived. But as he read the tenth commandment, he was caught suddenly by the truth of the law, to which sin immediately added killing guilt.

7:12 **The law is holy.** Although it was the instrument used to kill him, so to speak, Paul could not speak against the law. The law is holy because it reflects the character and will of God himself, who is holy. The commandment defines sin but is not sin (7:7). Instead it is **holy and just and good.**[NKJV] And the purpose of the law is to teach us right from wrong, to give us guidelines, and to show sin for what it is. The law helps us live for God, but it cannot save us.

If the law causes so much difficulty, what useful purpose does it serve? (1) It is a revelation of the nature, character, and will of God. (2) Its ethical components were incorporated in Christ's teaching. (3) It teaches us about sin. (4) It demolishes self-righteousness.

7:13 **Did that which is good, then, become death to me?**[NIV] Taking the last word from the last verse, Paul asks, "Did the commandment [referring to his example of coveting and used as a picture for the law as a whole], which is good, result in death?" Again he answers his own question, **By no means!**[NRSV] The law was given by God; it tells us what God desires of us, and it is *good.* Sin's deception and then application of the commandment brought death.

In order that sin might be shown to be sin.[NRSV] It is *sin,* not the law, that brings death, and it is only through the law that sin can be recognized as sin. Sin uses the commandments in the law, that are good, in order to continue to produce death in people because people cannot keep the law in their own strength. But, by using the commandments as instruments of death, sin reveals itself in all its ugliness.

7:14 **The law is spiritual; but I am unspiritual.**[NIV] Here Paul abruptly changes from writing in the past tense to writing in the present tense. By using the past tense in verses 7-11, Paul considered the effects of the law somewhat dispassionately. Then in the last two verses (7:12-13), he again strenuously defended the law's goodness. Paul's intense desire to view the law with high esteem helped fuel his next thoughts. He was making every effort to clarify the tension between the "holy and just and good" (7:12) law and the sin that uses the law for its deadly purposes. The law comes from God, has his character, and tells his will for his people. But as the majesty of the law fills Paul's mind, along with it comes the vision of his own standing before the law. Paul wants to make the point that sin does not besmirch the law. But he also realizes that he must clarify his own ongoing relationship to the law.

How can we be free from sin and yet continue to do wrong? In Christ, we are free from the penalty of sin (judgment) and the power of sin (hopelessness). But while still in the flesh, we are not free from the presence of sin (temptations) and the possibility of sin (failures). Paul never claimed that being under grace instead of under the law meant that a believer was somehow *above* the law. In fact, having described such a great distance between the law and sin, he realized that he was still far more acquainted with the reality of sin than the righteous standard of the law. Being under grace does not eliminate the law—it changes the purpose of the law in our lives, from a source of judgment to a source of guidance, from an unattainable moral standard of our judge to a character study of the one who loves us. So, Paul writes, **the law is spiritual** (*pneumatikos*); **but I am unspiritual** (*sarkinos*), "of the flesh," carnal. As such, he can write, **sold as a slave to sin.**NIV The expression is literally "being sold under sin," which is equivalent to saying "being given over to slavery." At one time sin was tyrannical in Paul's life. The law has an uncanny capacity for reminding us of what we once were, and of how captivating that old life can still appear. Our hope never shifts back to the law. We must daily focus on Christ.

> That man is perfect in faith who can come to God in the utter dearth of his feelings and desires, without a glow or an aspiration, with the weight of low thoughts, failures, neglects, and wondering forgetfulness, and say to him, "Thou art my refuge."
> —George MacDonald

7:15 **I do not understand.** Or, "I don't even recognize as mine some of the work I do!" By introducing his personal dilemma, Paul invites us to consider how well we understand our own behavior.

I do not do what I want, but I do the very thing I hate.^{NRSV} As
long as believers live in this world as men and women of flesh
and blood, they will face a constant tension—the conflict between their sinful nature and their new spiritual life. Paul wrote to
the Galatians, "The sinful nature desires what is contrary to the
Spirit, and the Spirit what is contrary to the sinful nature. They
are in conflict with each other, so that you do not do what you
want" (Galatians 5:17 NIV). In 7:6, Paul described conversion as
being "released from the law so that we serve in the new way of
the Spirit." This new service in the Spirit is not compulsory, but
the longer we are in this way, the clearer we see its necessity.
This growing awareness is itself a work of God's Spirit, "for it is
God who works in you to will and to act according to his good
purpose" (Philippians 2:13 NIV).

Paul shares three lessons that he learned in trying to deal with
his old sinful desires. (1) Knowledge is not the answer (7:9). Paul
felt fine as long as he did not understand what the law demanded.
When he learned the truth, he knew he was doomed. (2) Self-determination (struggling in one's own strength) doesn't succeed
(7:15). Paul found himself sinning in ways that weren't even attractive to him. (3) Becoming a Christian does not stamp out all
sin and temptation from a person's life (7:22-25).

Being born again starts in a moment of faith, but becoming
like Christ takes a lifetime. Paul compares Christian growth to a
strenuous race or fight (1 Corinthians 9:24-27; 2 Timothy 4:7).
Thus, as Paul has been emphasizing since the beginning of this
letter, no one in the world is innocent; no one deserves to be
saved—not the pagan who doesn't know God's laws, nor the
Christian or Jew who knows them and tries to keep them. All of
us must depend totally on the work of Christ for our salvation.
We cannot earn it by our good behavior.

Accepting the approach that Paul is speaking from personal experience in these verses presents us with another problem. From what
time in his relationship with God do these reflections come? Or,
How realistic is it to think that the thoroughly converted Paul might
actually have struggles that seem so strikingly familiar to our own?

Here are three possible answers:

1. Paul is reflecting on his preconversion state of mind.
    Defense—To accept this passage as a report of experiences Paul
    is having as a believer exposes him to the charge that he doesn't
    practice what he preaches, such as in Romans 5:1-5. Did or didn't
    Paul have peace, joy, and hope? It also seems to present one of
    the greatest Christian minds in a rather weak and frail condition.

Response—Remember, Paul is human. Rather than fearing that Paul's struggle somehow makes his faith less vital, we need to see this as rounding out our view of him. Paul is surprisingly human elsewhere, too! (See 2 Corinthians 12:1-10.) And as for Romans 5, isn't it possible that anguish over our own frailties might come under "sufferings" that must be passed through on the way to perseverance, character, and hope?

2. Paul is representing the immature, carnal, or even backslidden Christian.

Defense—Believers who are serving in the Spirit and are yielded to God simply do not experience what Paul is reporting here. And since Paul is not appealing to the Spirit and getting immediate relief, the problem must reside in him.

Response—In modern terms, who is in denial here? The history of the Christian church is full of godly men and women who have reported struggles remarkably like these. If there is one distinguishing characteristic of immature, carnal, and back-slidden Christians, it is that they are devoid of these struggles until the moment when they take up the cross again.

3. Paul was experiencing and reporting the normal Christian life.

Defense—This is the most straightforward reading of the text. The first person, present tense resonates with the reader. There is a heightened respect for the law of God. Its shocking openness is matched by its trusting conclusion. Its broader context (the entire letter) presents the experiences as part, but certainly not the whole, of Christian life. The depth of honesty highlights the magnificent message of 8:1, "Therefore, there is now no condemnation for those who are in Christ Jesus."

Response—If the ongoing struggle with sin is real, the temptation never to accept the gift of grace is also real.

Those who are really under grace take sin seriously. Sin is no longer their master, but it is still a powerful adversary. If we don't take sin seriously, we fall into it. If we don't take victory seriously, we fail to utilize the Holy Spirit's help.

Peter's words do not lead us to expect an easy Christian life; "Be self-controlled and alert. Your enemy the devil prowls around like a roaring lion looking for someone to devour. Resist him, standing firm in the faith, because you know that your brothers throughout the world are undergoing the same kind of sufferings" (1 Peter 5:8-9 NIV). We may be slaves of a new master, but we still live in enemy territory. The unique balance of the Christian life was described by Jesus himself when he said, "I have told you these things, so that in me you may have peace. In this world you will have trouble. But take heart! I have overcome the world" (John 16:33 NIV). Whatever the experience of each day, our hope is only real "through Jesus Christ our Lord!" (7:25).

:16-17 **If I do what I do not want to do, I agree that the law is good.**NIV We want to obey God's law, yet we still fail. Our failure is not the law's fault, nor is it our own fault: **It is no longer I myself who do it, but it is sin living in me.**NIV If sin did not exist, then the law would give us guidelines for living perfectly. But sin perverts everything. Paul is not abdicating responsibility for his sin; instead, he is making the point that his desires and the sin within him are in constant conflict. Sin is a power that, at times, can still win because his redemption is not yet complete.

The saints in the Old Testament expressed this struggle exquisitely. Jeremiah cried out, "The heart is deceitful above all things and beyond cure. Who can understand it?" (Jeremiah 17:9 NIV). David prayed, "Who can discern his errors? Forgive my hidden faults. Keep your servant also from willful sins; may they not rule over me. Then will I be blameless, innocent of great transgression" (Psalm 19:12-13 NIV).

One of the ongoing duties of God's Spirit is to convict us of our potential for wickedness. Serving "in the new way of the Spirit" (7:6) includes regular encounters with the Spirit's convicting ministry in our life (see John 16:7-15). When we are made aware of sin, we have a clear responsibility: "If we confess our sins, he is faithful and just and will forgive us our sins and purify us from all unrighteousness" (1 John 1:9 NIV).

:18-19 **Nothing good lives in me.**NIV In our sinful nature, there is nothing good. Paul sees this as part of being human. Although we belong to Christ and have died to sin, we still live in a sinful world and have a sinful nature. Picture the highly trained commander of a modern tank equipped with laser guidance systems, electronic wizardry, and atomic power. In preparation for a crucial battle he:

- loaded up with the wrong fuel
- filled his magazines with the wrong caliber ammunition
- picked up the wrong maps and directions
- left most of his crew in their bunks

How effective would he be under fire? Yet how often do we undertake spiritual warfare in our own strength, using our own tools

and resources, and making up our own directions as we go along?
We shouldn't be surprised if Satan quickly puts us out of commission! The tension continues—**What I do is not the good I want
to do . . . the evil I do not want to do—this I keep on doing.**^{NIV}
Paul describes the person who knows what is good and might
even desire to do it, but this person lacks the power. Without the
Holy Spirit's help, the person is dominated by the power of sin
and continues to do evil when he actually desires to do good.

NOTHING GOOD LIVES IN ME
Where am I battling in my own strength?
From time to time, it helps to list our major areas of struggle
and examine what our strategy has been:

- Childrearing
- Finances
- Church issues and problems
- Marriage
- Work Problems
- Personal temptation
- Aging

7:20 **It is sin living in me that does it.**^{NIV} Paul repeats his words from
verse 17. Believers still have a sinful nature that pulls them to do
what they do not want to do. The seeming contradiction of "I
do—I don't do" emphasizes how difficult it is to identify the
sources of our sinful behaviors. One way to think of it is, Until I
was under the grace of God, sin owned me. After I was under the
grace of God, I admit that I still owned sin. Before Christ, I was
responsible for being a sinner. Once Christ saved me, I'm still responsible for my sins.

EXCUSES
"The devil made me do it." "I didn't do it; the sin in me did it."
These sound like good excuses, but we are responsible for our
actions. We must never use the power of sin or Satan as an excuse because they are defeated enemies. Without Christ's
help, sin is stronger than we are, and we will be unable to defend ourselves against its attacks. That is why we should never
stand up to sin all alone. Jesus Christ, who has conquered sin
once and for all, promises to fight by our side. If we look to him
for help, we will not have to give in to sin.

7:21 **This law at work.**^{NIV} The law, or principle, at work here is the reality that evil is within us, even when we **want to do good.**^{NIV} In
fact, it is when we most want to do good that we become most

acutely aware of our propensity not to do so. A swimmer has no idea how strong the current is until she tries to swim upstream. When she faces the current, she finds this law at work: the current is against her.

7:22 **In my inner being I delight in God's law.**NIV Believers take delight in God's law (i.e., the path of obedience to God that the entire Old Testament presents) because they long to know it and do it and thus to please God. This is one of the marks of wisdom: "But his delight is in the law of the Lord, and on his law he meditates day and night" (Psalm 1:2 NIV). The problem is that there is . . .

7:23 **Another law at work in the members of my body.**NIV This other principle that is at work is the law of sin. Sin is constantly **at war.**NRSV We are at war because sin will not give up the control over us that it lost when we came to faith in Christ. Sin fights against the law of the **mind** because our mind is where we make our decisions and our moral judgments. We are prisoners of the law of sin at work with us. We cannot resist our sin nature in our own power. When we try, we will be defeated.

Paul does not say that these powers are equal, but he knows they are both there. We must do the same. One power must be resisted while relying on the other. When we fail to rely on Christ's strength for our daily strength, we in essence provide sin with more power over us. Sin's power will not have grown, but our relative weakness will make it seem that way. Sin's power is not an excuse for us to drift spiritually, or openly give in to temptation. Believers must not forget that "You, dear children, are from God and have overcome them, because the one who is in you is greater than the one who is in the world" (1 John 4:4 NIV).

WE MUST FIGHT!
All Christians struggle against sin. We must never underestimate sin's power; and we must never attempt to fight sin in our own strength. Satan is a crafty tempter, and we have a great ability to make excuses. Instead of trying to overcome sin with human willpower, we must take hold of the tremendous power of Christ that is available to us. This is God's provision for victory over sin—he sends the Holy Spirit to live in us and give us power. And when we fall, he lovingly reaches out to help us up.

7:24 **Who will rescue me from this body of death?**NRSV Our bodies are mortal; they are bodies *of death*. As long as we live on this earth in our human bodies, we will face this conflict with sin. Our place of residence is our place of least resistance. And, as seen above, as long as we are confined to this world, we will experience a measure of struggle and defeat. But, we are not left in defeat—rescue will come!

Sooner or later, almost every person asks this desperate question. How sad for those who cannot answer as Paul answered. His answer must also be ours, and we must share this truth with others. Paul made sure the Romans knew that he believed the gospel to be the answer.

7:25 **Thanks be to God through Jesus Christ our Lord!**NRSV The triumph is sweeter because the struggle is real. In the last few verses, we have glimpsed the struggle of a genuine believer. Now the answer is shouted in exclamation.

Many who claim to know Christ never see themselves well enough to appreciate as deeply as Paul did what they actually have in Christ. Because of Jesus Christ, we are assured of a great future. We will one day join him in eternity with a new body that is free from sin. In the meantime, however, we must realize that while in our mind we are **slave to God's law**, we still have a **sinful nature** that will remain **a slave to the law of sin.**NIV

The battle ends with a shout of victory. The winners *know* who really won. The winners also know the war isn't over. But in the meantime, there are more lessons to learn, and there is more freedom to experience.

AM I REALLY A SLAVE?
There is great tension in daily Christian experience. The conflict is that we agree with God's commands but cannot do them. As a result, we are painfully aware of our sin. This inward struggle with sin was as real for Paul as it is for us. From Paul we learn what to do about it. Whenever he felt overwhelmed by the spiritual battle, he would return to the beginnings of his spiritual life, remembering how he had been freed from sin by Jesus Christ. When we feel confused and overwhelmed by sin's appeal, let us claim the freedom Christ gave us. His power can lift us to victory.

Romans 8

At the end of chapter 7, Paul assures all believers of having power to overcome sin and the assurance of final deliverance from this evil world. But he includes the reminder that during this lifetime, there will be constant tension because in the sinful nature, even a believer is "a slave to the law of sin" (7:25). The question arises, *So, are we to spend our entire lives defeated by sin?* The answer is a resounding *no!* In this chapter, Paul describes the life of victory and hope that every believer has because of Christ Jesus.

With the suddenness of Pentecost, Paul begins his description of the victorious Christian life, referring repeatedly to the Holy Spirit. Up to this point in the letter, Paul has only mentioned the Spirit twice and not at all in 7:7-25; from here on, the Holy Spirit is mentioned specifically nineteen times. In the overall framework of the letter, Paul seems to have held this teaching in restraint. We must be aware of our need for the Holy Spirit before we are ready and willing to appropriate his help. The Holy Spirit's presence and power answers much of the momentary despair of chapter 7. "The law of sin" triumphed in chapter 7 but is defeated in chapter 8 by the power of the Spirit of life.

8:1 **There is therefore now no condemnation.**^{NKJV} We feel condemned because Satan uses past guilt and present failures to make us question what Christ has done for us. Our assurance must be focused on Christ, not our performance.

- Our own conscience reminds us of guilt.

- Non-Christian friends will notice (and point out) our inconsistencies.

- Past memories of how we lived can haunt us.

- Personal dysfunctions such as shame, low self-esteem, or compulsions will trip us up.

- The perfection of the law will show how imperfect we are.

- We can allow Christ's perfect example to discourage our efforts rather than encourage our trust.

- Unhealthy comparisons with other believers will make us feel inadequate.

"This then is how we know that we belong to the truth, and how we set our hearts at rest in his presence whenever our hearts condemn us. For God is greater than our hearts, and he knows everything" (1 John 3:19-20 NIV).

Often, we are like the criminal who hates his incarceration while at the same time denying that he finds any security in his cell. Then, beyond all expectations, the warden announces a pardon and unlocks the cell. As the door swings open, the prisoner meets the delight of freedom and a tinge of fear of the unknown. What will this new life be like? Many find a strange comfort in the familiar state of condemnation. Christ invites us to leave the cell behind. Some rush out joyfully, some calmly and thoughtfully, and others leave the cell of their old life with painful slowness. Once outside, most of us experience, from time to time, a strange longing for the old familiar cell. We must remember that what may seem appealing was actually a filthy holding cell on death row.

Because we have been rescued by Christ (7:24-25), and are thus **in Christ Jesus**, we are not condemned. To be *in Christ Jesus* means to have put our faith in him, becoming a member of his body of believers. Jesus said, "I tell you the truth, whoever hears my word and believes him who sent me has eternal life and will not be condemned; he has crossed over from death to life" (John 5:24 NIV). There can be no condemnation, for "we have been justified through faith" and "have peace with God through our Lord Jesus Christ" (5:2).

In the original manuscript, there was probably no break between Paul's summation in 7:25 of the struggle between the two allegiances (two minds) within himself and the proclamation in 8:1 that **in Christ Jesus**, there is no **condemnation** for our vacillations. We believers must never forget the reality of our rescue and our indebtedness to God's grace in Christ. We can persevere in our daily struggles knowing that "if we are faithless, he will remain faithful, for he cannot disown himself" (2 Timothy 2:13 NIV). Our need for the ongoing presence of the Holy Spirit is so clear at this point that some early manuscripts add, after *Jesus*, the phrase from verse 4, "who do not live according to the sinful nature but according to the Spirit." But putting that phrase here completes the thought too quickly, an approach Paul seldom used.

8:2 **Law of the Spirit of life in Christ Jesus has set you free from the law of sin and of death.**NRSV The *Spirit of life* is the Holy Spirit, who was present at the creation of the world as one of the agents in the origin of life itself (Genesis 1:2). He is the power behind the rebirth of every Christian, and the one who helps us live the Christian life. The Holy Spirit sets us free, once and for all, from sin and its natural consequence, death. How did this happen?

Paul has used the word *law* (*nomos*) with a variety of qualifiers in his letter: "God's law" (7:22); "law of sin" (7:25); "law of my mind" (7:23); and now *law of the Spirit*. A parallel can be found in 7:6, where Paul contrasts the freedom we have to "serve in the *new way of the Spirit*, and not in the old way of the written code." Paul must be referring to the binding authority of the law—I am liberated from the old authority and placed in the new. Paul is also referring to the consistent ways that the Holy Spirit works. These fall under two main functions: what the Holy Spirit does *for* us and what he does *in* us. First, this *law of the Spirit set you free*. What both we and the law were "powerless to do" (8:3), God did for us. Second, having been freed, "the Spirit of God lives in" us (8:9), so that we actually live "according to the Spirit" (8:4) (see Galatians 2:20).

8:3 **What the law was powerless to do.**NIV Freedom over sin never can be obtained by obedience to the law. The law cannot help us because **it was weakened by the sinful nature.**NIV But what the law can't do, **God did by sending his own Son in the likeness of sinful man.**NIV Jesus Christ was a "likeness" of us. This likeness (*homoious*) was not merely an appearance; he was completely human (John 1:14), with the same desires that yield to sin, yet he never sinned (see 2 Corinthians 5:21; Hebrews 2:17-18; 4:14-16).

> Grace was given that the law might be fulfilled.
> —Augustine

Christ took on humanity in order to be our **sin offering.**NIV Because Christ was sinless, his death passed the "death sentence" on sin for all of us, setting us free from sin's power over us: **he condemned sin in the flesh.**NRSV Jesus gave himself as a *sacrifice* ("sin offering") for our sins.

In Old Testament times, animal sacrifices were continually offered at the temple. These animals brought to the altar had two important characteristics: they were alive, and they were "without flaw." The sacrifices showed the Israelites the seriousness of sin: innocent blood had to be shed before sins could be pardoned (see Leviticus 17:11). But animal blood could not really remove sin (Hebrews 10:4); and the forgiveness provided by those sacrifices, in legal terms, was more like a stay of execution than a pardon. Those animal sacrifices could only point to Jesus' sacrifice that paid the penalty for all sin. Jesus' life was identical with ours, yet unstained by sin. So he could serve as the flawless sacrifice for our sins. In him, our pardon is complete. The tables are turned so that not only is there "no condemnation for those who are in Christ Jesus," but also the very sin that guaranteed our condemnation is itself condemned by Christ's sacrifice.

8:4 The righteous requirements of the law might be fully met in us.^{NIV} The requirement of the law is *holiness* (see Leviticus 11:44-45; 19:2; 20:7); but the law is powerless to make us holy because of our innate sinfulness. Only through Christ's death and the resulting freedom from sin can we no longer **live according to the sinful nature but according to the Spirit**^{NIV} and thus fulfill the righteous requirements of the law. The Holy Spirit is the one who helps us become holy. The Holy Spirit provides the power internally to help us do what the law required of us externally. The word translated *live (peripatousin)* means "walking" and suggests the entire course of one's life. Walking conveys the idea of action, daily behavior, and moral direction.

It is the Spirit who produces "fruit" in us; only in this way can we fulfill the requirements of the law. But Paul has already made it clear that the law is powerless to save. So why do its requirements still need to be met? The law is God's law and was never meant to be cast aside. Paul makes a distinction between two kinds of obedience to the law. He speaks against the obedience to the law that stays merely at the level of the flesh (such as being circumcised because the law required it) and the obedience that depends on God's Holy Spirit. Only the latter fulfills the law. When we live according to the Spirit, we actually do meet the requirements of the law. Or, as Paul puts it, the **requirements of the law are met in us.**^{NIV}

8:5 Live according to the sinful nature.^{NIV} We will struggle constantly with sin and its temptations until the resurrection. People who decide to follow their sinful nature **have their minds set on what that nature desires.**^{NIV} But believers do not need to live in sin because they can now **live in accordance with the Spirit**, setting their mind **on what the Spirit desires.**^{NIV} We must follow Christ daily in every area of our life, in our choices and moral decisions. Will you follow your former sinful nature or the Spirit's leading?

DIFFERENT WAYS TO HAVE YOUR MIND SET

When a person is determined to do something or to hold a certain belief or idea, we say that person has a certain mind-set. A mind-set:

- determines how a person acts
- motivates a person
- influences whom or what a person chooses as sources of
  knowledge and authority
- affects a person's view of every experience
- shapes a person's value system
- dominates a person's private and public life

Paul indicates that all mind-sets can be reduced to two categories: sinful and spiritual. The two mind-sets are not parts of a person or even forces within a person. They signify powers and
dominant features of two realms, the spirit and the flesh (former
sinful nature).

The sinful mind-set	*The spiritual mind-set*
Consciously and unconsciously life will be oriented toward:	Consciously and unconsciously life will be oriented toward:
Death	Life and peace
Hostility toward God	Friendship with God
Rebellion	Obedience to the Spirit's influence
Resistance to any form of submission	Guidance by the Holy Spirit
Actions and attitudes that will not please God	Love for God and neighbor
	Knowing and following the words of Jesus

8:6 **To set the mind on the flesh is death.**^{NRSV} The *mind* refers to our mind-set,
our goals. Choosing to follow our flesh (which is translated "sinful nature"
in the NIV) will result in death, both spiritual and physical.

To set the mind on the Spirit is life and peace.^{NRSV} Choosing to follow the Spirit's leading brings us full life on earth, eternal life, and
peace with God. Paul is not specific about how the Spirit controls because his emphasis here is in comparing the results of the two possible mind-sets. The phrases Paul uses are, literally, "the mind
belonging to the flesh" and "the mind belonging to the Spirit." Paul
forces an uncompromising choice and echoes Christ's words, "No
one can serve two masters. Either he will hate the one and love the
other, or he will be devoted to the one and despise the other. You cannot serve both God and Money" (Matthew 6:24 NIV).
  Elsewhere in Scripture we find the characteristics of a mind under
the Spirit's control. It will be a mind directed toward truth, aware of

the Spirit's presence (John 14:17). It will be a mind seeking to please the Holy Spirit (Galatians 6:8). It will be a mind active in memorizing and meditating on the words of Christ (John 14:26). It will be a mind sensitive to sin (John 16:7-11). It will be a mind eager to follow the Spirit's guidance (Galatians 5:16-22). The control of the Holy Spirit begins with voluntary commitment and submission to Christ.

HOW DO WE COOPERATE WITH THE SPIRIT'S CONTROL?
- Ask for greater openness and responsiveness to the Holy Spirit's guidance.
- Consciously humble ourselves before God, so we are not too proud to change.
- Look to God's Word for guidance.
- Obey where we have clear direction, so that our forward movement will enhance the Holy Spirit's leading. (It makes little sense to steer a parked car!)

When was the last time you prayed as Jesus did, "Nevertheless, may your will, not mine, be done"?

8:7-8 **The mind that is set on the flesh is hostile to God.**NRSV A sinful mind cannot submit to God because it is the seat of indwelling sin and is in permanent revolt against God. The "sinful mind" (NIV) instinctively recognizes in God's law the danger of judgment, and thus prefers willful ignorance. Living in sin, following one's own desires, and disregarding God boils down to hostility to him.

Does not submit to God's law, nor can it do so.NIV This statement supports the doctrine of total depravity. Every person not united to Christ is thoroughly controlled by sin's power. Thus, **those controlled by the sinful nature cannot please God** (NIV) because they are interested only in themselves and have cast aside the one and only power that can defeat sin. The mind directed by the flesh can only be devoted to its own self-gratification, which will lead to destruction.

Every human being has a sinful nature. But believers in Christ have access to the Holy Spirit. In fact, Paul says, "The Spirit of God lives in you" (8:9). Believers are still in the flesh, but because they are born again, they also have God's Spirit. The question is which will be in control.

TWO TYPES OF PEOPLE
Paul divides people into two categories—those who let themselves be controlled by their sinful nature and those who follow after the Holy Spirit. We would be in the first category if Jesus hadn't offered us a way out. After we say yes to Jesus, we want to continue following him because his way brings life and peace. We must consciously choose to center our life on God.

Use the Bible to discover God's guidelines, and then follow them. In every perplexing situation ask, "What would Jesus want me to do?" When the Holy Spirit points out what is right, do it eagerly. For more on our sinful nature versus our new life in Christ, see 6:6-8, Ephesians 4:22-24; Colossians 3:3-15.

8:9 Controlled . . . by the Spirit, if the Spirit of God lives in you.^{NIV} The Holy Spirit lives in us, taking over control from our *sinful nature*. This gives us great assurance. "We know that we live in him and he in us, because he has given us of his Spirit" (1 John 4:13 NIV). Paul is saying that the process of salvation has begun but is incomplete, for in order to have the Spirit within, a person already must have trusted Christ as Savior.

Anyone who does not have the Spirit of Christ does not belong to him.^{NRSV} This phrase may create doubt in our life. In our experience, we may feel a void, a conflict, a deficit, an overbearing problem. We can have such experiences and still have the Holy Spirit. The titles Spirit of God and Spirit of Christ both mean the Holy Spirit. Only the Holy Spirit can make us acceptable to God; therefore, anyone who does not have the Spirit cannot belong to Christ. Paul does not voice this as a threat or warning, but a statement of fact.

Having the Spirit of Christ is the same as belonging to Christ. This is not a criterion for judging others' lives, it is a helpful encouragement in our struggles. When facing times of doubt, Paul's statement supplies us with two questions that must be answered: (1) Do I have the Spirit of Christ? and (2) Do I belong to Christ? Paul's point is that answering yes to either determines the truth of the other. The first tends to be a less settled answer experientially; the second is clearly answered by the assurance given in God's Word.

In his writings, Paul often speaks of the Spirit and Christ synonymously. This is evident in Romans 8:9-10. The terms *Spirit of God, Spirit of Christ,* and *Christ* are all used interchangeably. The Spirit of God is the Spirit of Christ, and the Spirit of Christ is Christ. In Pauline terminology, being "in Christ" and being "in the Spirit" are the same thing because in Christian experience they are absolutely identical. There is no such thing as an experience of Christ apart from the Spirit.

WHEN DOUBTS ATTACK!
Have you ever worried about whether or not you are a Christian? A Christian is anyone who belongs to Christ by faith and has the Spirit of God living in him or her. If you have sincerely trusted Christ for your salvation and have acknowledged him as Lord, then the Holy Spirit has come into your life, and you are a Christian. You won't know that the Holy Spirit has come if you

are waiting for a certain feeling; you will know he has come because Jesus promised he would.

When the Holy Spirit is working within you, you will believe that
Jesus Christ is God's Son and that eternal life comes through him
(1 John 5:5); you will begin to act as Christ directs (Romans 8:5;
Galatians 5:22-23); you will find help in your daily problems and in
your praying (Romans 8:26-27); you will be empowered to serve
God and do his will (Acts 1:8; Romans 12:6ff.); and you will become
part of God's plan to build up his church (Ephesians 4:12-13).

THE TRINITY IN THE NEW TESTAMENT

In addition to Romans 8:9, where all three persons of the Trinity
are working together in our salvation, there are some other key
passages that portray the Trinity.

Baptism of Jesus—Matthew 3:17
    The Father Spoke.
    The Son was in the water.
    The Holy Spirit appeared as a dove.

Baptism of all believers—Matthew 28:19
    All believers are baptized in the name of
      the Father,
      the Son,
      and the Holy Spirit.

The angel Gabriel's words to Mary—Luke 1:35 NIV
    "The Holy Spirit will come upon you."
    "The power of the Most High will overshadow you."
    "The holy one to be born will be called the Son of God."

Paul's benediction—2 Corinthians 13:14 NIV
    "The grace of the Lord Jesus Christ"
    "The love of God"
    "The fellowship of the Holy Spirit"

8:10-11 **If Christ is in you, your body is dead because of sin, yet your
spirit is alive because of righteousness.**NIV Christ's Spirit lives
within our human spirits, but our fleshly bodies are still infected by
sin and are *dead*—that is, they are mortal. Sin has been defeated by
Christ, but sin and death still claim their hold on our mortal bodies.
Yet in these bodies we are alive spiritually and can live by the
Spirit's guidance. In addition, we are promised the physical resurrection of our bodies into eternal life, for God will **give life to [our]
mortal bodies** (NIV) because of the Holy Spirit within us. So there
is wonderful hope even for our prone-to-decay bodies. Elsewhere, Paul wrote, "So will it be with the resurrection of the dead.

The body that is sown is perishable, it is raised imperishable"
(1 Corinthians 15:42 NIV; see also 1 Corinthians 6:14; 2 Corinthians
4:14-16; 1 Thessalonians 4:14).

8:12   **So then, brothers and sisters.**NRSV Paul has just presented an overview of God's work in believers' lives (8:1-11). The Trinity is much
in evidence in these verses. God is the source of the law (8:7) and the
one against whom the sinful mind is hostile (8:7). God the Father acts
in "sending his Son" (8:3). God the Son was sent; having his Spirit
determines whether or not we belong to him (8:9); and "Christ is in" us
(8:10), the same Christ who was raised from the dead (8:11). God's
Spirit lives in us (8:9) and raised Jesus from the dead (8:11). God the
Spirit is the Spirit of life (8:2) who controls us (8:9)—he is called
both the "Spirit of God" and the "Spirit of Christ," and he lives in us
(8:11). God fully participated in our salvation and continues to participate in our sanctification.

We have an obligation.NIV Because God has done everything we
needed to be done, *we have an obligation* to respond. Because of all that
Christ has done and is going to do for us, we are obligated to live in the
power and control of the Holy Spirit. Paul first puts this in the negative—our obligation is **not to the sinful nature, to live according to
it.**NIV We are to refuse the drives and desires of our still attractive but crucified sinful nature, to say no to ungodliness and worldly passions, and
to live "self-controlled, upright and godly lives in this present age" (Titus 2:12 NIV). The old, sinful nature may present its demands, based
upon the past, but we have no obligation to cooperate.

HOW DO WE KEEP OUR OBLIGATION TO THE SPIRIT?
The Scriptures provide a picture of active response to God.
This works out as we:
- Train ourselves in godliness. Our response to the gospel does
  not involve *trying* to live a certain way, but *training* to live in the
  way of the Spirit. Much of the training schedule is created by
  God, through suffering, perseverance, and development of
  self-control. But God's Word gives training disciplines for us
  to do. Prayer, study, meditation, service, confession, and worship are all chosen actions that demonstrate spiritual growth
  and form the basis for further spiritual growth.
- *Constantly rely on the Holy Spirit.* Even our efforts in training
  are not independent acts. Along the way, we need the Spirit's
  presence, guidance, comfort, and encouragement. One way
  or another, no matter how far we have travelled in life, the Holy
  Spirit will always bring us back to an awareness of the grace
  we have in Christ Jesus. There we find no condemnation.

8:13 **If you live according to the sinful nature, you will die.**^{NIV} Death is both physical and spiritual. All people die physically, but only those with the Spirit will be resurrected. And those who live according to the sinful nature cannot enjoy God's presence in their lives, thus they are left to their own devices.

If by the Spirit you put to death the misdeeds of the body, you will live.^{NIV} Our sinful nature shows itself through the vehicle of the body. Therefore, we must put the body and its misdeeds to death—count ourselves "dead to sin" (6:11). These *misdeeds* are the practices (*praxeis*), the habitual responses, of the *sinful nature,* which must be terminated. In other passages, Paul provides lists of examples: "Put to death, therefore, whatever belongs to your earthly nature: sexual immorality, impurity, lust, evil desires and greed, which is idolatry" (Colossians 3:5 NIV; see Galatians 5:19-21; Ephesians 4:22–5:14). This is an action to be done, a moral decision to be made—every day we are to put to death the desires that draw us away from God. Phillips translated this phrase, "Cut the nerve of your instinctive actions by obeying the Spirit." This is the *obligation* mentioned by Paul in verse 12, and it is only possible *by the Spirit*. We cannot do this on our own.

> The Spirit works, the Son fulfills his ministry, and the Father approves; and man is thus brought to full salvation.
> —Irenaeus

INAPPROPRIATE RESPONSES TO THE MISDEEDS OF THE BODY

We should terminate the practices that the Holy Spirit points out as wrong. But instead, we often try to make excuses.

Response	Example
Denying that these habits or actions are part of our life	"I haven't done or couldn't do something like that."
Disclaiming our knowing participation	"I wasn't sure if it was right or wrong."
Continuing to give in to those patterns	"I'm weak, but at least I'm being honest about it."
Creating elaborate excuses	"I was deprived as a child. It's not really a habit. I tried to resist."
Minimizing or covering up the misdeeds	"At least I'm not as bad as *she* is."
Hiding behind a facade of legalism	"I'm doing so many things right; those wrong things don't count!"

14-15 **Those who are led by the Spirit of God are sons of God. For . . . you received the Spirit of sonship.**^{NIV} The Jews already considered themselves to be "sons of God" because of their heritage; but Paul explains that *sons of God* has new meaning. True sons of God are those who are *led by* the Spirit of God as evidenced in their life-style. Believers not only have the Spirit (8:9); they are also led by the Spirit.

Paul uses adoption or "sonship" to illustrate the believer's new relationship with God and his or her privileges as part of God's family. In Roman culture, the adopted person lost all rights in his old family and gained all the rights of a legitimate child in his new family. He became a full heir to his new family. Likewise, when a person becomes a Christian, he or she gains all the privileges and responsibilities of a child in God's family. One of these outstanding privileges is being led by the Spirit (Galatians 4:5-6).

You did not receive a spirit that makes you a slave again to fear, but you received the Spirit of sonship.^{NIV} This slavery *to fear* most likely refers to life under the law, obedience that was concerned for scrupulous exactness with a constant fear of failure. Paul implies that the absence of fear is an important indicator of the Spirit's presence: "God did not give us a spirit of timidity, but a spirit of power, of love and of self-discipline" (2 Timothy 1:7 NIV).

By whom we cry out, "Abba, Father."^{NKJV} We are not slaves who must cower in fear before their master. We are adopted sons who can call God our Father. *Abba* is from the Aramaic and is still a term used by Hebrew children to address their father (see Galatians 4:6). Jesus used the expression when he prayed to his Father (see Mark 14:36). "Abba" is a term of informal intimacy and respect spoken by children to their fathers. The equivalent expression in our language is "Daddy" or "Papa." Calling God "Daddy" indicates that we have an intimate relationship with him.

8:16 **The Spirit Himself bears witness with our spirit that we are children of God.**^{NKJV} The Holy Spirit within makes all the difference for believers. The Holy Spirit not only adopts us as God's children, but he also assures us of our family status (see Galatians 4:6). The Spirit within changes our obedience to God from slavery to a relationship where God is both our Master and our loving Father. The Scriptures indicate that believers can expect inward confirmation of the faith by the Spirit. Our very capacity and desire to approach God as our Father is itself evidence of the Spirit's *witness with our spirit that we are children of God.* We are motivated by the Spirit.

8:17 **We are heirs—heirs of God and co-heirs with Christ.**[NIV] The Jews
were convinced that they were the Lord's inheritance, and that as
such they would inherit the Promised Land. Paul explains that God's
promise includes all who believe in Christ—both Jews and Gentiles.
Because we are God's children, we are his heirs. "So you are no
longer a slave, but a son; and since you are a son, God has made you
also an heir" (Galatians 4:7 NIV). And we are co-heirs with Christ,
the Son of God. Heirs of what? The Jews thought it was to be the
Promised Land—instead, it is another "land," God's kingdom.

We are heirs of God only because of Christ's suffering on our behalf. As believers, **we suffer with him so that we may also be glorified with him.**[NRSV] We will enjoy our future inheritance if our relationship with Christ is genuine enough so that we will face suffering for
his sake. History has demonstrated that hatred for Christ has often resulted in terrible persecution of his co-heirs. The early Christians who
died in the arena shared in Christ's suffering because of their connection with Christ. There was no personally redemptive value in their
suffering, except that on occasion, the suffering of one believer was
the seed that bloomed with faith in another person. Jesus said, "Remember the words I spoke to you: 'No servant is greater than his master.'
If they persecuted me, they will persecute you also" (John 15:20
NIV). For more on this theme, see 2 Timothy 2:12; 3:12; 1 Peter 4:13.

THE PRICE
There is a price for being identified with Jesus. Along with the
great treasures, Paul mentions the suffering that Christians
must face. What kinds of suffering are we to endure? For first-
century believers, there was economic, social, and physical persecution; some even faced death. We too must pay a price for
following Jesus. In many parts of the world today, Christians
face pressures just as severe as those faced by Christ's first followers. Even in countries where Christianity is tolerated or encouraged, Christians must not become complacent. To live as Jesus
did—serving others, giving up one's own rights, resisting pressures
to conform to the world—always exacts a price. Nothing we suffer,
however, can compare to the great price that Jesus paid to save us.

THE FUTURE GLORY / 8:18-27

With hardly taking a breath, Paul proceeds to enlarge upon what
he calls "the glory which shall be revealed in us" (8:18). The last
paragraph ended with the shared connection between suffering
and glory. Sharing in the glory of Christ will come only after sharing in his sufferings (8:17 NRSV). For Paul, this matter of glory
has cosmic proportions, for the glorious destiny of believers will
signal a new day for all of creation. He wants his readers to real-

ize that sin has imprisoned all people and the entire environment. We must wait for God's timing to be free, depending on the Spirit, who helps us in ways we can hardly describe.

8:18 **The sufferings of this present time are not worthy to be compared with the glory which shall be revealed in us.**^{NKJV} In verse 17, Paul stated that believers will share in Christ's sufferings. He completes that thought with this verse, concluding that the sufferings we now face are completely overshadowed by the glory that awaits those who trust in Christ. The present suffering is temporary, while the future glory is eternal. Paul had written to the Corinthians, "For our light and momentary troubles are achieving for us an eternal glory that far outweighs them all" (2 Corinthians 4:17 NIV). Suffering is part of the process of sharing in Christ's death; it will culminate in sharing his glory. If *glory* is the majesty of God, his character seen for all that it truly is, then his *glory . . . revealed in us* will occur when we suddenly become exactly what God has intended us to be. God will allow us to share in the glory that belonged to Christ alone. We will share with Christ in the glory of sonship. In that day we will fully reflect God's image.

8:19 **The creation.** Human beings and the rest of creation presently face suffering, and both will be glorified in the future. When Adam sinned, God sentenced all of creation: "Cursed is the ground because of you" (Genesis 3:17 NRSV). Since then, the world has suffered decay and pollution, largely because people have forgotten or ignored their responsibilities as stewards of the earth.

Waits with eager longing.^{NRSV} This form of the Greek verb (*apekdexetai*) for this phrase is used seven times in the New Testament. Each time it is used in connection with the believers' anticipation of Christ's return (see Romans 8:19, 23, 25; 1 Corinthians 1:7; Galatians 5:5; Philippians 3:20; Hebrews 9:28). Here it is used in connection with creation awaiting that day. In the meantime, the created order functions in spite of its flaws. But diseases, deformities, and suffering constantly remind us that all is not right with us or with the world. When people treat nature with care, the environment displays a remarkable willingness to cooperate. All creation looks forward to its liberation from the effects of the Fall.

For the revealing of the sons of God.^{NKJV} This will occur at the second coming of Christ when he returns for his people. We will share in his glory (8:18) and receive our complete redemption (8:23). The entire universe is looking forward to the conclusion of God's plan. People are the largest group of holdouts in anticipating that time. It is humbling to realize that as creatures developing an eager expectation for Christ's return, we humans are the last to respond.

8:20-21 **The creation was subjected to frustration . . . by the will of the one who subjected it.**[NIV] When Adam sinned, God decreed that all of creation would be subjected to *frustration*; that is, to futility, change, and decay. Creation is frustrated because it is unable to attain the purposes for which it was made. When Solomon was seeking for wisdom and meaning within the limits of the world, his conclusion was "Everything is meaningless" (Ecclesiastes 1:2 NIV). The word translated "meaningless" in the Greek Old Testament is the same word that Paul uses here for *frustration*. The original sense of perfect order in the world was marred by sin; therefore, fallen people had to live in a fallen world. This was **not by its own choice** because it was God's doing and part of his plan of salvation.

> I beg of you for the love and reverence of God our Lord to remember the past, and reflect not lightly but seriously that the earth is only the earth.
> —Ignatius Loyola

Translating Paul's complex thought here into English is not easy. Paraphrasing has been the most helpful. For example, Phillips has, "The world of creation cannot as yet see reality, not because it chooses to be blind, but because in God's purpose it has been so limited—yet it has been given hope. And the hope is that in the end the whole of created life will be rescued from the tyranny of change and decay, and have its share in that magnificent liberty which can only belong to the children of God!"

In hope that the creation itself will be liberated from its bondage.[NIV] The word for *hope* indicates anticipating a future event. Eventually this frustration will end and creation will be **brought into the glorious freedom of the children of God**[NIV]—freedom from sin, evil, decay, and death. Revelation 22 describes the future removal of the curse from the earth.

Adam and Eve were the first polluters of the environment when they sinned. Their act of rebellion affected the entire world. It has taken many centuries to realize the inter-relatedness of this global village, but the Bible begins with that assumption. Having the same Creator links us with the rest of the created order. But as much as we do personally and corporately to clean up and care for the environment, we must realize that the creation will require the same kind of transformation that we require in order to be set straight again. The world is wearing down, and God has a recycling plan in mind. One of the psalmists contemplated creation's future in this way: "In the beginning you laid the foundations of the earth, and the heavens are the work of your hands. They will perish, but you remain; they will all wear out like a garment. Like clothing you will change them and they will be discarded. But you remain the same, and your years will never end" (Psalm 102:25-27 NIV). Making creation a god is only worshiping a power that is finite and destructible. We have been charged to care for the world, and to worship her Creator.

The ultimate answers about the meaning to life cannot be found among the wonders of earth, nor in the far reaches of the universe. For those, we must turn to God.

8:22 **The whole creation has been groaning in labor pains until now.**NRSV Paul pictures the fallen earth in pain. Consider earthquakes, floods, fire, drought, famine—these are surely not what creation was meant to be, but sin and evil now rule. Just as the pains of childbirth end at the birth of the child, so the groaning and pain of the creation will end at the birth of the new earth. This *groaning* is not impatient, but "eager" (8:23). It is not the *groaning* of hopelessness, but the sound of total concentration on a painful, but hopeful conclusion. It is not the despairing cry of the hopeless, but the eager longing of the hopeful. Before the glory is revealed there is a time of groaning. Creation groans and longs for its release and transformation into the new heaven and new earth. We groan, longing for our own release from the cycle of sin and decay (8:23). We long for the full redemption of our bodies in the resurrection. In this process we are not alone, for the Holy Spirit groans with us, expressing our unutterable longing to God. But until the time of our release and redemption, we must groan, wait, and hope.

THE REAL WORLD
Christians see the world as it is—physically decaying and spiritually infected with sin. But Christians do not need to be pessimistic, because they have hope for future glory. They look forward to the new heaven and new earth that God has promised, and they wait for God's new order that will free the world of sin, sickness, and evil. In the meantime, Christians go with Christ into the world, where they heal people's bodies and souls and fight the evil effects of sin.

8:23 **We also who have the firstfruits of the Spirit.**NKJV This verse returns to the train of thought Paul began in verse 18, the present

sufferings of believers. We know that God will fulfill his promises of future glory because of the witness of the Holy Spirit
within us. The Holy Spirit is like the firstfruits of a farmer's harvest—a guarantee of more to come. To the Ephesians, Paul described the Holy Spirit as "a deposit guaranteeing our inheritance
until the redemption of those who are God's possession" (Ephesians 1:14 NIV).

**Groan inwardly as we wait eagerly for our adoption as sons,
the redemption of our bodies.**NIV To creation's groaning is now
added ours. Like creation, we have the promises but lack the final
realization of glory. Our sufferings cause us to groan inwardly;
God's promises cause us to wait eagerly. Although we have already received adoption into God's family (8:15), we are still
awaiting our completed adoption, identified here as *redemption*
(see also 8:19, 21). Paul discusses this principle of *adoption* at
length in Galatians 3:26–4:7. This will occur when Christ returns,
when our bodies will be transformed, and we will live with him
forever (see 1 Corinthians 15:42-54; 2 Corinthians 5:1-5; 1 Thessalonians 4:13-18). In the meantime, our groans are not imaginary. We see, touch, hear, and smell the destruction of our
environment; we watch our aging bodies decay and fail; we see
the destructive elements in nature. They remind us of Jesus'
words, "Heaven and earth will pass away, but my words will
never pass away" (Mark 13:31 NIV).

8:24 **In this hope we were saved.**NIV When we put our faith in Christ
as Savior, we receive this hope: that we will be redeemed. Paul
wrote of this assurance in other letters: "By faith we eagerly
await through the Spirit the righteousness for which we hope"
(Galatians 5:5 NIV); and "Christ in you, the hope of glory" (Colossians 1:27). We already have the presence of the Holy Spirit, who
is unseen, but we must eagerly wait for our new bodies, that are
also unseen.

The redemption of our bodies.NRSV Our bodies will be redeemed
in the resurrection (see 2 Corinthians 4:7–5:10). In Ephesians
4:30 Paul calls it the day of our redemption. When that day
comes, we will fully realize all that our sonship guarantees.

**Hope that is seen is no hope at all. Who hopes for what he al-
ready has?**NIV Our full redemption has not yet happened; it will
happen when Christ returns. That is why it is still a *hope* for believers.

CAN'T WAIT!
We keep looking in confidence for what we cannot see. Our eager anticipation is like that of the person who drives all night and eagerly looks forward to the sunrise, when the mist and darkness will be driven away. He knows it will happen and can't wait. His assurance of it carries him on. We look forward to:
- Our new bodies.
- The new heaven and the new earth.
- Rest and the rewards of service.
- Our eternal family and home.
- The absence of sin and suffering.
- Being face to face with Jesus Christ.

8:25 **If we hope for what we do not yet have, we wait for it patiently.**[NIV] Our salvation is both present and future. It is present because the moment we believe in Jesus Christ as Savior we *are* saved (3:21-26; 5:1-11; 6:1-11, 22-23); our new life (eternal life) begins. But at the same time, we have not fully received all the benefits and blessings of salvation that will be ours when Christ's new kingdom is completely established. While we can be confident of our salvation, we still look ahead with hope and trust toward that complete change of body and personality that lies beyond this life.

Waiting for things *patiently* is a quality that must be developed in us (see Romans 5:3-4; James 1:3-4; 5:11; Revelation 13:10; 14:12). Patience is one of the Spirit's fruit borne in our lives. It includes fortitude, endurance, and the ability to bear up under pressure in order to attain a desired goal.

BE PATIENT
It is natural for children to trust their parents, even though parents sometimes fail to keep their promises. Our heavenly Father, however, never makes promises he won't keep. Nevertheless, his plan may take more time than we expect. Rather than acting like impatient children as we wait for God's will to unfold, we should place our confidence in God's goodness and wisdom. Yet even the most patient children will groan in anticipation when what they are waiting for is wonderful.

8:26 **Likewise, the Spirit also helps in our weaknesses.**[NKJV] In the same way that our "hope" gives us fortitude, the Holy Spirit strengthens us and sustains us through times of trial. Our weakness (evidenced by our "groaning," 8:23) may be physical, emotional, or spiritual. While we were yet sinners, Christ interceded for our sins; as believers, the Spirit intercedes for our weakness. At times, our weakness is so intense that **we do not know what we ought to pray for, but the Spirit himself intercedes for us with groans that words cannot express.**NIV At those times when we don't know what to pray for or how to pray because we don't know what God's will for us is, the Spirit voices our requests for us. He intercedes by appealing to the only one who can help us, God himself. We may not know the right words to say, but the Holy Spirit does. His groanings to God become effective intercession on our behalf.

> The Holy Spirit lays hold of our weaknesses along with us and carries his part of the burden facing us as if we were carrying a log, one at each end.
> —A. T. Robinson

The companionship of the Spirit in prayer is one of the themes of this chapter. It is the Spirit who urges us to call *"Abba*, Father" (8:15). Here, the Spirit literally "joins in to help" us, expressing for us what we can't fully express for ourselves. How should we pray?

- Utilize all the forms prayer takes: adoration, confession, petition, thanksgiving, and meditation. As we pray, we should trust the Spirit to make perfect what is imperfect.

- Listen during prayer. We should ask the Spirit to search our hearts and minds, and then we should be silent.

- Practice prayer as a habit.

- Combine prayer with other regular spiritual disciplines (see Philippians 4:4-8).

- Confess sins that the Spirit points out.

8:27 **He who searches our hearts knows the mind of the Spirit.**NIV The One who searches our hearts is God, and he also knows what the Spirit is requesting (see 8:26). God can look deep, past our inarticulate groanings, to understand the need we face, our hidden feelings.

The Spirit intercedes for the saints in accordance with God's will.NIV This is a beautiful picture of the Trinity. The Father knows what is being requested because he knows the Holy Spirit; elsewhere we read that Jesus Christ also intercedes for us (8:34).

HELP IN PRAYING
As believers, we are not left to our own resources to cope with problems. Even when we don't know the right words to pray, the Holy Spirit prays with and for us, and God answers. With God helping us pray, we don't need to be afraid to come before

him. We simply ask the Holy Spirit to intercede for us "in accordance with God's will." Then, when we bring our requests to
God, we trust that he will always do what is best.

NOTHING CAN SEPARATE US
FROM GOD'S LOVE / 8:28-39

Alongside the theme of glory in the Christian life is the theme of
victory. We get to be on the winning side, though our contribution
is almost insignificant. We are protected by a God whose love
cannot be measured and from which, as Paul will eloquently explain, absolutely nothing can separate us.

This section begins with some concluding remarks on how
God responds to our prayers and the trials that motivate them.
Paul briefly outlines God's plan, emphasizing God's effective
work in our behalf. Following this, Paul asks, "If God is for us,
who can be against us?" (8:31). His answer includes a listing of
problems and situations that might threaten us, but are unable to
ever "separate us from the love of God that is in Christ Jesus our
Lord" (8:39). Even though we don't know how to pray according
to God's will, the Spirit does. That is why it all works for the
good. God gives us what we truly need, not what we want.

8:28 **We know that in all things God works for the good of those
who love him.**^{NIV} This verse develops the thought introduced at
the end of verse 27. Paul emphasizes that the Spirit's efforts on
our behalf are carried out in full agreement with God's will, to
bring us to maturity. This is expressed elsewhere by Paul: "He
chose us in him before the creation of the world to be holy and
blameless in his sight" (Ephesians 1:4 NIV).

Everything that happens to us in this life is directed toward that
goal. What happens may not itself be "good," but God will make
it work to our ultimate good, to meet his ultimate goal for our
life. In the KJV this well-known verse reads, "All things work together for good to them that love God . . . "The wording is
smooth and familiar but, unfortunately, can lead to a misunderstanding of Paul's point. God works all things for good, not "all
things work out." Suffering will still bring pain, loss, and sorrow,
and sin will bring shame. But under God's control, the eventual
outcome will be for our good.

God works behind the scenes, ensuring that even in the middle
of mistakes and tragedies, good will result for *those who love
him*. At times this will happen quickly, often enough to help us
trust the principle. But there will also be events whose results for
good we will not know until eternity. Paul knew this from his

own experience: "Now I want you to know, brothers, that what has happened to me has really served to advance the gospel" (Philippians 1:12 NIV); "I will boast all the more gladly about my weaknesses, so that Christ's power may rest on me. That is why, for Christ's sake, I delight in weaknesses, in insults, in hardships, in persecutions, in difficulties. For when I am weak, then I am strong" (2 Corinthians 12:9-10 NIV).

Who are called according to his purpose.NRSV God's Spirit called us, convinced us of our sinfulness, showed us what Christ could do for us, and then helped us to accept Christ. Our ultimate destiny is to be like Christ. God's design is more than just an invitation; God summons us with a purpose in mind: we are to be like Christ and share his glory.

IN ALL THINGS

God works in all things—not just isolated incidents—for our good. This does not mean that all that happens to us is good; evil is prevalent in our fallen world. But God is able to turn it around for our long-range good. Note that God is not working to make us happy, but to fulfill his purpose. Note also that this promise can be claimed only by those who love God and are "called according to his purpose." Those who are called are those the Holy Spirit convinces and enables to receive Christ. Such people have a new perspective on life. They trust in God, not life's treasures; they look to their security in heaven, not on earth; they learn to accept, not resent, pain and persecution, because God is with them.

8:29 **Those whom he foreknew.**NRSV Believers are those people whom God foreknew. God's foreknowledge refers to his intimate knowledge of us and our relationship with him based on his choosing us. God **predestined** believers to reach a particular goal: **to be conformed to the image of his Son.**NRSV "Now we are children of God, and what we will be has not yet been made known. But we know that when he appears, we shall be like him, for we shall see him as he is" (1 John 3:2 NIV).

What does predestination mean? What keeps foreknowledge and predestination from being determinism? How can belief in predestination avoid leading someone to despair over the futility of any human choice? God's foreknowledge does not imply determinism—the idea that all our choices are predetermined. Since God is not limited by time as we are, he "sees" past, present, and future at the same time. Parents sometimes "know" how their children will behave before the fact. We don't conclude from these parents' foreknowledge that they made their children act that way. God's foreknowledge, insofar as we can understand it, means that God knows who will accept the offer of salvation. The plan of predestination begins when we trust Christ and comes to its conclusion when we become fully like him. Receiving an airline ticket to Chicago means we have been predestined to arrive in Chicago.

To explain foreknowledge and predestination in any way that implies that every action and choice we make has been not only preknown, but even predetermined, seems to contradict those Scriptures that declare that our choices are real, that they matter, and that there are consequences to the choices we make.

That he might be the firstborn among many brothers.[NIV] Some families have such distinct characteristics (for example, Dad's brown eyes or Mom's blonde hair) that everyone immediately knows the children are all related. In the case of believers, the distinguishing family characteristic is that we all are becoming like our oldest brother. When all believers are conformed to Christ's likeness, the resurrected Christ will be the firstborn of a new race of humans, who are purified from sin. Because we are God's children, we are Christ's brothers and sisters.

Some believe these verses mean that before the beginning of the world, God chose certain people to receive his gift of salvation. They point to verses like Ephesians 1:11, which says we are "predestined according to the plan of him who works out everything in conformity with the purpose of his will" (NIV). Others believe that God *foreknew* those who would respond to him; upon those he set his mark (predestined). What is clear is that God's *purpose* for human beings was not an afterthought; it was settled before the foundation of the world. Humankind is to serve and honor God. If we have trusted Christ as Savior, we can rejoice that God has always known us. His love is eternal. His wisdom and power are supreme. He will guide and protect us until we one day stand in his presence.

8:30 **Those whom he predestined he also called.**[NRSV] God's plan for the salvation of those who believe in Christ has three steps: **called** (see 1:6; 8:28), **justified** (3:24, 28; 4:2; 5:1, 9), and **glorified** (8:17; Colossians 1:27; 3:4). While being *glorified* is a future event, Paul writes it in the past tense to show that it is so certain to happen that it is as good as done. When we are finally conformed to the image of Christ, we will be glorified. Paul's description of God's meticulous plan for our future underscores the length God will go to work "for the good of those who love him" (8:28). In his original summary of the gospel, Paul described a constant component of salvation, "faith from first to last" (1:17). Faith is at work in each segment of the way of salvation: by faith we recognize we have been *called* (the message of the gospel is personalized); by faith we are *justified* (God reckons us righteous which we could never achieve by our efforts); by faith we are *glorified* (we arrive at the destination that God intended all along)— we become "conformed to the image of his Son" (8:29). In each of these steps, God is the active agent, while we are the responsive subject.

WANTED
Predestination is God's plan whereby his purpose is carried out. The emphasis is on God's choosing, like the illustrations that Jesus used of the feast and banquet in Luke 14. We are chosen to participate so that we might say, "I was wanted," not, "I deserve this."

8:31 **What then are we to say about these things?**[NRSV] Paul's questions fall into three categories:
   1. Will opposition from people or Satan be too great? (8:31-32)
   2. Will we fail because of our tendency to sin? (8:33-34)
   3. Will we be overcome by difficult times? (8:35-39)

In broad terms, Paul may be encouraging specific reflection on the evidences we have that **God is for us**. One way of doing this is to replace *these things* with some of the phrases Paul has used earlier in this chapter. For example, **what then shall we say in response to** [NIV] the fact that "there is now no condemnation for those who are in Christ Jesus" (8:1)? Or, what then shall we say in response to the fact that "the Spirit helps us in our weakness" (8:26)? What then shall we say in response to the fact that "in all things God works for the good of those who love him" (8:28)?

The other option for considering what to *say in response* is the choice Paul makes. He asks rhetorical questions, the answers to which require application of the pattern God has already established for our day-to-day experiences. So, for instance, since *God* has shown that he *is for us, who* of any real significance *can be against us?* Or, since God "did not spare his own Son . . . how will he not also, along with him, graciously give us all things?" (8:32). Paul wants to let believers know, in no uncertain terms, that their salvation is sure and secure. When we fully realize that

God has called, justified, and glorified us, we can do nothing but fall before him in humble gratitude.

If God is for us, who can be against us?[NKJV] Satan and those under his power are against us, but in the end, God promises the victory. No one will oppose God and his followers forever; their dreadful end is also sure.

8:32   **He who did not spare his own Son, but gave him up for us all.**[NIV] How much is God "for" us? So much that he gave us his only Son to die for us. (The Greek word behind "for" is *huper*, a benefactive pronoun meaning "on behalf of.") Only through Christ's death are we been made acceptable to God. The word for *spare* is the same word for "withheld," used in Genesis 22:12, when God said to Abraham, "You have not withheld from me your son, your only son" (NIV).

Our major struggle with prayer is not that God doesn't answer. What upsets us is that he seldom answers in line with our plans or schedule. At those times we may think that God is intentionally withholding something from us. But God has already given us the greatest gift of all. Remembering God's gift will help us see that God is working for our good even when we can't immediately see it. So when we are most tempted to doubt God's love for us, we ought to express our love to him. This allows us to apply the lesson of verse 28, trusting that God is working in all things for our good.

How will he not also, along with him, graciously give us all things?[NIV] God sacrificed his Son to save us; will he now invalidate that sacrifice by refusing to help and guide believers? No, instead, he promises to *give us all things* to bring us to the ultimate goal—our sanctification and glorification. These *things* come under the guideline as the *things* in verse 28; they are experiences God will give us as he "works for the good" that he has planned for us (see also Matthew 6:33). When the Bible promises that God will answer our prayers, it does not oblige God to give us anything we ask of him. Rather, these promises are reminders that we are presenting requests to someone who is infinitely free and powerful to act. The fact that his grace motivates his giving ensures that his gifts are best for us.

8:33   **Who will bring any charge against those whom God has chosen?**[NIV] Paul's next question is, Who can press charges or accuse us? At first we might think of Satan because he is our accuser (Revelation 20:10). And his charges will contain truth, because despite being saved, we still will sin. But the charges won't stick—God will throw Satan's accusations out of court because he has *chosen* us. The word *chosen* (*eklekton*) has been transliterated from Greek and Latin into English as the word *elect*. In the Bible, election refers to God's choice of an individual or group for a specific purpose or destiny (see 9:10-13). God is the one who chooses us, and he is also the Judge who has already declared us "not guilty." When Satan accuses us, Jesus, the advocate for our defense, stands at God's right hand to present our case (8:34). Thus, the result is that no one can bring a charge against God's chosen ones. (See also Isaiah 50:8-9. For more on the concept of Christ as our advocate, see the notes in Hebrews 4:14-16.)

8:34 Who is he who condemns?NKJV Like the last question, this one focuses on charges, but in Greek it carries a future tense: Who *will* condemn? Jesus Christ has been appointed by God to judge the world (John 5:22, 27; Acts 17:31), but **Christ Jesus, who died . . . is at the right hand of God, who indeed intercedes for us.**NRSV This is a divine court. God has already declared us "not guilty." Any further charges of guilt are thrown out of court. Jesus would not condemn those for whom he died. Because he **was raised to life,**NIV Christ Jesus is at God's right hand interceding for us in heaven (see also Psalm 110:1; Mark 12:35-37; Hebrews 4:14-16). The Spirit intercedes for us (8:27) and Christ intercedes for us. How much more advocacy do we need?

A LETTER TO YOU
Do you ever think that because you aren't good enough for God, he will not save you? Do you ever feel as if salvation is for everyone else but you? At those times, make verses 31-34 your constant companions. If God gave his Son for you, he isn't going to hold back the gift of salvation! If Christ gave his life for you, he isn't going to turn around and condemn you! Christ will not withhold anything you need in order to live for him. The book of Romans is more than a theological explanation of God's redeeming grace—it is a letter of comfort and confidence addressed to you.

8:35 Who shall separate us from the love of Christ?NIV The next questions help seal our assurance in God. Nothing can separate us from Christ's love for us. Then Paul lists several situations we might think could come between us and God. Paul knew from experience that these could not separate believers from God—he had already experienced them (see 2 Corinthians 11:23-28). This means that *the love of Christ* doesn't separate us from these experiences, but that even in the most devastating of these, *the love of Christ* is with us.

Shall trouble or hardship or persecution or famine or nakedness or danger or sword?^{NIV} These words are almost eerily prophetic. The Roman church would face severe persecution within just a few years. But no matter what happens, believers can never be lost to God's love. When suffering comes, it should not drive us away from God, but rather help us to identify with him further and allow his love to reach us and heal us.

8:36 As it is written . . . Paul quotes from Psalm 44:22 to remind the believers that people who trust in God must expect to face persecution, even death. In that psalm, the poets made the specific point that difficulties and suffering were coming to people who had been faithful. The two verses preceding the one that Paul quotes say, "If we had forgotten the name of our God or spread out our hands to a foreign god, would not God have discovered it, since he knows the secrets of the heart?" (Psalm 44:20-21 NIV). Believers who suffer are the rule, not the exception.

8:37 We are more than conquerors through him who loved us.^{NRSV} No, instead of being separated from Christ through *all these things* (the trials and hardships mentioned in 8:35), we are the conquerors. This does not mean that we will be superheroes, but that our victory will be intensified by virtue of our union with Christ.

WHAT MEANS MORE THAN VICTORY?
Paul tells us that through Christ we are more than conquerors. Paul is saying that we surpass Alexander the Great and Caesar because of our faith in Christ. For high achievers, this is good news indeed. There is something better than winning. Perhaps the best way to grasp what Paul means is to realize that the experience of victory can be extremely selfish. To be more than conquerors means that our moments of spiritual achievement coincide with moments of realization that we have succeeded through him who loved us. The glow of the greatest victory dims in the light of Christ's love for us.

8:38 I am convinced.^{NIV} Or, "I have been persuaded," implies a deep and settled frame of mind. When we express our beliefs, we may say, "I think." When speaking of the most important matters of time and eternity, we need to become not people who happen to think a certain way, but people who are *convinced*. For Paul, conviction was a matter of faith confirmed by God's Word, experience, and a transformed mind. In a similar context, when Paul is explaining to Timothy the tension between being a servant of the gospel of Christ and yet experiencing suffering, he shares his conclusions: "Yet I am not ashamed, because I know whom I have believed, and am convinced that he is able to guard what I have entrusted to him for that day" (2 Timothy 1:12 NIV; see also 2 Corinthians 5:11-15; Galatians 5:7-9; 2 Timothy 3:14-17).

> It is very hard for a man to defend anything of which he is entirely convinced . . . but a man is not really convinced of a philosophic theory when he finds that something proves it. He is only really convinced when he finds that everything proves it.
>
> —G. K. Chesterton

Neither death nor life, neither angels nor demons, neither the present nor the future, nor any powers.NIV Yes, we are secure in Christ—Paul was *convinced,* and so should we be. Nothing will separate us from God's love for us (8:39). In both *death* and the trials of *life* in this evil world, we will be in God's presence. No spiritual forces, such as *angels* or *demons,* are powerful enough to undo what God has done for us. Nothing in the sphere of time itself can threaten us; nothing that can happen in *the present* and nothing that can happen in *the future*, such as persecution and hardship, would cause God to leave us. No *powers* that exist (Satan, human governments, etc.) are more powerful than God; they can have no effect on our relationship with him.

8:39 **Neither height nor depth, nor anything else in all creation, will be able to separate us from the love of God that is in Christ Jesus our Lord.**NIV Nothing in space, from *height* or *depth,* can take us away from God's love; these words denoted astronomical terms that cover the entire heavens; thus, no supposed astrological powers that might have been thought to determine people's fate have any power over God. Nothing *in all creation* can take us away from God's love or thwart his purposes for us.

Here Paul defends the claim of Christ's love against all that might seem to offer a threat. Elsewhere, he describes that love itself: "And I pray that Christ will be more and more at home in your hearts, living within you as you trust in him. May your roots go down deep into the soil of God's marvelous love; and may you be able to feel and understand, as all God's children should, how long, how wide, how deep, and how high his love really is; and to experience this love for yourselves, though it is so great that you will never see the end of it or fully know or understand it. And so at last you will be filled up with God himself" (Ephesians 3:17-19, TLB). Paul's point is simple and compelling: once in his care, it is impossible to be separated from Christ. His death for us is proof of his unconquerable love. Nothing can stop his constant presence with us. God tells us how great his love is so that we will feel totally secure in him.

Romans 9

The end of chapter eight marks the conclusion of the first major section of Romans. Paul has discussed the doctrines of justification, sanctification, and glorification. But before Paul moves on to address practical concerns of local church life (in chapters 12-15), he feels compelled to speak about God's plan for the Gentiles and the Jews, Paul's very own people.

Had God abandoned the Jews? Paul had already resolutely answered no to such a conclusion in chapter 3. Yet if the Jews were God's chosen people, why did most of them oppose the gospel? If the gospel really is the fulfillment of the Hebrew Scriptures, why don't the Jews recognize it as such? And how does one make sense of God's choice of Israel and his promise to bless the world through them when the Jews had rejected the gospel?

Paul completely understood the feelings of the Jews who refused to accept Jesus as their Messiah—he had once been so opposed to Christ that he had hunted down and imprisoned Christians. But then Paul was confronted by Christ and became a changed man. Though he was the "apostle to the Gentiles," Paul was still so concerned for his people that he was willing to be "cursed" (9:3) to bring Jews to the Savior. Furthermore, Paul knew that the church at Rome had a unique opportunity to use the diverse personal backgrounds of its members to strengthen the cause of Christ. Paul tackled many of the issues in this letter for the sake and unity of both Jewish and Gentile Christians.

The key verse in chapter 9 is verse 16: "It does not, therefore, depend on man's desire or effort, but on God's mercy." For Paul, every question sooner or later led the inquirer to accept or reject God's sovereignty.

9:1 My conscience confirms it by the Holy Spirit.[NRSV] Paul uses *conscience* to refer to that inner prompting that confirms or disapproves of our conduct. Believers should have well-tuned consciences because they also have the Holy Spirit within. The words Paul would write bear the truth—he is **not lying,** as his conscience confirms. Paul reveals his depth of feeling here; as the apostle to the Gentiles, with his great zeal for preaching to the Gentiles, he was probably often accused of turning his back on his own people.

9:2 **Great sorrow and unceasing anguish.**^{NRSV} Despite his great success as a missionary to the Gentiles, a church planter, and a writer of letters of teaching and assurance to those churches, Paul still feels great sorrow. Most of the Jews, his people, the chosen people of God, were rejecting the gospel. The Jews should have been the first to recognize the gospel as the promised fulfillment of their Scriptures, but somehow they missed it. They were missing out on salvation, and this hurt Paul deeply.

Though his commission to preach the gospel took him outside Jewish boundaries, Paul never lost his love for his Jewish brothers and sisters. Later in this letter, Paul writes of his plan to visit Palestine in order to deliver a special financial gift to the saints in Jerusalem. Acts 21 records his return to Zion and his arrest in the temple. The next day (Acts 23) he confronted the Sanhedrin in God's name. In his travels for the gospel, Paul always kept the door of the gospel open to those from his own race.

9:3 **I could wish that I myself were accursed.**^{NKJV} Paul's agony was so intense that he was willing to be **accursed and cut off from Christ** (NRSV) if, by doing so, his brothers, the Israelites, would be saved. Paul has just written of the dependability of God's love (8:35-39); here he expresses desire that his people could take his place in knowing God. Paul knew that it was only a short step of faith from all the past blessings the Jews already had to the infinitely greater gift that God wanted to give them. Yet that small step might as well have been a vast gulf, for very few Jews were responding to Christ. For his people's sake, Paul would have borne the curse himself if it would have ensured their salvation. Of course, he knew it would be impossible for God to curse him, but his expression shows the intensity of his affection for his people. (Compare Moses' similar attitude about Israel in Exodus 32:32.)

God has given you friends, acquaintances, and loved ones that he wants to reach through you. Can you have the same love, concern, and compassion that Paul had for his Jewish brothers and sisters?

IN THEIR PLACE
To what lengths will we go to offer the gospel to someone else? Paul consistently loved the Jews. They are one group that still needs to hear the gospel. But there are others, too. Sometimes the barriers to overcome are racial, linguistic, or cultural. Other times the distance is nothing more than social or geographical. Our lack of compassion is directly addressed in Scripture: "If anyone says, 'I love God,' yet hates his brother, he is a liar. For anyone who does not love his brother, whom he has seen, cannot love God, whom he has not seen" (1 John 4:20 NIV). One of our persistent prayers needs to be for more love.

9:4-5 **Theirs is the adoption as sons.**NIV With this phrase, Paul begins a list of eight benefits of being a Jew (see the chart on the next page). Last on this list of blessing is **the patriarchs** (NRSV)— Abraham, Isaac, Jacob, and Jacob's twelve sons. From the patriarchs **is traced the human ancestry of Christ**NIV (see Matthew 1:1-16; Romans 1:3), thus all Israel is in line to receive God's promises. And it is in Christ that all God's promises to Israel are fulfilled.

Paul made the point earlier that those who share Abraham's faith will share his inheritance (4:11-17). This makes believers co-heirs of Abraham along with Jews. But we have problems in our churches similar to the ones Paul faced. The church has its own share of noncommitted members who practice a religion that relies on membership as a substitute for personal faith and spiritual discipline. At a certain point, the amount of nominal belief in a church cripples it almost entirely as a vehicle for the gospel. (If faith isn't personal, it may disappear.) The privileged children of faith who have no sense of sacrifice, vision for missions, personal commitment, surrender of time and comfort, or renunciation of rest and reward, will eventually stray from home.

Christ, who is God over all, forever praised!NIV For some, Christ is really not a separate benefit, but the reason behind all the other benefits. Everything that God had given the Jews prepared the way for Christ. Because of the lack of punctuation in Greek, there have been differences of opinion over what Paul meant to say with this phrase. Some translators choose to make the phrase refer to God the Father, "May God, supreme above all, be blessed for ever!" (NEB), while others decide in favor of a reference to Christ, "Christ who is God over all, blessed for ever" (Phillips). Both are possible. Sometimes, an ambiguous original is most honestly translated with the ambiguity preserved. For example, "from whom is the Christ according to the flesh, who is

BENEFITS OF BEING A JEW

- They are sons of God by adoption.
    - "Israel is my firstborn son" (Exodus 4:22).
    - "Yet the Israelites will be like the sand on the seashore, which cannot be measured or counted. In the place where it was said to them, 'You are not my people,' they will be called, 'sons of the living God'" (Hosea 1:10).
    - "When Israel was a child, I loved him, and out of Egypt I called my son" (Hosea 11:1).
- They had the divine glory, or visible presence of God, dwelling among them.
    - "By day the Lord went ahead of them in a pillar of cloud to guide them on their way and by night in a pillar of fire to give them light, so that they could travel by day or night. Neither the pillar of cloud by day nor the pillar of fire by night left its place in front of the people" (Exodus 13:21-22).
    - "Then the cloud covered the Tent of Meeting, and the glory of the Lord filled the tabernacle" (Exodus 40:34-35).
    - "The glory of the Lord filled his temple" (1 Kings 8:11).
- They were given the covenants. God made covenants with his people. God's promises never go unfulfilled. The Old Testament records five covenants:
    - The Abrahamic covenant—"On that day the Lord made a covenant with Abraham and said, 'To your descendants I give this land'" (Genesis 15:18, see also 17:4-21).
    - The Mosaic covenant—The Ten Commandments (Exodus 20:1-17).
    - The Reestablished covenant—"I am making this covenant, with its oath, not only with you who are standing here with us today in the presence of the Lord our God but also with those who are not here today" (Deuteronomy 29:14-15).
    - The Davidic covenant—"Your house and your kingdom will endure forever before me; your throne will be established forever " (2 Samuel 7:16).
    - The New covenant through Jeremiah—"'This is the covenant I will make with the house of Israel after that time,' declares the Lord. 'I will put my law in their minds and write it on their hearts. I will be their God, and they will be my people'" (Jeremiah 31:33).
- They received the law. God gave his law to Israel (see Exodus 20:1ff.; Deuteronomy 5:1-22).
- They worshiped in the temple. Israel also was given the worship ceremony prescribed for the tabernacle and the temple (see especially the book of Leviticus).
- They were given God's promises. This refers especially to the promised Messiah—promises of his arrival are found throughout the Old Testament (see Luke 24:27).
- Last in this list of blessings is the patriarchs—Abraham, Isaac, Jacob, and Jacob's twelve sons. From the patriarchs is traced the human ancestry of Christ (Matthew 1:1-16; Romans 1:3), thus all Israel is in line to receive God's promises. And it is in Christ that all God's promises to Israel are fulfilled.
- They have Christ, who is God over all, forever praised! For some, Christ is really not a separate benefit, but the reason behind all the other benefits. Everything that God had given the Jews prepared the way for Christ.

Note: Above Scripture quotations from NIV.

over all, God blessed forever" (NASB, also KJV). This last allows
the reader to choose. God the Father can be the focus as long as
our choice is not against inferring that Christ is divine. And
Christ remains, always, worthy of our praise.

9:6 It is not as though God's word had failed.NIV The Jewish nation as
a whole did not respond to the gospel, even though God's gifts had
made them better prepared than any other nation to receive Christ.
On the surface, the covenants and promises seem not to have accomplished their purpose, but this does not mean that God's word had
failed. Human beings failed. Earlier in this letter, Paul clarified that
not all who are descended from Israel are Israel—that is, not all
Jews are part of spiritual Israel (see 2:28-29; 11:5-6; Galatians 3:7-9). Israel's history demonstrates that God was fulfilling his promises,
apart from human failures and misunderstandings. Paul illustrates
this from three Old Testament events: (1) verses 7-9, the lineage
passing from Abraham to Isaac, rather than Ishmael (see Genesis 16–
21); (2) verses 10-16, the lineage passing from Isaac to Jacob, rather
than Esau (see Genesis 25–28); (3) verses 17-18, the hardening of
Pharaoh's heart (see Exodus 7–12).

THE INFALLIBLE WORD
As long as there have been Scriptures, there have also been
those unwilling to submit to the Scriptures' authority. Many treat
the Bible as an old book, a leatherbound relic to display and
keep dusted. Others turn to it only in times of crisis or in
church. But even studying the Bible and knowing it well doesn't
guarantee a right relationship with God. Obedience proves
whether or not a person considers the Bible to be, in fact,
God's Word. So people who do not read, study, understand,
and obey God's Word may doubt its power. But God's Word
never fails, even though some doubt it. If you want to see
God's Word *succeed* in your life, if you want to experience
God's power, treat the Bible as though it is what it claims to be,
the infallible Word from almighty God—read it, study it, understand its principles for living, and apply those truths to your life.
In short, do what the Bible says—LIVE it.

**9:7 Nor because they are his descendants are they all Abraham's
children.**NIV Paul's first illustration of God's sovereign choice is
Abraham and his children. Just being Abraham's physical descendants did not guarantee an inheritance. The line of natural descent
was not the same as the line of promise. Abraham had children by
three different women (Isaac, by Sarah—see Genesis 21:1-7; Ishmael, by Hagar—see Genesis 16; and six sons by Keturah—see

Genesis 25:1-4). But God made it clear that the line of promise would be through Isaac only: "It is through Isaac that your offspring will be reckoned" (Genesis 21:12 NIV). God made a sovereign choice regarding who among Abraham's physical descendants would carry the line of promise, the line that would result in the Messiah. God did not choose Isaac because he was better than his half brothers; the choice was made before Isaac was even born. Instead, it was simply God's sovereign choice.

The Jews were chosen as special recipients and emissaries of God's grace. Their opportunity to participate in that plan arrived with the coming of Christ. As John puts it, "He came to that which was his own, but his own did not receive him. Yet to all who received him, to those who believed in his name, he gave the right to become children of God—children born not of natural descent, nor of human decision or a husband's will, but born of God" (John 1:11-13 NIV). That gracious opportunity to receive Christ and become a child of God is still producing offspring today!

9:8 Not the natural children who are God's children, but it is the children of the promise who are regarded as Abraham's offspring.NIV Paul repeats the statement of verse 7 in other words. The "children of promise" are the spiritual offspring of Abraham, including all true believers. It is not by being *natural children*, born in the line of Abraham and Isaac, that the Jews can be saved and considered *God's children* and *children of the promise* (notice the distinction between "natural children" and "God's children"). Instead, it is by believing in God's Son, Jesus Christ.

9:9 This is what the promise said.NRSV God made a promise to Abraham when he and Sarah were childless and very old. The promise said, **"At the appointed time I will return, and Sarah will have a son"**NIV (see Genesis 18:10). Abraham believed this promise. As Paul has already explained in chapter 4, it was Abraham's faith—his belief in God's promise—that justified him before God. Abraham is a helpful model of faith in two ways: (1) he believed the specific promise that God gave to him and his descendants (Genesis 12:1-7); (2) more significant, he trusted in the God who keeps promises. Between Abraham and God there was an agreement, but there was also a personal relationship.

Trusting God will also push us beyond our comfort zone. Abraham trusted God when the covenant was made, but his trust grew when he packed his bags and traveled into the unknown. How often do you act simply out of trust that your action is what God wants you to do?

9:10   **Rebekah's children had one and the same father ... Isaac.**^{NIV}
Paul's second illustration of God's sovereign choice focuses on
Isaac and Rebekah's twin sons, Jacob and Esau. God chose to
continue the line of blessing through the younger son, Jacob,
rather than Esau (Genesis 25:23). This was quite unusual in the
Hebrew culture, where the firstborn son was highly honored. In
Abraham's case, Isaac and Ishmael were sons of different
women—each was a firstborn, so a choice had to be made. But
Isaac and Rebekah were the parents of children over whom God
had a sovereign purpose. Again, this had nothing to do with either
son's character, because the choice had already been made.

9:11   **Before they had been born or had done anything good or bad.**^{NRSV}
Jacob was not chosen because he was "better" than Esau; he was
chosen **not by works but by him** [God] **who calls**^{NIV} (see 9:12).
Jacob's future conduct does not even enter into the discussion because it was unrelated to God's choice.

In order that God's purpose in election might stand.^{NIV} God's
sovereignty, not people's works or character, is the basis for election. The Jews were proud of the fact that their lineage came from
Isaac, whose mother was Sarah (Abraham's legitimate wife),
rather than from Ishmael, whose mother was Hagar (Sarah's
maidservant). Paul asserts that no one can claim to be chosen by
God because of his or her heritage or good deeds. God freely
chooses to save whomever he wills. The doctrine of election
teaches that it is God's sovereign choice to save us by his goodness and mercy, and not by our own merit.

The word *election* actually takes on a technical sense within
the letter to the Romans. The fact of God's choice was important
to Paul, but the words he uses (*eklektos, ekloge*) are the natural
expressions for "choice." We find them in this letter in the following sequence: 8:33; 9:11; 11:5, 7, 28; 16:13. The doctrine of election emerges when we use the entire Bible as a source. But,
assuming that the original readers did not have other Pauline letters to consult for corroboration, what would they have learned
from this letter about the ways that God chooses?

▪ Once God chooses, no charges against that person will hold (8:33).

▪ God's choices are not based on the character or actions of the
  one chosen, but on his own merciful purposes (9:11; 11:5).

▪ God's chosen ones will be faithful, while others, with the same
  evidence, will turn away (11:7).

- God's love for his original chosen ones (Israel) is based on his promises to the patriarchs (11:28).

- God's choosing is personal and specific, not general (16:13).

Election is like receiving an invitation for a banquet that we know will be wonderful. But the invitation comes unearned. No friendship or effort has created an expectation that we ought to be on the invitation list. The choice to invite is purely the host's. After all, it is his banquet. The invitation comes with the traditional R.S.V.P. God's gracious invitation does request our response and attendance.

9:12 By him who calls.^{NIV} When Paul uses *call,* the context often indicates that he also has *response* in mind (see 8:28ff.), emphasizing the effectiveness of the call. The source of the call is God, and the vehicle of the call is the gospel that sets into motion a life of faith. Salvation and sanctification make the call effective. Jesus explained the other side of this concept when he differentiated between the "called" ("those who hear") and the "chosen" ("those who respond") (Matthew 22:14).

She was told, "The elder shall serve the younger."^{NRSV} God told Rebekah, while the twin boys were still in her womb, that Esau (the elder twin) would serve Jacob. Esau himself did not serve Jacob, but Esau's descendants, the Edomites, did serve Jacob's descendants, the Israelites (see 1 Samuel 14:47; 2 Samuel 8:14; 1 Kings 11:15-16; 2 Kings 14:7).

Was it right for God to choose Jacob, the younger, to be over Esau? God chose Jacob to continue the family line of the faithful because he knew that Jacob was teachable. But he did not exclude Esau from knowing and loving him. We must remember what God is like: he is sovereign; he is not arbitrary; in all things he works for our good; he is trustworthy; he will save all who believe in him. When we understand these qualities of God, we will know that his choices are good even if we don't understand all his reasons.

9:13 As it is written, "Jacob I have loved, but Esau I have hated."^{NKJV} These words refer to the nations of Israel and Edom rather than to the individual brothers (see Malachi 1:2-3). God chose Jacob to continue the family line of the faithful. *Esau I have hated* refers only to God choosing Jacob and rejecting Esau for continuing the line of promise. The choice of Jacob for such a great privilege made the rejection of Esau seem like hatred by

comparison. God did not exclude Esau from knowing and loving
him. God was not rejecting Esau's eternal salvation; he was
choosing Jacob to lead the nation. (Other such uses for *hate* and
hatred are found in Luke 14:26 and John 12:25.)

Paul answers the concern voiced in verse 6 and shows that God's
Word has *not* failed. The Jews have simply misunderstood it. They
missed the truth that God's election *never* has anything to do with
works of the law, rituals, even family or community ties. They misunderstood their own election as God's people. They settled on enjoying the benefits of God's promises, rather than fulfilling their role
as emissaries for sharing God's promises with the world. While we
enjoy the gracious benefits of our salvation, we must not ignore the
others whom God wants to reach through us.

9:14 **Is God unjust?**[NIV] God chose Isaac over Ishmael and Jacob over
Esau, not because of their character or their actions, but simply
because that was his choice. "Doesn't that seem a bit unfair?" we
might ask. "Surely those Jews who are working so hard to follow
all of God's laws should be chosen. Isn't it rather arbitrary of
God to just choose some and reject others?"

Paul's wording of the question in Greek expects a negative answer, which he emphatically supplies: **Not at all!**[NIV] If God gave anyone exactly what they deserved the results would be disastrous! Both
Isaac and Jacob were scoundrels. God demonstrated unexpected
grace when he chose these men in spite of their weaknesses and failures. That same grace is available to us in God's offer of salvation. If
we were to receive what we deserve, we would have no hope. We
should come to God for mercy, not for justice.

9:15 **He says to Moses.** God is absolutely sovereign. He had explained to
Moses, **"I will have mercy on whom I have mercy, and I will have
compassion on whom I have compassion"**[NRSV] (see Exodus 33:19).
We might still be tempted to say, "Doesn't that seem a bit unfair?"
But by asking such a question we are claiming a higher understanding of fairness than God himself. We must remember that God
has no obligation to show mercy or compassion to any of us—not
one of us deserves his slightest concern. For God to even choose
anyone is evidence of his great mercy. These words of God reveal
that he *does* show mercy and compassion, but they are by *his* sovereign choice.

We tend to read God's statement to Moses (which was a response to Moses' request to see God's glory) as if it were an expression of God's withholding mercy rather than a statement of
his merciful generosity. In the context of this statement in Exo-

dus, God was not justifying himself, but saying in effect, "I will have mercy on people you would not expect, and I will have compassion in ways that will surprise you, especially when I am compassionate with you!" No one can know the heart of a person in the way that God knows. No individual, court of law, or group can perfectly assess the righteousness of a person. So we must leave the choosing and judging to God.

9:16 **It does not . . . depend on man's desire or effort.**ᴺᴵⱽ God chose Israel out of mercy, and he will keep his promises to them regardless of their works. God chose them, but they still held on to the belief that their strict adherence to the law was a condition for them to maintain their "chosen" status. Paul makes it clear that God's mercy and compassion have nothing to do with what people want or try to achieve.

GOOD INTENTIONS
This fallacy remains as strong as ever—people still think good intentions are the key to unlock the door to eternal life. By the time they get to try the lock, they will find that their key does not fit. Others imagine that their efforts are building an invisible ladder to heaven made up of service, family, position, reputation, good work, and desire, although none of these rungs will support a feather. People are so busy trying to reach God that they completely miss the truth that God has already reached down to them. We cannot earn God's mercy—if we could, it would not be mercy.

9:17 **For the Scripture says to the Pharaoh.**ᴺᴷᴶⱽ For a third illustration of God's sovereign choices, Paul recalls Pharaoh. Through Moses, God told Pharaoh, **"I raised you up for this very purpose, that I might display my power in you and that my name might be proclaimed in all the earth"**ᴺᴵⱽ (see Exodus 9:16). God had purposely placed that particular Pharaoh in that particular position at that particular time in history so God's great power would be displayed (through the miracles witnessed in Egypt and by the incredible release of the Hebrew slaves), and so his name would be known over all the world. God put up with Pharaoh's fickleness and defiance for quite some time, but all for the same purposes. Pharaoh became mired in his own rebelliousness. In fact, part of God's judgment on Egypt was the hardening of Pharaoh's heart. Eventually, those nations who heard what God had done for his people in Egypt greatly feared the Israelites and their God (see Joshua 2:10-11; 9:9; 1 Samuel 4:8).

THE TRAGEDY OF A HARDENED HEART
God gave Pharaoh many opportunities to heed Moses' warnings. But finally God seemed to say, "All right, Pharaoh, have it
your way," and Pharaoh's heart became permanently hardened. Did God intentionally harden Pharaoh's heart and over-
rule his free will? No, he simply confirmed that Pharaoh
freely chose a life of resisting God. Similarly, after a lifetime
of resisting God, we may find it impossible to turn to him. We
can't wait until just the *right* time before turning to God, because we won't see it when it comes. The *right* time is now. If
you continually ignore God's voice, eventually you will be unable to hear it at all.

9:18 God has mercy on whom he wants to have mercy.[NIV] Again someone might ask, "Doesn't it seem a bit unfair that God would just use
somebody to glorify himself?" But Paul answers the implicit question as before: God has mercy on whomever he chooses; and con-
versely, **he hardens whom he wants to harden.**[NIV] God's judgment
on Pharaoh's great sinfulness was to "harden" his heart, to confirm
his disobedience so that the consequences of his rebellion would be
his own punishment. "Hardening" occurs when a person has a track
record of disobedience and rebellion. From the human perspective, it
is difficult to know exactly at what point God confirms our own resistance as hardness. Paul's implicit warning is to avoid attitudes that
lead to hardness of heart (see 1 Corinthians 10:6; Hebrews 3:8).

Everything comes from God's sovereign choices. Israel, as
God's chosen people, had made a grave mistake in acting with superiority over others who were not of God's "chosen" nation. It
was that pride that made them misunderstand their own Scriptures that said that God would offer salvation beyond Israel, to
people from all nations.

9:19 Why then does he still find fault?[NRSV] Paul probably had countless discussions with fellow Jews about these issues. So he can
anticipate their questions. If God simply chooses those on whom
he will have mercy and those whom he will harden, why would
he punish those whom he has hardened? They were acting in accordance with his will, right? How can God hold people responsible for *his* choices—**for who has resisted His will?**[NKJV]

Occasionally these questions are asked by those who are genu-
inely seeking to understand God and his ways with people. Usually, however, they are used to excuse certain behavior—"It's not
my fault, God; it's your fault!" In either case, as Paul explains,
the answer is the same. We ourselves are to blame because we are
guilty of trying to reject or resist God. And even this questioning

of God is an attempt to bring him down to our level. It is impossible for finite beings to totally understand an infinite God and how he works. We *do know,* however, that we have made choices to do what we know is wrong, to disobey God. Therefore, we are guilty. In fact, our consciousness of blame is practically an admission of blame. We ask why God blames us, while inside our consciences are blaming us. We may sincerely wonder just how much freedom we have to act within God's sovereignty, but there is little doubt that we use the freedom we do have to sin.

STAGES IN THE HARDENING PROCESS

Stage 1 Abandoning God's guidance from his Word or believers	*Example* "I don't read the Bible or attend church." "Who are they to tell me what to do?"
Stage 2 Willfully disobeying God, based on desire for sin or unresolved conflict with God	"I know it's wrong, but I want it." "Where was God when I needed him?" "How could he do this to me?"
Stage 3 Justifying sin as not really being sin, but as being essential for the person's welfare	"I'm not sure this is really wrong." "I'm not as bad as others." "I'll feel better."
Stage 4 Rejecting the Holy Spirit's conviction	"I know I'll feel guilty, but I don't care." "I'll just ignore it."
Stage 5 Becoming entrenched in the sinful behavior	"I'm in too deep to get out." "I might as well finish what I started."

9:20 Who indeed are you, a human being, to argue with God? Paul has little patience for such questions, and he supposes that God doesn't either. When it comes down to it, we cannot question God. He is absolutely sovereign. We are extremely privileged to have any relationship with him at all. His dealings with all the world are not to be judged by us. Quoting from Scripture, Paul illustrates the absurdity of such questions: **"Will the thing formed say to him who formed it, 'Why have you made me**

like this?"NKJV This passage was taken from Isaiah 29:16 and/or Isaiah 45:9; in context it expresses God's response to his rebellious people. Isaiah 64:8 conveys the correct attitude, "O LORD, you are our Father. We are the clay, you are the potter; we are all the work of your hand" (NIV).

While God welcomes our sincere questions and concerns (see for example, John the Baptist in Matthew 11:1-6, and Thomas in John 20:24-29) and patiently answers us, he will not allow sinners to question his sovereignty. The creature has no right to sit in judgment on the Creator.

9:21 **The potter.** To further illustrate God's sovereignty, Paul compares God to a potter (a very common and necessary vocation in ancient times, since most cooking and storage was done in various types of clay pots). The potter has every right to take one large lump of clay and use part of it to make a delicate vase (**one object for special use**) and another part of it to make a pot for cooking (**and another for ordinary use**).NRSV Neither vase nor pot has any right to complain and ask why the potter did what he did. The potter has every right to do what he pleases with the clay; and God has every right to do what he pleases with people, who are his creation. The lesson of the *potter* points to equal worth among lumps of clay, while the artist's purpose and design may differ. The proper attitude for clay is to be pliable rather than stiff, receptive rather than rebellious, and grateful for the potter's touch rather than resentful of the potter's purpose for us.

Jeremiah 18:1-10 also refers to a potter and clay. In this case, the potter began making a pot, but it "was marred in his hands; so the potter formed it into another pot, shaping it as seemed best to him" (Jeremiah 18:4 NIV). Not only does the potter make whatever he wants; he may also change and reform the clay as needed. Paul points out that all people must humbly submit to their Creator, performing the tasks for which they have been made. God wants all his creation to be flawless—for some that means being remade. We should look to God to discern his ultimate purpose for our life instead of comparing ourselves with others.

> Though justice be thy plea, consider this,
> That in the course of justice, none of us
> Should see salvation.
> —William Shakespeare
> (*The Merchant of Venice*)

9:22 **What if God . . . bore with great patience the objects of his wrath.**NIV The two "what if" questions in verses 22 and 23 again focus on God's sovereignty. What if God does these things? Who

has the right to question him? The Creator can do as he chooses
with his creation.

The *objects of his wrath* are unbelievers, and especially, in context, Jewish unbelievers (1:18). God has been patient with their
antagonism, rebellion, blasphemy, and hatred because he is giving them time to repent (2 Peter 3:9). But those who refuse to repent are **prepared for destruction.**^{NKJV} Their doom is coming.
They had rebelled and refused to turn to God for salvation, and
thus they took responsibility for their own destruction. So God
has prepared the punishment for their sin. They will experience
his *wrath* for their sins and his **power** that they had constantly refused to acknowledge.

Without God's mercy and *great patience*, shown to us completely apart from our performance, we would have no hope at
all. If God did not do this for his own purposes, we would be in-
stantly destroyed.

**9:23 What if he did this to make . . . his glory known to the objects
of his mercy.**^{NIV} In contrast, *the objects of his mercy* are Gentile
believers **whom he prepared in advance for glory.**^{NIV} The objects of his mercy are true believers, whether Jews or Gentiles, so
no one can claim God by right of birth. Three of God's purposes
are mentioned in verses 22-23: (1) **to show his wrath**; (2) to
make his power known; and (3) **to make . . . his glory
known.**^{NIV} But what is the *this* to which Paul is referring? *This* is
God's sovereign choosing when he works with "pots" prepared
for destruction (9:22) or with "pots" prepared for glory. The key
point to remember is that all this has been in God's plan from the
beginning. When God's dealings with his creation have been
summed up, there will not be a shred of doubt about his wrath,
power, and glory. God did not change his plans just because his
people were disobedient. Instead, God knew all that would happen to both Jews and Gentiles, and God does everything to display his great mercy.

Believers still may wonder why they would be chosen
while others were rejected. Paul's point is that God is sovereign and that *no one* has any claim on his mercy. He prepared us in advance by his gift of salvation, and he will
reveal his glory when we are finally with him for eternity. Instead of focusing on God choosing some and rejecting others, we should stand in awe at God's offer of grace to any of
us. Thus, no one can demand that God explain why he does
what he does. He makes all the rules. But he loves to show
mercy to us—what an amazing God he is!

MAKING GLORY KNOWN
To what lengths will our sovereign God go to make his glory
known? We may assume that God will show his anger before
his mercy. Consequently, when unexpected hardships come,
we may think that God is punishing us for something. We find it
difficult to believe that God would allow us to experience pain in
order that we might grow in our understanding of his mercy and
himself.

That was certainly the disciples' problem in John 9. They as-
sumed that the man born blind was suffering the consequences of some sin that he or his parents had committed.
Jesus surprised them with the true explanation: "Neither this
man nor his parents sinned, . . . but this happened so that the
work of God might be displayed in his life" (John 9:3 NIV). Jesus
used a healing touch to demonstrate the mercy of God. When
you are experiencing difficulties, remember that your response
to your problems and God's work in your life can glorify God.

9:24 **Including us whom he has called.**^{NRSV} Paul and the Roman Christians were a part of that group of *objects of mercy* whom God had
called and was preparing for glory. This group obviously was made
up **not only from the Jews but also from the Gentiles.**^{NIV} God's
choices are always sovereign. He sovereignly chose a messianic line
from Abraham, and he sovereignly chose many Gentiles to receive
salvation. Only those who respond to God's call receive the gift of
salvation; it is "by invitation only." It comes to us completely undeserved so that we might have no basis for pride. When we understand God's mercy, we respond with humility and gratitude that God
would be merciful to even us.

:25-26 **He says in Hosea.**^{NRSV} To back up the statement that God also
calls the Gentiles, Paul quoted two verses from the prophet
Hosea. Several hundred years before Jesus' birth, Hosea told of
God's intention to bring Gentiles into his family after the Jews
would reject his plan. God was not surprised by Israel's rejection.
Israel thought that they alone were God's chosen because of their
lineage and their laws. But God's plan never was to save only the
Jews. His call was for people from all nations. Verse 25 is a quotation from Hosea 2:23, and verse 26 is from Hosea 1:10.

Hosea had married Gomer. Hosea named their firstborn child
Jezreel. But the next two children were not his, so he obeyed God
and named them Lo-Ruhamah and Lo-Ammi, meaning, as the
words of verse 25 indicate, **not my people** and **not my loved one**.^{NIV}

Hosea's situation and his children's names pictured God's attitude toward Israel—they had turned away from him and were no
longer called his people or his loved ones. But God would not let

this situation remain forever; one day he would call Israel back to himself. God would also turn to the Gentiles, those who are outside his chosen nation. Some day, many Gentiles would be considered God's people, his loved ones, his children. Paul saw that while God's plan had always made room for the Gentiles, with the advent of Christ, the doors to the kingdom were opened wide. Those not known as God's people were becoming his people by God's mercy and grace, shown through Christ.

9:27 Isaiah also cries out concerning Israel.^NKJV But the Jews, the people who were in number **like the sand of the sea** in number (NIV; see Genesis 32:12; Isaiah 10:22), will not be forgotten. God's sovereign choice always includes some Jews, but his promises were not a blanket guarantee for all Israel. Isaiah prophesied that only a small number—a **remnant**—of God's original people, the Jews, **will be saved**. Paul saw this happening in every city where he preached. Even though he went first to the Jews, relatively few ever accepted the gospel message. Quoting from Isaiah 10:22-23 and 1:9, Paul explained that the majority of Israel had turned away from God. But God always preserves a remnant for himself, "a remnant chosen by grace" (11:5). The remnant are those people who remain faithful to God whenever the majority doesn't (see Micah 5:7-8).

9:28-29 Carry out his sentence.^NIV Continuing the quote from Isaiah (Isaiah 10:23), God will punish his people for turning away from him. In the captivity and the exile, much punishment had been meted out.

Had left us descendants.^NIV If God had not spared a remnant of faithful believers, all of Israel would have been destroyed. But God always saved a remnant. Having chosen Israel, God remained faithful to her. If he had not, Israel would have been **like Sodom** and **Gomorrah**, the ancient cities that were completely destroyed by God for their horrible wickedness (see Genesis 19:24-29; Isaiah 1:9). Nothing was left of Sodom and Gomorrah. But God never completely destroyed his people. Today the Gentiles are the majority in the church, but one day, many Jews too will come to their Savior. There is a final judgment to come, and God will carry it out. There is no time to delay. A remnant will be saved—who of God's people, the Jews, will become part of that remnant? Paul explores this further in chapter 11.

ISRAEL'S UNBELIEF OF THE GOSPEL / 9:30–10:21

This section provides a summary in the middle of Paul's exposition on God's sovereign plan and an expanded explanation of the present position of the Jews. He realized that his teaching was creating a paradox, especially for his Jewish audience. How could it be that the acknowledged experts in righteousness would find their way to God barred, while those who were ignorant of righteousness were welcomed by God as long-lost children? Paul here contrasts the way of faith with the way of the law. Israel, following after a law of righteousness, did not attain it—while the Gentiles, not seeking righteousness by the law, found it by faith in Christ.

Whereas chapter 9 has focused primarily on God's sovereignty, chapter 10 outlines the extent of human responsibility.

9:30 Gentiles, who did not pursue righteousness [i.e., a law that produces righteousness], **have attained to righteousness.**NKJV The gospel was preached to both Jews and Gentiles, but it was being accepted by far more Gentiles than Jews. The Gentiles did not have God's law, did not even know God, and were not even "trying to be righteous," yet they were obtaining righteousness. Why? Because they were coming *in faith* to God.

9:31 Israel, who pursued a law of righteousness, has not attained it.NIV In contrast to the Gentiles, the Jews tried to obtain righteousness by obeying the law, only to never attain it. They had incorrectly understood righteousness in terms of works. They could not keep the law perfectly, therefore they could not keep it at all. Thus God could not accept them.

9:32 They pursued it not by faith.NIV Instead of admitting that they could not keep God's law and pursuing righteousness by faith in God, the Jews kept trying to pursue righteousness by their **works.** They had a worthy goal—to "obtain" God's righteousness. But they tried to achieve it the wrong way—by rigid and painstaking obedience to the law. Thus some of them became more dedicated to the law than to God. They thought that if they kept the law, God would have to accept them as his people. But God cannot be obligated by us. The Jews did not see that their Scriptures, the Old Testament, taught salvation by faith and not by human effort—the point Paul made in the first part of this letter. As a result they **stumbled over the stumbling stone**NRSV—the Lord Jesus Christ (see 1 Peter 2:4-8). Jesus was not what they expected, so they missed him. In so doing they missed their only way of salvation. Jesus is a stumbling block to Jews and to all who by pride would rather have recognition for doing it on their own than for trusting Christ and his goodness.

Some people still stumble over Christ because salvation by faith doesn't make sense to them. They would rather try to work their way to God, or else they expect him simply to overlook their sins. Others stumble over Christ because his values are the opposite of the world's. Christ asks for humility, and many are unwilling to humble themselves before him. He requires obedience and many refuse to put their will at his disposal. The "stone" has caused them to stumble. They heard about Christ and misunderstood, so they tripped over the one thing that could have saved them.

NEVER GOOD ENOUGH
Sometimes we are like those people who try to achieve God's approval by keeping his laws. We may think that going to church, doing church work, giving offerings, and being nice will be enough. After all, we've played by the rules, haven't we? But Paul's words sting—this approach never succeeds. Paul explained that God's plan is not for those who try to earn his favor by being good; it is for those who realize they can never be good enough and so must depend on Christ. Only by putting our faith in what Jesus Christ has done will we be saved. If we do that, we will never be "put to shame" or disappointed.

9:33 **As it is written.** Paul quotes from Isaiah 28:16. Isaiah declared God's warning of destruction to Israel by Assyria. Then he said, **"See, I lay in Zion a stone that causes men to stumble and a rock that makes them fall."**[NIV] This *stone* refers to the righteous remnant and to Christ.

"The one who trusts in him will never be put to shame."[NIV] When we put our trust in Christ, we need never fear that we have put it in the wrong place. When we have placed our feet on the Rock of Zion, the Lord Jesus Christ himself, we can be confident of our salvation.

THE STUMBLING OR HUMBLING STONE
Jesus is a stumbling block to Jews and to all who would rather have the satisfaction of gaining God's acceptance on their own than admit their inability and then submit to God's grace. When we are presented with Christ, we have only two possible responses, to reject or accept. Any form of rejection will result in our stumbling over him, resulting in judgment. But trusting submission to him will gain for us what we could never hope to gain by ourselves—a righteous standing with God. Isaiah showed the way by personally applying the phrase he used above, "I will put my trust in him" (Isaiah 8:17 NIV). Are you stumbled or humbled by Jesus?

Romans 10

10:1 **Brothers.** Though fully engaged in matters concerning his fellow Jews, his blood brothers, Paul also includes his broader audience in the Roman church by calling them *brothers*. He knows that neither Jews nor Gentiles can claim superiority in the church. And any unity apart from Christ would not be real. Meanwhile, Paul's concern for the Jews is genuine and heartfelt; his **desire** and **prayer** is **that they may be saved** (see also 9:1-3).

What will happen to the Jewish people who believe in God but not in Christ? Since they believe in the same God, won't they be saved? If that were true, Paul would not have worked so hard and sacrificed so much to teach Jews about Jesus Christ. Because Jesus is the most complete revelation of God, no one can fully know God apart from knowing Jesus; and because God appointed Jesus to bring God and human beings together, no one can come to God by another path. The Jews, like everyone else, can find salvation only through Jesus Christ (John 14:6; Acts 4:12). Just as Paul did, we should wish that all Jews might be saved. We should pray for them and lovingly share the Good News with them. In fact, we should ask ourselves, *Who do I desire to be saved, and am I regularly praying for them?*

10:2 **They are zealous for God.**[NIV] The Jews certainly were zealous in their devotion to God and their practice of the law—Paul knew that from his own experience. However, **their zeal is not based on knowledge.**[NIV] The people Paul loved (the Jews) were so busy trying to keep the law that their zeal was actually keeping them from understanding God's way of salvation. This was exactly Paul's state of mind before Christ confronted him. He was so zealous for God and for his religion that he persecuted Christians (see Acts 9:1-2; 22:3-5; 26:4-11). His zeal was based on a misunderstanding of God's Word, and so was the zeal of his fellow Jews (see chapter 9).

WHY GOOD INTENTIONS CAN'T SAVE US
- Starting out with good intentions does not ensure the results will be good.
- Possessing good intentions does not guarantee that any action will be taken.
- Good intentions by themselves do not fulfill the demand to love God with all our heart, soul, mind, and strength.
- Our ever-present bad intentions are often hidden from us.
- Good intentions can lead to false pride.
- Good intentions can seek to bypass and alter God's clear commands.
- Good intentions can be a cover-up for ignoring or willfully disregarding God's desires.
- Good intentions may appear to do so, but they cannot actually make up for bad deeds.

Many people claim that they are acting with good intentions when, in fact, their efforts are halfhearted. They want to dictate the way God should accept them. But none of our best intentions can save us.

10:3 **Being ignorant of the righteousness that comes from God.** NRSV The Israelites did not understand the extent of God's righteousness, how it would be achieved, and how it would be made available to all people (the point Paul explained in chapters 3–6). Instead, they sought **to establish their own**. They were not creating some new kind of righteousness; rather, they wanted to achieve God's righteousness by observing the law and their rituals. Once their minds were set, they could no longer **submit to God's righteousness,** NIV the righteousness that God provided for them through faith in Jesus Christ.

We are made righteous by humbly submitting to God. The Israelites had understood the need for obedience, but they had become so zealous in carrying out their duties and rituals without love that they had actually become disobedient. And when they tried to make God's righteousness exclusively theirs, they were putting themselves out of its reach. They misunderstood their own Scriptures: they saw righteousness in terms of outward actions, rituals, and customs; they did not see that their Scriptures pointed to Jesus as the Messiah. When Israel rejected Christ, they rejected their own Scriptures with the promises and blessings in them. According to Philippians 3:1-9, Paul remembered being stuck on the treadmill of effort. By human standards he had been quite successful in what he later realized was actually a self-styled, self-approved, and self-justified religion. In order to believe in Christ, Paul had "lost" all those things, only to discover that what he had gained was of immeasurable value. "What is

more," he said, "I consider everything a loss compared to the sur-
passing greatness of knowing Christ Jesus my Lord, for whose
sake I have lost all things" (Philippians 3:8 NIV).

RECEIVE THE GIFT
Rather than living by faith in God, the Jews established customs and traditions (in addition to God's law) to try to make
themselves acceptable in God's sight. Regardless of our sincer-
ity, no human effort can ever substitute for the righteousness
that God offers us by faith. The only way to *earn* salvation is to
be perfect—and that is impossible. We can only hold out our
empty hands and receive salvation as a gift.

10:4 **Christ is the end of the law.** There are at least three possible explanations for what Paul meant by Christ being the **end of the
law**. In Jesus, the law was:

(1) *Terminated.* Instead of seeking justification through the
law, we receive justification by faith and use the law to guide our
obedience to God. Through Christ, the offer of grace is universal.

(2) *Replaced.* The law literally pointed to Christ. The law was
only the teacher, or mentor, until Christ came (see Galatians
3:24). Now we follow his lead.

(3) *Fulfilled.* Christ was the law in human form. He met every
criteria of the law, completing it and transcending it (see Matthew
5:17-20). He spoke with authority to divide the unchangeable law
from the human additions and twisted interpretations.

While each of these is a valid explanation of part of the relationship of Christ to the law, Paul seems to have had the first in
mind at this point in Romans. The law, however, is terminated
only in the sense of 7:6—that is, we have been released from the
law to serve in the newness of the Spirit. We no longer seek justification by keeping the law.

Whatever reasons Israel had for misunderstanding God's law
and God's righteousness, those ended with Christ. Christ is the
end of the law in several possible ways (see the chart on page
197). Christ fulfills the purpose and goal of the law (Matthew
5:17) in that he perfectly exemplified all that the law requires.
But he is also the termination of the law, because with the coming
of Christ, the law became powerless to save (3:20; 7:7).

However, Paul does *not* mean that the law has been cast aside
and is no longer of any value. Jesus completed the law. With the
coming of Christ, the puzzle that looked like it was going to be a
picture of human righteousness suddenly turned out to be a picture of God's grace. Jesus did not change the law—he changed

our way of seeing the law. Paul has amply explained this in such verses as 3:31 and 8:4. What ended was the view that the law was the way to achieve righteousness and the belief that Israel was the only recipient of that righteousness.

Righteousness for everyone who believes.^{NRSV} Christ perfectly fulfilled the law; then he gave his life to pay the penalty that we deserved for breaking the law. So, instead of "seeing" ourselves fearfully attempting to meet the demands of the law (with death as the consequence for failure), we are now freely invited to "see" ourselves in Christ. His righteousness becomes our righteousness. When we believe in him, he gives us righteousness (8:3-4) and makes us acceptable to God.

10:5   Moses writes concerning the righteousness that comes from the law.^{NRSV} Paul quotes freely from Moses. The first quote is from Leviticus 18:5, a section in Leviticus that gives God's instructions to the people for how they should live in the Promised Land. He explains that they are not to be like the people of the land, but are to obey God's laws because **"the person who does these things will live by them."**^{NRSV} In Leviticus, this phrase is preceded and followed by God's self-affirmation, "I am the LORD your God." From Paul's repeated insistence, we know that he was not demeaning the law. So how are we to understand this reference to Moses? The meaning hinges on what was intended by *live.* Was God promising that the person who lived by the law would live eternally? Or was God stating that obeying the law was the best way to live on earth, without reference to eternity. So the idea might be paraphrased, "In following the law, a person will find a godly way of life, rather than the ungodly life of following the ways of the Egyptians or Canaanites." This was what God required for them if they were to obtain his blessings and flourish in the Promised Land (see also Nehemiah 9:26).

The Jews carried the concept further, however, trying to obtain more than godly living by a *righteousness that comes from the law.* In essence, they interpreted God's statement to mean, "Keep the law and you will live eternally by it." But in order to do so, they would have to live perfectly, not sinning once—and that is impossible (see James 2:10). *Righteousness that comes from the law* is the ideal way of life, but it cannot be achieved well enough to merit God's acceptance. For that level of righteousness, supernatural help is needed.

Why did God give the law when he knew people couldn't keep it? According to Paul, one reason that the law was given was to show people how guilty they are (Galatians 3:19). In addition, the law was a shadow of Christ—that is, the sacrificial system educated the people so that when the true sacrifice came, they would be able to understand his work (Hebrews 10:1-4). The system of ceremonial laws was to last until the coming of Christ. The law points to Christ, the final sacrifice for sin, the reason for all those animal sacrifices.

HEBREW WORDS FOR LAW

Hebrew law served as the personal and national guide for living under God's authority. It directed their moral, spiritual, and social life. Its purpose was to produce better understanding of God and commitment to him.

Word	Meaning	Examples	Significance
Torah	Direction, Guidance, Instruction	Exodus 24:12; Isaiah 30:20	Need for law in general; a command from a higher person to a lower
Mitsvah	Commandment, Command	Genesis 25:5; Exodus 15:26; 20:2-17; Deuteronomy 5:6-21	God's specific instruction to be obeyed rather than a general law; used of the Ten Commandments
Mishpat	Judgment, Ordinance	Genesis 18:19; Deuteronomy 16:18; 17:19	This refers to the civil, social, and sanitation laws
Huqqim	Statutes, Oracles	Leviticus 18:4; Deuteronomy 4:1	Dealt with the royal pronouncements—mainly connected to worship and festivals

10:6 Righteousness that comes from faith.NRSV Moses also wrote about righteousness by faith. In verses 6-8, Paul recalls phrases from Deuteronomy 30. The book of Deuteronomy includes Moses' final speeches to Israel as they were about to enter and subdue the land that God had promised to them many years before. Moses recited the blessings they could look forward to for their obedience to God, as well as the curses they could expect if they disobeyed and turned away from him.

At the conclusion of his third address to the people, Moses explained, "Now what I am commanding you today is not too difficult for you or beyond your reach. It is not up in heaven . . . . Nor is it beyond the sea . . . . No, the word is very near you; it is in your mouth and in your heart so you may obey it" (Deuteronomy 30:11-14 NIV). In other words, the people knew what they had to do to please God. The message was as near as their mouths and hearts. No one would have to go up to heaven or cross the sea to get it so that they would know what to obey. They knew what God required of them, and they could do it if they chose. But they also knew what God had committed himself to do, which is the point of Deuteronomy 30. There God spoke of his intention to "circumcise your hearts and the hearts of your descendants, so that you may love [God] with all your heart and with all your soul, and live" (Deuteronomy 30:6 NIV). From the beginning, the law had been given with the understanding that it would guide those who submitted to God. Without that submission, the law's effectiveness was nullified.

Paul applies those words to the people of his generation, speaking of a relationship to Christ. The truth of righteousness by faith in Christ is now known. And the way to achieve it is not beyond our abilities.

"Do not say in your heart, 'Who will ascend into heaven?'" (that is, to bring Christ down).NIV No one has to go up to heaven to bring Christ down as though he had never been incarnated; Christ himself has already come in the flesh (John 1:14). The attitude that Paul is attacking is the assumption that one's righteousness can contribute to God's saving plan. Self-righteousness goes looking for God, seeking to find him. Righteousness by faith begins by submitting to God, allowing him to find us.

10:7   **"Or 'Who will descend into the deep?'" (that is, to bring Christ up from the dead).**NIV The *deep* (literally "the abyss") as used here refers to the grave or Hades, the place of the dead. No one has to go into the grave to bring Christ up from the dead; Christ has already been resurrected.

The extent of the quest in verses 6 and 7 is reminiscent of the psalmist's recognition of the universal presence of God: "Where can I go from your Spirit? Where can I flee from your presence? If I go up to the heavens, you are there; if I make my bed in the depths, you are there" (Psalm 139:7-8 NIV). Before people even begin to look for God, he is already present, and no matter how far they go out of their way to find him, he is never farther away than when they first started

out. As long as we insist on doing the finding, we will discover that
the search never ends. But if we begin by trusting God, we discover
he is to be found right where we are.

FINDING CHRIST
Paul adapted Moses' farewell challenge from Deuteronomy
30:11-14 to apply to Christ. Christ has provided our salvation
through his incarnation (coming to earth) and resurrection (coming back from the dead). God's salvation is right in front of us.
He will come to us wherever we are. All we need to do is to respond and accept his gift of salvation.

10:8 **"The word is near you, in your mouth and in your heart."**[NKJV]
Just as God's message was already clear to the people of Moses'
day, so it is as near as the mouths and hearts of Paul's readers, including us. The words convey an immediate opportunity to respond.
It is as close and available to us as it can possibly be without over-
ruling our will. What message is that? **The word of faith that we
proclaim.**[NRSV] Salvation is available through *faith* in Jesus Christ.

10:9 **If you confess with your mouth, "Jesus is Lord."**[NIV] The word
is near—as near as your mouth and heart (10:8; Deuteronomy
30:14). To "confess" (*homologeo*) means to "give verbal affirma-
tion,"—in this case to acknowledge *with your mouth* that Jesus
Christ died and was raised for you. Anyone can say he or she believes something, but God knows each person's heart. In this confession, it is not enough to merely utter the words; they must be
declared, professed, proclaimed "from the heart," expressing our
full conviction. For salvation you must truly **believe in your
heart that God raised him from the dead.**[NRSV] In 1 Corinthians
15:17 Paul asserts how the Resurrection is totally interrelated
with our salvation: "If Christ has not been raised, your faith is futile; you are still in your sins" (NIV). Jesus is distinct from all
other religious leaders: he is the only "Lord" to have risen from
the grave. This makes Christianity more than a philosophy of life
or a religious option; it is the only way to be saved.

You will be saved. The gospel message in a nutshell is "believe
and confess Jesus as Lord, and you will be saved." There is no
reference to works or rituals. The point of decision is between a
person and God, but the point of confession implies another person. It is true that God is often our first confessor, but having others witness our confession confirms our belief. In fact, to *confess*

and to *believe* become mutually related responses. If one is true, the other follows.

Jesus is Lord. The title *Lord* (*kurios*), though rarely used outside of diplomatic circles today, carried great weight in Paul's day. It was a title of respect (similar to sir), a form of address for Roman emperors (similar to "royal highness"), a title given to Greek gods, and the title used in the Greek translation of Old Testament to translate the Hebrew word *YAHWEH*. When we confess that *Jesus is Lord*, we are acknowledging his rank or supreme place. We are pledging our obedience and worship; we are placing our life under his protection for safekeeping. We are pledging ourselves and our resources to his control for direction and service. *Lord* is intended to represent the highest authority to whom we submit.

BECOMING A CHRISTIAN
Have you ever been asked, "How do I become a Christian?" These verses give the beautiful answer—salvation is as close as your own mouth and heart. People think it must be a complicated process, but it is not. If we believe in our heart and say with our mouth that Christ is the risen Lord, we will be saved.

10:10 **It is with your heart that you believe and are justified.**^{NIV} You must first believe with your heart—that belief justifies you (God declares you "not guilty" for your sins).

It is with your mouth that you confess and are saved.^{NIV} By prayer to God, you confess with your mouth your belief in God and what he has done for you. As in verses 8-9 above, belief and confession lead to salvation.

As has already been noted, neither of these components that establish our personal relationship with God can be reduced to reciting certain words or assenting to the facts. To *believe* and to *confess* involve whole-person commitment. Neither are these components described in such a way that a person might accomplish one without accomplishing the other. They are two parts of a single step, just as lifting the foot and then placing it back down are two movements in the one act of taking a step. Likewise, one cannot be *saved* without being *justified*, nor *justified* without being *saved*.

10:11 **As the Scripture says, "Anyone who trusts in him will never be put to shame."** ^{NIV}To summarize the transaction that he has just described, Paul quotes again from Isaiah 28:16, as he did at the end of chapter 9. Anyone who trusts in Christ will be saved.

What appears momentarily in verse 10 to be two separate actions turns out to be two parts to the response the Bible calls *trust* (or belief).

Paul is not saying that Christians will never be disillusioned or disappointed. At times people will let us down and circumstances will take a turn for the worse. Paul is saying that God will keep his side of the bargain—those who call on him will be saved. God will never fail to provide righteousness to those who believe.

10:12 **No difference between Jew and Gentile.**[NIV] The "anyone" of verse 11 includes both Jews and Gentiles. In 3:22-23, Paul also writes that "there is no difference." But the focus is on all people's sinfulness, for "all have sinned and fall short of the glory of God." Here, there is *no difference* because God's salvation is available to all who believe (the point Paul has been making throughout this letter), for **the same Lord is Lord of all.**[NRSV] Every person is confronted with the need to acknowledge Jesus as Lord. Because sin is a universal condition, the remedy of justification by faith universally applies.

Richly blesses all who call on him.[NIV] To call on the Lord is to trust him for salvation. Paul is keeping the parallel between confession and belief, heart and mouth, and trust and call. Those who are saved will be richly blessed—in this world (although not always materially, as some might hope or expect), and most certainly in the world to come. Paul also keeps the parallel when describing the results: justification and salvation, not put to shame and blessed.

10:13 **"Whoever calls on the name of the LORD shall be saved."**[NKJV] A final quotation taken from the Hebrew Scriptures (Joel 2:32) serves well for Paul's conclusion. God's special relationship with Israel will continue, but it has been broadened to include everyone who calls on the name of the Lord. God's plans for Israel had their climax in Christ. Access to God, for all people, now comes through Jesus Christ. With this last reference, Paul neatly lays the foundation for the necessity of worldwide evangelism. Joel 2:32 is an Old Testament mandate for missions. To call on the Lord is to ask the Lord to come to you and be real to you. Those who call on Jesus as their Lord want him to be their Lord and Savior.

10:14 **How, then, can they call on the one they have not believed in?**[NIV] If God's salvation is to "everyone who calls on the name of the Lord" (10:13), how can people call on God for salvation if they have not been moved to believe in him? **And how can they believe in the one of whom they have not heard?**[NIV] There can be no call, no belief, if these people have not heard about God ("heard" means a hearing that understands the significance of the words and realizes that a response is required), and been given the offer of salvation. And **how can they hear without someone preaching to them?**[NIV] There can be no call, no belief, no hearing, unless someone communicates the truth.

> What is the best general method of preaching? (1) to invite, (2) to convince, (3) to offer Christ, (4) to build up; and to do this in some measure in every sermon
> —John Wesley

 NEEDED: MORE THAN MODELS
In the task of evangelism, an effective witness must include more than being a good example. Eventually, someone will have to explain the content, the *what* and the *how* of the gospel. Modeling the Christian life is important, but someone will need to make the connection between the mind of the unbeliever and the message of the gospel. There should never be a debate between those who favor life-style evangelism (one's living proclaims the gospel) and confrontational evangelism (declaring the message). Both should be used together in promoting the gospel. Do people know of your faith by your actions? To whom can you communicate the life-changing message of Christ?

10:15 **How shall they preach unless they are sent?**[NKJV] There can be no call, no belief, no hearing, no preaching, unless there are those sent to share the Good News. The Greek word for "preach" (*kerusso*) is not limited to the Sunday morning sermon from the pulpit; rather, it means to announce or proclaim something. All believers are sent to announce this Good News. The process of salvation begins with the one who tells another the Good News.

As it is written, "How beautiful are the feet of those who bring good news!"[NRSV] Like Paul and the early Christians, who spread the message of Christ despite persecution and even death, we should be eager to share this Good News of salvation to all who will listen. In the verse quoted from Isaiah 52:7, the herald is bearing good news to Judah about the end of their exile in Babylon and their return to their own land. His *feet* were *beautiful* to them, for his good news was so welcome. The message was what he brought, but it was those worn and dusty feet that brought him.

Those *feet* were *beautiful* because they represented the messenger's willingness to be *sent* with *good news*. Only now the message was not just for Israel, but for the whole world.

TAKING AND TELLING
We must take God's great message of salvation to others so that they can respond to the Good News. How will our loved ones and neighbors hear about Christ unless someone tells them? Is God calling you to be a part of making his message known in your community? Besides thinking of a person who needs to hear the Good News, think of something you can do to help that person hear it. Then take that step as soon as possible.

10:16 **Not all the Israelites accepted the good news.**NIV Many Jews did not accept the gospel of Jesus Christ—they heard it but refused to believe and submit to it. The failure of Jews to respond to God's warnings of impending judgment was true in Isaiah's day, **for Isaiah says, "Lord, who has believed our message?"**NRSV It was true while Jesus preached (John 12:37-41), and it was true in Paul's day. We can expect the same today. Bringing people *good news* does not guarantee a welcome. But having been changed by the message ourselves ought to change the way we see those who have not yet heard. As Paul writes earlier in Romans, "I am obligated both to Greeks and non-Greeks" (1:14). We are not held responsible for how others respond, but we are expected to carry the *Good News*.

10:17 **Faith comes from hearing the message.**NIV This statement expresses the main theme of this section. People need to hear the Good News of salvation in Christ in order to believe it (10:14). Faith does not respond in a vacuum or respond blindly. Faith is believing what one has been told about God's offer of salvation and trusting the one who has been spoken about.

The message is heard through the word of Christ.NIV The word *of* Christ is the word *about* Christ and what he has accomplished to give salvation to all who believe in him.

10:18 **Have they not heard?**NKJV Some might argue that the Jews weren't given enough chances to hear or that somehow the message should have been made clearer for them. Perhaps Isaiah's complaint ("Who has believed?" 10:16) was the fault of the messenger. But Paul emphatically responds that **of course** they heard. The message had been preached far and wide, first to the Jews and then to the Gentiles (see 1:16). Then Paul quotes from Psalm 19:4: **"Their voice has gone out into all the earth, their words to the ends of the world."**NIV When Luke ended the book of Acts with Paul in Rome, this was probably considered a culmination of the great commission to take the gospel to the ends of the earth (Acts 1:8). At this time in history, the Good News had been preached to Jews and Gentiles for about twenty years, and it had spread throughout the Mediterranean areas where Jews lived. There may have been some Jews who truly had not yet heard, but to use that as an excuse for the large number of Jews who had rejected the gospel did not sit well with Paul (see also Romans 1:18-20).

As the loopholes close for the Jews, they close for everyone else, too. If the Jews are not excused for their unbelief, how can the rest of us think there might be some excuse for us? In the end, some may wish they had heard more, but God will declare that what they heard was enough. In the meantime, those of us who have heard have little excuse for our apathy in passing on the Good News!

10:19 Did Israel not understand?NRSV Someone might then argue, "Okay, so the Jews heard, but perhaps they didn't understand that God's message was salvation not by the law, but by faith, and that it was for the Gentiles too." Paul didn't like that excuse either. The Jews' knowledge of their own Scriptures should have led them to believe in Christ. He quotes again from their Scriptures to answer the argument. First, from Deuteronomy 32:21: **"I will make you envious by those who are not a nation; I will make you angry by a nation that has no understanding."**NIV The Gentiles were not a single nation; they consisted of everyone who was not part of the Jewish nation. The Jews would be envious that God would offer salvation to the world at large and not just to his chosen people. They would be angry that the pagan peoples whom they considered to have *no understanding* would be accepted by God. In all of this, God's purpose would not be to reject his people, but to cause them to return to him.

10:20 Isaiah boldly says, "I was found by those who did not seek me; I revealed myself to those who did not ask for me."NIV The second quote is from Isaiah 65:1. Paul was sure that **those** were the Gentiles. Although they had previously ignored God as simply the God of Israel and so had never sought him out, the Gentiles would recognize God as the one true God, and God would reveal himself to them.

The next statement in Isaiah 65:1 reads, "to a nation that did

not call on my name" (NIV). Israel considered itself to be the only
people of God, but the time would come when other nations
would seek him. Paul points out that these other nations would
seek him. God's people today are those who accept Jesus as Savior and Lord whether they are Jews or Gentiles. Since the gospel
is for everyone, we must seek to proclaim it to every nation and
race, and man and woman.

10:21 **Concerning Israel he says, "All day long I have held out my**
hands to a disobedient and obstinate people."NIV Finally, from
Isaiah 65:2, Paul explains that God had been gracious to his people, patiently holding out his hands to them and calling them,
only to have them turn away. God *held out* his *hands* to his people indicates a gesture of dual purpose: one of welcome and one
of giving. But God's welcome was spurned and his gifts were rejected.

The disobedience of *Israel* was judged by God's welcome to
the Gentiles (even though that was in his plan all along). But he
will still accept his chosen people if they will only return to him.
He remains faithful to his promises to his people, even though
they have been unfaithful to him. God still holds out his hands.

Romans 11

In this section Paul points out that not all Jews have rejected God's message of salvation. He draws upon the experience of Elijah to show that there had always been a faithful remnant among the people. In Paul's day, there was still a remnant living by faith, under the law (11:5). After all, Paul was a Jew; so were Jesus' disciples and nearly all of the early Christian missionaries. Part of God's sovereign choice involves bringing a remnant of his people back to himself. This truth forbids any hint of anti-Semitism—God's plan still includes the Jews.

11:1 **I ask, then.**NRSV Paul continues his "I ask" format that he used in 10:18 ("I ask: Did they not hear?") and in 10:19 ("I ask: Did Israel not understand?"). Paul now asks: **Has God rejected his people?**NRSV

The Jewish nation had heard such words before. In the depths of their sinfulness when King Manasseh ruled the northern kingdom of Israel, God said, "I will forsake the remnant of my inheritance and hand them over to their enemies . . . because they have done evil in my eyes and have provoked me to anger from the day their forefathers came out of Egypt until this day" (2 Kings 21:14-15 NIV). Indeed, Jeremiah had warned the people: "Cut off your hair and throw it away; take up a lament on the barren heights, for the Lord has rejected and abandoned this generation that is under his wrath" (Jeremiah 7:29 NIV). With this question Paul expresses a deep concern—has God finally grown tired of Israel's constant disobedience and rejected them forever?

Paul responds, **By no means!**NRSV—literally, "May it never be!" One proof of this is Paul's experience. Paul had received salvation, and he is **an Israelite . . . a descendant of Abraham, from the tribe of Benjamin.**NIV Paul is a full-blooded Jew (who had even gone so far as to persecute Christians before he became a believer). Surely if God was going to reject someone, Paul would have been a good choice. But God, in his sovereignty, called Paul and rearranged his entire life.

11:2-3 **God has not rejected his people.**^{NRSV} God did not reject his people in the days of Moses, nor in the days of the prophets. And he is not rejecting them now. Regardless of Israel's unfaithfulness, God always keeps his promises.

- Samuel told Israel, "For the sake of his great name the LORD will not reject his people, because the LORD was pleased to make you his own" (1 Samuel 12:22 NIV).

- A psalmist wrote, "For the LORD will not reject his people; he will never forsake his inheritance" (Psalm 94:14 NIV).

- Jeremiah prophesied, "'Only if these decrees vanish from my sight,' declares the LORD, 'will the descendants of Israel ever cease to be a nation before me.' This is what the LORD says: 'Only if the heavens above can be measured and the foundations of the earth below be searched out will I reject all the descendants of Israel because of all they have done,' declares the LORD" (Jeremiah 31:36-37 NIV).

Whom he foreknew.^{NRSV} God's foreknowledge of his people implies his special relationship with them. God chose Israel to be the people through whom all other nations of the world could know him. He made this promise to Abraham, their ancestor (Genesis 12:1-3). Israel didn't have to do anything to be chosen. God had given them this privilege because he wanted to, not because they deserved special treatment (Deuteronomy 9:4-6). God knew beforehand that Israel would be unfaithful; if God's faithfulness to Israel was going to be dependent on *their* faithfulness, God would never have chosen them in the first place. God will remain faithful to his promises to Israel, despite Israel's failure.

Elijah . . . appealed to God against Israel.^{NIV} Paul then reminds his readers of a time when all Israel had deserted God, but God had preserved a remnant. After Elijah's stunning demonstration of God's power over Baal's prophets at Mount Carmel (and the killing of all of Baal's prophets), Elijah fled for his life from the wrath of Israel's evil Queen Jezebel who threatened to have him killed. He ran for many miles and then stopped to rest. In his terror and exhaustion, he cried out to God, **"Lord they have killed your prophets and torn down your altars; I am the only one left, and they are trying to kill me."**^{NIV} "They" actually refers to the evil leadership in the northern kingdom of Israel, but Elijah was holding the entire nation responsible for the actions of many. He had concluded that he was the only person left in Israel who believed in God.

YOU ARE NOT ALONE

The prophets of Israel, for all their severity, consistently revealed God's ongoing commitment to a remnant. The messages God used to remind the people of his faithfulness were varied and persistent. You are not the *only* faithful follower of Christ; God has others. Together you are the remnant that he wants to use to impact the world.

Isaiah	Named his son Shear-Jashub, which means "a remnant will return" (Isaiah 7:3 NIV).
Jeremiah	Wrote of God as one who "will gather the remnant of my flock out of all the countries where I have driven them" (Jeremiah 23:3 NIV).
Micah	Recorded God saying, "I will surely bring together the remnant of Israel. I will bring them together like sheep in a pen, like a flock in its pasture; the place will throng with people" (Micah 2:12 NIV).
Zephaniah	Told Israel that God would "leave within you the meek and humble, who trust in the name of the LORD. The remnant of Israel will do no wrong; they will speak no lies, nor deceit be found in their mouths" (Zephaniah 3:12-13 NIV).

11:4 And what was God's answer to him? "I have reserved for myself seven thousand who have not bowed the knee to Baal."^{NIV} God shared some very important information with Elijah. Elijah was not the last of God's people left on the earth—God had seven thousand believers who had not turned to idol worship. That was not a large number, but it was a faithful "remnant." Notice that God *reserved* these faithful followers for himself—the remnant existed because of his sovereign choice.

When we experience conflict and antagonism, it is likely that we will feel alone. That is especially the case when we focus on the failure of others to recognize that we may be the last of the real followers. When we think this way, we overestimate our importance and underestimate God's power. It is shocking to discover, at times, that verbalizing our faith causes others to reject us. But we also discover, much to our delight, that until we verbalize our faith, we don't really know how many other believers there are that surround us. God always has his remnant in places we might least expect.

11:5 **There is a remnant, chosen by grace.**^{NRSV} Just as God had preserved a remnant of his people when almost the entire nation had turned to idolatry, God is restoring a remnant through Christ—and only because of God's sovereign choice and by his grace. The remnant is a small group who have remained faithful, yet it is by God's grace that the remnant stands firm. The Jewish believers in this faithful remnant are proof that God has not rejected his people (2 Kings 19:4, 19). What Paul could say with confidence in his day, we can repeat today. No matter how grim and hopeless the situation might seem, because of God's sovereignty we can say with confidence that at the present time there is still a remnant chosen by grace!

11:6 **If it is by grace, it is no longer on the basis of works.**^{NRSV} Jews who struggled to gain God's acceptance by good works and adherence to the law have lost the grace of God. But the "remnant chosen by grace" (11:5) understand that God's choice is not on the basis of works, but by his grace and mercy—his generosity to them. Salvation is *never* on the basis of works; it is always by God's merciful choice, as Paul has explained earlier in this letter. Jews who believe in Christ are not denying their faith or their heritage; instead, they are discovering what these were truly meant to be.

Otherwise, grace would no longer be grace.^{NRSV} If God's grace in choosing us depended on our works or obedience to the law, it would not be grace. "For it is by grace you have been saved, through faith—and this not from yourselves, it is the gift of God—not by works, so that no one can boast" (Ephesians 2:8-9 NIV).

GOD'S GOOD GIFT
Do you think it's easier for God to love you when you're good? Do you secretly suspect that God chose you because you deserved it? Do you think some people's behavior is so bad that God couldn't possibly save them? If so, you don't entirely understand that salvation is by grace, a free gift. It cannot be earned, in whole or in part; it can only be accepted with thankfulness and praise.

11:7 **What Israel sought so earnestly it did not obtain.**^{NIV} This verse provides an excellent summary of Romans 9–11. The nation had earnestly sought God's acceptance by doing works of the law (see 10:2-3). But God did not accept them. Instead, he accepted **the**

elect—the remnant chosen through his sovereignty and grace. Throughout the Old Testament, God dealt with the people of Israel in two ways:
(1) as individuals, and (2) as a corporate community. At times, God emphasized the responsibility that each person bears for his or her own
sins. At other times, God emphasized the fact that the entire nation
might be affected by the acts of a few. Paul uses the name *Israel* to indicate the community of Jews, most of whom rejected Jesus and most of
whom were busily but hopelessly pursuing righteousness under the law.

But the elect did.^{NIV} There was a chosen remnant among the
chosen people, however, who did respond, who did **obtain.**

The rest were hardened.^{NKJV} Israel's failure was foreseen by
God and, in fact, brought about by him (see 9:22-23, 33). This
"hardening" was confirmation of their inablility to understand
and their insensitivity to God's Word and God's call. When God
judged them, he removed their ability to see, hear, and repent;
thus they would experience the consequences of their rebellion.
But this "hardening" is not the same as rejection; rather, it confirms their response to God. Paul illustrates this "hardening"
from two passages in Scripture (as follows).

11:8 **As it is written.** This verse describes the punishment for hardened
hearts that was predicted by the prophet Isaiah.

"God has given them a spirit of stupor."^{NKJV} Paul is quoting from
Deuteronomy 29:4 and Isaiah 29:10. This *stupor* is a kind of numbness
that results in blindness (**eyes ... could not see**) and deafness (**ears
... could not hear**).^{NIV} When people repeatedly refuse to listen to God's
Good News, they eventually will be unable to hear and understand
it. Israel's present misinterpretation of their Scriptures and refusal to
accept Christ as their Messiah is a continuation of their tendency to
misunderstand God's plans and purposes for them. Paul saw this happening in the Jewish congregations he visited on his missionary journeys.

LEAVE ME ALONE!
Resisting God is like saying to him, "Leave me alone!" But because God is always and everywhere present, his answer to
that prayer might be to agree and make that person less sensitive,
more hardened to him. The very possibility of that happening
ought to keep us asking God specifically for ears that really hear
and eyes that really see—openness and responsiveness to
him.

WARNING SIGNS OF DEVELOPING HARDNESS

Hardening is like a callus or like the tough bone fibers that bridge a fracture. Spiritual hardening begins with self-sufficiency, security in one's self, and self-satisfaction. The real danger is that at some point, repeated resistance to God will yield an actual inability to respond, which the Bible describes as a hardened heart. Insensitivity indicates advanced hardening. Here are some of the warning signs:

Warning Sign	Reference
Disobeying–Pharaoh's willful disobedience led to his hardened heart.	Exodus 4:21
Having wealth and prosperity–Taking God's blessings for granted can cause us to feel as if they were owed to us.	Deuteronomy 8:6-14
Rebelling and being discontented–Suffering or discomfort can create an attitude that blames God.	Psalm 95:8
Rejecting a deserved rebuke–Rejecting God's gift makes our neck stiff and our heart hard.	Proverbs 29:1
Refusing to listen–Refusing to listen leads to a loss of spiritual hearing.	Zechariah 7:11-13
Failing to respond–Listening to God with no intention of obeying produces an inability to obey.	Matthew 13:11-15

11:9-10 **David says.** Verses 9 and 10 are from Psalm 69:22-23 (a psalm thought to be prophetic about the suffering of the Messiah). These words of David were originally a curse directed at Israel's enemies. Paul turns the curse around and points it at the Jews!

Their table. This refers to the blessings that God had given Israel. These blessings should have drawn Israel to him and thus led them to Christ; instead, they became **a snare and a trap, a stumbling block and a retribution for them.**NIV Israel's blessings had led to pride that led them away from God. Thus, not only did they miss the Messiah when he came, but they also persecuted and killed him.

Eyes be darkened . . . and keep their backs forever bent.^{NRSV}
The Jews refused to see God's truth when it was set before them
(Isaiah 6:9-10), so they are cursed with eternal blindness and the
back-breaking burden of their self-imposed law keeping and regulations, their sins, and their guilt. John 9 records Jesus confronting the Pharisees with their spiritual blindness. He had healed a
blind man, but the religious leaders had invalidated the healing
because it broke their Sabbath work rules. Eventually, the healed
man came to realize Jesus was the Son of Man, the Messiah
(John 9:35-38). Jesus used the man's experience to explain his
own ministry: "'For judgment I have come into this world, so
that the blind will see and those who see will become blind.'
Some Pharisees who were with him heard him say this and asked,
'What? Are we blind too?' Jesus said, 'If you were blind, you
would not be guilty of sin; but now that you claim you can see,
your guilt remains'" (John 9:39-41 NIV). For Jesus, those who
claimed to see but could not recognize his true identity were af-
flicted with the worst possible blindness.

GOD'S MERCY ON THE GENTILES / 11:11-24

Paul had a vision for the church, and thus for local churches, to
be a place where all Jews and Gentiles would be united in their
love of God and in obedience to Christ. While respecting God's
law, this ideal church would look to Christ alone for salvation. A
person's ethnic background and social status would be irrelevant
(see Galatians 3:28)—what mattered would be his or her faith in
Christ. In this section, Paul describes a large olive tree, from
which some branches had been pruned and to which other
branches had been grafted. That tree represents Paul's vision for
the church.

   True Christians have no basis for persecuting others. Attempting to force Christian belief only destroys that belief. "Evangelism" does not justify hurting others. Both Gentiles and Jews have
done so much to damage the cause of the God they claim to serve
that Paul's vision of unity seems very distant. Yet God chose the
Jews, just as he chose the Gentiles, and he still works to unite
Jews and Gentiles in a new Israel, a new Jerusalem, ruled by his
Son (see Ephesians 2:11-22).

   But Paul's vision has not yet been realized. Many Jewish people rejected the gospel. Depending on their works and heritage
for salvation, they did not have the heart of obedience that was so
important to the Old Testament prophets and to Paul. After Gentiles became dominant in many of the Christian churches, they be-

gan rejecting Jews and even persecuting them. Unfortunately, this practice has recurred through the centuries.

11:11 **Did they stumble . . . beyond recovery?**^{NIV} This is the tenth time in this letter that Paul has asked a question only to respond in a strong negative: **Not at all!**^{NIV} No, Israel's stumbling did not cause them to fall so that God has declared the nation *beyond recovery.* Their blindness is not permanent (11:8); their fall is not fatal. Israel's stumbling, **their transgression** (rejecting Christ so strongly that they killed him) means that **salvation has come to the Gentiles.**^{NIV} Israel's rejection of Christ was a part of God's plan all along, as essential as God's sovereign choice of Jacob over Esau (9:10-13) and his hardening of Pharaoh (9:17-18).

When Paul preached in various cities, he usually went to a synagogue first to speak to the Jews. Many times their unbelief would turn to hostility toward Paul. Then Paul would take the message to the Gentiles: "Then Paul and Barnabas answered them boldly: 'We had to speak the word of God to you first. Since you reject it and do not consider yourselves worthy of eternal life, we now turn to the Gentiles'" (Acts 13:46 NIV). But the salvation of the Gentiles is not the end of the story. It too has a purpose.

To make Israel jealous.^{NRSV} Both the news that salvation is in Christ and that God accepted pagan Gentiles served to provoke Israel to jealousy. Israel had lost sight of the reason for their election as a nation; God had told Abraham, "All peoples on earth will be blessed through you" (Genesis 12:3 NIV). Instead of accepting Jesus as Messiah and Savior and then taking that good news to all peoples on earth, the Jews were "hardened" for a time while God got the Good News out in other ways. But this was God's plan all along. The blessings offered to the Gentiles would spur Israel to end their hostility toward the gospel and ultimately bring them to faith. God desires to restore Israel to himself.

11:12 **Their transgression means riches for the world.**^{NIV} The Jews' rejection of the Christ meant that the gospel was given to the rest of the world. The world was greatly blessed—those who received the gospel received great riches for eternity; and believers, in turn, have an influence for good on the rest of the world.

Their loss means riches for the Gentiles.^{NIV} God took the riches that the Jews should have received and offered them to the Gentiles, who gladly received them.

How much greater riches will their fullness bring!^{NIV} Paul
looks beyond the present to a future time when Israel will accept
the riches of salvation that God offers (see 11:26). The word *fullness* is to be understood in the same sense as "the full number of
the Gentiles" in verse 25; in other words, all those chosen by God
to receive salvation. Israel's acceptance does not mean that the
riches given to the Gentiles will be taken away; rather, when the
Jews are saved, the Gentiles will enjoy even greater blessings
along with them.

UNITED AROUND CHRIST
Paul visualized a church in Rome where Jews and Gentiles
would be united in their love of God and in obedience to Christ.
There were plenty of spiritual riches for everyone. If either
group tried to claim sole ownership of the truth, both groups
would be impoverished. God's plan involves a large, healthy
tree of life, with both Jewish and Gentile branches growing vigorously. Healthy churches come in many shapes and
sizes, and the power of Jesus Christ is often demonstrated in the sheer variety of people who gather around
the Cross for worship. It is spiritually healthy to ask, from
time to time, "Who, or what, is at the center of the church
where you worship?"

13-14 **I am speaking to you Gentiles.**^{NRSV} We can almost sense the intensity of Paul's words as he defines his audience. If we are not
Jews, we know that the next words are meant for us. Paul singles
out the Gentile believers to listen carefully to what he is going to
say. They (and we) are being given an opportunity to understand
their role in the divine plan. Paul will explain that the salvation of
the Gentiles both depends on Israel and contributes to Israel's salvation.

I am an apostle to the Gentiles.^{NKJV} All of the apostles were
preaching both to Jews and non-Jews, but Paul had been specially
chosen and commissioned by God to go to the Gentiles: "This
man is my chosen instrument to carry my name before the Gentiles and their kings and before the people of Israel" (Acts 9:15
NIV; see also Galatians 2:3-10). Before his conversion on the road
to Damascus, Paul's "mission" was to persecute the followers of
Jesus. Once he became a Christian his ministry was to proclaim
the Good News to the Gentiles. Throughout this mininstry he had
been a strong (and at first lone) advocate for Gentile freedom
from the Jewish law.

I glorify my ministry.NRSV Paul is emphasizing God's sending him to the Gentiles in order to **somehow arouse** his people **to envy and save some of them.**NIV Paul's reference to *envy* means that he hopes to cause the Jews to recognize that God greatly blessed the Gentiles when they believed in the Jews' own Messiah. The Jews might then realize that those blessings are still promised to them as part of God's covenant with them, but they can only be obtained by faith in Jesus Christ. Again Paul is revealing his great desire to see his people be saved (see 9:1-3; 10:1).

11:15 **If their rejection is the reconciliation of the world.**NRSV Israel's rejection by God meant that all other people could hear the Good News and be reconciled to God. But how can Paul make this statement when 11:1 states in forceful terms that God did not reject his people? In verse 1, the word translated "reject" is *aposato,* "putting away," while in this verse, *rejection* translates the Greek word *apobolei,* "casting away or setting aside." In spite of our use of the same word, Paul must have meant two different ideas. The context of the first "rejection" indicates that Paul was responding to the charge that God's acceptance of the Gentiles meant abandoning his chosen people. This idea of "rejection" Paul does not support. In this verse, Paul presents the idea that God had always planned to include the Gentiles, even if that meant a temporary setting aside of the Jews. When the chosen people, who were designated as the vehicles of God's blessing to the world, actually blocked that message from getting through, God made sure that the message arrived anyway. The "riches" that have been made available to the world (11:12) are found in reconciliation with God. (See the discussion on Romans 5:11; see also 2 Corinthians 5:18-20 for more on reconciliation.)

What will their acceptance be but life from the dead? NKJV The Jews had been moved aside, so God offered salvation to the Gentiles. When Jews come to Christ and God accepts them back, there is great rejoicing, as if dead people had come back to life. The structure of this verse is almost identical to verse 12, where Paul writes that the "transgression" and "loss" of the Jews brings "riches to the world," but that their "fullness" (*pleroma*) will bring "much greater riches." Several possible meanings have been suggested for *life from the dead:* (1) spiritual awakening in the world, (2) resurrection of the dead, and (3) the conversion of the Jews. But it is clear from the context that Paul has in mind the future role of the Jews in God's plan. As Paul goes on to illustrate by his grafting metaphor, the "rejection" of the Jews actually allows them another opportunity to fulfill God's purpose for them. Their terrible failure in rejecting Christ will make their eventual *acceptance* as vivid as the resurrection that all believers will experience.

Though we may not grasp all the nuances of Paul's extensive argument, his purpose is unmistakable. He wants to give Gentiles every reason possible to welcome their Jewish brothers and sisters in the faith with open arms. At the same time, he wants to help his Jewish brethren reciprocate that welcome. Neither group is to claim supremacy in the church. The message is: God has made room in his family for *both* of you, so you must get along together.

11:16 **If the part . . . is holy, then the whole . . . is holy.**NRSV Paul believes that Israel's refusal to accept Christ is temporary and that one day the nation will be brought back to God. He explains this through two illustrations: the firstfruits and the olive tree (with its branches).

In Numbers 15:20, Moses had instructed Israel about their offerings to the Lord. After Israel entered the Promised Land, they were to show their thanks to God for the bounty of food by presenting a portion of the food to the Lord as an offering: "Present a cake from the first of your ground meal and present it as an offering from the threshing floor" (NIV). If the first part of the dough (the firstfruits) offered is holy, *then the whole batch is holy.* It is set apart for the Lord, and the whole batch is blessed.

If the root is holy, so are the branches.NKJV The second illustration is a tree. The root obviously is the first part of a tree, and it will form the "character" of the branches. Abraham's faith was like the root of a productive olive tree, and the Jewish people are the tree's natural branches. As a result of God's choice and Abraham's response, the nation that descended from him was set apart for God.

Each of these illustrations conveys a different idea. In the first, a sample, or tithe, or **firstfruits** represents the whole. In the second, the foundation, source, or **root** determines the quality of the particulars (branches).

In the Old Testament, God made his rightful ownership over everything clear, but he only required token gifts that acknowledged his ownership. The gift represented the whole. If given to God, it was declared holy and served to sanctify the whole. Paul extends the principle to cover the fate of his people. If the *firstfruits*, the remnant of Jews who since Abraham had lived by faith, were called holy by God, then there is still hope for the whole, proving that God has not rejected the dough (Israel). If the *root*, the tree of justification by faith, is *holy*, then any branch attached to and nourished by that *root* will also be *holy*. In the first illustration, the part affects the fate of the whole; in the second, the whole affects the fate of its parts.

Note the present parallel to how an unbeliever comes in contact with the church. He or she may meet the church as a corporate body by attending a worship service and draw certain conclusions about the individual members from their experience with the whole. Or the person may meet the church through one or more individual members and draw certain conclusions about the whole from particular believers. What might unbelievers think about Christianity from knowing you? What might they think of Christians from attending your church?

11:17 **Some of the branches were broken off.**[NRSV] God did not tear down the entire tree, but some of the *branches* were broken off because of sin and unbelief. These *branches* are Jews who failed to respond in faith to God's mercy. In their place, the Gentile believers, likened to a **wild olive shoot were grafted in.**[NRSV] Grafting involves inserting a bud or shoot of one plant into a slit in the stem or trunk of another plant. The shoot shares in the nourishment from the main stem or trunk (**the nourishing sap**[NIV]) and grows. Usually the cultivated olive shoots were grafted into wild olive trees (11:24), not vice versa. But Paul is emphasizing God's special work.

11:18 **Do not boast over those branches.**[NIV] But the Gentiles, the wild olive shoots who have been grafted into the cultivated olive tree (Israel), have no grounds for boasting. The Gentile "shoots" need to remember that they are just as dependent on "the root," for their survival as the Jewish branches they have replaced. God has not changed his original plan; salvation stems from the promise to Abraham and God's choice of Israel. Hence Paul's warning and explanation: **You do not support the root, but the root supports you.**[NIV] Both Jews and Gentiles share the tree's nourishment based on faith in God. For Paul, the only appropriate attitude for any "branch" is humble thankfulness. Any attitude of superiority is to be avoided, for it might indicate that grafted-in branches are candidates for the same fate as the original ones that had been broken off (see 11:21).

SINNERS AND SAVIOR
Whether in worship, prayer, or our relationships with nonbelievers, from time to time all believers need to be reminded of
who are the sinners and who is the Savior. There must never be
any doubt who is the dependent one and who is the Sustainer.
We are to share with the world a gospel they don't deserve,
while remembering that we don't deserve it either!

11:19 **"Branches were broken off that I might be grafted in."**NKJV A
Gentile believer might make this argument. It is true that it was
necessary to break off some branches in the grafting process. But
it would be a mistake to assume that Paul is limiting God's acceptance, as if there was only so much room on the tree for branches.
The point is not so much replacement as opportunity. The idea is
not that Jews were *broken off* so *that* we could take their place;
but rather that they were *broken off* so *that* the Gentile opportunity for justification by faith might become clear. This is under-
scored by Paul's assertion that even *broken off* branches can be
grafted back in (see 11:23).

11:20 **Broken off because of unbelief.**NIV The real reason some of the
branches of the tree, some of the nation of Israel, were broken off
was because of their stubborn unbelief.

You stand by faith.NKJV The Gentiles that were grafted in are
only there by their faith and by God's grace. Thus they are
warned, **Do not be arrogant, but be afraid**.NIV Those who are arrogant cherish proud thoughts about themselves; they do not have
a proper fear and respect for God. Our relationship with God is to
be one of humble dependence (see 12:3).

Jesus used many of these images to explain his own role as the
vine (John 15:1-8). He spoke of his Father, the Gardener who
cuts off every branch that is unproductive. He also reminded the
disciples that a branch cannot survive on its own, but is entirely
dependent on the vine for its survival and nourishment. The
branches serve their purpose in bearing fruit.

11:21 **If God did not spare the natural branches**. God willingly set
aside Israel because of their stumbling and blindness to the Good
News. The Gentiles should remember that God will set them
aside as well if they became arrogant—he will **not spare** them
either. Some readers may wonder if Paul is speaking of apostasy
in this verse. According to the context, it is not absolutely clear
whether Paul is refering to those who have fallen away from the

faith or those whose faith was never real. What is clear is that he
is warning Gentiles not to arrogantly think that their being
grafted in is irreversible. The only way they can remain in the
tree is by continuing to trust in God's grace.

DISGUISED ELITISM

To remember that God bases our salvation on faith and not on
any merit in ourselves provides an effective antidote for elitism.
But knowing some of the subtle ways that elitism can take root
will keep us on guard.

When we say this	We're actually doing this . . .
"They're not welcome in our church!"	Rejecting people because of race
"Everybody knows *that* at our church."	Excluding people on the basis of knowledge
"You're not part of *that* denomination?"	Rejecting people on the basis of denominational affiliation, with no reference to their personal relationship with Christ
"This is our family's church."	Excluding people because they are not in the "family"
"We need to dress up for church and use only the best for God."	Excluding people on the basis of wealth
"Our church is growing so fast that soon we'll be the biggest and best."	Rejecting people on the basis of success
"We have the best people."	Excluding people because of their reputation
"*We* know the truth."	Rejecting people because of doctrinal pride

11:22 **Sternness to those who fell, but kindness to you, provided
that you continue in his kindness.**[NIV] God sovereignly decided
to put Israel aside for a time and offer salvation through faith to
all the world. This was a stern act, but it was done in judgment
on those who "stumbled over" Jesus Christ (9:32-33). He has
been kind to the Gentiles, but Gentile believers must *continue in
his kindness*. This refers to steadfast perseverance in faith—continual and patient dependence on Christ. Steadfastness is a proof
of the reality of faith. If Gentile believers do not continue in their

perseverance in faith, they **will be cut off**, just as the natural branches were cut off because of their unbelief. This does not mean individual believers can lose their salvation and be cut off from God; rather, Paul is speaking from a generalized standpoint, picturing Gentiles as a group turning away from God as the nation of Israel had. God's *sternness* was demonstrated in that faith was not automatic for the chosen people; and his *kindness* was demonstrated in providing Gentiles with the opportunity for faith.

APPROACHING GOD
Christianity is monotheistic, but God is not a monolithic deity. His character is infinitely varied. He is utterly consistent in the diversity of his personality. He manages to be divinely stern and kind without contradiction. It is healthy for us to worship him while contemplating as much of his awesome variety as possible. We approach him humbly, knowing that his love will motivate his sternness with us. We approach him joyfully, knowing that his kindness is wonderful to us.

:23-24 **If they do not persist in unbelief, they will be grafted in.**[NIV] Returning to Israel, Paul says if they will stop persisting in their unbelief, God may decide to *graft them in again*. If, **contrary to nature**, wild olive shoots can be grafted into a cultivated olive tree, certainly the natural branches can be grafted back into root stock of the cultivated tree. We become part of God's "tree" by faith; we forfeit any potential relationship with God by unbelief. Gentiles are orphans graciously adopted into God's family. A wayward Jew who discovers the faith of Abraham is coming home.

GOD'S MERCY ON ALL / 1:25-32

The best way to summarize this section is to quote the first and last phrases:
  I do not want you to be ignorant of this mystery, brothers. . . . God has bound all men over to disobedience so that he may have mercy on them all.[NIV] As difficult as it may be for us to understand, God's handling of the Jews and the Gentiles is intended to expose all of us to his mercy. Paul wraps up his argument by saying that in the end there will be room for both Jews and Gentiles in the plan of God. The details of exactly how God will do all this are aptly called by Paul a *mystery!*
  When trying to understand the marvels of God's dealings with people, we are never far from uttering the words of the disciples,

"Who then can be saved?" (Matthew 19:25 NIV). At those times we also need to remember Jesus' response, "With man this is impossible, but with God all things are possible" (Matthew 19:26 NIV). We understand what we can; where we can't, we trust.

11:25 **This mystery**. The temporary stumbling of Israel is part of what Paul calls a *mystery* (*mysterion*)—the word here means a truth that has been unrevealed up to this point but is now being made known. The *mystery* reveals, for example, that Israel's stumbling has always been part of God's plan. God put Israel aside for a time in order to offer salvation to the Gentiles. Paul reviews this *mystery* so the Gentiles will **not be conceited**.NIV Conceit would be a sign that they were **ignorant** of God's master plan that included everyone (see 11:32).

Israel has experienced a hardening in part.NIV The Greek word for "hardening" used here is not the same as the Greek word used in 9:17-18 describing the "hardening" of Pharaoh's heart. The word in 9:18 suggests stubbornness; the word for "hardening" in this verse (and in 11:7) suggests a dullness in understanding.

This *hardening* is only partial (see also 11:7) because there is always a remnant that God promises to save. And the hardening is temporary, because it will only be experienced **until the full number of the Gentiles has come in**NRSV—that is, when all the elect of the Gentiles have come to salvation (see Acts 15:14). Then will come the "fullness" of the Jews (11:12). Everything will occur according to God's plan.

God knows the size of that number of Gentiles who will be grafted into God's tree of faith. We only know that the number will be complete (*full*). As many will have come in as are going to come in. Our main concern begins with our earnest interest in being one of that number. Here are several possible indicators that the number could be nearly full:

- A worldwide, sweeping revival among Gentiles.

- A prophetic fulfillment of what Christ called the "times of the Gentiles" (Luke 21:24).

- The point at which the gospel has been proclaimed in every tongue and nation (Mark 13:10).

There will be a marked increase in evangelization before Christ returns.

11:26 **All Israel will be saved.** This statement has provoked a variety of interpretations. The most widely held are as follows:

- "And so all Israel will be saved" means that the majority of Jews in the final generation before Christ's return will turn to Christ for salvation.

- Paul is using the term *Israel* for the "spiritual" nation of Israel made up of everyone—Jew and Gentile—who has received salvation through faith in Christ. Thus *all Israel* (or all believers, the church) will receive God's promised gift of salvation.

- *All Israel* means that Israel as a whole will have a role in Christ's kingdom. Their identity as a people won't be discarded. God chose the nation of Israel, and he has never rejected it. He also chose the church, through Jesus Christ, and he will never reject it either. This does not mean, of course, that all Jews or all church members will be saved. It is possible to belong to a nation or to an organization without ever responding in faith. But just because some people have rejected Christ does not mean that God stops working with either Israel or the church. He continues to offer salvation freely to all.

- "And so" means "in this way" or "this is how," referring to the necessity of faith in Christ.

These explanations do not exclude one another, and they all serve to underscore Paul's clear intention: to demonstrate that God had not rejected Israel. Indeed, Paul believed the nation of Israel would be restored to God. Both Jews and Gentiles will make up the flourishing tree that stands for the kingdom, as well the brush pile of broken branches prepared for burning that represents those who have rejected God's gracious offer of forgiveness.

As it is written. To confirm his statement, Paul quotes from Isaiah, first from 59:20-21.

The deliverer will come from Zion; he will turn godlessness away from Jacob.NIV Jesus Christ is the deliverer who comes from Zion (Jerusalem). For the first and only time in this letter, Paul speaks of the second coming of Christ. At that time, Christ will purge Israel (here identified with the ancestor Jacob) of all godlessness (see also Psalm 14:7; 53:6). The mention of *Jacob* seems to indicate that Paul has primarily the actual descendants of Abraham in mind, rather than the broader spiritual Israel of whom he had spoken previously (see chapter 4).

11:27 **Take away their sins.** God also promises to cleanse his people from all sin. God had also spoken through the prophet Jeremiah:

"This is the covenant I will make with the house of Israel . . . I will forgive their wickedness and will remember their sins no more" (Jeremiah 31:33-34 NIV).

God's promise to *take away . . . sins* is a helpful description of forgiveness. Because we often continue to remember our sins long after we have confessed them, we assume that God also remembers them. But Scripture promises the opposite. What we keep are only memories. Confession allows God to remove the sins from our life. They are as gone as a demolished house that has been hauled to the landfill. If we continue in those sins, we are rebuilding a structure that already has been destroyed.

11:28 **As far as the gospel is concerned, they are enemies on your account.**^NIV Paul is still speaking to the Gentiles in his audience (11:13). In order for God to bring the gospel to them, he had to set the Jews aside—as if they were his enemies for having rejected the Good News.

As far as election is concerned, they are loved on account of the patriarchs.^NIV But as far as God's choice, his election, is concerned, Israel is loved by God because of his covenants with the patriarchs—Abraham, Isaac, and Jacob. Because God chose those men through whom he would carry out his promises, he will keep his promises to their descendants.

11:29 **The gifts and the calling of God are irrevocable.**^NKJV The privileges and invitation given to Israel can never be withdrawn. God will not take back his gifts or withdraw his call. He will keep his promises. The important word is *irrevocable*, not irresistible. While God will not take back what he has offered, we are certainly able to reject it. Paul is making an application from God's characteristic faithfulness to the Jews that anyone can rely on. God will do what he promises. The writer of Hebrews spoke of this same consistent purpose in God's actions when he said, "Because God wanted to make the unchanging nature of his purpose very clear to the heirs of what was promised, he confirmed it with an oath" (Hebrews 6:17 NIV). If God's *gifts* were revocable, we could call into question his character.

11:30 **Just as you who were at one time disobedient to God have now received mercy as a result of their disobedience.**^NIV The Gentiles were disobedient before they knew God, but they received God's mercy and offer of salvation because of Israel's *dis-*

obedience. Having received from God something that they had
lacked previously, they could expect to keep on enjoying God's
mercy. By the same logic, however, the Jews could also expect
God to be consistent with his promises, even though they had, for
a time, rejected his mercy.

**31 They too have now become disobedient in order that they
too may now receive mercy as a result of God's mercy to
you.**NIV From Paul's time onward, Israel has been disobedient
to God because of their refusal to accept salvation in Christ.
Though they began with an advantage due to God's gracious
choice of them as his people, by being *disobedient,* the Jews
had proved themselves equally needing God's mercy. And Israel
will receive mercy because as soon as all the elect of the Gentiles have come (see 11:25), then God's mercy will again be directed to Israel.

In these verses, Paul shows how the Jews and the Gentiles
benefit each other. Whenever God shows mercy to one
group, the other shares the blessing. In God's original plan,
the Jews would be the source of God's blessing to the Gentiles (see Genesis 12:3). When the Jews neglected this mission, God blessed the Gentiles anyway through the Jewish
Messiah. He still maintained his love for the Jews because of
his promises to Abraham, Isaac, and Jacob ("on account of
the patriarchs"). But someday the faithful Jews will share in
God's mercy. God's plans will not be thwarted; he will "have
mercy on them all" (11:32).

32 God has imprisoned all in disobedience.NRSV When Adam
sinned, all humanity sinned with him (5:19). We are all sinners: "All have sinned and fall short of the glory of God"
(3:23); "Jews and Gentiles alike are all under sin" (3:9). When
people choose to follow their own passion and desires, they
are **bound**NIV in their disobedience. People who deliberately
choose to disobey God imprison themselves. It is those who
understand that they have been saying *no* to God who are in
the best position to say *yes* to him.

That he may be merciful to all.NRSV God can only show
mercy to people who know they have been *bound* in their disobedience. This is God's ultimate purpose. He is willing to
have mercy on all who come to him. For a beautiful picture
of Jews and Gentiles experiencing rich blessings, see Isaiah
60.

EVERYONE NEEDS THE SAVIOR
When in a large crowd, it is humbling to look around and think, "Everyone here needs the Savior!" Until we recognize profoundly God's mercy in our own life, it is unlikely that we will seriously consider letting others know about that mercy.

HYMN OF PRAISE / 11:33-36

At this point, Paul has thoroughly spoken about God's sovereign plan for the Jews and Gentiles. So he pauses before exploring a number of practical issues that occupy the remainder of the letter. For a moment, his mind is filled with the majesty of God. Paul remembers familiar phrases from the Old Testament, and he is caught up in an expression of heartfelt praise.

11:33 **Depth . . . of the wisdom and knowledge of God!**[NIV] Here Paul bursts into a song of praise as he concludes his entire treatise in chapters 1–11 on God's sovereign plan for our salvation. It is beyond our understanding. God's wisdom and knowledge are far too deep for us to understand; they are **unsearchable** and **beyond tracing!**[NIV] Nonetheless, we can appreciate their value, for even our limited knowledge has the effect of **riches** in our life. We can't know or understand everything about God, but the *wisdom and knowledge* that God allows us to have constantly affects how we live.

11:34 **"Who has known the mind of the Lord? Or who has been his counselor?"**[NRSV] Paul quoted from Isaiah 40:13, pointing out that God alone knows the plan. In his unsearchable wisdom he designed it. No human being was, is, or will ever be involved in giving him advice or making new suggestions.

11:35 **"Who has ever given to God, that God should repay him?"**[NIV] Paul quoted loosely from Job 41:11 to point out that God is in sovereign control. He is not in our debt, *we* are in *his!*

The implication of this series of questions is that no one has fully understood the mind of the Lord. No one has been his advisor. And God owes nothing to any one of us. Isaiah and Jeremiah asked similar questions to show that we are unable to give advice to God or criticize his ways (Isaiah 40:13; Jeremiah 23:18). God alone is the possessor of absolute power and absolute wisdom.

From him and through him and to him are all things.[NRSV] the Creator, Sustainer, and Omega of all life. Everything m him and is for him to use for his glory. God is almighty and all-powerful, but even more, he cares for us personally. No person or power can compare with God.

Paul began his letter with the statement that God left his imprint on the world he created, but that the human beings of that creation had chosen rebellion. In the past eleven chapters, Paul has examined God's marvelous plan for bringing the rebels home. God has chosen to "have mercy on them all" (11:32). Each one of us is one of the "all." What more can any believer, saved by grace, say than, **To him be the glory forever. Amen.**[NRSV]

Romans 12

Next, Paul moves from a doctrinal discussion to a practical discussion, for Christian doctrine translates into action. The first eleven chapters of this letter reveal God's mercy to sinners in that he sent his Son to die on the cross for our sins. The last five chapters explain our obligation to God. If the early message of the letter is the way we all can come to God through Christ, then the closing part of the letter is the way we all can live for God in Christ. In view of all God has done for us, how can we respond in a way that is pleasing to him?

WHAT IS SACRIFICIAL LIVING?
Romans 12 offers an outline for breaking the world's mold. To put these directions in motion means going against the flow of society. Yet God does not hesitate to confront us with the choice. The option is not whether we will conform; rather, the choice is to whom will we conform? Will our lives follow the pattern of this world or God's pattern? The following are components of God's pattern:

- *Offer our bodies*—Delivering both the inner and outer self into God's control. Divers and gymnasts know that where their head goes, the rest of their body will eventually follow
- *Be nonconformists*—Consciously resisting the suggestions and pressures of the world around us
- *Renew our minds*—Constantly asking God to teach us to think as he thinks
- *Estimate ourselves honestly*—Having neither false humility nor inappropriate pride in our serving relationships with others
- *Utilize our gifts*—Identifying those gifts to be used in helping others; finding a purpose, a place, and a position to serve other believers

12:1 Therefore, brothers and sisters.^{NRSV} Therefore, because of God's great compassion on both Jews and Gentiles in offering salvation through Christ, Paul urges believers to please God in their daily lives. The evil world is full of temptation and sin. Paul helps believers understand how they can live for God.

SACRIFICES COMPARED

In the old sacrifices	*But for the new sacrifice*
An altar was required	There is no altar
Animals were slain	The sacrifice lives
Sacrifices were cut up	The sacrifice is whole
Sacrifices were burned up	The sacrifice serves
It was based on a legal obligation	It is based on mercy and gratitude
Death was not defeated	Eternal life is celebrated

By the mercies of God.NKJV Or, literally, "through the compassions [*oiktirmon*] of God," refers to all that Paul has already written. Our Christianity is not based on pride in what we can do, but entirely on God's mercy to forgive us.

Present your bodies as a living sacrifice.NRSV Paul had already told the Roman believers, "Do not offer the parts of your body to sin, as instruments of wickedness, but rather offer yourselves to God, as those who have been brought from death to life; and offer the parts of your body to him as instruments of righteousness" (6:13). Our bodies are all we have to offer—we live in our bodies. The body enfolds our emotions, our mind, our thoughts, our desires, and our plans. Thus, the body represents the total person; it is the instrument by which all our service is given to God. In order to live for God, we must offer him all that we are, represented by our body. The word *offer* has also been translated "give," "yield," or "present." If our body is at God's disposal, he will have our free time, our pleasures, and all our behavior.

When sacrificing an animal according to God's law, a priest would kill the animal, cut it in pieces, and place it on the altar. Sacrifice was important, but even in the Old Testament God made it clear that obedience from the heart was much more important (see 1 Samuel 15:22; Psalm 40:6; Amos 5:21-24). God wants us to offer ourselves as *living* sacrifices—daily laying aside our own desires to follow him, putting all our energy and resources at his disposal, and trusting him to guide us (see Hebrews 13:15-16; 1 Peter 2:5). Our new life is a thank-offering to God. Offering our body as a living sacrifice is **holy and pleasing to God.**NIV To be a *holy* sacrifice is to be completely set apart for God and dedicated to his service. Those who are dedicated to God are *pleasing to God* because they can particiapte in his service. If we are not set apart from our old life, we will not be useful to God.

This is your spiritual act of worship.^NIV The Greek word for "worship" (*latreian*) here refers to any act done for God, such as work that priests and Levites performed. *Spiritual* (*logiken*) can also mean "reasonable" (NKJV). To serve God is the only reasonable way to respond to his mercy.

12:2 **Do not conform any longer to the pattern of this world.**^NIV When believers offer their entire self to God, a change will happen in their relation to the world. Christians are called to a different life-style than what the world offers with its behavior and customs, which are usually selfish and often corrupting (Galatians 1:4; 1 Peter 1:14). Christians are to live as citizens of a future world. There will be pressure to *conform*, to continue living according to the script written by the world, but believers are forbidden to give in to that pressure.

Many Christians wisely decide that much worldly behavior is off limits for them. After all, it is not our objective to find out just how much like the world we can become yet still maintain our distinctives. But refusing to conform to this world's values must go even deeper than the level of behavior and customs—it must be firmly planted in our minds—**be transformed by the renewing of your minds.**^NRSV The Greek word for "transformed" (*metamorphousthe*) is the root for the English word *metamorphosis.* Believers are to experience a complete transformation from the inside out. And the change must begin in the *mind,* where all thoughts and actions begin. Paul wrote to the Ephesians, "You were taught, with regard to your former way of life, to put off your old self, which is being corrupted by its deceitful desires; to be made new in the attitude of your minds; and to put on the new self, created to be like God in true righteousness and holiness" (Ephesians 4:22-24 NIV). One of the keys, then, to the Christian life is to be involved in activities that renew the mind. *Renewing* (*anakainosei*) refers to a new way of thinking, a mind desiring to be conformed to God rather than to the world. We will never be truly *transformed* without this *renewing* of our mind.

Much of the work is done by God's Spirit in us, and the tool most frequently used is God's Word. The Bible claims the ability to judge "the thoughts and attitudes of the heart" (Hebrews 4:12 NIV). As we memorize and meditate upon God's Word, our way of thinking changes. Our minds become first informed, and then conformed to the pattern of God, the pattern for which we were originally designed.

DO NOT CONFORM
What causes us to conform to the world's pattern?

- We believe that the world is more likely to allow us pleasure than God is.
- We find a certain exhilaration in rushing along with the world.
- We are afraid of what might happen if we really think about life and change.
- We are crippled by pride or a negative self-image and believe there really *isn't* an alternative.
- We reject the life of service and humility necessary to conform ourselves to God's pattern.

Conforming to the world's pattern will involve the following ways of thinking:

- We have a right to have all our desires fulfilled (see Romans 8:5; 1 Peter 4:3-4).
- We have a right to pursue and use power (see Mark 10:42-45).
- We have a right to abuse people (see Luke 11:43, 46-52).
- We have a right to accumulate wealth for purely selfish reasons (see Matthew 16:26).
- We have a right to use personal abilities and wisdom for self-advancement rather than for serving others (see 1 Corinthians 3:19).
- We have a right to ignore or even hate God (see James 4:4).

Then you will be able to test and approve what God's will is.NIV When believers have had their minds transformed and are becoming more like Christ, they will want God's will, and not their own will, for their lives. And only as they are being transformed will they be able to know, do, and enjoy what God desires for them. Knowing God's will

> The main problem with a living sacrifice is that it keeps crawling off the altar.
> —Anonymous

isn't always easy, and even less so when it is not defined in every aspect by a set of laws and regulations. But it is possible if we willingly submit to and depend on God. Only then can we know it; only then can we begin the even more difficult task of doing it.

His good, pleasing and perfect will.NIV In the Greek text the three adjectives *good, pleasing, and perfect* are used as substantives (nouns). God's will *is* what is good, what is pleasing (to God), and what is perfect for each believer. Believers who are being transformed, who know and do God's will, also discover that what God plans for them is good, pleasing to God, and perfect for them.

12:3 **By the grace given to me I say.**NRSV Paul is here speaking as an apostle (see 1:5). The authority he was about to exercise was not his own by right, but was an evidence of God's grace. He firmly claimed to speak for another.

Do not think of yourself more highly than you ought.[NIV] Inflated pride has no place in a believer's life (see 3:27; 11:18, 20). This is especially significant in light of Paul's teaching up to this point in his letter. The Jews are not better than the Gentiles; the Gentiles are not better than the Jews. Rather, all are dependent on God's mercy for their salvation, thus there is no room for pride. Any such pride would undermine the oneness vital to the growth of the church.

Think of yourself with sober judgment, in accordance with the measure of faith God has given you.[NIV] Each believer's personal appraisal ought to be honest. Neither an inflated ego nor a deflated person is free to obey. God has given each believer a *measure of faith* with which to serve him. This expression refers to the spiritual capacity and/or power given to each person to carry out his or her function in the church. The concept of "measure" is described further in 12:6, where Paul uses the terminology "different gifts, according to the grace given us." It is God's discernment, not ours, that gives out the measure for service. Whatever we have in the way of natural abilities or spiritual gifts— all should be used with humility for building up the body of Christ. If we are proud, we cannot exercise our faith and gifts to benefit others. And if we consider ourselves worthless, we also withhold what God intended to deliver to others through us.

> Don't let the world around you squeeze you into its own mould, but let God re-mould your minds from within, so that you may prove in practice that the plan of God for you is good, meets all his demands, and moves towards the goal of true maturity (Romans 12:2).
> —J. B. Phillips

SELF-WORTH
Healthy self-esteem is important because some of us think too little of ourselves; on the other hand, some of us overestimate ourselves. The key to an honest and accurate evaluation is knowing the basis of our self-worth—our identity in Christ. Apart from him, we aren't capable of very much by eternal standards; in him, we are valuable and capable of worthy service. Evaluating ourselves by worldly standards of success and achievement can cause us to think too much about our worth in the eyes of others and thus miss our true value in God's eyes.

12:4 **We have many members in one body.**^{NKJV} Replacing the national identity that had once set apart God's people, Paul gives a
new picture of the identity of God's re-
deemed people. They are like a *body*. Each
of us has one body, but it has many parts—
eyes, ears, fingers, toes, blood vessels, muscles.
And **all the members do not have the same
function.**^{NKJV} Not every part of our body can
see; not every part hears. Instead, each part
has a specific function, and they all must
work together if the body is going to move
and act correctly. (See also 1 Corinthians
12:12-27.)

> We are called to
> bear that image as
> a Body because
> any one of us
> taken individually
> would present an
> incomplete image,
> one partly false
> and always
> distorted, like a
> single glass chip
> hacked from a
> mirror. But
> collectively, in all
> our diversity, we
> can come together
> as a community of
> believers to
> restore the image
> of God in the world.
> —Paul Brand

12:5 **In Christ we who are many form one
body.**^{NIV} Just as our physical bodies are com-
posed of many parts, so the "body of Christ" is
made up of many believers who all perform
different yet vital functions. And as our bodies
cannot be taken apart, so **each member,** each
believer in the body of Christ, **belongs to all
the others.**^{NIV} The members work together to
make the body work; the body doesn't exist to
serve the members, and the body is not dependent on one or two of its members to run
the show. Every person has his or her part to
do. When it is not done, the body suffers.

Even a superficial grasp of this *one body* imagery demolishes
much of the individualized religion of our day. The overemphasis
given to personal opinion tends to create an all-too-fragile unity,
given the real nature of those being brought together. As sinners,
we are naturally divisive; so it is only through the presence and
work of Christ that we can remain together. Only *in Christ* is
there basis for unity that transcends differences. Perhaps more
churches and relationships between believers would be preserved
if we ended every disagreement with a genuine question, "Are we
still together in Christ?"

12:6 **Different gifts.**^{NIV} We must be humble and recognize our partner-
ship in the body of Christ. Only then can our gifts be used effec-
tively, and only then can we appreciate others' gifts. God gives us
gifts so we can build up his church. To use them effectively, we
must:

- realize that all gifts and abilities come from God

- understand that not everyone has the same gifts nor *all* the gifts
- know who we are and what we do best
- dedicate our gifts to God's service and not to our personal success
- be willing to utilize our gifts wholeheartedly, not holding back anything from God's service.

According to the grace given to us.NRSV God's gifts differ in nature, power, and effectiveness according to his wisdom and graciousness, not according to our faith. The "measure of faith" (12:3) or the "proportion" of faith means that God will give the spiritual power necessary and appropriate to carry out each responsibility. We cannot, by our own effort or willpower, drum up more

> It is only rarely that prophecy in the New Testament has to do with foretelling the future; it usually has to do with *forthtelling* the word of God.
> —William Barclay

faith and thus be more effective teachers or servants. These are God's gifts to his church, and he gives faith and power as he wills. Our role is to be faithful and to seek ways to serve others with what Christ has given us.

Prophesying ... in proportion to his faith.NIV The gifts Paul mentions in this list fall into two categories: speaking and serving. Gifts are given that God's grace may be expressed. Words speak to our hearts and minds of God's grace; acts of service show that grace in action. This list is not exhaustive; there are many gifts, most of them hidden from the public, those "behind the scenes" words and actions that serve and magnify God.

Prophesying, according to the New Testament, is not always predicting the future. Often it means effectively communicating God's messages (1 Corinthians 14:1-3). Another translation of *in proportion to his faith* would be "in agreement to the faith"; in other words, the message communicated must be true to the tenets of the Christian faith. The way that Paul refers to each of these gifts focuses on their importance in use. These gifts are not for having, but for using. In other words, God's gifts fulfill their value as they are utilized for the benefit of others. Discovery of God's gifts to us ought to be followed by putting them to work.

12:7-8 **Serving ... serve.**NIV If a person has the gift of serving, then he or she should use it where and when it is needed, and use it to its best and fullest capacity. The same goes for the other gifts that Paul mentions: **teaching ... encouraging ... contributing to**

GIFT DISCOVERY

Believers will respond differently in the same circumstances. Recognizing what our initial response might be will help us identify the general nature of our gifts. For example, imagine that a destitute family attends your worship service next Sunday. How will different believers respond? The responses that are most similar to what you would do will give you clues to your gifts.

The *prophets* will ask the congregation . . .	"What went wrong here that needs to be corrected? What caused this family to experience these problems?"
The *servers* will ask the person . . .	"Are there others we need to help?"
The *teachers* will ask the person . . .	"What can we do for you?"
The *encouragers* will say to the person . . .	"How can we help you avoid this situation in the future? What skills, wisdom, and spiritual insights will give you better direction?"
The *givers* will ask the person . . .	"You must be feeling bad. Please know that we will care for you any way we can. Before you know it, you will be helping someone else."
The *leaders* will ask the church . . .	"How much will you need to meet your needs? How can we respond to this need in the most effective manner?"
The *merciful* . . .	will probably not ask any questions, but welcome the person with smiles, hugs, warm acceptance, and understanding.

the needs of others . . . leadership . . . [and] showing mercy.^{NIV} Whatever gift a believer has, he or she should faithfully use it in gratitude to God. By focusing on the application of the gifts, Paul is removing the tendency toward unhealthy self-congratulation in the discovery of gifts. If we are busy using our gifts, we will be less taken up with concerns over status and power. Genuine service controls pride.

When studying this list of gifts, one might imagine the characteristics of the people who would have them. Prophets are often bold and articulate. Servers (those in ministry) are faithful and loyal. Teachers are clear thinkers. Encouragers know how to motivate others. Givers are generous and trusting. Leaders are good organizers and managers. Those who show mercy are caring people who are happy to give their time to others.

This list of gifts is representative, not exhaustive. It would be difficult for one person to embody all these gifts. An assertive prophet usually would not make a good counselor, and a generous giver might fail as a leader. When people identify their own gifts and their unique combination of gifts (this list is far from complete), they should then discover how they can use their gifts to build up Christ's body, the church. At the same time, they should realize that one or two gifts can't do all the work of the church. Believers should be thankful for each other, thankful that others have gifts that are completely different. In the church, believers' strengths and weaknesses can balance each other. Some people's abilities compensate for other people's deficiencies. Together all believers can build Christ's church. But all these gifts will be worthless if they are used begrudgingly out of duty, or if they are exercised without love (see also 1 Corinthians 13:1-3).

OVERCOME EVIL WITH GOOD / 12:9-21

As it has done elsewhere (1 Corinthians 12-13), Paul's thinking progresses from the use of gifts to the motivation behind those gifts—love. Whereas the previous section pointed to individual contributions that each believer can make to the body, this section includes practical commands that require application by all believers. These commands cover two distinct concerns: among believers, there must be evidence that love is being practiced and that evil is being defeated. In verse 9, Paul presents the theme of this section, in verses 10-13 he applies it to the relationship among the believers, and in verses 14-21 he applies it to the relationship believers have with unbelievers.

12:9 **Let love be genuine.**NRSV The key ingredient in interpersonal relationships is love—God's love (*agape*). This kind of love is a self-sacrificial love, a love that cares for the well-being of others. All the gifts that are exercised in the body should be expressed in this love. This love is the most accurate indicator of spiritual health in the body of Christ. To the Ephesians Paul wrote, "Speaking the truth in love, we will in all things grow up into him who is the Head, that is, Christ. From him the whole body, joined and held together by every supporting ligament, grows and builds itself up in love, as each part does its work" (Ephesians 4:15-16 NIV). Believers have God's love within because "God has poured out his love into our hearts by the Holy Spirit, whom he has given us" (5:5). For our love to be different from most of what is called "love" in the world, it must be *genuine*—without hypocrisy, deceit, falseness. Sincere love is genuine love. Jesus was referring to this kind of love when he said, "A new command I give you: Love one another. As I have loved you, so you must love one another. By this all men will know that you are my disciples, if you love one another" (John 13:34-35 NIV).

GENUINE LOVE
Most people know how to pretend to love others—how to speak kindly, avoid hurting their feelings, and appear to take an interest in them. We may even be skilled in pretending to feel moved with compassion when we hear of others' needs, or to become indignant when we learn of injustice. But God calls us to real and sincere love that goes far beyond politeness. Sincere love requires concentration and effort. It means helping others become better people. It demands our time, money, and personal involvement. No individual has the capacity to express love to a whole community, but the body of Christ in your town does. Look for people who need your love, and look for ways you and your fellow believers can show your Christian love to others.

Hate what is evil; cling to what is good.NIV The words here are clear and forceful, and they continue the thought of the first phrase. The whole might be translated, "Your love must be genuine, hating what is evil, clinging to what is good." *Genuine* love is not blind, but able to recognize evil and good. To *hate* and *cling* call for emotional involvement and energetic action. Believers are to hate evil (see Psalm 97:10; Proverbs 8:13). Turning from evil means turning toward what is good and clinging to it. This principle is practiced when we are able to detest an evil act while practicing compassion toward the one who has done it. This principle is also important regarding the exercise of spiritual gifts. Believers must always be careful that the use of their gifts does not lead them to unloving or evil motives, attitudes, or actions.

12:10 **Be devoted to one another in brotherly love.**NIV Paul's charge goes against the value of rugged individualism—the attitude of "doing it all by myself." Believers are to show brotherly love to fellow believers, and respect all the gifted people in the church, not just those whose gifts are visible. That's the only way that the body of Christ can function effectively and make a positive impact on the unbelieving world. The Greek word for "be devoted" (*philostorgoi*) means the type of loyalty and affection that family members have for one another. This kind of love allows for weaknesses and imperfections, communicates, deals with problems, affirms others, and has a strong commitment and loyalty to others. Such a bond will hold any church together no matter what problems come from without or within.

Honor one another above yourselves.[NIV] God's command for us to honor others also involves love. To *honor* means to give a person high value and respect. As Christians, we honor people because they have been created in God's image, because they are our brothers and sisters in Christ, and because they have a unique contribution to make to Christ's church (see also Ephesians 5:21; Philippians 2:3).

12:11 Never be lacking in zeal, but keep your spiritual fervor.[NIV] These two phrases are opposites. As believers are **serving the Lord,**[NIV] they should never become lazy or lose their diligence. Instead, their service should be enthusiastic. Paul is not advocating activity for activity's sake. Rather, we should consistently use our spiritual gifts to serve the body. We have been called (1:6-7), challenged (12:1-2), and equipped (12:4-6) for serving the Lord. Fatigue may be part of the cycle of service, but apathy (lack of zeal) should not be part of a believer's life. Christians must fight against discouragement, depression, and negativeness; they must do their utmost to keep their spiritual temperature high.

12:12 Rejoicing in hope.[NKJV] This means that we should look forward with happy anticipation to all that God has in store for us. We don't have to fear our future when it is in God's hands. Christ is the reason that we can be joyful.

Patient in suffering.[NRSV] When believers face trials or persecution, they are to endure patiently, for they know God is in control (see also 5:2-5).

Faithful in prayer.[NIV] A trademark of believers is prayer, for it is their lifeline to God. They must be persistent in praying, both individually and corporately.
    The only way we can be patient in affliction is by faithful prayer and joyful hope. When afflictions come our way, the only joy may be our hope for the future unveiling of God's plan (8:18-27).

12:13 Share with God's people who are in need.[NIV] For believers, the challenges of the Christian life are constantly shifting between what we experience personally and what we experience because we are part of the body of Christ. Gifts, love, hope, patience, and prayer are valuable, but they do not take precedence over other believers' needs. Because we are members of Christ's body, we must take care of one another in every way. When some are in need, others who have the means should share what they have in order to meet that need (whether financial or daily necessities). This was another trademark of believers, and it was often what drew nonbelievers to Christianity (see Acts 2:44-45; 4:34-37; 11:27-30).

Practice hospitality.NIV Hospitality means being friendly to strangers, not just having friends over. Christian hospitality differs from social entertaining. Entertaining focuses on the host— the home must be spotless; the food must be well prepared and abundant; the host must appear relaxed and good-natured. Hospitality, in contrast, focuses on the guests. Their needs—whether for a place to stay, nourishing food, a listening ear, or acceptance—are the primary concern. Hospitality can happen in a messy home. It can happen around a dinner table where the main dish is canned soup. It can even happen while the host and the guest are doing chores together. Believers should not hesitate to offer hospitality just because they are too tired, too busy, or not wealthy enough to entertain. The word *practice* is instructive, for it reminds us that *hospitality* improves with *practice*.

Both of Paul's commands are generally unheeded today. We would do well to return to biblical Christianity by taking inventory of what we can do without. Do we have clothes to spare? Can we give away a used car rather than sell it to buy a new one? Do we have toys or other possessions that others need more than we do? Can we help with ready cash or gifts of food? Above all, can we help without expecting to be thanked or rewarded ourselves?

12:14 Bless those who persecute you ... do not curse them.NRSV Paul now broadens his perspective to the world where the believers live—in this case, the capital of the empire, Rome itself. The community of believers was a tiny segment, vulnerable to the edicts of pagan emperors and persecution by any who disagreed with them. Paul, aware of these realities, counsels believers to avoid trouble by refusing to retaliate when persecuted and to respond with good when they are treated with evil.

By doing this, believers would be obeying Christ's words, for he said, "Love your enemies and pray for those who persecute you" (Matthew 5:44 NIV). They would also be imitating Christ, who when he was on the cross said, "Father, forgive them, for they do not know what they are doing" (Luke 23:34 NIV). Stephen, Christianity's first martyr, said nearly the same thing as he was being stoned, "Lord, do not hold this sin against them" (Acts 7:60 NIV).

BLESS THEM!
Most of us have trouble visualizing exactly what Paul had in mind when he commanded us to *bless* persecutors. This trouble intensifies when we are under personal attack. If we decide beforehand how we will respond in times of crisis, we will not be delayed by trying to define what we ought to be doing. Instead, we will simply have to do it.

In context, to *bless* means to not *curse*. Instead of hoping for the worst to happen to our enemies, we are to willfully hope that the best will befall them. Instead of speaking words of hatred, we are to choose to speak words of truthful good towards those intending to hurt us. Finally, we are to pray for those who we feel are preying on us.

12:15 **Rejoice with those who rejoice.** Believers need to be able to empathize with others—to join in with the feelings of others as if we were experiencing it oursleves. Christians should rejoice with others, with no hint of jealousy; and they should **mourn with those who mourn** (NIV), offering kindness, concern, compassion, and a shoulder to cry on if needed. The believers needed to have this as they dealt with the ups and downs of daily life in their surroundings.

Following Jesus will mean that believers will pass through a kaleidoscope of experiences in life. Christianity is neither denying life's hardships, nor dulling life's excitements. Our perspective of eternity in Christ can free us to enter into the full variety of living. Both laughter and tears are appropriate before God. Each has an important place in representing our feelings. Identifying with the joys and heartaches of others is also an important way to show them our love.

12:16 **Live in harmony.**NRSV In order to live in harmony with others, and especially with fellow believers, we cannot **be proud** (NIV). Instead, we are to **be willing to associate with people of low position.** In other words, **do not be conceited,** for then empathy and harmony are impossible. James leveled a scathing indictment on believers who were practicing favoritism and elitism in the church (James 2:1-9). *People of low position* are only identified as such by the world's standards. Christ thought they were worth dying for, and so we can associate with them.

BE WILLING TO ASSOCIATE
Many people use their contacts and relationships for selfish ambition. They select those people who will help them climb the social ladder. Christ demonstrated and taught that we should treat all people with respect—those of a different race, the handicapped, the poor, young and old, male and female. We must never consider others as being beneath ourselves. Are we able to do humble tasks with others? Do we welcome conversation with unattractive, nonprestigious people? Are we willing to befriend newcomers and entry-level people? Or do we relate only to those who will help us get ahead?

12:17 **Do not repay anyone evil for evil.**NRSV The commands in verses 17-21 relate mainly to dealings with unbelievers. When people do evil against us, we are not to repay in kind, as much as we might like to (see also 1 Peter 3:9). Repaying *evil for evil* makes us participants in an evil economy. We will not be able to hate evil (12:9) while actively using it as a method of exchange with others. Instead we are to **be careful to do what is right in the eyes of everybody**NIV (see 1 Peter 2:11-12). The word for *right* could also be translated "noble" or "honorable." Paul is certainly not using the word *everybody* as it is used in the common expression "Everybody's doing it." Paul's standard for behavior was not common consensus, but godliness. The point being made here is that the behavior of believers must be such that no one can rightfully make a claim of wrongdoing. To commit the same *evil* that was committed against us makes us indistinguishable from the original offenders.

12:18 **Live at peace with everyone.**NIV Paul counsels believers to have as peaceful relations as possible with their unbelieving neighbors and associates. In a perfect world, all people could live peacefully together. Realistically this is impossible in our imperfect world. However, believers, as the salt of the earth, should do their best **if it is possible** and **as far as it depends on** them.NIV They certainly are not to be the *cause* of dissension. Believers should do their utmost to seek reconciliation.

12:19 **Never avenge yourselves, but leave room for the wrath of God.**NRSV We may want to take revenge and repay evil for evil (12:17), but Paul reminds us to leave that in God's hands. Refusing to take revenge avoids grudges and feuds. This attitude makes possible the actions Paul recommends in 12:20. In human practice, revenge is repaying evil for evil, with interest. Because our personal demands for justice are mixed with wounded pride, hatred, and sinfulness, opportunities for revenge ought to be consciously turned over to God. This advice is helpful to us not only in dealing with opponents, but in family situations. It is so easy to strike back verbally (or in our minds) when a family member dominates, criticizes, or belittles us. Paul's advice is to not act vengefully.

It is written. Quoting from Deuteronomy 32:35: **"It is mine to avenge; I will repay," says the Lord.**NIV Vengeance, when taken into human hands, only serves to destroy the good it tries to defend and make evil grow by feeding on itself. Paul challenges believers to trust that ultimately God will ensure that his just vengeance will be given.

12:20 **On the contrary.**NIV Just the opposite of repaying with evil and taking revenge is caring for our enemies. Believers are not simply expected to abstain from evil; rather, they are expected to actively pursue opportunities to benefit their enemies.

"If your enemy is hungry, feed him; if he is thirsty, give him something to drink"NIV (see Proverbs 25:21-22). The principle here is that we should care for our enemy's needs. God invites us to observe our enemies and at the very points of weakness, where a counterattack of revenge might be most effective, we should mercifully meet that need.

THE CORE
These verses summarize the core of Christian living. If we love someone the way Christ loves us, we will be willing to forgive. If we have experienced God's grace, we will want to pass it on to others. And remember, grace is *undeserved* favor. By giving an enemy a drink, we're not excusing his misdeeds. We are recognizing him, forgiving him, and loving him in spite of his sins— just as Christ did for us.

By doing this you will heap burning coals on their heads.NRSV This statement comes from Proverbs 25:21-22. It has been interpreted in at least three ways: (1) It may refer to an Egyptian tradition of carrying a pan of burning charcoal on one's head as a public act of repentance. By referring to this proverb, Paul is say-

ing that we should treat our enemies with
kindness so that they will become ashamed
and turn from their sins. Even if they don't,
we are doing right. (2) It could signify an act
of kindness that would increase an enemy's
sense of guilt. But this interpretation doesn't
fit the context, wherein Paul is enouraging
believers to love their enemies. (3) It could

> Everyone says
> forgiveness is a
> lovely idea, until
> they have
> something to
> forgive.
> —C. S. Lewis

mean befriending an enemy so as to win him or her to Christ. Of
the three interpretations, the first seems the most plausible.

12:21 **Do not be overcome by evil, but overcome evil with good.**[NIV] Do
not give in to your desire to take revenge or retaliate with evil; instead, act in a positive way. Paul comes full circle back to his point
of verse 9. To hate evil is to overcome it with *good*. When we hang
on for dear life to those things that are *good* and to God, we will be
overcoming evil. All of this will be accomplished to the degree that
we allow God to create in us sincere love.

FORGIVENESS
When someone hurts you deeply, instead of giving him what he
deserves, Paul says to befriend him. Why does Paul tell us to
forgive our enemies? (1) Forgiveness may break a cycle of re-
taliation and lead to mutual reconciliation. (2) It may make the
enemy feel ashamed and change his or her ways. (3) In contrast, repaying evil for evil hurts you just as much as it hurts
your enemy. Even if your enemy never repents, forgiving him or
her will free you of a heavy load of bitterness.

Chapter 13

Paul ends chapter 12 by exhorting his readers about their Christian life-style as they relate to unbelieving neighbors, employers, and others. In chapter 13, he discusses how Christians should relate to the government. Remember, Paul's immediate audience was in Rome, the capital city of the mighty Roman empire.

Before the spread of Christianity, Judaism was a permitted religion in the Roman empire and thus protected by Roman law. Although Jewish observances and practices were generally safeguarded, imperial edicts could change anything. In A.D. 19, all Jews were expelled from Rome by the emperor Tiberius. Another expulsion occurred about A.D. 49-50, for when Paul went to Corinth on his second missionary journey, "he met a Jew named Aquila . . . who had recently come from Italy with his wife Priscilla, because Claudius had ordered all the Jews to leave Rome" (Acts 18:2 NIV). The situation for any minority religious sect was tenuous at best, depending on the particular ruler.

During the rest of the first century after the death of Christ, Christianity was regarded by Rome as a sect of Judaism. Through this entire letter, Paul has explained the makeup of the new people of God—they are not like the Jews, an ethnic sect set apart by their ancestry and heritage. Therefore, they were in an awkward political position—how should they fit in? They could not expect any legal protection such as that afforded (at times) to Judaism. Besides that, Christianity was suspect as being seditious.

- The founder of this Christian sect, Jesus Christ, had been crucified under Roman law for leading a movement that challenged Caesar as ruler and God—the inscription on Jesus' cross read, "The King of the Jews" (Mark 15:26 NIV).

- Christians had been accused of defying Caesar. When Paul had visited Thessalonica a few years prior to writing this letter, his enemies stirred up trouble by going to the city officials and exclaiming, "These men who have caused trouble all over the world have now come here. . . . They are all defying Caesar's decrees, saying that there is another king, one called Jesus" (Acts 17:6-7 NIV).

- Wherever the gospel was taken, it usually caused a spiritual upheaval because both pagan and Jewish systems were threatened by this new religion based on faith (see Acts 16:16-22; 19:23-41).

- Christians often were blamed for social disturbances. Businesspeople, like silversmiths, who made a living off of religion were threatened by Christianity. Riots often ensued when the gospel was preached, not because the speakers stirred up the people, but because someone's power or livelihood was affected when people began following Christ and rejecting pagan idols. Leaders in other cities found that mere accusations against Christians could be used effectively against them.

Paul urges believers to be careful in their relationships with the governing authorities. There would come enough persecution without them bringing it on themselves by rebelling against authorities who could just as well serve them.

In addition, modern-day readers must take special note of what life in the Roman empire was like. The political powers were there by birth, connection, wealth, or ruthlessness. The masses had no power, could never expect to have any power, and could never think that *they* could change the status quo. Their best strategy was to live within the structure and take advantage of the protection offered by it. Because people still believed in "the divine right of kings," most authority went unquestioned. And those in authority usually had a well-developed system of spies and informers who would not hesitate, in the name of good citizenship, to turn in anyone who complained or rebelled. It may be difficult for us to understand the political realities in ancient Rome, but the mind-set of the times caused Paul to exhort believers to be careful. Christians were not to rebel against godless Rome—Roman law was the only restraint against the lawless.

13:1 **Submit . . . to the governing authorities.**[NIV] Paul basically commands believers to submit to the governing authorities. Submission means cooperation, loyalty, and a willingness to obey. These were wise words to this small group of believers living within the massive structure of the Roman empire. It wouldn't take much for an imperial edict to fall on a group who might become known for causing unrest within the empire. Their quiet submission would not guarantee peace, but at least it might allow them to continue to spread the gospel freely for a time.

Paul does not recommend either of the two possible extreme responses to the presence of a hostile authority. He does not favor believers becoming like the Zealots, Jewish rebels who fought (often violently) for freedom from Rome; neither does he suggest that they withdraw to the desert to set up their own community far from the evil city. Instead, Paul explains how Christian should live *within* the structure. Only then would they be able to share the gospel and transform society.

Recent rapid political changes in the world have demonstrated that even under the most restrictive and hostile forms of government, the gospel continues to bear fruit. In fact, the faith evidenced by oppressed believers exhibits a vitality missing in many who have political and religious freedom.

Although submitting to God is our most basic responsibility, God has placed us in situations that offer daily lessons in submission. If we don't learn proper submission in those areas, our submission to God may be imaginary. To measure our progress in learning practical submission we can ask:

- Which of the following challenge me to practice submission: family, school, work, sports, civil government?

- To what persons in authority am I personally accountable?

- How submissive is my attitude toward each of those authorities?

- How well am I able to separate issues of authority from matters like personality differences, disagreements, envy, and ambition?

- In what specific ways can I demonstrate respect for the authority of even those whom I do not admire?

We can learn how to submit to God by submitting to those whom God has placed in authority over us. What grade would you give yourself for how you are doing in God's class on submission?

There is no authority except from God.^{NKJV} God sets all authorities in place. He allows all governments and leaders to function under his sovereign will. Government is ideally in place to protect and serve its citizens. When governments distort or betray this function, those who run them will answer to God. They are under God's constraint *and* under his final judgment (see also Psalm 2; Daniel 4:34-35).

13:2 **He who rebels against the authority is rebelling against what God has instituted.**^{NIV} Citizens of any government should respect their government and obey its laws. If they choose to break a law, they can expect to **bring judgment on themselves.**

Christians understand Romans 13 in different ways. All Christians agree that we are to live at peace with the state as long as the state allows us to live by our religious convictions. For hundreds of years, however, there have been at least three interpretations of how we are to do this.

(1) Some Christians believe that the state is so corrupt that Christians should have as little to do with it as possible. Although they should be good citizens as long as they can do so without compromising their beliefs, they should not work for the government, vote in elections, or serve in the military.

(2) Others believe that God has given the state authority in certain areas and the church authority in others. Christians can be loyal to both and can work for either. They should not, however, confuse the two. In this view, church and state are concerned with two totally different spheres—the spiritual and the physical—and thus complement each other but do not work together.

(3) Still others believe that Christians have a responsibility to make the state better. They can do this politically, by electing Christian or other high-principled leaders. They can also do this morally, by serving as an influence for good in society. In this view, church and state ideally work together for the good of all.

None of these views advocates rebelling against or refusing to obey laws or regulations unless those laws clearly require a person to violate the moral standards revealed by God. Wherever we find ourselves, we must be responsible citizens, as well as responsible Christians.

Are there times when we should not submit to the government? Paul does not address this question here, but other passages of Scripture give guidelines and examples. The government can demand respect, obedience, taxes, and honor from its citizens inasmuch as God appoints governments to protect people. When a government demands allegiance that conflicts with a believer's loyalty to God, Christians must respond in a different way. Believers should never allow the government to force them to disobey God. Jesus and his apostles never disobeyed the government for personal reasons; when they disobeyed, they were following their higher loyalty to God (Acts 5:29). Their disobedience was not cheap; they were threatened, beaten, thrown into jail, tortured, and executed for their convictions. If we are compelled to disobey, we must be ready to accept the consequences (see 1 Peter 2:13-14; 4:15-16).

CONSCIENTIOUS OBJECTORS
In the Bible, God's faithful people resisted or disobeyed corrupt
political or religious structures:

Daniel	declined the food fit for a king (Daniel 1:8-21)
Daniel's friends	refused to bow to the king's image (Daniel 3:1-30)
Jesus	healed on the Sabbath (Luke 6:6-11; 14:1-6)
Jesus' disciples	picked grain on the Sabbath (Luke 6:1-5) and refused to be silenced (Acts 1-22; 5:17-32)

13:3 **Rulers are not a terror to good conduct.**^{NRSV} Verses 3 and 4 focus on officials who are doing their duty. Society needs leader-
ship and positive constraints in order to ensure the safety and
well-being of its citizens. When these officials are just, people
who are doing right have nothing to fear. Therefore, in order to be
free from fearing **the one in authority**, people should simply **do
what is right**^{NIV}—i.e., obey the laws of the land. Governments
that serve well facilitate and encourage citizens to do right. That
is their purpose. If citizens are conscientiously seeking to do what
is *right*, and the *rulers* disagree, citizens must respectfully appeal
to the higher authority of God.

History records many instances where Christians have taken
submission to government far beyond the point of reasonable cooperation. They have gone along willingly when those in authority were clearly breaking God's commands. In passing judgment
on their errors, we must acknowledge how easy it is to criticize
with hindsight. We condense the developments of years into single sentences and imply that those who lived through those times
experienced them at the same speed that we have summarized
them. After judging the past, we must conclude with a clear answer to the question, How well do we passionately pursue what is
right?

Perhaps most widely discussed is the response of Christians to
Nazi rule in Germany. At first, the Christian response varied; some
believers did suffer and die while protecting Jews and resisting Na-
zism. But, on the whole, Christians responded slowly and ineffec-
tively to what their government was doing. In Germany, as in other
totalitarian governments, many citizens had lost the capacity to view
the authority structure critically. Some were so dependent on the

benefits and generosity of the central government that they had lost their will to criticize its goals or actions. They cooperated rather than risk their security. Many were so uninformed or isolated that they were unable to take a stand until it was too late.

Today believers live under tyranny. Others live in societies that have recently thrown off totalitarian rule. Every government makes mistakes. God passes judgment and grace on these human institutions as well as those in authority, and the citizens. God is for right and good in every sphere of living. He is against every form of evil. We must side with God, constantly depending on him to help us see and act on the difference. We are to pursue right living and resist evil.

Christians are not to use their freedom in Christ as a handy excuse for disobeying the laws of the state. Civil disobedience should come only after submission to authority has been practiced. We should be informed and willing to question the motives of those who govern us, but we should be more demanding and more suspicious of our own motives. We must be careful not to be ruled by our sinful desires. Our protest may not be spiritual but rooted in our offended pride or hatred of any authority. This response is not directed by Christ or the Holy Spirit.

13:4 **He is God's servant to do you good.**NIV Rulers are in their position only because God has placed them there, and they are ultimately responsible to God. God is sovereign, and the church may grow even in a hostile environment under an atheistic leader. "The king's heart is in the hand of the LORD; he directs it like a watercourse wherever he pleases" (Proverbs 21:1 NIV). All earthly governments are temporary—only Christ's reign will be eternal. To rebel against them is to rebel against their God-given authority. In practice, the responsibilities and opportunities of the politically powerful and the politically powerless will differ. For believers in a hostile environment, cooperation may be the most realistic approach. Believers who have the opportunity to affect change must challenge, speak out, offer solutions, and confront the power structure.

So **if you do wrong, be afraid.**NIV Paul's guidelines are directed toward seeing human government as a control on blatant evildoing. People can become so oriented to evil, so completely out of control, that they will only be brought to accountability by sheer power.

He does not bear the sword in vain.NKJV When properly used, force shown by a good government prevents tyranny, maintains

justice, protects and commends those who do right (13:3), and
brings **punishment on the wrongdoer.**^{NIV}

SERVING GOD'S SERVANTS
Willingly or unwittingly, people in authority are God's servants.
They are allowed their positions in order to do good. This provides our principal motivation to pray for our rulers. Paul instructed Timothy, "I urge, then, first of all, that requests,
prayers, intercession and thanksgiving be made for everyone—
for kings and all those in authority, that we may live peaceful
and quiet lives in all godliness and holiness" (1 Timothy 2:1-2 NIV).
Praying for those in authority over us will also mean that we will
watch them closely. If we pray diligently for those in authority
over us, we will be functioning as God's sentinels. We must
avoid ignorance of and apathy toward our world.

13:5 **Submit to the authorities ... because of possible punishment but also because of conscience.**^{NIV} Believers have two
good reasons to submit to their government: to avoid punishment and to heed their own conscience, for it will prod them to
do what is right. Believers know in their consciences that obeying the authorities pleases God. However, a believer's conscience answers to a higher, divine authority; if ever the
human authority contradicted the divine authority, a believer
must be true to his conscience in following the higher authority.

True citizenship is rarely rewarded. Faithfully carrying out
our small duties may not gain recognition. But Paul reminds
the Romans that God notices every action. When we obey
the government because it serves God, God knows our real
motives.

13:6 **Pay taxes**. Believers are called not only to submit to authorities,
but also to support them by paying taxes (see also Matthew
22:21; Mark 12:17). Taxes pay the salaries for those who **give
their full time to governing.**^{NIV} This was a heated topic at the
time Paul wrote—he does not refer to this in any other letter. Government taxation, and abuses of taxation, were causing great unrest in the city. Christians might be thinking that they could get
away with not paying the inflated taxes, but that would inevitably
draw the attention of the authorities and put the believers at unnecessary risk. So Paul says to pay. In this regard Paul followed
Jesus, who told Peter to pay taxes so as not to offend the governing authorities (Matthew 17:24-27).

For the authorities are God's servants.NRSV *God's servant* (*theou diakonos*) is used twice in verse 4, while here, *God's servants* (*leitourgoi theou*) are specifically God's public servants. The difference may be that earlier Paul emphasized the way that believers relate to rulers, while here he is pointing out that rulers serve God by being responsible for the entire population. Paul is not teaching that all the authorities in Rome are God's servants in the same sense as the believers are God's servants. The powers in Rome were arbitrary and often self-serving. But they were God's servants, ultimately responsible to the one who set them in place.

13:7 **Pay to all what is due them.**NRSV Christians are not exempt from fulfilling the expectations of any government: **taxes . . . revenue . . . respect**, and/or **honor**.NIV

This verse also prepares for Paul's idea of debt in the next section. We must certainly pay taxes to the government, but our obligation also extends to others to whom we may **owe** a debt of gratitude, *honor*, *respect*, money, or an assortment of "borrowed" items, from books to garden tools. What is borrowed must be repaid or returned.

LOVE FULFILLS GOD'S REQUIREMENTS / 13:8-14

Paul's practical directions for Christian living have a distinct pattern. Each time he focuses on a set of applications, whether it is gifts (chapter 12), government (chapter 13), or personal convictions (chapter 14), Paul always anticipates the question, Why should we do this? Consistently he answers, Because that is what love does! Throughout his writings, Paul demonstrates that believers can practice their faith in a multitude of ways, but they can never get too far from the great commandment:

- *"The most important one," answered Jesus, "is this: 'Hear, O Israel, the Lord our God, the Lord is one. Love the Lord your God with all your heart and with all your soul and with all your mind and with all your strength.' The second is this: 'Love*

> God did not make the first human because he needed company, but because he wanted someone to whom he could show his generosity and love. God did not tell us to follow him because he needed our help, but because he knew that loving him would make us whole.
> —Irenaus

your neighbor as yourself.' There is no commandment greater than these" (Mark 12:29-31 NIV).

In this section, Paul teaches that love is an urgent requirement for believers. Love is not to be withheld for later. We must live as if this were our last day on earth. One day will be the last day—will Christ find us loving others?

> The debt of charity is permanent, and we are never quit of it; for we must pay it daily and yet always owe it.
> —Origen

13:8 **Owe no one anything.**[NKJV] If we owe something, we should pay the debt. But we must ask, Is Paul against home mortgages and school loans? Paul is not teaching against borrowing, except as it applies to borrowing things or money that we cannot hope to repay. Careless or deceitful debt is not acceptable behavior among believers. To this point Jesus adds the command that his followers ought to be known as willing lenders and givers (Matthew 5:42). We are to be responsible to make payments and not borrow beyond our ability to pay.

The continuing debt to love one another.[NIV] One debt should never be paid in full; we should not fall short in displaying God's love in all our relationships (see also John 13:34-35; Galatians 5:22; Ephesians 5:1-2; 1 John 3:11-24; 4:7-21).

THE DEBT OF LOVE
Why is love for others called a debt? We are permanently in debt to Christ for the love he has lavished on us. The only way we can even begin to repay this debt is by loving others. Because Christ's love will always be infinitely greater than ours, we will always have the obligation to love our neighbors.

The one who loves another has fulfilled the law.[NRSV] Love is the basis of the law. Paul quotes several laws to show how these can be kept if a person simply acts in love.

13:9 **The commandments.** The commandments against adultery, murder, stealing, and coveting that Paul quotes are directly from the Ten Commandments. They apply to our relationships with others (see Exodus 20:13-15, 17). Paul lists them to show that they all fit under a broader commandment. Living according to the great commandment makes us responsible for its applications, such as the ones Paul mentions.

Are summed up in this word, "Love your neighbor as yourself."^{NRSV} All the laws about interpersonal relationships can be summed up by this one law from Leviticus 19:18. When asked about the most important law, Jesus answered, "'Love the Lord your God with all your heart and with all your soul and with all your mind.' This is the first and greatest commandment. And the second is like it: 'Love your neighbor as yourself.' All the Law and the Prophets hang on these two commandments" (Matthew 22:37-39 NIV).

Then some might ask, "Who is my neighbor?" as the Pharisee did. Jesus illustrated his meaning with the parable of the Good Samaritan. There was deep hatred between Jews and Samaritans. The Jews saw themselves as pure descendants of Abraham, while the Samaritans were a mixed race, produced when Jews from the northern kingdom intermarried with other peoples during the Exile. In the parable, a Jew was beaten and robbed as he traveled. Two other Jews, a priest and a Levite, passed him by. But a Samaritan who happened along, the person least likely to help, was the one who stopped and cared for the unfortunate Jew.

Thus, Jesus was explaining that a *neighbor* is not just the person next door or across the street. A neighbor can be of any race, creed, or social background. And we are called to *love*. Lack of love is often easy to justify, even though it is never right. To love we must act with love.

SELF-LOVE AND SELF-ESTEEM
Somehow many of us have gotten the idea that self-love is wrong. But if this were the case, it would be pointless to love our neighbors as ourselves. Paul explains what he means by self-love. Even if you have low self-esteem, you probably don't willingly let yourself go hungry. You clothe yourself reasonably well. You make sure there's a roof over your head if you can. You try not to let yourself be cheated or injured. And you get angry if someone tries to ruin your marriage. This is the kind of love we need to have for our neighbors. Do we see that others are fed, clothed, and housed as well as they can be? Are we concerned about issues of social justice? Loving others as ourselves means actively working to see that their needs are met. People who focus on others rather than on themselves rarely suffer from low self-esteem.

13:10 Love does no harm to a neighbor.^{NKJV} When we love others, we will not purposely harm or do evil to them. **Therefore love is the fulfillment of the law.**^{NKJV}

Christians must obey the law of love, which supersedes both religious and civil laws. It is easy to excuse our indifference to others merely because we have no legal obligation to help them, and even to justify harming them if our actions are technically legal! But Jesus does not leave loopholes in the law of love. Whenever love demands it, we are to go beyond human legal requirements and imitate the God of love. See James 2:8-9, James 4:11, and 1 Peter 2:16-17 for more about this law of love.

13:11 **Do this, understanding the present time.**NIV Paul wants believers to realize their constant need to show love, especially considering the *time*—Christ's return is near. New Testament passages on the return of Christ center on our responsibility to be morally prepared, spiritually alert, and diligently serving (1 Peter 4:11; James 5:8; 1 John 2:18).

The hour has come for you to wake up from your slumber.NIV Believers must be vigilant, alert, and not caught unaware. Paul knows that the old sinful nature will still cause problems from time to time, but he requires believers to stay "awake." Remaining too long in a state of spiritual lethargy, where sin is tolerated and good works are not pursued, can lead to a spiritual coma, rendering us unresponsive to God (see Ephesians 5:14; 1 Corinthians 15:34).

Salvation is nearer to us now.NRSV The return of Christ and our ultimate and final salvation is nearer now **than when we first believed.**NKJV Each day that passes brings us closer to the time of Christ's return, when we will be taken to heaven to be with him forever. (See also Mark 13:13; Luke 21:28; 1 Thessalonians 5:4-11; Hebrews 9:28.) When reading the biblical warning of the imminent return of Christ, many Christians picture this as waiting for an alarm clock to sound. This image focuses too much on waiting and creates too much room for inactivity and discouragement. A better picture is a minute hand on a watch, reminding us that time is short and to make every minute count.

13:12 **The night is nearly over; the day is almost here.**NIV The *night* refers to the present, evil time. The *day* refers to the time of Christ's return. Believers in Paul's day, as well as believers today, are living in the night, the time of darkness characterized by Satan's evil work (see 2 Corinthians 4:4; Ephesians 2:2).

Put aside the deeds of darkness.NIV The deeds of darkness are all evil and sin. We are to **put on the armor of light.**NIV We are to "take off" sin and "put on" good deeds as though they are protective armor for battle. As Paul explained in Ephesians 6:10-17, this *armor of light* or "weapons of light" represent all the features that make up God's gift of justification by faith (see also John 12:36; Ephesians 5:8; 1 Thessalonians 5:4, 5; 1 John 1:7; 2:10). We should depend on God's strength and use every resource that he has given us.

PEOPLE OF THE LIGHT
In Scripture, light provides a very powerful image, for light represents all that opposes darkness and evil. We must utilize God's light.

- We must follow Christ's leadership and point people to God: "Put your trust in the light while you have it, so that you may become sons of light" (John 12:36 NIV). Jesus claimed to be the true source of guidance.
- We have a new loyalty to doing right. Our conduct should reflect our new allegiance. Christ has "rescued us from the dominion of darkness and brought us into the kingdom of the Son he loves" (Colossians 1:13 NIV).
- According to Christ's new standards, we should live above reproach. "You were once darkness, but now you are light in the Lord. Live as children of light" (Ephesians 5:8 NIV).
- Our testimony should radiate God's goodness. We are to be "blameless and pure, children of God without fault in a crooked and depraved generation, in which you shine like stars in the universe" (Philippians 2:15 NIV).
- We are to serve without becoming enthralled with ourselves and with no compromise. "Do not be yoked together with unbelievers. For what do righteousness and wickedness have in common? Or what fellowship can light have with darkness?" (2 Corinthians 6:14 NIV).

13:13 **Behave decently, as in the daytime.**^NIV To put on the armor of light (13:12) means to behave correctly, *decently,* with life-styles that please God. Even though "the night is nearly over," the world is still in darkness. Jesus said, "This is the verdict: Light has come into the world, but men loved darkness instead of light because their deeds were evil" (John 3:19 NIV). The "deeds of darkness" get their name from the illusion that they cannot be seen by the one who really matters. But, says Paul, even though we live in the final darkness before dawn, we are to *behave decently,* or walk or live in a way that will stand up to examination. For believers, the surrounding darkness is no excuse for indecent behavior.

Most high, glorious God, enlighten the darkness of my heart and give me, Lord, a correct faith, a certain hope, a perfect charity, sense, and knowledge, so that I may carry out your whole and true command.
—Francis of Assisi

Not in orgies and drunkenness, not in sexual immorality and debauchery, not in dissension and jealousy.NIV These are examples of what does not please God; actions, activities, and attitudes that belong to the darkness. These have no place in the believer's life. (See also Galatians 5:19-21.)

> It is not our body which feels, not our mind which thinks, but we, as single human beings, who both feel and think.
> —Thomas Aquinas

Some people are surprised that Paul lists dissension and jealousy with the gross and obvious sins of orgies, drunkenness, and sexual immorality. Like Jesus in his Sermon on the Mount (Matthew 5–7), Paul considers attitudes to be as important as actions. Just as hatred leads to murder, so jealousy leads to strife, and lust to adultery. When Christ returns, he wants to find his people clean on the inside as well as on the outside.

13:14 **Clothe yourselves with the Lord Jesus Christ.**NIV So how do we put on this armor of light (13:12)? How do we behave decently (13:13)? The answer: We clothe ourselves with Christ; we "put on" Christ (Ephesians 4:24; Colossians 3:10). Between the warrior and his armor was special protective clothing. Inside our armor of spiritual resources we need to be "in Christ" (2 Corinthians 5:17). This is deliberate, conscious acceptance of the lordship of Christ, so all our desires and actions are under his control. We live in conformity to his mind and will. Then, we should live as Christ would live, as though Christ lived within us—which he does (Colossians 1:27)!

HOW DO WE CLOTHE OURSELVES WITH THE LORD JESUS CHRIST?
First, we identify with Christ by being baptized (Galatians 3:27). This shows our solidarity with Christ and other Christians.

Second, we exemplify the qualities Jesus showed while he was here on earth (love, humility, truth, and service). In a sense, we role-play what Jesus would do in our situation (see Ephesians 4:24-32; Colossians 3:10-17). We also must not give our desires any opportunity to lead us into sin, avoiding situations that open the door to gratifying sinful desires.

Third, we train ourselves in the use of spiritual weapons: prayer, Bible study and meditation, fellowship with other believers, and other specific habits that we can learn from Jesus.

Fourth, we need to train our minds not to be persuaded by our desires for gratification.

Little children who try on their parents' clothes are demonstrating their desire to grow up. We need to experiment with Christ's habits. Praying for others' healing may be a big first step, but pausing to say thanks to the Father every time we have a meal is a habit well within our reach. Our loving care may not heal the sick physically, but it may work wonders in other areas. How often can we respond, if asked why we are doing something, "Because Jesus did it"? Clothing ourselves with Jesus Christ ought to be an exciting adventure!

Do not think about how to gratify the desires of the sinful nature.[NIV] Living in the light means thinking about how to avoid gratifying sinful desires. Sinful actions and sinful attitudes all start with a single thought. Just as in violent crimes, where premeditation is a factor, premeditation is the first step toward gratifying our desires. A temptation becomes an opportunity to plan to sin. But as harmless as imagination may seem to be, it actually impels us towards sin. If we don't make plans, we can't carry them out.

HOW DO WE PREVENT GRATIFYING OUR DESIRES?
As long as we are wrapped up in Christ, we will find it difficult to gratify our sinful desires. From time to time, we ought to ask some probing questions:
- Does God's love fill me?
- Am I serving others the way Jesus did?
- Am I saying no to my improper desire?
- Can I think of specific examples in each of these categories:
  - whatever is true
  - whatever is noble
  - whatever is right
  - whatever is pure
  - whatever is lovely
  - whatever is admirable (see Philippians 4:8)

Our objective should be to see Christ clearly, so that our sinful desires fade from view.

Romans 14

As any believer knows, relationships with fellow believers can sometimes be strained. Paul knew that unity and harmony among believers is vital for the strength of the church and the success of its mission.

Paul had already established the equality of Jewish and Gentile believers. In this chapter he continues to discuss how that equality could work out in daily living. Paul focuses on two issues: dietary restrictions and observance of special days. Next to circumcision, diet and calendar were the most sensitive issues that separated Jews from all Gentiles. Now, as Jews and Gentiles attempted to work out their distinctive character as Christians, these issues had to be resolved.

Paul wrote the Epistle to the Romans from Corinth, where a similar situation occured (see 1 Corinthians 8–10). Some believers wondered if eating meat previously offered to idols meant that they had participated in idolatry. Furthermore, some Jewish believers still were concerned about the *kosher* preparation of food and the observance of special Jewish holidays. On the other side, some Gentiles were totally unconcerned about special days or the type of food preparation, yet they might worry about whether meat being served had been offered to idols prior to its being sold in the marketplace. If they came out of a pagan background, this would cause them special concern. There were as many potential disagreements over small matters as there were believers in the church. These could develop into impossible divisions. In this chapter, Paul counsels the Roman believers about how to maintain harmony in their very diverse church. In the process of helping the Romans, he also helps believers today maintain unity in our churches. The issues may be different today, but the principles of God's Word still apply.

14:1 **Accept him whose faith is weak.**NIV The key word is *accept* (*proslambanesthe*), which also means "receive" or "welcome." Believers in the church in Rome came from a wide variety of backgrounds. As we've already seen, the major differences were

between Jewish believers and Gentile believers. But there were other differences. Some
believers were slaves, some were masters;
some were wealthy, most were poor. In addition, they were all at different stages of spiritual maturity. Growing in the spirit is like
growing physically—everyone grows at dif-

> In things
> necessary, unity;
> in things not
> necessary, liberty;
> in all things grace.
> —Peter Meiderlen

ferent rates as God works in each life. So the first instruction Paul
gives the church is to *accept,* welcome, and love one another
without judging or condemning—no matter how *weak,* immature,
or unlearned someone's faith may seem. Acceptance creates room
for growth to continue; rejection stunts growth.

Who is weak in faith, and who is strong? Every believer is
weak in some areas and strong in others. A person's faith is
strong in an area if he or she can survive contact with sinners
without falling into their patterns. The person's faith is weak in
an area if that individual must avoid certain activities, people, or
places in order to protect his or her spiritual life.

Without passing judgment on disputable matters.[NIV] This statement assumes that the church will contain differences of opinion
(*disputable matters,* scruples). These kind of disputes are not about
doctrines essential to salvation, but are discussions about differences
of life-style. Paul says we are not to quarrel about issues that are matters of opinion. Differences should not be feared or avoided, but accepted and handled with love. We shouldn't expect everyone, even
in the best church, to agree on every subject. Through sharing ideas
we can come to a fuller understanding of what the Bible teaches.
Our basic approach should be to *accept,* listen to, and respect others.
Differences of opinion need not cause division. They can be a source
of learning and richness in our relationships.

HOLY CAUTION
It is important to take self-inventory in order to find out our
strengths and weaknesses. Whenever in doubt, we should ask,
"Can I do that without sinning? Can I influence others for good,
rather than being influenced by them?" But self-inventory alone
is not enough. We also need the kind of intimate spiritual relationships with at least a few other believers whom we know will
accept us while telling us the truth about the strengths and weaknesses they see in us. In areas of strength, believers should
not fear being defiled by the world; rather, we should go and
serve God. In areas of weakness, believers need to be cau-
tious.

14:2 Some believe in eating anything.^{NRSV} Eating *anything* may refer to freedom from certain Jewish dietary restrictions. When Jews became Christians, many still would be concerned about the proper preparation of food according to their laws. Such restrictions made it impossible for Jewish and Gentile believers to even sit down at a meal together. On the other side, meat that had been offered to idols could pose a problem for Gentile believers—not to mention Jewish Christians.

While the weak eat only vegetables.^{NRSV} The person weaker in the faith eats only vegetables and refuses to eat meat for fear that it had been improperly prepared or that it had been offered to idols.

How could Christians end up eating meat that had been offered to idols? An ancient sacrificial system was at the center of religious, social, and domestic life in the Roman world. After a sacrifice was presented to a god in a pagan temple, only part of it was burned. Often the remainder was sent to the market to be sold. Thus a Christian might easily, even unknowingly, buy such meat in the marketplace or eat it at the home of a friend. Should a Christian question the source of his meat?

> It is foolish to judge those who will be judged by Christ. But also be careful in order that you who judge may not be judged yourself by God.
> —Martin Luther

Some thought there was nothing wrong with eating meat that had been offered to idols because idols were worthless and phony. Others carefully checked the source of their meat or gave up meat altogether to avoid a guilty conscience. This problem was especially acute for Christians who had once been idol worshipers. For them, such a strong reminder of their former paganism might weaken their newfound faith (see also 1 Corinthians 8).

Paul is speaking about immature faith that has not yet developed the strength it needs to stand against external pressures. For example, if a person who once worshiped idols were to become a Christian, he might understand perfectly well that Christ saved him through faith and that idols have no real power. Still, because of his past associations, he might be badly shaken if he knowingly ate meat that had been used as part of a pagan ritual. The same would be true for a Jew whose strict observance to the law would cause him to be concerned about the preparation of the meat.

NEW LEGALISM
It was very difficult for Jews to get kosher meat (from animals killed under the supervision of a rabbi), so many Jews chose to eat only vegetables. Jewish Christians had an additional problem: it was nearly impossible to tell whether meat had come from animals sacrificed to idols (and was later sold in the common meat market). So they ate vegetables to avoid the problem. For some Jews, strict adherence had become a badge portraying loyalty to Judaism. We should not take elements of conduct beyond the scope of Scripture and make them badges of loyalty to Christianity. To do so would be to create a new legalism.

14:3 Must not look down on . . . must not condemn.^{NIV} When believers differ over scruples or matters of opinion, they should not look down on or condemn each other. The Greek for *look down on* means "despise" (see NRSV) or "reject with contempt." The stronger one faces the temptation to despise the weaker brother or sister. The weaker one is in danger of condemning the stronger brother or sister. Neither attitude is acceptable. Believers should not despise or condemn, because God does not; instead, **God has accepted** them both. (The Greek word for *accepted* here is the same word used in verse 1, where Paul explains what we must do.) They all need to remember, first of all, their corporate status as believers, forgiven and saved by God. God accepts people who some of us might feel are unacceptable because of their beliefs or practices.

Paul responds to both brothers in love. Both are acting according to their consciences, but their honest scruples do not need to be made into rules for the church. Our principle should be: In essentials, unity; in nonessentials, liberty; in everything, love.

MUSIC OFFERED TO IDOLS
Conflicts between believers today over the uses and styles of music clearly parallel the concerns of early believers over meat offered to idols. The same principles for resolving the conflict hold true:

- Believers can accept each other without all liking the same music.
- When music strongly reminds some believers of their pagan past, it ought to be used carefully.
- When music demonstrates a special capacity to carry the gospel into the pagan world, it ought to be used prayerfully.
- Differing convictions between believers can be respected.

> Condemnation and looking down on other believers should
> not be part of church life.
> ■ Sometimes both sides of an issue have valid points. Have
> we really listened to each other?

14:4 Who are you to judge?NKJV Every believer will be judged by
God alone (14:10); therefore, believers have no right to judge one
another. Each believer is **someone else's servant**NIV—that is,
God's servant. And before God, he or she **stands or falls.**NKJV
Each person is accountable to Christ, not to others (see also Matthew 7:3-5; Luke 6:37, 41-42; 1 Corinthians 4:3-5). While the
church must be uncompromising in its stand
against activities that are expressly forbidden by Scripture (such as adultery, homosexuality, murder, theft), it should not create
additional rules and regulations and give
them equal standing with God's law. Often
Christians base their moral judgments on
opinion, personal dislikes, or cultural bias,
rather than on the Word of God. When they
do this, they show that their own faith is

> A Christian is a
> most free lord of
> all, subject to none
> . . . A Christian is
> a most dutiful
> servant of all,
> subject to all.
> —Martin Luther

weak, and they demonstrate that they do not think God is powerful enough to guide each of his children. When we stand before
God's judgment seat (14:10), we won't be worried about what
our Christian neighbor has done (see 2 Corinthians 5:10).

He will stand, for the Lord is able to make him stand.NIV No
matter what one believer thinks of another believer's scruples in
some matters, the Lord, as Judge, will defend each person. What
matters is each believer's individual accountability before God.

14:5 One person esteems one day above another.NKJV For Jews, this
day would have probably been the Sabbath; for Christians, the
Lord's day (Sunday). The believers had differing opinions about
the sacredness of certain days. For example, if a Jew who once
worshiped God on the required Jewish holy days were to become
a Christian, he might well know that Christ saved him through
faith, not through his keeping of the law. Still, when the feast
days came, he might feel empty and unfaithful if he didn't dedicate those days to God. Other believers might not have any concern about that and might consider **every day alike**NKJV—in other
words, every day is holy to the Lord. (See also Colossians 2:16-
17.)

The position of each is no matter to Paul, but he does add that **each one should be fully convinced in his own mind**^{NIV}— through prayer and careful thought examining whether that action is what he or she believes God wants him or her to do. People must decide for themselves before God and be convinced of the rightness of their position, even if it means disagreeing with other believers. Believers can disagree on some points and can still be acceptable to God.

14:6 Does so to the Lord.^{NIV} This puts limits on what is acceptable and not acceptable. When it comes to differences of opinion between believers on matters of conscience, each believer should respond *to the Lord*, doing as his or her conscience dictates. It is his or her own personal conscience and accountability to God that matters, not what everyone else thinks. Acceptability should be defined by what we determine God is saying. God desires obedience, and the range of what obedience requires varies greatly in matters of tradition, ritual, or conduct.

This great principle of freedom should guide us: we are to dedicate our actions, attitudes, and habits *to the Lord*. The questions that others ask us about our convictions should cause us to ask, "Am I doing this out of respect for God?" Jesus repeatedly confronted the extreme religious observance of the Sabbath in his day. "Remembering the Sabbath" had become a tool of religious tyranny. Jesus did not legislate the details or method for keeping the Sabbath. He was concerned for the attitude of keeping the Sabbath in its proper place as a gift from God for the rest and spiritual renewal of people (Mark 2:23-28).

14:7 We do not live to ourselves.^{NRSV} We do not live in a vacuum; everything we do affects others. We need to consider our responsibility to others. We can demand freedom for ourselves, but we must also allow other believers that same freedom. If demonstrating our freedom causes us to act in an uncaring, hurtful way towards other believers, we are not yet free.

14:8 If we live, we live to the Lord; and if we die, we die to the Lord.^{NIV} Our lives are ultimately for Christ alone. Our entire life, from beginning to end, belongs to the Lord. We live to him and die to him. Our relationship with the Lord is more important than life or death, and life and death are more important than religious observances. So all our discussions must never interfere with our relationship to Christ, who is our Lord.

Whether we live or die, we belong to the Lord.^{NIV} It is the
Lord's judgment that matters. With respect to the way we treat
other believers, we ought to consider the question, "Am I treating
people as though they also *belong to the Lord?*"

14:9   **For this very reason, Christ died and returned to life.**^{NIV} Christ
died to free us and to deliver us from judgment. He alone is our
judge. For any believer to claim to have the authority to tell others how they should think or act in matters of opinion is to usurp
the position that Christ alone holds.

14:10   **Why do you pass judgment on your brother or sister?**^{NRSV} Believers are not to judge one another, because all of us will be
judged by Christ. **We will all stand before God's judgment seat**
(NIV) to give an accounting of our actions. This is not where God
judges the eternal destiny of all people, but where believers' lives
will be judged for what they have done (see also Matthew 12:36;
1 Peter 4:5).

JUDGMENT
Jesus has been given the authority to judge all the earth. Although his judgment is already working in our lives, there will
be a future, final judgment when Christ returns (Matthew 25:31-
46) and everyone's life is reviewed and evaluated. This will not
be confined to unbelievers; Christians, too, will face a judgment. Their eternal destiny is secure, but Jesus will look at how
they handled gifts, opportunities, and responsibilities in order to
determine their heavenly rewards. On judgment day, God will
deliver the righteous and condemn the wicked. But it is not for
us to judge others' salvation; that is God's work.

14:11   **It is written.** Quoting from Isaiah 45:23, Paul explains that a
time of judgment will come. Isaiah referred to the day when all
the nations (or Gentiles) would bow before God. It was God's
original intention to bring all the peoples to himself through Abraham, but the Jews had discarded God's message to the Gentiles.
We must never participate in rejecting those whom God has accepted. We must be convinced that we will be held responsible
for our own lives before God. Each person will give an account
for himself or herself (14:12; Matthew 12:36). We are to confront
one another in love, concern, and truth, but not in judgment.

14:12   **Each of us will be accountable to God.**^{NRSV} Each believer
will answer for himself or herself alone. Each of us will have

enough to explain without also adding condemning or mocking attitudes toward other believers. We need each other, so we simply cannot afford to be undercutting each other. If anything, we ought to be busy helping ourselves and our fellow believers so that we can give a good account of ourselves to God. In the front lines of a battle, all the soldiers on your side look good.

14:13 **Stop passing judgment.**^{NIV} Believers are to not judge one another regarding their convictions on matters of opinion. Here Paul directs his words to the "strong" believers, explaining that they need to be sensitive about how their convictions affect other believers. Each believer, though free to have his or her own convictions, must also be careful that those convictions don't hinder the spiritual growth of other believers. And if they do, then those freedoms must be reevaluated.

> Scruples . . . serve as purgatives—very active ones sometimes—to a soul which has just risen from sin. They are useful to him for some time, and inspire him with fear and aversion as regards even the shadow of sin.
> —Ignatius Loyola

Not to put any stumbling block or obstacle in your brother's way.^{NIV} Both "strong" and "weak" Christians can cause their brothers and sisters to stumble. A *stumbling block or obstacle* refers to something that might cause someone to trip or fall into sin. The strong but insensitive Christian may flaunt his or her freedom, be a harmful example, and thus offend others' consciences. The scrupulous but weak Christian may try to fence others in with petty rules and regulations, thus causing dissension. Paul wants his readers to be both strong in the faith and sensitive to others' needs. Because we are all strong in certain areas and weak in others, we constantly need to monitor the effects of our behavior on others (see also 1 Corinthians 8:9).

14:14 **No food is unclean in itself.**^{NIV} Referring back to the issue of food (14:2-3, 6), Paul states his own conviction. But not all believers felt the same way. At the Jerusalem council (Acts 15), for example, the Jewish church in Jerusalem asked the Gentile church in Antioch not to eat meat that had been sacrificed to idols. Paul accepted this request, not because he felt that eating such meat was wrong in itself, but because this practice would deeply offend many Jewish believers. Paul did not think the issue was worth dividing the church over; his desire was to promote unity. So, he concludes, **it is unclean for anyone who thinks it unclean**NRSV (see also Mark 7:14-23). Paul's practice was to honor, as far as possible, the convictions of others.

Believers are called to accept one another without judging our varied opinions. However, when the situation has to be faced, how should we deal with those who disagree with us? Paul's response is that all believers should act in love so as to maintain peace in the church.

14:15 **If your brother is distressed because of what you eat, you are no longer acting in love.**NIV If one believer has no scruples about where meat comes from or how it is prepared, but flaunts his or her belief in order to cause one who is concerned to be distressed, then the stronger individual is not acting in love. The conduct of stronger believers is not to be decided by what they feel is their better insight into the Scriptures, or what they feel would "strengthen" those weaker ones. Rather, it is to be decided by love and sensitivity.

Do not by your eating destroy your brother for whom Christ died.NIV The stronger believer must not let what he or she wants to do, when it is a minor matter such as whether to eat meat or not, become a stumbling block that could destroy a weaker brother or sister. The Greek verb *apollue* often means "to bring about destruction." It could also mean a "ruin" of one's conscience if the weaker believer goes against his or her scruples. We are to act in love. That other person, no matter how much we may disagree with him or her, is still someone for whom Christ died. If Christ gave his life for that person, surely no believer has the option to ruin him or her because of food!

Mature Christians shouldn't flaunt their freedom. They should be sensitive to younger converts whose faith can be destroyed by such freedom. For example, a young Christian addicted to gambling may be damaged by our freedom to play cards. Some activities may be alright in and of themselves, but not around weaker new converts.

14:16 **Do not allow what you consider good to be spoken of as evil.**NIV When believers persist in flaunting their freedom in certain areas, this could result in that very freedom being slandered because of their unloving attitude. This has no place in Christian congregations and would be a poor advertisement of Christianity to unbelievers.

This verse also indicates that honesty must be part of our communication with other believers. Convictions are our feelings

about actions that we consider *good*. Whether abstaining from
meat or enjoying meat, both parties were free to speak their mind.
But they were not to insist theirs was the only possible exercise
of freedom. In disputable matters, believers are free to partake or
abstain.

14:17 **The kingdom of God is not a matter of eating and drinking.**NIV
After all, says Paul, if we let those little scruples become major
points of contention, we have forgotten what the kingdom of God
is all about. It has nothing to do with what we eat or drink (Matthew 6:31, 33). Instead, it is **righteousness, peace and joy in the
Holy Spirit.** Arguing over scruples does not contribute to righteousness (a right relationship with God), peace (unity with fellow
Christians), or joy (spiritual contentment) in the churches. The believers need to concern themselves with doing what is right in the
essentials, maintaining harmony, and sharing God's joy, not in
forcing their scruples and life-styles on others.

14:18 **Anyone who serves Christ in this way is pleasing to God and
approved by men.**NIV Those who serve Christ by doing right before God, maintaining peace among the believers, and sharing joy
with others are the ones who will accomplish the acceptable service to Christ—they will please both God and people.

14:19 **Let us pursue the things which make for peace and the things
by which one may edify another.**NKJV Christian fellowship
should be characterized by peace and building up one another
(see also 1 Thessalonians 5:11). False believers and immature
Christians have been known to use the "weaker brother argument" to support their own opinions, prejudices, or standards.
"You must live by these standards," they say, "or you will be offending the weaker brother." In truth, the person would often be
offending no one but the speaker. While Paul urges us to be sensitive to those whose faith may be harmed by our actions, we
should not sacrifice our liberty in Christ just to satisfy the selfish
motives of those who are trying to force their opinions on us.
Strong believers need not judge their own liberty by the troubled
consciences of the weak. Each believer is to follow Christ.

14:20 **Do not destroy the work of God for the sake of food.**NKJV Food
and our feelings about it, or any scruples that are not specifically
condemned in scripture, are not worth arguing about, flaunting,
or judging—these should never be allowed to tear down other believers or tear apart the church.

It is wrong for you to make others fall by what you eat.[NRSV] It is wrong for one believer to insist on his or her freedom when it causes others' faith to falter. If it causes someone else to fall, then put it aside for the other's sake. Paul wrote to the believers in Corinth: "'Everything is permissible'—but not everything is beneficial. 'Everything is permissible'—but not everything is constructive. Nobody should seek his own good, but the good of others. . . . So whether you eat or drink or whatever you do, do it all for the glory of God. Do not cause anyone to stumble, whether Jews, Greeks or the church of God" (1 Corinthians 10:23-24, 31-32 NIV).

INTERDEPENDENCE
Sin is not just a private matter. Everything we do affects others, and we have to consider the impact of what we do. God created us to be interdependent, not independent. We who are strong in our faith must, without pride or condescension, treat others with love, patience, and self-restraint. Nothing like food should be so important to us that we insist on having it even at the risk of harming another.

The matter of personal convictions among believers is sometimes complicated by the variety of audiences who watch our behavior. An example of this can be seen in the life of Eric Liddell, who died while interned in a Japanese POW camp during World War II. He was a missionary in China when he was taken captive.

In his earlier years Eric demonstrated an unusual ability to run. He was a world-class sprinter in the longer distances. He postponed his intended departure for China for what he saw as an immediate opportunity to serve God in some way by representing the British empire in the 1924 Olympics. When Eric discovered that the qualifying heat for the 100 meters (his speciality) was scheduled for Sunday, he withdrew because of his personal convictions. He was forced to weigh the effect that ignoring his convictions could have on many believers who were watching him against the effect of disappointing multitudes of his countrymen whose hopes for victory were riding on him. He held to his convictions, was replaced by another runner, and eventually ran in a longer race that did not involve the same complication. Eric won that race, much to the delight of everyone.

But even that second opportunity was not as valuable as the indelible lesson he demonstrated to the world about the importance of having convictions and standing firmly by them.

14:21   **Better not to eat meat or drink wine or to do anything else
that will cause your brother to fall.**^NIV Paul followed his own advice, for he had told the Corinthians, "Therefore, if what I eat
causes my brother to fall into sin, I will never eat meat again, so
that I will not cause him to fall" (1 Corinthians 8:13 NIV). Truly
strong believers can restrict their freedoms for the sake of others.

14:22   **Whatever you believe about these things keep between yourself and God.**^NIV In those areas of disagreement, Paul counsels
the believers to keep their beliefs between themselves and God.
The brother or sister who believes in certain freedoms should not
be trying to influence others with scruples to "loosen up." Those
bothered by some actions should not be judging or condemning
those with freedom, nor should they be trying to force their scruples on the entire church. Instead all believers should seek a clear
conscience before God. The believer who does so is **blessed**
(NIV) and **does not condemn himself in what he approves.**^NKJV
This person has a good, but not insensitive, conscience.

14:23   **Those who have doubts are condemned if they eat, because
they do not act from faith.**^NRSV If a believer does something that
he or she is not sure is right or wrong, that action will bring condemnation.

Whatever does not proceed from faith is sin.^NRSV We try to
steer clear of actions forbidden by Scripture, of course, but sometimes Scripture is silent. Then we should follow our conscience.
To go against a conviction will leave a person with a guilty or uneasy conscience. When God shows us that something is wrong
for us, we should avoid it. But we should not look down on other
Christians who exercise their freedom in those areas.

Romans 15

LIVE TO PLEASE OTHERS / 15:1-13

Paul continues his discussion from chapter 14 on how believers should relate to one another, especially when there are disagreements on matters of opinion. There is no question that a variety of opinions on many matters will be represented in any church—and the church in Rome was no exception. Paul uses "strong" and "weak" to describe the believers. "Strong" believers are those who understand their freedom in Christ and who are sensitive to the concerns of others. They realize that true obedience comes from the heart and conscience of each individual.

"Weak" believers are those whose faith has not yet matured so as to be free of some of the rituals and traditions. "Strong" believers can function in a variety of situations and be influences for good; "weak" believers find that they need to stay away from some situations in order to maintain a clear conscience. But both are still *believers*, and both are still seeking to obey God.

As long as these matters of conviction do not entail disobedience to God, strong believers must not look down on their weaker brothers and sisters, and weak believers must not judge and condemn the freedom of stronger brothers and sisters (14:1-12). Also, strong believers must not flaunt their freedom in a way that hinders the spiritual growth of the weaker brother or sister (14:13-23). Our best example for dealing with others in the church is Jesus Christ. We should imitate him.

15:1 We who are strong.^{NRSV} Paul identifies himself as one of the "strong." He was comfortable in any company because his main goal was to win others to Christ. To the Corinthians he wrote:

- *Though I am free and belong to no man, I make myself a slave to everyone, to win as many as possible. To the Jews I became like a Jew, to win the Jews. To those under the law I became like one under the law (though I myself am not under the law), so as to win those under the law. To those not having the law I became like one not having the law (though I am not free from God's law but am under Christ's law), so as to win those not having the law. To the weak I became weak, to win the weak. I have become all things to all men so that by all possible means I might save some. (1 Corinthians 9:19-22* NIV*)*

Ought to put up with the failings of the weak, and not to please ourselves.NRSV The word for *ought* is present tense, showing that stronger believers always have this obligation. They may find themselves frustrated by the *failings of the weak*—their concerns and worries over what, to the strong, seems trivial. But the responsibility lies with the strong to maintain harmony in the church by bearing with these brothers and sisters (see Galatians 6:1-2). The stronger believers demonstrate their spiritual strength precisely at those moments when they are practicing compassion for those who are weaker. The kind of strength modeled by Christ allowed him to *put up with* our *failings*. We ought to do the same for one another.

15:2 **Please his neighbor for his good, to build him up.**NIV The strong believer must never be self-centered, but must be concerned for the spiritual welfare of his *neighbor*—the weaker person beside him or her in the congregation. This "pleasing" is done with a goal in mind—to encourage and build up that other believer in the faith. There is a fine line to walk—the stronger person should not push the weaker one to change his or her ways before he or she is ready; neither should the stronger person pander to the scruples of that weaker one by allowing such scruples to become rules for the church. Instead, the stronger believers should bear with (15:1) and work to help the weaker believers in their faith; this will benefit the church as a whole.

It is not always possible to predict exactly how acceptance and encouragement will help another believer grow, but it is certainly the way to *build him up*.

15:3 **Christ did not please himself.** Christ was the "strongest" human who ever lived—he did not please himself, but did God's will. Certainly death on a cruel cross was not the path he would have chosen to please himself, but his mission was to please God (see John 4:34; 5:30; 8:29). Most of the world can't recognize the *strength* God calls for (1 Corinthians 1:25). Christ's *strength* showed itself most graphically in his death and resurrection (2 Corinthians 13:4). God's *strength* is made perfect in weakness—so he allowed Paul to minister with an infirmity (2 Corinthians

12:7-10). Those who are *strongest* are actually servants of all (Mark 10:42-45).
Strength is not independence *from* God, but
total dependence *on* God. Strength in the
church doesn't come from each believer being completely independent, but from mutual interdependence. Truly strong believers
are those who are willing to limit their free-

> You will not
> understand what it
> means to be a
> servant until
> someone treats
> you like one.
> —Gerry Fosdal

doms in order to care for and love their weaker brothers and sisters.

**As it is written, "The insults of those who insult you have
fallen on me."**NRSV Paul quotes from Psalm 69:9. This messianic
psalm prophesied the Messiah's coming into the world and what
would happen to him. Christ faced reproach and insults because
he did not choose to please himself; instead, he chose to do what
God had called him to do. How much more should we, who are
called by his name, also choose to please God rather than ourselves.

NOT OUR WILL
Real Christian freedom means inconvenience. In the complexities of relationships, a free person will limit his or her actions in
one area in order to accomplish a more important goal in another. Bearing with weaknesses, identifying with those who are
persecuted for the cause of Christ, and seeking others' good
demonstrate a life of love. Maturity develops when we don't allow our convictions to become excuses for treating poorly our
brothers and sisters in Christ.

15:4 **Everything that was written in the past was written to teach
us.**NIV All of Scripture (here referring to the Old Testament) was
written and preserved for future generations. Our scriptural
knowledge affects our attitude toward the present and the future.
The more we know about what God has done in years past, the
greater will be our confidence in what he will do in the days
ahead. We should read our Bible diligently to increase our trust
that God's will is best for us.

To Timothy, who was with Paul when he wrote Romans
(16:21), Paul later expands what he means by *written to
teach us*. He reminds his youthful assistant of the Scriptures'
divine origin and describes their purpose: "The whole Bible
was given to us by inspiration from God and is useful to
teach us what is true and to make us realize what is wrong in

our lives; it straightens us out and helps us do what is right"
(2 Timothy 3:16 TLB).

**So that by steadfastness and by the encouragement of
the scriptures we might have hope.**^{NRSV} How does the Bible
encourage us? (1) God's attributes and character constantly remind us in whom our hope is based (Psalm 46:1-2).
(2) The biographies of saints who overcame great obstacles
give us examples of what can be done with God's help (Hebrews 11). (3) The direct exhortation of Scripture calls for
endurance and speaks encouragement (James 1:2-4; Hebrews 12:1-2). (4) The prophetic statements support our
hope for a wonderful future planned for us in eternity (Romans 5:1-5).

Paul admonishes strong believers not to please themselves but
to please God and others. Scripture records stories of those who
pleased God, those who didn't, and those who failed but learned

PROFILE OF A STRONG CHURCH

A place of refuge, where people find help	15:1
A place of instruction, where people's faith and lives are built up	15:2
A place centered on Christ, where Jesus is held up as a model	15:3
A place filled with the Word, where the Scriptures are known and applied	15:4
A place of prayer, where endurance and encouragement are sought from God	15:4-5
A place of acceptance, where there is an atmosphere and understanding of hope	15:4
A place of togetherness, where unity is recognized as a product of God's work	15:5
A place of witness, where acceptance of others is Christlike	15:8

from their mistakes. We are to endure as Christ endured and be
encouraged by the examples of other believers. This gives us
hope as we look toward the future.

15:5 **May the God who gives endurance and encouragement give
you a spirit of unity among yourselves as you follow Christ Jesus.**^{NIV} The endurance and encouragement received from the
Scriptures (15:4) have their ultimate source in God, for the Scriptures are his. Paul asks God to give the believers an attitude of
unity—Jews and Gentiles, weak and strong, conservative and lib-
eral—as they seek to follow Christ. This prayer is strikingly similar to the one Jesus prayed with his disciples at the end of his
final meal with them, "I have given them the glory that you gave
me, that they may be one as we are one: I in them and you in me.
May they be brought to complete unity to let the world know that
you sent me and have loved them even as you have loved me"
(John 17:22-23 NIV). Unity is not an optional behavior for believers.

LORDSHIP
To accept Jesus' lordship in all areas of life means to share his
values and perspectives. Just as we take Jesus' view on the
authority of Scripture and the resurrection, we are to have his
attitude of love toward other Christians as well (have a "spirit of
unity"). As we grow in faith and come to know Jesus better, we
will become more capable of maintaining this attitude of loving
unity throughout each day. Christ's attitude is explained in more
detail in Philippians 2.

15:6 **So that with one heart and mouth you may glorify the God
and Father of our Lord Jesus Christ.**^{NIV} The unity Paul prays
for is unity of heart (worship and fellowship) and mouth (witness
and teaching) that continually glorifies God and Jesus Christ.
This should be the ultimate purpose of each believer and of the
entire church.

15:7 **Accept one another . . . just as Christ accepted you.**^{NIV} If our goal
is to glorify God, we cannot be caught up in dissension, disagree-
ments, or arguments, especially about trivial matters. Instead, we
should lovingly accept one another—there is to be no one-sided acceptance. *All* are to accept one another and live in harmony. At one
time, we all were weak. And many strong believers are still weak in
some areas. Christ is our model of what acceptance means. When
we realize that Christ accepted us, as unlovely and sinful and immature as we were when we came to him (see 5:6, 8, 10), then we will

accept our brothers and sisters. The world sits up and takes notice
when believers of widely differing backgrounds practice Christlike
acceptance. This brings **praise to God.**NIV

MUTUAL ACCEPTANCE
The Roman church was a hybrid community. It was made up of
Jews and Gentiles, slaves and free, rich and poor, strong and
weak. So it was difficult for them to accept one another. Accepting means taking people into our homes as well as into our
hearts, sharing meals and activities, and avoiding racial and
economic discrimination. We must go out of our way to avoid favoritism. Consciously spend time greeting those you don't nor-
mally talk to, minimize differences, and seek common ground
for fellowship.

15:8-9 **Christ has become a servant of the Jews on behalf of God's
truth.**NIV Having referred to unity again, Paul feels compelled to
remind his readers that the greatest example of unity brings both
Jews and Gentiles under the lordship of Christ. Jesus came to
bring the truth to the Jews and to show that God is true to his
promises—**the promises given to the patriarchs.**NRSV At the
same time, Christ came so **that the Gentiles might glorify God
for His mercy.**NKJV The promises, the covenants, were made to
the patriarchs of the Jewish nation alone, but God, in his mercy,
made them available to the Gentiles as well. God's offer of salvation to the Gentiles would cause them to glorify him for his
mercy. Without God's mercy, the Gentiles could never receive his
blessings and his salvation.

To offer final proof, Paul quoted four Old Testament passages,
taken from the three divisions of the Old Testament—the Law,
the Prophets, and the Psalms. The Old Testament pictured the
Gentiles as receiving blessings from God.

**As it is written: "Therefore I will praise you among the Gen-
tiles; I will sing hymns to your name."**NIV Paul quotes from
Psalm 18:49 and 2 Samuel 22:50. In this psalm and the parallel
passage in 2 Samuel 22, David praises God for delivering him
from his enemies and from King Saul who was trying to kill him.
He writes that he would praise God among the Gentiles, not just
among his own people.

15:10 **"Rejoice, O Gentiles, with his people."** This is a quote from
Deuteronomy 32:43, sometimes called "The Song of Moses,"
where Moses poetically recites a brief history of Israel, reminds

the people of their mistakes, warns them to avoid repetition of those mistakes, and offers the hope that comes only in trusting God. Moses calls the Gentiles to rejoice with the Hebrews.

15:11 **"Praise the Lord, all you Gentiles, and let all the peoples praise him."**NRSV In this quote from Psalm 117:1, the psalmist calls the Gentiles to sing praises to God. It must have been startling, at times, for Jews to be reminded from their own Scriptures that the God who had chosen them was not theirs alone. Since God's unlimited love has been extended to all people, Jewish Christians should accept the Gentile Christians as full-fledged participants in God's kingdom.

15:12 **Isaiah says, "The Root of Jesse will spring up, one who will arise to rule over the nations; the Gentiles will hope in him."**NIV Paul quotes from Isaiah's prophecy of the Messiah in Isaiah 11:10. The *Root of Jesse* refers to Christ as the heir from the family line of Jesse, David's father (1 Samuel 16:1). Isaiah prophesied that the Gentiles would also *hope in* or believe in the Messiah.

In the foregoing quotations, Paul demonstrated that the Old Testament spoke of the Gentiles being included in the messianic kingdom. Since Christ would rule over both the Jews and the Gentiles, they should accept each other as members of God's family.

15:13 **May the God of hope fill you with all joy and peace as you trust in him.**NIV Paul again prays for the believers (as in 15:5). This time Paul prays that the God who gives hope will give them joy (as they anticipate what God has in store for them) and peace (as they rest in the assurance that God will do as he has promised). Then, the believers can **overflow with hope by the power of the Holy Spirit.**NIV It is by the power of the Holy Spirit that God accomplishes his care for his people—giving them endurance, encouragement, unity (15:5), hope, joy, and peace. *Hope* comes as a by-product of the Holy Spirit's work. It does not come from our own senses or experiences. This is Paul's benediction to his letter. What follows from this point are his personal plans and greetings.

PAUL EXPLAINS HIS REASON FOR WRITING / 15:14-32

Although Paul referred briefly to his reason for writing earlier in the letter, here in his closing remarks, he says more about his rea-

sons for writing. He also explains his writing style. In these
verses, we feel the heartbeat of Paul's missionary zeal.

15:14 **I myself feel confident about you, my brothers and sisters.**NRSV
Although Paul had never met most of the be-
lievers in Rome, he was convinced (most
likely from reports he had heard of them)
that they were spiritually mature.

> In the poor man
> who knocks at my
> door, in my ailing
> mother, in the
> young man who
> seeks my advice,
> the Lord himself is
> present: therefore
> let us wash His
> feet.
> —C. S. Lewis

**You yourselves are full of goodness, filled
with all knowledge, and able to instruct
one another.**NRSV Paul knew they were doing
good and living to please God, that they had
a full understanding of the truth of the gospel, and were able to counsel and help guide
one another. Paul was practicing the kind of
encouragement that he had just asked them
to use with each other.

15:15-16 **Written you quite boldly . . . to remind you.**NIV Paul knew these
believers were mature, but he wrote this lengthy letter on the basics of Christianity to *remind* them. It may have seemed bold of
him to write in this manner to a church he had not founded, but
he was the apostle to the Gentiles, and it was in that capacity that
he wrote to them. (See also 2 Peter 1:12; 3:1-2.)

**Because of the grace given me by God to be a minister of
Christ Jesus to the Gentiles.**NRSV Paul is qualified to write to
them because God had allowed him the special privilege of being
a *minister* to the Gentiles. The Greek word here is *leitourgon*,
meaning "public servant."

Priestly duty of proclaiming the gospel of God.NIV Paul viewed
his ministry to the Gentiles as a *priestly duty*. The Greek here is
hierourgounta, meaning "to work in sacred things." Paul's ministry was a sacred task because he was *proclaiming the gospel* to
the Gentiles.

**Gentiles might become an offering acceptable to God, sancti-
fied by the Holy Spirit.**NIV Paul faithfully proclaimed the gospel
to the Gentiles so that they would receive the Good News, and become acceptable to God, sanctified (literally "having been sanctified" or "having been set apart") by the Holy Spirit. Paul's
missionary work was an act of worship. He viewed the Gentile

church as a consecrated, sacrificial offering which he presented to
God for his acceptance.

ACCEPTABLE OFFERINGS
From Paul we learn that to produce offerings acceptable to
God:
- Our motives must be clear and cleansed—the love of Christ
  must be what compels us (2 Corinthians 5:14).
- Our preparation and participation should be wholehearted de-
  sire to serve God, not human beings.
- Our expectations and results must be left in God's control.
- Our objective should be to glorify God by what he has done
  in us.

15:17 **Therefore I glory in Christ Jesus in my service to God.**^{NIV} Paul
did not glory in what he had done, but in what God had done
through him. The word *therefore* ties this sentence to Paul's previous explanation of his work among the Gentiles and the fact
that God had accepted them. This caused him to glory in his service because of what Christ was accomplishing through him. We
should reevaluate our attitudes in service and ministry. How often
do we view our efforts as giving glory to God?

:18-19 **I will not venture to speak of anything except what Christ has
accomplished through me.**^{NRSV} Being proud of God's work is
not a sin—it is worship. Paul knew that all the glory for his ministry went to Christ alone, for it was Christ who was accomplishing
the work of **leading the Gentiles to obey God.**^{NIV} (The word for
obey here refers to coming to Christ for salvation.) But Paul well
understood that he was the vessel through whom God was working because the mission to the Gentiles was being accomplished
by what Paul had **said and done.**^{NIV}

**By the power of signs and wonders, by the power of the Spirit
of God.**^{NRSV} Paul had, by the power of God's Spirit, done *signs*
(the Greek word is *semeia*, miracles to show God's truth) and
wonders (the Greek word is *terata*, miracles to catch people's attention so they want to know more).

The words *signs, wonders,* and *miracles* are used throughout
the book of Acts to describe what the apostles did—these verified
the authenticity of their words. Paul wrote to the Corinthians,
"The things that mark an apostle—signs, wonders and miracles—
were done among you with great perseverance" (2 Corinthians
12:12; see also Hebrews 2:3-4).

From Jerusalem all the way around to Illyricum, I have fully proclaimed the gospel of Christ.^{NIV} Because of the Holy Spirit's empowerment, Paul had taken the Good News from Jerusalem to Illyricum. Also known as Dalmatia (see 2 Timothy 4:10), Illyricum was a Roman territory on the Adriatic Sea between present-day Italy and Greece. It covered much the same territory as present-day Yugoslavia. See the map in the introduction.

15:20 **My ambition to preach the gospel where Christ was not known.**^{NIV} The reason for the extent of Paul's ministry was the driving ambition to share Christ in territories where Christ was not known or heard of yet. Paul saw his mission as moving into the centers of population, starting a church, being sure it had a good foundation, then allowing it to continue the work of evangelization in its area while Paul moved on to areas uncharted by the gospel.

AMBITION
Paul says that he has "ambition." Ambition can be a difficult topic for Christians because we see so many bad examples of ambitious people who claw their way to the top. But certainly that isn't the kind of ambition one sees in Paul. Instead of looking out for himself and working hard for personal advancement, he was ambitious to serve God—for Paul that meant to "preach the gospel where Christ was not known." Are you ambitious for God? Do you want, more than anything else to please him, to do his will? Ask God for "holy ambition."

I do not build on someone else's foundation.^{NRSV} Other preachers would have brought the gospel to some areas that Paul had not gone to; they would be involved in the follow-up and spiritual growth of the believers there. Paul did not want to move into those areas when it was more important for him to preach where people had not yet heard the Good News.

15:21 **It is written: "Those who were not told about him will see, and those who have not heard will understand."**^{NIV} Paul quotes from part of Isaiah 52:15 to show that those who had been ignorant of God's Word would respond positively to the Messiah. Isaiah predicted how surprised the Gentile nations would be when they saw the humiliation and exaltation of God's Servant, the Messiah. Paul uses this prophetic word to affirm the need for his missionary efforts to the Gentiles.

15:22 **I also have been much hindered from coming to you.**^{NKJV} Because
of his driving force to bring the gospel to people who had not yet
heard, Paul had been *hindered* from going to Rome. He had much territory to cover in Asia Minor and around Greece, so it seems likely that
he postponed his trip to Rome because there was already a strong
church there. However, it is possible that Satan had hindered him
from coming to Rome (as in 1 Thessalonians 2:18) or that the imperial edict of Rome (in A.D. 44), which mandated the expulsion of the
Jews from Rome, had hindered him from going to Rome.

15:23 **No more place for me to work in these regions.**^{NIV} But now
Paul feels that enough local churches have been established
throughout the area (not just by him, but by the other apostles and
other missionaries) that these churches could complete the work
of evangelization.

I have been longing for many years to see you.^{NIV} Because he
feels that his work in the regions of Jerusalem and Greece has
been accomplished, and because of his great desire to meet the believers in Rome, he will visit them on his next trip. The fact that
he knows so many of them personally is reason enough for his desire (see chapter 16). But up to this point, his pioneering missionary work has taken all his time.

15:24 **I plan to do so when I go to Spain.**^{NIV} The planned destination
of Paul's next trip is Spain. The Greek word for *when* is more indefinite, better translated "whenever." On the way, he will stop in
Rome to **visit** with the believers there **while passing through.**^{NIV}
Apparently Paul did not plan to stay long in Rome, but he hoped
that the believers there would **assist** him (i.e., encourage him,
help financially with the trip, be a home base) as he continued on
to Spain. This statement should dispel any concern that Paul
would try to assume some sort of permanent leadership position
or take advantage of the church's hospitality. Instead, he was planning to move through, to the next uncharted territory for the gospel, at the western limit of the Roman empire.

Spain was a Roman colony, and there were Jews there. Paul
wanted to take the Good News there. Also, Spain had many great
minds and influential leaders in the Roman world (Lucan, Mar-
tial, Hadrian), and perhaps Paul thought Christianity would advance greatly in such an atmosphere.

15:25 **I am going to Jerusalem in a ministry to the saints.**^{NRSV} Paul
was indefinite about exactly when he would visit Rome because

he was busy with another matter at present. Paul was on his way to Jerusalem from Corinth (from where he had most likely written this letter; he had been in that city for about three months, see Acts 20:3) with a delegation of men chosen by each church to deliver offerings from those churches to the believers (*saints*) in Jerusalem (see Acts 24:17; 1 Corinthians 16:1-4; 2 Corinthians 9:13). Paul considered his delivery of this offering as an act of worship. Indeed, it was a fitting climax to his ministry in the east before he moved west.

It is quite evident that Paul was not aware that his plan to go to Rome was about to be accomplished in a way he did not foresee. His imprisonment in Jerusalem and in Caesarea and his eventual travel to Rome was completely at the expense of the Roman empire.

15:26   **It pleased those from Macedonia and Achaia to make a certain contribution for the poor among the saints who are in Jerusalem.**NKJV Paul had collected voluntary offerings from various churches, including the ones in Macedonia and Achaia, and would be taking that to the poor believers in Jerusalem. He mentioned these two provinces in particular because he had been in close contact with them during his months in Corinth. (See 2 Corinthians 8 and 9.)

15:27   **They were pleased to do this, and indeed they owe it to them.**NRSV Paul again stressed the voluntary nature of the offering by repeating that the churches were *pleased* to give. But Paul also considered it an obligation.

If the Gentiles have shared in the Jews' spiritual blessings, they owe it to the Jews to share with them their material blessings.NIV That is, if the Gentiles had received the gospel (*spiritual blessings*) originally from Jerusalem (where Christianity began), surely they would want to offer financial help to the needy poor there (*material blessings*).

Not only that, but Paul hoped that such generosity and caring among the churches would strengthen the ties between them. The Jerusalem church, obviously made up mostly of Jews, at first had a difficult time even accepting ministry to the Gentiles (see Peter's situation in Acts 10:1–11:18). Some were still concerned about these mostly-Gentile churches. Gentile churches helping to meet the needs of the Jerusalem church was a sure way to maintain harmony among the believers and strengthen the bond of brotherhood.

This was not the first time a collection was taken to the church

in Jerusalem. About ten years earlier, Paul and Barnabas brought
a collection from the church in Antioch of Syria to help the Jerusalem church during a time of famine (Acts 11:30; 12:25). It
seems that being Christian and being poor went together if one
lived in Jerusalem. Christianity was not well accepted by the Jewish authorities, and when Jews became Christians they were often
cut off from family and friends. The Jerusalem church probably
had little means of support, so help from the other churches was
needed and greatly appreciated.

15:28 **When I have completed this, and have delivered to them what
has been collected.**NRSV After making sure the church in Jerusalem received the offerings from the other churches, Paul would
take his anticipated trip.

I will go to Spain and visit you on the way.NIV Paul was looking
forward to taking the gospel to new lands west of Rome. But
even the best-laid plans may not happen as we anticipate. Eventually Paul got to Rome, but it was after having his life threatened,
becoming a prisoner of Rome, enduring a shipwreck, getting bit
by a poisonous snake on the island of Malta, and landing finally
in Rome under arrest (see Acts 27–28)! Tradition says that Paul
was released for a time, and that he used this opportunity to go to
Spain to preach the Good News. This journey is not mentioned in
the book of Acts.

15:29 **I know that when I come to you, I will come in the fullness of
the blessing of Christ.**NRSV Paul knows that when he arrives in
Rome, he will come with blessings to share: "I long to see you so
that I may impart to you some spiritual gift to make you strong—
that is, that you and I may be mutually encouraged by each
other's faith" (1:11-12 NIV). The sense of this verse can be read in
two ways: Paul will be bringing a fresh awareness of all the benefits of being united with Christ; or Paul is expecting to experience
with the Romans a rich time of fellowship in Christ. The benefits
of spending time with other believers, even those we do not
know, are very real. From time to time, Christians should worship
in unfamiliar places, just to be reminded how oneness in Christ
overcomes the barrier of meeting strangers.

15:30 **I urge you . . . by our Lord Jesus Christ and by the love of the
Spirit, to join me in my struggle by praying to God for me.**NIV
Paul asked his readers to pray for him, a request he made in many of
his letters (Ephesians 6:19-20; Colossians 4:3-4; 1 Thessalonians

5:25; 2 Thessalonians 3:1-2; Philemon 22). Paul needed their intercessory prayer; he needed them to join him in promoting the cause of Christ. The Greek term *sunagonisasthai* ("to strive together with him") was often used in connection with athletic events where a team had to put forth a great, concerted action. Though the Roman believers could not be physically with Paul, they could join his efforts through prayer. This is a subtle but effective emphasis that Paul was not an independent agent. He was part of the body, and he needed the body's help.

STRUGGLING TOGETHER
Too often we see prayer as a time for comfort, reflection, or making our requests known to God. But here Paul urges believers to join in his *struggle* by means of prayer. Prayer is a weapon that all believers possees and should use in interceding for others. Many of us know believers who are living in difficult places in order to communicate the gospel. Sending them funds is part of joining them in their struggles. But prayer is also a crucial way of being with them. Missionaries are unanimous in desiring the prayers of those who have sent them out. Do our prayers reflect that urgency?

15:31 **That I may be rescued from the unbelievers in Judea, and that my ministry to Jerusalem may be acceptable to the saints.**[NRSV] Paul's specific prayer requests pertain to his return to Jerusalem. Paul knew of the potential danger awaiting him there (see Acts 20:22-24; 21:27ff.), so he asked them to pray for his safety. Paul was still regarded as a traitor to his faith, and some of his fellow Jews might have considered it their religious duty to get rid of him for good. He also asked the Roman Christians to pray that the offering he was bringing to the Jerusalem church would be received and distributed acceptably. He may have been fearing that the church would not want to accept the money.

15:32 **By God's will I may come to you with joy and together with you be refreshed.**[NIV] If all went well in Jerusalem, Paul hoped to then visit the church in Rome, finally to be able to relax with them and be refreshed. Paul's anticipation of being with other believers puts to shame our halfhearted efforts at preparing for worship and looking forward to the time we spend with other believers. Could it be that most of the lack of vitality in church life is created by the very ones who notice its absence? If we don't mentally prepare ourselves to be with Christ and his people, how can we expect to be refreshed by those encounters?

15:33 **The God of peace be with you all. Amen.**[NKJV] Paul closes this
section of the letter with another personal benediction for the believers. *The God of peace* was a Jewish benediction, and Paul offers it here to his Jewish and Gentile Christian readers. This
phrase sounds like it should signal the end of the book, but the
epistle continues on for another chapter. However, this benediction pronounces the end of Paul's teaching—the last chapter is an
extended salutation. His greeting at the opening of the letter was
"Grace and peace to you" (1:7). Most of the letter had explained
the nature and results of God's grace. It was natural, then that he
close by referring also to the *God of peace.*

Romans 16

Rome was the capital of the empire. As Jerusalem was the center of Jewish life, Rome was the world's political, religious, social, and economic center. There the major governmental decisions were made, and from there the gospel spread to the ends of the earth. The church in Rome was a dynamic mixture of Jews, Gentiles, slaves, free people, men, women, Roman citizens, and world travelers; therefore, it had potential for both great influence and great conflict.

The Romans had built a tremendous system of roads between the various major cities of its vast empire, so movement by people from place to place was not unusual. As Paul preached in the eastern part of the empire, he went first to the key cities—Jerusalem, Antioch in Syria, Philippi, Corinth, Athens, Ephesus. Along the way he met many believers who eventually ended up in Rome. The fact that Paul knew the whereabouts of so many of his friends and co-workers gives us a glimpse into the interest this great missionary had in the people to whom he ministered and who ministered to him. This final chapter reveals a treasury of friends Paul expected to see in Rome.

Paul had not yet been to Rome to meet all the Christians there, and, of course, he has not yet met us. We too live in a cosmopolitan setting with the entire world open to us. We also have the potential for both widespread influence and wrenching conflict. We should listen carefully to and apply Paul's teaching about unity, service, and love.

16:1 **I commend to you Phoebe our sister, who is a servant of the church at Cenchrea.**NKJV Phoebe was known as a servant or "deacon." The Greek word used here is *diakonon* (masculine gender); literally she was a deacon, not a deaconess. However, this description could suggest her entire service, not just an office in the local church at Cenchrea. Apparently she was a wealthy person who helped support Paul's ministry. Phoebe was highly regarded in the church (suggested by the phrase *a servant of the* *church*). Furthermore, because Paul specifically commends her to the Romans it is likely that she delivered this letter from Corinth to Rome. This provides evidence that women had important roles in the early church, as well as important roles in business. Paul mentions by name nine women among his friends in Rome, calling them all "fellow workers." *Phoebe* was wealthy, and she apparently had some business in Rome to attend to. Paul, knowing that her itinerary would bring her to Rome before he could get there, asked her to personally carry this letter for him. The letter, then, served as an introduction for *Phoebe* to the church in Rome.

> It's amazing what could get done for God if no one worried who got the credit.
> —Unknown

Cenchrea. Cenchrea, the town where Phoebe lived, was the eastern port of Corinth, six miles from the city center (see Acts 18:18). The church here was probably a daughter church of the one in Corinth.

16:2 Receive her in the Lord in a manner worthy of the saints.^{NKJV} Paul here asks that the believers welcome Phoebe and **give her any help she may need from you, for she has been a great help to many people, including me.**^{NIV} Believers who traveled from one place to another could always be assured of a warm welcome and kind hospitality from other believers. How Phoebe helped Paul and others is unknown, but those she helped were obviously very grateful. Life within the body of Christ is a constant exchange of help. Those who are helped one day are given the privilege in Christ of being the helpers the next day. We need to make sure we are participating in both roles in the local church where we worship.

16:3 Priscilla and Aquila, my fellow workers.^{NKJV} Priscilla and Aquila were a married couple who had become Paul's close friends. They, along with all other Jews, had been expelled from Rome in A.D. 49 by Emperor Claudius (Acts 18:2-3) and had moved to Corinth. There they met Paul while he was on his second missionary journey, and they invited him to live with them. Priscilla and Aquila were Christians before they met Paul, and probably told him much about the Roman church. Like Paul, Priscilla and Aquila were missionaries, and they all shared the same trade—tentmaking. They went with Paul when he left Corinth, and when they arrived in Ephesus, decided to stay and help the believers there (Acts 18:19). Priscilla and Aquila helped explain the full gospel to the powerful preacher, Apollos (Acts 18:26). Paul probably stayed with them when he visited Ephesus on his third missionary journey. At some point, they moved back to Rome when they were allowed to return (the Emperor Claudius died five years after issuing the edict expelling Jews from Rome, so it is possible that many returned then). Later, they went back to Ephesus (2 Timothy 4:19).

BEHIND THE SCENES
Priscilla and Aquila were a couple who accomplished effective ministry behind the scenes. Their tools were hospitality, friendship, and person-to-person teaching. They were not public speakers, but private evangelists. For at least some of the Romans, their home was used for church meetings (16:5). Priscilla and Aquila give us a challenging model of what a couple can do together in the service of Christ. How often do we see our families and homes as gifts through which God can accomplish his work? How does God want to use your home and family to serve him?

16:4 They risked their lives for me.^{NIV} Paul was indebted to these dear friends, even explaining to the others that they risked their lives for him. What they did is no longer known, but Paul had faced plenty of danger and had heard many threats against himself. This was certainly true in Ephesus (see Acts 18:6-10; 19:28-31; 1 Corinthians 15:32). Somehow Priscilla and Aquila intervened at one time to save Paul.

Not only I but all the churches of the Gentiles are grateful to them.^{NIV} Paul is grateful that they saved his life, and the Gentile churches would also be grateful that Paul's life was spared.

16:5 Greet also the church that meets at their house.^{NIV} A common characteristic of the early church was that the believers met in people's homes. Priscilla and Aquila had also had a church in their home in Ephesus (1 Corinthians 16:19).

Epenetus, who was the first convert to Christ in the province of Asia.^{NIV} Whoever this man was, Paul calls him **my dear friend** (NIV), and he has the legacy of being the first convert in Asia! Paul was in Asia on his third missionary journey (Acts 19:10); he had wanted to travel there during his second missionary journey but had been prevented (Acts 16:6).

WHO WAS FIRST?
When we think of being first, we invariably think about athletic records. Paul thought of converts. He went to places in which there was not a single believer in Jesus. The people who first heard the gospel in those places were important to him. Recognizing firsts in our lives is a valuable exercise. Do we know who planted the church where we worship? Do we know who was the first believer in our family? Do we remember who first communicated the gospel to us? Do we remember who was the first one we told about our relationship with Christ? Have we taken time to thank God for each of those first people in our lives?

The personal greetings that follow went to people (twenty-six in all) who were Romans and Greeks, Jews and Gentiles, men and women, prisoners and prominent citizens. The church's base was broad: it crossed cultural, social, intellectual, and economic lines. From this list we also learn that the Christian community was mobile. Though Paul had not yet been to Rome, he had met these people in other places on his journeys. Tradespeople, such as Priscilla and Aquila for example, were very mobile. What these believers had in common was a willingness to be taught and a willingness to serve fully as members of the body of Christ.

16:6 **Mary, who has worked very hard among you.**NRSV Paul would not know firsthand who had worked hard among the believers in Rome, so he is probably speaking from information given him by others, possibly Priscilla and Aquila.

16:7 **Andronicus and Junia, my relatives who were in prison with me.**NRSV These two may have been a husband and wife team. *Junia* (or even "Julia," which is the reading in certain ancient manuscripts) was a widely used female name at the time. Paul's references to them as relatives (see also 16:21) could mean that they were also Jews, possibly from the same tribe. When they were imprisoned with him is not known, because Paul had been imprisoned numerous times (see 2 Corinthians 11:23).

They are prominent among the apostles, and they were in Christ before I was.NRSV Andronicus and Junia distinguished themselves as apostles ("sent ones") in their ministry. They belonged to that larger group of apostles who had seen the risen Christ (a credential of an apostle—see Acts 1:22; 1 Corinthians 15:5-8). Quite interestingly, this is the only mention of a female apostle (Junia) in the New Testament. If Andronicus and Junia were believers before Paul was, they would have been Christians for about 25 years.

16:8 Ampliatus, whom I love in the Lord.^{NIV} This was a common Roman name at this time period, and it often showed up in the imperial household. It is possible that this man was part of Caesar's household because the gospel had reached even there. When Paul later wrote to the Philippian church from Rome, he said, "All the saints send you greetings, especially those who belong to Caesar's household" (Philippians 4:22 NIV).

16:9 Urbanus, our fellow worker in Christ.^{NKJV} Another common Roman name, Urbanus is greeted as a fellow worker—most likely another missionary for the early church.

Stachys. This name was not so common; some people in association with the imperial household were named Stachys.

16:10 Apelles, approved in Christ.^{NKJV} This is a typical Jewish name, common among the Jews in Rome.

Those who are of the household of Aristobulus.^{NKJV} This person may have been related to the Herods, perhaps a brother of Herod Agrippa I. He lived in Rome as a private citizen. To greet a "household" would mean greeting both the family and the servants.

16:11 Herodion, my relative.^{NIV} This person was probably a Jew, and a relative by tribe, not family.

Those in the household of Narcissus who are in the Lord.^{NIV} Perhaps some in Narcissus's household were not believers, because Paul specifies his greetings to those who are. This person has been identified as Tiberius Claudius Narcissus, a wealthy and powerful man during the reigns of emperors Tiberius and Claudius. But he was executed under Nero (sometime after A.D. 54). At that point, all his possessions, including slaves, would have been confiscated and become imperial property. So Paul sent his greetings to the believers among Narcissus's household who are now the property of Rome.

16:12 Tryphena and Tryphosa, those women who work hard in the Lord.^{NIV} These probably were sisters, maybe even twins because of the close relation of the names.

Persis, another woman who has worked very hard in the Lord.^{NIV} This name has appeared both among slaves and wealthy people, but never in connection with the imperial household.

16:13 **Rufus, chosen in the Lord.** This is an extremely common name. But it is possible that this is the same Rufus as mentioned in Mark 15:21. If so, then this is a son of Simon of Cyrene, and thus a North African.

His mother, who has been a mother to me, too.^{NIV} If Rufus is the same as the one mentioned in Mark's gospel, Paul may have met his mother in Antioch of Syria. Rufus's father, Simon, has been identified as the Simeon who was a teacher in the church there (Acts 13:1). Paul was brought to Antioch of Syria by Barnabas, where they spent a year (Acts 11:25-26). Perhaps Paul lived with them, and Rufus's mother had special concern and love for Paul—seeming like a mother to him.

16:14 **Asyncritus, Phlegon, Hermes, Patrobas, Hermas, and the brothers with them.**^{NIV} Perhaps these men were leaders of other house churches. The names are common names, especially among slaves.

16:15 **Philologus, Julia, Nereus and his sister, and Olympas, and all the saints who are with them.**^{NKJV} Philologus and Julia may have been married. Olympas may have been another leader in a house church.

16:16 **Greet one another with a holy kiss.** The "holy kiss" was a common form of greeting, much like the handshake today. (See also 1 Corinthians 16:20; 1 Thessalonians 5:26.)

All the churches of Christ greet you.^{NRSV} The churches Paul is referring to would most likely be those who were joining together in delivering the offering to Jerusalem (see 15:25-27).

Taken together, the list above represents a cross-section of Roman culture, from slaves to those of high social status. The church to whom Paul was writing had all the potential for unity in Christ in spite of every possible barrier. Even this list serves as another example of the theme of Paul's letter: God's plan includes the entire world. Justification by faith is the greatest proof of the truth of the theme, but the repeated theme of this letter is the great news that the Good News is for everyone!

16:17   **Watch out for those who cause divisions and put obstacles in your way that are contrary to the teaching you have learned.** NIV Jesus had told the disciples that false teachers would come (Matthew 24:11; Mark 13:22-23). Just as false prophets had contradicted the true prophets in Old Testament times (for example, see Jeremiah 23:16-40; 28:1-17), telling people only what they wanted to hear, so false teachers were twisting Christ's teachings and the words of his apostles. These teachers were belittling the significance of Jesus' life, death, and resurrection. Some claimed that Jesus couldn't be God; others claimed that he couldn't have been a real man. These teachers allowed and even encouraged all kinds of wrong and immoral acts, especially sexual sin.

Avoid them.NKJV Paul had not yet been to Rome, but he certainly realized that the ubiquitous false teachers would make their way there. He urges believers to be careful about the doctrines they listen to and to check all teachers' words against the Scriptures. And then they were to keep away from those trying to cause divisions. The severe problem of false teaching in some of the other churches Paul visited caused him to include this in the closing lines of his letter, for he knew it could certainly become a problem.

ENDLESS TALK
The false teachers were motivated by their own interests rather than Christ's. They embroiled the church in endless and irrelevant questions and controversies, taking precious time away from the study of the truth. Today we could also enter into worthless and irrelevant discussions, but such disputes quickly crowd out the life-changing message of Christ. We must stay away from religious speculation and pointless theological arguments. Such exercises may seem harmless at first, but they have a way of sidetracking us from the central message of the gospel—the person and work of Jesus Christ. And they expend time we should use to share the gospel with others. We should avoid anything that keeps us from doing God's work.

16:18   **Such people do not serve our Lord Christ, but their own appetites.**NRSV Teachers should be paid by the people they teach, but false teachers were attempting to make more money by distorting the truth and saying what people wanted to hear. They were more interested in making money than in teaching truth, motivated by a desire to gain power and prestige. In contrast, genuine Christian teachers are motivated by sincere faith and a desire to do what is right. Both Paul and Peter condemned greedy, lying teachers (see 1 Timothy 6:5).

By smooth talk and flattery they deceive the minds of naive people.^{NIV} Paul warns the Roman believers that when they listen to teachers, they should check the content of what is said and not be fooled by smooth style or flattery. Many cult leaders have led Christians astray by teaching things that sound like truth but are actually falsehoods. Christians who study God's Word will not be fooled, even though superficial listeners may easily be taken in. For an example of those who carefully checked God's Word, see Acts 17:10-12.

16:19 **Everyone has heard about your obedience, so I am full of joy over you.**^{NIV} Paul quickly adds that he knows the Roman believers are not naive (16:18) because their obedience to God is well known.

I want you to be wise about what is good, and innocent about what is evil.^{NIV} Believers are to *be wise* in their understanding of what is good, that is, in what God wants them to do. On the reverse, they are to be *innocent* about evil. The Greek word for innocent is *akeraious*, meaning simple or pure. The word was used to describe wine that was undiluted. Believers are to be innocent; "Do not conform any longer to the pattern of this world" (12:2).

16:20 **The God of peace will crush Satan under your feet shortly.**^{KJV} This langauge echoes Genesis 3:15, wherein God declares that the serpent's head would be crushed by the seed of the woman. These false teachers, servants of Satan, would try to sow discord in the churches, but God is the God of peace. The false teachers will be destroyed when Christ establishes his peace upon his return (see Revelation 20:1-6).

16:21 **Timothy, my fellow worker, sends his greetings to you.**^{NIV} Timothy was a key person in the growth of the early church, traveling with Paul on his second missionary journey (Acts 16:1-3). Later Paul wrote two letters to him (1 and 2 Timothy) as Timothy worked to strengthen the churches in Ephesus. Paul wrote of him, "Timothy has proved himself, because as a son with his father he has served with me in the work of the gospel" (Philippians 2:22 NIV). Acts 20:4 places Timothy with Paul prior to Paul's departure to Jerusalem.

Lucius and Jason and Sosipater, my relatives.^{NRSV} Again these are fellow Jews, not family relations. These names are also mentioned in other places: Acts 13:1; 17:5-9; 20:4.

16:22 **I, Tertius, who wrote down this letter, greet you in the Lord.**NIV This was Paul's secretary, who wrote the letter as Paul dictated it.

16:23 **Gaius, whose hospitality I and the whole church here enjoy, sends you his greetings.**NIV This is most likely *not* the same Gaius who was from Macedonia (Acts 19:29), nor the one from Derbe (Acts 20:4), nor the one addressed in 3 John. It is probably the Gaius whom Paul baptized in Corinth (1 Corinthians 1:14).

Erastus, the treasurer of the city.NKJV Erastus would have been a powerful and influential man. A civic official of this name is mentioned on the inscription on a marble paving-block in Corinth. The name was common enough that he need not be identified with the Erastus mentioned in other places (Acts 19:22 and 2 Timothy 4:20).

There is no verse 24 in most modern translations because it is not found in the most trusted Greek manuscripts. It is a scribal addition repeating the words of 16:20.

> The great thing is to be found at one's post as a child of God, living each day as though it were our last, but planning as though our world might last a hundred years.
> —C. S. Lewis

16:25 **Now to him who is able to establish you according to my gospel and the preaching of Jesus Christ.**NKJV Paul had explained his gospel at length in this letter to the Romans (see 2:16). Paul's gospel *was* the proclamation of Jesus Christ. Paul knew that the gospel and Christ himself would *establish* (strengthen and stabilize) them in the faith.

According to the revelation of the mystery hidden for long ages past.NIV Parts of that gospel were a mystery for many ages, hidden in the Old Testament (see also Ephesians 3:8-11; Colossians 1:25-27).

16:26 **Now revealed and made known through the prophetic writings by the command of the eternal God.**NIV The prophets who wrote various books of the Old Testament were not fully aware of the meaning of their own words; but they wrote, at God's command, much about the fulfillment of the mystery—the coming of the Messiah, the salvation of the Gentiles, and the return of the Jews (see 11:25). Now, after the coming of Christ and the growth of the church, what they wrote is being understood (1:2). (See also Luke 24:44-45; 1 Peter 1:10-12.)

So that all nations might believe and obey him.NIV This was the ultimate goal, all part of God's plan from the beginning (see 1:5). Paul exclaims that it is wonderful to be alive when the mystery, God's secret—his way of saving the Gentiles—is becoming known throughout the world! All the Old Testament prophecies are coming true, and God is using Paul as his instrument to tell this Good News.

16:27 **To the only wise God be glory forever through Jesus Christ! Amen.**NIV God's glory is displayed through Jesus Christ. William Tyndale reflected on what might be the appropriate application of the entire letter to the Romans when he wrote, "Now go to, reader, and according to the order of Paul's writing, even so do thou. First behold thyself diligently in the law of God, and see there thy just damnation. Secondarily turn thine eyes to Christ, and see there the exceeding mercy of thy most kind and loving Father. Thirdly remember that Christ made not this atonement that thou shouldest anger God again: neither cleansed he thee, that thou shouldest return (as a swine) unto thine old puddle again: but that thou shouldest be a new creature and live a new life after the will of God and not of the flesh. And be diligent lest through thine own negligence and unthankfulness thou lose this favour and mercy again."

Paul had not yet been to Rome to meet all the Christians there, and, of course, he has not yet met us. We can easily count ourselves among the strangers to whom he was writing. We too live in a cosmopolitan setting with the entire world open to us. We also have the potential for both widespread influence and wrenching conflict. We, too, belong to churches that exhibit an all-too-embarrassing tendency towards disunity and ineffectiveness. There is plenty of work to be done if we will listen carefully to and apply Paul's teaching about unity, service, and love. Any effort in that direction is bound to bring glory to God!

BIBLIOGRAPHY

Barclay, William. *The Letter to the Romans.* Philadelphia: The Westminster Press, 1975.

Barrett, C. K. *Commentary of the Epistle to the Romans.* New York: Harper and Row, 1957.

Bauer, Walter, William F. Arndt, Wilbur F. Gingrich, Danker. *A Greek-English Lexicon of the New Testament and Other Early Christian Literature.* Chicago: University of Chicago Press, 1979.

Bruce, F. F. *The Epistle of Paul to the Romans.* Tyndale New Testament Commentaries. Grand Rapids: Eerdmans, 1985.

Calvin, John. *Commentary on the Epistle of Paul the Apostle to the Romans.* Reprint, Grand Rapids: Eerdmans, 1947.

Donfried, K. P., ed. *The Romans Debate.* Peabody, Mass.: Hendrickson Publishers, 1991.

Douglas, J. D., and Philip W. Comfort, eds. *New Commentary on the Whole Bible: New Testament Volume.* Wheaton, Ill.: Tyndale House Publishers, 1990.

Dunn, James D. G. *Romans 1-8.* Word Biblical Commentary Series. Dallas: Word Books, 1988.

Edwards, James R. *Romans.* The New International Biblical Commentary Series. Peabody, Mass.: Hendrickson Publishers, 1992.

Ferguson, Wright, and Packer. *New Dictionary of Theology.* Downers Grove, Ill.: InterVarsity Press, 1988.

Foreman, Kenneth J. *The Layman's Bible Commentary: Romans, 1 Corinthians, 2 Corinthians.* Atlanta: John Knox Press, 1961.

Gutzke, Manford G. *Plain Talk on Romans.* Grand Rapids: Zondervan, 1976.

Harrison, Everett F. "Romans." In *The Expositor's Bible Commentary*, vol. 10. Frank E. Gaebelein, ed. Grand Rapids: Zondervan, 1976.

Hughes, R. Kent. *Romans: Righteousness from Heaven.* Wheaton, Ill.: Crossway Books, 1991.

Johnson, Alan F. *Romans, Volumes 1 and 2: The Freedom Letter.* Everyman's Bible Commentary Series. Chicago: Moody Press, 1985.

Luther, Martin. *Commentary on the Epistle to the Romans.* Reprint. Grand Rapids: Kregel Publications, 1954.

Moo, Douglas. *Romans 1-8.* Wycliffe Exegetical Commentary Series. Chicago: Moody Press, 1991.

Robertson, A. T. *Word Pictures in the Greek New Testament.* Nashville: Broadman Press, 1932.

Sanday, William, and Arthur C. Headlam. *A Critical and Exegetical Commentary on the Epistle to the Romans.* Edinburgh: T. & T. Clark, 1964.

Vine, W. E. *Expository Dictionary of New Testament Words.* Old Tappan, N.J.: Fleming H. Revell, 1966.

Walvoord, John F., and Roy B. Zuck. *Bible Knowledge Commentary: New Testament Edition.* Wheaton, Ill.: Victor Books, 1983.

Wuest, Kenneth S. *Wuest's Word Studies: Romans.* Grand Rapids: Eerdmans, 1955.

GENERAL INDEX

Abba—157
Abraham
believed God's
promises—91-93, 180
declared righteous—87, 89
father of all believers—87-91,
177, 214, 221, 223
God chose him and promised
many descendants—81-82,
89, 90, 207, 224
his physical descendants are
not guaranteed the
promises—179-192
not perfect, but trusted in
God—92-93
justified by his faith and not by
his works—82-95, 180, 217
Chart: Steps of Abraham's
Faith—88
Accountable
whole world will be held
accountable before God—69,
265-266
application for today—70
Adam
all are born into his family—108,
119
and Eve rebelled against
God—24, 26, 106-107,
138-139, 160
sin and death came into the
world by—106-111, 160, 225
Adoption
believer's new relationship with
God—157-158
Adultery—132
Ambition—280
Ananias—*xiv*, 8
Anger
God's anger at sin—24-40

Antioch—*xiv*
Aquila and Priscilla—*xvii, xx, xxi,*
10, 288-289
Ashamed
Paul was not ashamed of the
gospel—19-20
application for today—19-20
Atonement
Jesus Christ is our sacrifice
of—75
Baal—209
Baptism
believers baptized into
Christ—115-118
in the church today—116
Barnabas—*xiv,* 100, 214, 283
Belief
Abraham's belief in God's
promises—91-93, 180
must be from the heart—199
no excuse for not believing in
God—27-28
results of unbelief—28-40
application for today—27, 28,
92, 93, 129, 153-154
Bible
is completely trustworthy—93-94
written to teach us—273-275
application for today—179, 231,
274-275
Blessed
what it means—85-86
Blood
the blood of Christ saved
us—75-76, 104, 149-150
Boasting (see Pride)
Body of Christ
all believers are members
of—234

Branches
as illustration of Jews and
Gentiles—217-221
Called/Calls
Paul was called by God—3,
17-18
believers are called—9, 10-11,
166, 163-168, 169, 182, 224
"called" meaning "known
as"—132
application for today—3
Cenchrea—288
Chamula Culture—98
Character
how it is produced—102
what it is—102, 217
Christian Life
believers are to "clothe"
themselves with
Christ—257-258
Holy Spirit helps us live—149,
150-158
how to live to please
God—229-234
two sides of/old self vs. new
self—97-98, 118-129, 131-165
application for today—119, 120,
121, 122, 133, 139, 145, 152,
166, 229, 243, 256, 257-258,
279, 289
Church (Today)
all people equal before
God—213-214
differences of opinion on minor
matters should not cause
division—260, 275-276
application for today—215, 218,
260, 262-263, 267, 276
Chart: Disguised Elitism—220
Chart: Profile of a Strong
Church—274
Church in Jerusalem (see
Jerusalem)
Circumcision
Abraham was declared righteous
before—87, 89
physical vs. spiritual/of body vs.
of heart—58-60, 61
what it is—57-58
Claudius (Emperor)—*xvii, xviii*
Condemnation
no condemnation for those in
Christ Jesus—147-148

Confess/Confession
believers are to confess that
Jesus is Lord—199-200
of sin—143, 224
Conform
believers are not to—231-232
Chart: Do Not Conform—232
Conscience—50-51, 175-176, 251
Corinth
Paul's ministry in—*xvi-xvii,*
113-111
Paul wrote letter to Romans
from—259
Council of Jerusalem—*xiv,* 53,
266
Creation
tells about God—25-27
awaiting its own
redemption—26, 159-161
David
his line produced the
Messiah—5-6, 277
his writings—63, 85, 143,
212-213
Death
believers need not fear—109,
119-120, 172
comes to all people—108, 109
how death entered the
world—106-111
physical vs. spiritual—128-129
Debt—253
Deep, The (see Grave)
Diatribe—41
Eagerness
Paul's to go to Rome—18, 281,
283-284
application for today—18, 19
Elect/Election—169-170,
181-190, 210-211, 222, 224
Elijah—108, 207, 208-210
Encouragement
Paul hoped to give and
receive—15
application for today—15-16,
272, 274-275
Enoch—108
Ephesus—*xvii*
Esau—181, 182-183, 214
Eternal life
given by God to his
followers—47, 108, 109, 119,
128-129
what it is—129

Faith
  Abraham's faith—82, 82-95,
    180, 217
  accomplishes our salvation—90,
    168, 191-201
  as the law of God's
    kingdom—77-78
  comes from hearing the Good
    News—203
  does not nullify the law—78-79
  God's gifts received by—109
  makes us righteous before
    God—22-24
  measure of—233
  we are justified by—78, 98
  what it is—8-9, 23-24, 73, 76,
    83-84, 98
  application for today—9, 13, 23,
    84, 88, 102, 177, 191-192, 199
  Chart: Steps of Abraham's
    Faith—88
Faithfulness
  of God—62-63, 94, 201, 208,
    224
  of people—64
  application for today—63,
    209-210
  Chart: You Are Not Alone—209
False Teachers—292-294
Favoritism
  God does not show—48-52
Forgiveness
  available because of
    Jesus—108
  God forgives us—85, 223-224
  application for today—85, 237
Fruit
  evil deeds—133-134
  good deeds—46-47, 133
  application for today—134
Gaius—*xvii*
Gamaliel—*xi, xii,* 1
Gentiles
  God's judgment of—49, 52
  no difference between Jews
    and—74, 201, 221-225, 233,
    259
  Paul was apostle to—*xii, xiv-xv,*
    1, 3-4, 8, 16-17, 21
  salvation is also offered to—21,
    78, 188, 190, 191-192,
    203-205, 213-225, 276-277

Gifts (see Spiritual Gifts)
Glory
  believers will be glorified with
    Christ—158-162, 163-168,
    169, 188
  creation will be
    glorified—159-161
  people created for glory, but fell
    short—74, 100, 225
  what is God's glory?—74
  application for today—161, 189
God
  angry at sin—24-40
  believers can rejoice in their
    relationship with—100,
    105-106, 221
  compared to a potter—187-189
  consequences when we reject
    him—28-40
  controls all
    governments—247-252
  does not show favoritism—48-52
  faithfulness of—62-63, 94, 201,
    208, 224
  forgiveness of—85, 223-224
  grace of—75, 85, 99, 103, 108,
    110, 144, 210
  giver of life—91, 128-129,
    226-227
  glory of—74, 226-227
  justice of—76-77, 107, 183-192
  kindness of—44
  love of—11, 27, 103-104,
    165-173, 237
  mercy of—224-225, 230
  patience of—44, 188
  power of—20
  revealed in the creation—25-27
  righteousness of—21-24, 50,
    63-66, 76, 194
  sovereignty of—94, 103, 175,
    181-192, 210, 214
  works all things together for
    good—165-166
God's Will
  believers can know—232
God's Word (see Bible)
Good Deeds
  are the proper response to
    God's grace—46-47, 133
  cannot save us—78, 93, 210-211
  application for today—47, 86,
    184, 194

Gospel
brings people to the point of repentance and forgiveness—24-25, 111
message of—199
Paul not ashamed of—19-20
power of—20, 113
reveals the righteousness of God—21-22
taken first to the Jews, then to the Gentiles—21, 190, 203-204

Governments
believers are to obey—245-252
controlled by God—247-252
application for today—247, 248, 250, 251
Chart: Conscientious Objectors—249

Grace
given to Paul—7
given to believers—7, 90, 122-123, 235
not to be taken for granted—113-115
of God—75, 85, 99, 103, 108, 110, 144, 210
relationship of law and—*xxiv*, 122-124, 131-152
what it is—11, 123, 210
application for today—7-8, 86, 111, 210

Grave—198

Greece—*xvii*, 281

Hades (see Grave)

Hard Heart
how people become hardened—184-185, 211
of the Jews—214, 222
application for today—185, 211
Chart: Stages in the Hardening Process—186
Chart: Warning Signs of Developing Hardness—212

Heirs
believers are heirs of the promises to Abraham—177
believers are heirs of God and co-heirs with Christ—158

Holy/Holiness
God's law is—139
how we can be—128, 150
what it is—126-127, 217-218

Holy Spirit
convicts us of sin—143
does signs and wonders—279
encourages us—103
empowered Paul—*xxi*, 278, 280
guarantees our future glory—161-162, 277
helps us become holy—150
helps us in our weaknesses—163-164
helps us live the Christian life—149, 150-158
helps us overcome sin and temptation—*xxv*, 147-159
intercedes for us in prayer—164-165
outpouring at Pentecost—*xx*

Homosexuality
is a perversion of God's natural order—34-36
application for today—35

Hope
all believers have—160-163, 277
believers rejoice in the hope of sharing God's glory—100
will never disappoint us—102-103
application for today—102, 163

Hosea—189-190

Hospitality
believers are to care and share—239-240, 288
application for today—240

Hypocrisy
how Jews were being hypocritical—55-60
application for today—57-58

Idols/Idolatry
eating meat offered to—259, 261
in ancient Israel—208-210
in Rome—29-30
why people worship idols—29-30, 33-34
application for today—30, 34

Images (see Idols)

Isaac—181, 224

Isaiah—190, 192, 204-205, 211, 277

Israel (see Jews/Jewish)

Jacob—181, 182-183, 214, 223, 224

Jerusalem
money collected for believers in—*xv, xvii*, 176, 281-283, 284
Paul educated in—1

Jesus Christ
descendant of David—5-6
died for our sins—71-77, 95,
103-104, 120-122, 146,
149-150, 169, 197
end of the law—195-196
firstborn among many—163
gives us peace with God—98
is exalted as Lord—7, 12, 199,
200
is our Savior—74, 75-76, 104,
105, 149-150
human and divine—5-7, 149
our sacrifice of atonement—75
rose from the dead—6-7, 94-95,
115, 116, 198, 199, 265
Son of God—5-6
stumbling stone—191-192, 212
Jews/Jewish
advantages of being—61-62,
177-183
God's judgment of—49, 52
gospel taken first to—21, 190,
203-204
had been called to be the guides
of the Gentiles—55, 78, 180,
184, 208
if they do not believe, they will
not be saved—179-192, 193,
203-205, 213
no difference between Gentiles
and—74, 201, 221-225, 233,
259
Paul's imaginary questioner in
this letter is a Jew—41-42
rejection of the gospel by
many—214-217, 216, 224-225
remnant will be saved—190,
207-213, 216-226, 276
Chart: Benefits of Being a
Jew—178
Jezebel, Queen—208
Joy
response for all God has done
for us—105-106
Judgment
God's judgment of
sinners—42-48, 51-52, 64-66,
109, 263, 265
judging others is wrong—41-46,
55-56, 65, 260, 262-270
application for today—42, 44,
63, 265, 267

Justice
of God—76-77, 107, 183-192
Chart: God's Justice—65
Justification
how we receive—74-75, 76, 77,
84, 95, 98, 104, 108, 109,
148, 163-168, 169, 200
is by faith apart from works—78,
98
what it does for the
believer—98-103
Kingdom of God
believers are citizens
of—*xxv-xxvi*
Jews thought they were ensured
entrance into—44
Paul as citizen of—*xiii-xiv, xvi*
what it is and isn't—268
Law
breaking the law dishonors
God—56-57
cannot bring salvation—70-71,
72-73, 87, 89-90, 107-108,
132, 135-145, 149, 150, 191,
195-197, 210-211
explanation of—57, 131, 149
love fulfills—254-255
obedience to—50-51, 55, 77-79
relationship of grace and—*xxiv,*
122-124, 131-152
reveals sin—107-108, 110,
135-145
application for today—70, 111,
124
Chart: Hebrew Words for
"Law"—197
Chart: Why Do God's Laws
Arouse Our Sinful
Desires?—135
Living Sacrifice
believers are to present their
bodies as—230-231
Chart: Sacrifices
Compared—230
Love
commanded for all
believers—252-258
God's contrasted with
human—103-104
God's for us—11, 27, 103-104,
165-173, 237
maintaining through
persecution—102

Love cont.
no one can separate us from
God's—170-173
what genuine love is—237-239
application for today—11, 102,
104, 171, 176, 177, 238, 253,
254
Lust (see Sin)
Mercy
of God—224-225, 230
application for today—226
Mind/Mind-set
believers are to have renewed
minds—231-232
on the flesh vs. on the
Spirit—151-155
application for today—153-154
Chart: Different Ways to Have
Your Mind Set—151
Missionaries
why we need them—26-27
Morality
Chart: Moral Alternatives—39
Moses—107, 108, 176, 183, 184,
196, 197-198, 217
Nature (see Creation)
Nero (Emperor)—*xix*
Obedience
and righteousness—49-50, 122
correct response to gospel
message—8
how it can become
disobedience—194-196
results of—10, 49-50
to the government—245-252
to the law—50-51, 55, 77-79
two kinds of—150
application for today—50, 125,
247, 248, 250, 251
Obligated/Obligation
Paul's obligation to Christ and to
the world—17-18
people's obligation to respond to
God—155
application for today—18, 155
Patience
God's patience with us—44, 188
waiting patiently for God's
promises—163
application for today—45, 163,
239
Paul
as a Jew—*xi-xii,* 62, 175, 207
as a Pharisee—*xi,* 1

Paul cont.
as apostle to the Gentiles—*xii,
xiv-xv,* 1, 3-4, 8, 16-17, 21,
175, 176, 215, 232-233, 278
as author—*xi, xx-xxii,* 176,
277-285
as persecutor of believers—*xi,
xii,* 2, 207, 215
as Roman citizen—*xii-xiii,* 1, 2
conversion of—*xiii, xiv,* 2, 215
death of—*xvi*
goal in life—17-18, 280, 296
imprisonments in Rome—*xv*
missionary journeys of—*xiv-xv,
xvi-xvii,* 16, 280-283, 294
prevented from going to
Rome—16, 281
sorrow over Jews not
believing—176, 193
voyage to Rome—*xv,* 14, 283
Pax Romana (see Roman peace)
Peace
among believers—268
believers are to live at peace
with everyone—242
given to believers—48, 98, 277,
285
what it is—11
Persecution
believers are to bless those who
persecute them—240-241
believers can rejoice in
suffering—100
believers will share in Christ's
suffering—158, 159
of believers in Rome—*xvi,
xviii-xix,* 100, 240-241
of Paul—*xv-xvi*
results of—100
application for today—*xvi,* 101,
158, 239, 241
Chart: Suffering with Christ—101
Perseverance
develops character—102
produced by suffering—100
Peter
and church in Rome—*xix*
death of—*xvi*
Pharaoh—184-185, 214
Phoebe—*xxi,* 287-288
Power
of God—20
of the gospel—20, 113
application for today—105

Prayer
  believers in Rome for
    Paul—283-284
  Holy Spirit intercedes in our
    prayers—164-165
  Paul's for the believers—13-15
  application for today—14, 15,
    164-165, 169, 239, 284
Predestined/Predestination—166-
  168
Pride
  no place in believer's life—233,
    241-242
  no pride in salvation—77, 78,
    82, 230
  application for today—242
Priscilla and Aquila (see Aquila
  and Priscilla)
Prophets
  the gospel is rooted in God's
    promises through the
    prophets—4-5, 295
  Chart: The Prophets Wrote of
    God's Plan—4
  Chart: You Are Not
    Alone—209
Rebekah—181, 182
Reconciliation
  how sinners are reconciled
    with God—104-105, 106
  steps in reconciliation
    process—105
Redemption
  how we receive—75
  of believers' bodies—162
Rejoice/Rejoicing
  three occasions for—100
  application for today—101, 221,
    239, 241
Repentance
  first step to forgiveness—51
  God's kindness leads us
    toward—44
  application for today—51
Resurrection
  of believers—116-114
  of Jesus Christ—6-7, 94-95,
    115, 116, 198, 199, 265
  application for today—7
Revenge
  believers are not to
    seek—242-237
Righteousness
  and obedience—49-50, 122

Righteousness cont.
  available to everyone who
    believes—196
  Gentiles received it by
    faith—191-201
  how we can be—22-24, 50,
    73-77, 73-74, 84, 93-95, 104,
    194-195
  Jews could not attain it by
    obeying the law—191-201
  of Abraham—83-84, 87, 89
  of God—21-24, 50, 63-66, 76,
    194
  what it is—22
  application for today—64, 71, 95
  Chart: How Can God Accept
    Us?—72
  Chart: Righteousness and
    Wickedness—43
Roman Empire
  life in—246
  power of—*xxv,* 10, 18, 19
  slavery in—*xviii-xix,* 126
  territory of—*xii, xvii,* 10, 287
Roman Peace
  importance of for the
    church—*xviii,* 98
Romans
  Paul's reason for writing this
    letter—*xx-xxii, xxviii,* 1, 12-13,
    14, 18, 41, 277-285
  to whom Paul wrote the
    letter—*xvii*
  when the letter was written—*xvii*
Rome, Church in
  beginnings of—*xix-xx,* 1
  dangers to—292-294
  make-up of—*xvi, xx,* 5, 10,
    287-296
  met in people's homes—289
  reputation of—13, 294
Rome, City of
  allegiance of the citizens—*xviii*
  being a Christian in—*xvi,*
    xviii-xix, 100, 240-241,
    246-252
  description of—*xvii-xix*
  history of Christianity in—1,
    245-246
  history of Judaism in—*xviii,* 245
  Paul's first imprisonment in—*xv,* 283
  Paul's second imprisonment
    in—*xv*
  religions of—*xviii, xxiii,* 10

Rome, City of cont.
 slavery in—*xviii-xix,* 126
 symbol of paganism in
  Scripture—*xix*
Root of Jesse—277
Sacrifice, Living (see Living
 Sacrifice)
Saints
 believers are called to be—10-11
Salvation
 available to all—*xxiii-xiv,* 108
 how to receive—20-21, 41, 46,
  74, 78, 90, 99, 105, 168,
  191-201, 216
 is sure and secure—168-173
 theme in Romans—*xxiii-xxiv*
 application for today—*xxiv,* 61,
  71, 170, 191-192, 195, 199,
  200
Sanctification
 what it is—113
Scripture (see Bible)
Second Coming
 believers are to be ready
  for—159-160, 162, 255-258
Self-righteous
 God hates
  self-righteousness—53-57
 application for today—54, 54-55
Self-seeking
 leads to judgment—47
Self-worth—233, 254
Servant
 Paul calls himself—1, 2-3
 application for today—3
Service
 believers are to serve with
  enthusiasm—239
 believers serve Christ out of
  love—134-135
 theme in Romans—*xxvii*
 application for today—*xxvii-xxviii,*
  132, 135, 268
Sexual Impurity
 in ancient world—31-33
 what it is—31-33, 34-36
 application for today—32, 56
Sin
 all have sinned—41-44, 66-71,
  74, 107
 confession of—143, 224
 consequences of—36-40, 74,
  107-111, 114, 128-129
 freedom from—114-129

Sin cont.
 Holy Spirit helps us
  overcome—*xxv,* 147-159
 how it entered human
  race—106-111
 makes God angry—24-40
 seriousness of—114
 sexual impurity—31-33
 sinful desires—120-123
 theme in Romans—*xxii-xxiii*
 unbelievers given over to sinful
  desires—30-40
 what it is—107
 application for today—*xxiii,* 32,
  65, 66, 114, 118, 144
 Chart: Inappropriate Responses
  to the Misdeeds of the
  Body—156
 Chart: Make Heavenly Truth an
  Earthly Reality—123
 Chart: What Has God Done
  about Sin?—121
Slavery
 believers are no longer slaves to
  fear—157
 in the Roman empire—*xviii-xix,*
  126
 we are slaves of God or of
  evil—123-129
 application for today—146
 Chart: Slavery vs. Spiritual
  Freedom—134
Sodom and Gomorrah—190
Sons of God/Sonship
 who are true sons of
  God?—157-158
Sovereignty
 of God—94, 103, 175, 181-192,
  210, 214
 theme in Romans—*xxv-xxvii*
 application for today—*xxvi-xxvii*
Spain
 Paul's plan to visit—*xv, xvii, xx,*
  281, 283
Spirit of Christ (see Holy Spirit)
Spirit of Holiness—6
Spiritual Gifts
 examples of—235-237
 how we should use our
  gifts—234-244
 Paul's hope in his visit to
  Rome—15, 283
 purpose of in the body of
  Christ—233-237

Spiritual Gifts
application for today—236-237
Chart: Gift Discovery—236
Spiritual Growth
theme in Romans—*xxiv-xxv*
application for today—*xxv*
Stephen—*xi,* 2
Strength—272-273
Strong and Weak Believers
Paul's advice about—259-272
application for today—260, 262,
269, 273
Stumbling Stone—191-192, 212
Suffering (see Persecution)
Tarsus—*xi, xii, xiv,* 1
Taxes—251-252
Ten Commandments—57, 59,
124, 253
Tertius—5, 295
Thankfulness
cannot thank God if we don't
believe—28
Timothy—*xv,* 62, 273, 294
Titus—*xv*
Trinity
all persons of Trinity work in our
salvation—155, 164

Trinity cont.
Chart: The Trinity in the New
Testament—154
Truth
characteristics of truth as
revealed in nature—25-27
suppressing it—25, 27
results of suppressing it—27
Unity
among believers—275-276
believers are united with Christ
in his death and
resurrection—116-129
application for today—117, 275,
276
Chart: United in Christ—117
Weak and Strong Believers (see
Strong and Weak Believers)
Witnessing for Christ
how people come to
believe—201-203
Paul's main goal—17-18
application for today—17, 202,
203, 219
Worship
what it is—231